101 DIVES
from the mainland of Washington
and British Columbia

S0-ADM-070

TWO NEW GUIDEBOOKS . . .

101 DIVES and its companion, *99 DIVES,* are expanded and updated editions of Betty Pratt-Johnson's *141 DIVES,* which has sold more than 40,000 copies. The new books include more than 80 new dives.
Of *141 DIVES,* reviewers have noted:

"This must be considered THE BIBLE for skin divers in the Pacific Northwest . . ."
VICTORIA TIMES

"Betty Pratt-Johnson has written a very comprehensive book on the fabulous underwater treasures (flora, fauna and wrecks) to be discovered and appreciated in Puget Sound waters and the straits between Vancouver Island and the British Columbia mainland . . ."
PADI UNDERSEA JOURNAL

". . . thorough, accurate, and above all – interesting."
PACIFIC SEARCH

"The author has obviously dived at every site discussed and provides information concerning tidal conditions, currents . . . invaluable to the diver – beginner or veteran."
DIVER

". . . a must if you're going to dive in the Pacific Northwest. It has local information about wrecks, marine life, bottles . . ."
SKIN DIVER

". . . most comprehensive reference for Northwest divers . . . extensive sections on dive charters and resorts, safety information, tides, equipment and boat rentals, wrecks, bottle and junk collecting, underseas photography . . ."
SUNSET

". . . well-illustrated, nicely laid-out, informative package . . ."
QUILL AND QUIRE

"I like to think . . . my book *Diving Around Britain* was the first of its kind; but recent competitors, admittedly in other countries, have been producing stuff that I frankly envy. *Red Sea Diver's Guide,* for example, is eye-popping. *141,* although not as lavish, is even better; without doubt the best of its kind . . ."
SUB-AQUA

The most authoritative guides to
underwater fun in Washington and British Columbia

Betty Pratt-Johnson

101 DIVES
from the mainland of Washington
and British Columbia

Heritage House Publishing Company Ltd.

FRONT COVER: Red snakelock anemones near Saltery Bay, south of Powell River
Photograph by Dale Sanders

SPINE: The red-and-white dive flag marks an area where scuba diving is in progress, and is flown from a float. It is recognized throughout North America.
The blue-and-white dive flag is flown from a vessel when scuba divers are in the water. It is recognized throughout the world.

Copyright © 1995 Betty Pratt-Johnson, Vancouver, Canada. All rights reserved.

Canadian Cataloguing in Publication Data

Pratt-Johnson, Betty.
   101 dives from the mainland of Washington and British Columbia

   Includes index.
   ISBN 1-895811-20-1

   1. Scuba diving–British Columbia–Pacific Coast–Guidebooks. 2. Scuba diving–Washington (State)–Pacific Coast–Guidebooks. 3. Pacific Coast (B.C.)–Guidebooks. 4. Pacific Coast (Wash.)–Guidebooks. I. Title.
   GV840.S782B74 1994   797.2'3   C94-910292-X

Library of Congress Catalog Card Number: 94-79773

First Edition 1995

Published in Canada and the United States by
HERITAGE HOUSE PUBLISHING COMPANY LTD.
Unit #8, 17921-55 Avenue, Surrey BC Canada V3S 6C4

HERITAGE HOUSE PUBLISHING COMPANY LTD.
1916 Pike Place, Suite 73, Seattle Washington 98101

Printed in Canada

To all the wonderful people
working to protect our
precious underwater marine life

It has started here
at Whytecliff Park

Wall of plumose anemones at Whytecliff Park: marine life may not be taken from Whytecliff Park, nor from Porteau Cove Marine Park, by any means – sport diving, sport fishing or commercial fishing. In 1994, the shore off these popular dive sites became the first coastline in Canada where marine life is fully protected.

Books by Betty Pratt-Johnson

99 Dives from the San Juan Islands in Washington to the Gulf Islands and Vancouver Island in British Columbia

101 Dives from the mainland of Washington and British Columbia

Whitewater Trips and Hot Springs in the Kootenays of British Columbia: For Kayakers, Canoeists and Rafters

Whitewater Trips for Kayakers, Canoeists and Rafters in British Columbia: Greater Vancouver through Whistler, Okanagan and Thompson River Regions

Whitewater Trips for Kayakers, Canoeists and Rafters on Vancouver Island

Everybody Loves an Octopus, her popular natural-history article which was published first in the United States, was translated into French and German and reprinted in a scuba diving magazine in Switzerland. It was then made available to readers around the world in twelve additional languages as well as in big print and it was selected as an example of good writing for the college anthology *Read to Write.* It is also included in the *1979 Science Annual* of the Americana Encyclopedia.

WARNING – DISCLAIMER AND LIMITATION OF LIABILITY

This guidebook is intended to provide recreational divers and snorkelers with some general information about the diving services and diving sites discussed in this book in order to help them have a safe and enjoyable time. **This guidebook is not meant to teach the reader to become a certified scuba diver and it is not meant to be used by scuba divers or snorkelers for non-recreational purposes.** Neither the author nor the publisher, Heritage House Publishing Company Ltd., are engaged in providing teaching or professional guide services.

Scuba diving and snorkeling can be very dangerous and demanding recreations and may involve serious injury or death. The user of this guidebook acknowledges both an understanding of and an assumption of the risks involved in these sports.

The information contained in this guidebook is supplied merely for the convenience of the reader and must not be the only source of information for the diving services and sites described in this book. The author has endeavored to ensure that the information contained in this book is accurate at the time of publication. However, the user is cautioned that this information may be incorrect or incomplete and that it may change after the date of publication. Users of this book and their diving buddies must evaluate for themselves the potential risks and dangers of each site listed in this book and the accuracy, suitability and applicability of any service information contained in this book, including the availability of adequate or appropriate emergency services.

Neither the publisher, Heritage House Publishing Company Ltd., nor its directors, officers, and employees have any knowledge of or expertise with scuba diving and snorkeling and are not qualified to check or confirm the information contained in this guidebook which is solely within the knowledge of the author.

This guidebook is sold with the understanding that the author and the publisher, Heritage House Publishing Company Ltd., disclaim any responsibility with respect to the completeness or accuracy of the information provided in this guidebook and will not be liable with respect to any claim, action or proceeding relating to any injury, death, loss of property or damage to property caused or alleged to be caused, directly or indirectly, by the information contained in or omitted from this guidebook whether caused by negligence or otherwise.

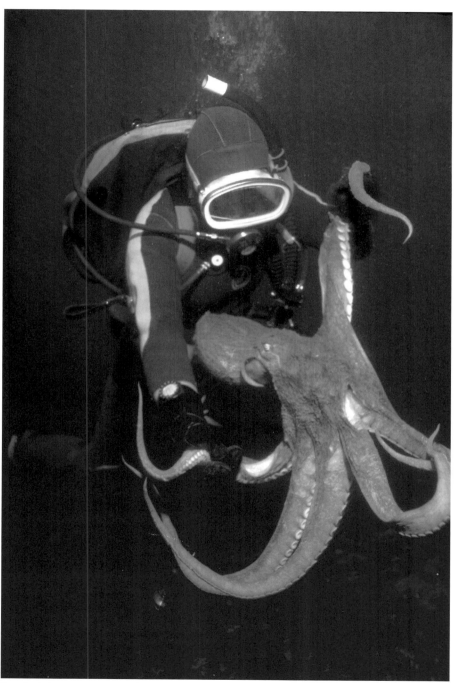

Everybody loves an octopus – diver gently playing with the delicate giant, but for its sake, do not handle. Octopuses are abundant throughout the Strait of Georgia and Puget Sound.

CONTENTS

Come Dive with Me

COME DIVE WITH ME

Scuba diving is growing and changing – it is forever new – and I feel lucky to have been involved with this remarkable recreation for so long, lucky to still be wandering around under water. I have enjoyed twenty-seven years of scuba diving in the Strait of Georgia and Puget Sound, as well as many other parts of the world.

This new *101 Dives* where-to-go guidebook is based on *141 Dives in the Protected Waters of Washington and British Columbia,* a guide I started writing in 1974 when I first became excited about diving in the North Pacific. No guide was available for the region, and the best excuse I could find to dive as much as I wanted to was to write the very book I wanted to buy, a book containing basic information about facilities and sites. The book grew as my skills increased: it was first published in 1976, and since that time has been used by beginner to expert divers. That guidebook is still growing.

More than eighty new dive sites are in two new volumes that replace it. The original guide has outgrown its binding and is now transformed into two smaller books that will easily fit in your pocket or dive bag. Forty-two new dive descriptions are in *101 Dives,* forty-five new sites in its companion volume *99 Dives.* Again the guide format is deliberately designed with each dive described on two opposing pages. If you don't want to take the whole book, you can photocopy it and take just the photocopy when you go for your dive. Both books contain the same type of information as in *141 Dives,* but the two new guides are fully updated and expanded, reflecting the changes in diving. The number of dive-guide and charter-boat offerings has increased. A great deal is now known about formerly difficult-to-dive sites and how to dive them. A couple of high-current dives requiring expert skills are included in each of the new guides. You will also find new, easy-but-excellent shore dives like Kelvin Grove and Tramp Harbor where beginning divers can go, and experts will also want to.

Wherever there is water there is a potential dive site. This endless possibility for exploration is one of the great joys of diving. It also means I could not possibly list every location. However this book – like *141 Dives* – offers something better than a mere list. It gives clues about how to dive different types of sites. And it offers a diverse sampling of various kinds of diving available from shore, by dive-kayak and boat. It includes many of the better-known and more accessible dives sites, and some not-so-well-known spots on the mainland side of the protected inland sea which stretches from Desolation Sound at the top of the Strait of Georgia in British Columbia to the southern tip of Puget Sound in Washington.

If you like doing things with groups, you will find clubs dedicated to special interests such as wreck diving, marine life conservation, activities with physically challenged divers, creating artificial reefs. If you are a non-club-joiner type, you can go quietly with one other diver to explore. Charter boats are available for day-trips and live-aboard trips. Clues to all of these things and more are offered in this guide. I personally have dived every site described in this guidebook, some sites many times. I include information to help you find and dive these places, but I also give you the tools to go beyond the described sites.

Diving is unlimited. Use this guidebook, dive with charter operators who are constantly finding new sites, and also find your own sites. Study charts; see the important sections in the introduction with information on local conditions, wrecks, bottle collecting, kayak-diving and more; see lists of rental boats and expanded information on launching ramps included in the service information of each chapter, as well as lists of charter boats.

To obtain information for this guide, once again I talked with local divers about each site; where changes were reported I dived the sites. Many old favorites are still in it but with enhancements such as at Porteau Cove Marine Park. It has been fun revisiting these sites, and a thrill to visit many new sites. A few places I've had minor difficulties in determining whether some properties crossed in gaining access to diving waters are public or private property. Treat with respect, therefore, any new signs advising that property is private or stating that no trespassing is allowed.

My observations of marine life are the observations of an interested layperson. I refer to all animals by common names. In the absence of an authoritative common name I have used the common name most descriptive to me.

A portion of nautical chart in the actual chart size is included in each site description. These charts are for reference only and are not to be used for navigation. All soundings are in meters unless stated otherwise. The scale varies because the charts themselves vary. Therefore I have added a small scale bar under each chart. An arrow has been added to each chart to indicate the dive-entry point described.

The tide table or current table to refer to for every site is given at the top of the first page of each dive description. When a time correction is required, wherever possible, a simple rule-of-thumb figure is given. These corrections have usually been derived from locals. Such information is always easier to use and often more reliable than trying to pin down dive time to precisely what you find in the current tables – often currents are measured mid-channel and that is not where you are diving.

Although this is a where-to-go guidebook, I include information about possible hazards to beware of at each site. One note regarding safety: It is possible but not proven that heavy exertion after diving could bring on signs and symptoms of decompression sickness. I know of several people who suspect this problem has happened to them. Therefore I include cautions in the hazards section of some of the descriptions of dives that are most likely to require heavy physical exertion, but consider it on all dives. Each site description incorporates the best of current knowledge for your safety. All information has been checked by one or more experienced divers in addition to myself. But as noted in the disclaimer, this book is not meant to teach you how to dive. Proper training and certification are required before you can rent or purchase equipment or obtain air fills. And you must have good equipment.

All dives are rated for skill and experience required. This skill level requirement cannot be measured by the number of years you have been diving. It can only be measured by the variety of diving situations you have encountered. Any certified diver should be able to attempt the dives classified "All Divers". Beginners and visitors should have experience with a number of these dives before doing any of the more difficult ones. When a dive site has *some complications* but does not require intricate planning, I have rated it for "Intermediate Divers". I expect an intermediate to know how to use tide and current tables – and to know the difference between them – as well as to know techniques to use when diving in current. Dives that require *precision* because of current or depth or boat traffic or any other variable described in hazards, dives that present several difficult hazards, and dives that require great strength and fitness are classified for "Expert Divers".

Kayak-divers will find eighteen kayak dives, which could also be reached by larger boat, described in this guide.

Divers who use wheelchairs will find descriptions of sixteen shore dives that might be accessible to them. I say "might" because on some dives I could have misjudged suitability. Though I have dived every one of these sites, as I have dived every site in the book, not all locations have been checked out by divers using wheelchairs. eleven more sites described are possible for divers who use wheelchairs and who paddle dive-kayaks as well. Boat charter operations and dive resorts that welcome divers with wheelchairs are noted in the service information listings but none of them are specifically equipped for it and the capabiities differ. Wheelchair access to dive sites or boats often requires assistance from able-bodied personnel. So ask any charter boat or resort operator you plan to use exactly what their situation is.

All dives are within sport diving limits, no dive descriptions are for greater depth than 125 feet (38 meters). Many sites are suitable for snorkeling or skin diving as well as scuba diving: when this is so, I have mentioned it. When I state that a dive is suitable for all divers, or intermediate divers "with guide", I indicate that divers who go under water with an experienced guide can enjoy a dive that is otherwise above their skill and experience level: this presupposes that the guide will have a great deal of local knowledge and will be capable of summing up the visiting diver to help him or her deal with the dive situation. Be aware that I have made no value judgments about the capabilities of any dive guides or charter operators – I simply list them. Finally, I have tried to present a balanced number of dives for divers of all skill levels in each locale. The greatest number of dives are in and around cities where there are the most divers looking for places to get wet.

101 Dives and *99 Dives* are a starting point for coastal divers who have just learned to dive, dropouts who are returning to diving, and visiting divers from around the world. These guides contain useful service information for all divers. They are an open invitation to enjoy some of the most varied and remarkable diving found anywhere. Producing the expanded update of *141 Dives* has been a second experience of discovery for me. I have loved repeating many dives I've enjoyed before, still seeing creatures new to me even after twenty-seven years of diving, and visiting places I never dreamed divers would ever be able to go.

Come dive with me, with this book as a guide, and we'll go on and on discovering the colorful, still world known only to North Pacific divers.

After diving Whiskey Rock, off to see petrified palms

WHAT'S DIFFERENT ABOUT NORTH PACIFIC DIVING?
WHAT'S OLD? WHAT'S NEW?

A kaleidoscope of color – hot pink, red, yellow and orange; cool blue, mauve, purple and white covers the ocean floor. The emerald sea is bursting with life. You keep seeing things under water that you can't find in any book. Fascinating creatures, many still unnamed. It's fabulous to feel you're on the edge of discovery on every dive. Perhaps the other most striking feature of diving in the North Pacific inland sea is the sheer magnitude of protected coastline which makes this region one of the safest and most accessible diving areas in the world. It has always been that way – so what's new?

Adventuring by diving to see wild creatures like sea lions is "in". Technical diving and use of Nitrox, becoming popular. Spearfishing is "out". Gone, too, are the skin-diving spearfishermen who hunted in competitions at depths of 60 to 100 feet (18 to 30 meters). A loss. I admired the amazing skills of those breath-hold divers, hope they are still doing it in remote locales. But, happily, this era is marked by conservation. No more rape and pillage of wrecks or marine life. Wreck divers of today are ardent preservers of our underwater heritage. They are documenting wrecks, not tearing them apart and taking them away, and some are *making* wrecks. Creating artificial reefs is a developing diving specialty. While the newest frontier of diving is exploring archaeological sites – prehistoric artifacts from 6,800 years ago have been found.

Divers have different expectations. Many divers don't want to snorkel as far as they used to. But now divers use dive-kayaks to eliminate difficult swims and to reach sites that are a much greater distance away than they could ever have snorkeled. Many people are diving – it has become mainstream, and diving facilities have increased enormously.

More features of this enormous inland sea are included in the information listed below, as well as some suggestions about how to use them to your advantage in pursuing a variety of diving activities. Details about local conditions are in the site descriptions which comprise most of the book. However, before you start selecting specific sites, read the following summary of basic information every diver will want to know. It includes a great deal of information:

General Conditions
Water Salinity
Water Temperature
Seasons
Visibility
Bull Kelp
Currents and Riptides
Boats and Log Booms
Broken Fishing Line
Surge and Surf
Marine Life
Diver Traffic
Public Access
Kayak-Diving
Diving Regulations and Safety

Diving Activities
Underwater Photography
Marine Life Conservation
Spearfishing and Shellfish Collecting
Bottle, China and Junk Collecting
Archaeological Diving
Wreck Diving
Artificial Reefs
Clubs and Associations
Night Diving

WATER SALINITY – All dives covered in this book, except two, are in salt water. Divers accustomed to diving in fresh water will find they need to wear 1 to 4 pounds (½ to 1¾ kilograms) more weight when diving in the sea. Probably most divers should start by adding 2 pounds (1 kilogram) to accommodate for the increased density of salt water. Experiment until you find the right amount.

WATER TEMPERATURE – Water temperature is affected by several factors including depth and currents. Surface temperatures of North Pacific waters vary from 39° to 46° Fahrenheit (4° to 8° Celsius) in winter to 54° to 64° Fahrenheit (12° to 18° Celsius) in summer, depending upon location. However, below a depth of 30 to 40 feet (9 to 12 meters) the temperature varies little, winter or summer, from about 45° Fahrenheit (7° Celsius).

It is just a matter of where the temperature drop, or thermocline, comes – at 30, 40, 50 or 60 feet (9, 12, 15, or 18 meters), usually not deeper than that. Then if you are diving below the thermocline you will want to dress warmly year-round. Another factor for wet-suit divers to consider is that you will probably feel the cold more quickly when diving where there is a current. The current constantly forces a change of water under any gaps in your suit. And the water itself will probably be colder because shifting water never becomes warm.

Most local divers dive comfortably year-round in all locations wearing custom-fitted dry suits. Some wear custom-fitted wet suits of neoprene. Wet-suit divers usually wear the "farmer Jane" or "farmer John" style of suit which covers the trunk of the body with a double thickness. Some divers obtain extra warmth for winter by wearing an Arctic hood with a large flange around the neck, or by wearing a vest under their wet-suit jacket. Others wear lightweight neoprene five-finger gloves in summer and ¼-inch (⅔-centimeter) neoprene mitts in winter. In very cold weather, wet-suit divers warm themselves for entry by pouring warm water into their gloves and hood, and down the backs of their necks.

Many wet suits manufactured in California and other warmer parts are of less than ¼-inch (⅔-centimeter) neoprene and will not be comfortably warm in winter waters of the North Pacific. Visiting divers may want to rent a dry suit or buy or rent a vest or an Arctic hood for added warmth while diving in Puget Sound and the Strait of Georgia.

SEASONS – Year-round diving is enjoyed in the Strait of Georgia and Puget Sound and a variety of diving activities is possible. Winter is best for photography since low

Photographer descending into clear emerald sea in winter

plankton activity and low river runoff levels make visibility best then. Because summer visibility can be poor, summer is a good time to combine a dive with a picnic on an unspoiled beach, or pursue some diving activity like bottle collecting. Because much bottle collecting is done at muddy sites by touch alone, visibility does not matter. Sunny September days are considered best all-round by some, as that season can be most beautiful both above and below the surface. I opt for year-round diving, choosing sites and diving activities suitable to each season.

VISIBILITY – Water clarity is probably the most significant variable in North Pacific diving. It can vary from "faceplate" visibility when you cannot see 1 foot ($\frac{1}{3}$ meter) ahead, up to a crystal clear 100 feet (30 meters). Poor visibility may be the result of several factors: the type of bottom, river runoff, industrial pollution, and plankton growth.

• **Type of bottom** – Muddy substrates are liable to be stirred up when current is running, or when a lot of divers are swimming close to the bottom. In many locations, diving at the end of the outgoing tide will help you obtain the best possible visibility. When diving at a silty site near a wall, if possible, head out at one level and back at a shallower level. A buoyancy compensation device, which gives neutral buoyancy at any depth, should be worn by all divers at all times. It is particularly useful when diving in muddy areas.

• **River runoff** – Both melting snows and rainstorms cause murky surface water, especially near river and creek mouths. In spring, early summer and after rainstorms, check your chart and avoid sites near large rivers like the Fraser or Skagit. A small, clear stream of fresh water flowing into the sea creates a shimmery appearance like scotch and water, but does not impede vision – or match the taste!

• **Industrial pollution** – Effluents, tailings and other solid wastes from mines, factories and logging operations can impair visibility. Avoid these areas.

• **Plankton growth** – Two "waves" of plankton growth or "bloom" come to protected waters of North Pacific seas each spring and summer. Prolonged sunny weather encourages these blooms. The spring bloom invariably occurs each year throughout the Strait of Georgia and Puget Sound. It begins any time from March through April or May, and clouds the top 20 to 30 feet (6 to 9 meters) with a green growth of plankton making the water look like pea soup. Later, the plankton aggregates in white clumps and looks like a snowstorm in the water. This may last only two weeks or a month. However, often just as the plankton bloom fades away, river runoff comes to cloud surface waters.

The second wave of plankton is less predictable and more localized. It may come in late summer, August through September or October, making the water look slightly red. This second bloom may come to one area and not to another, usually lasting a very short while. The water may be turbid one day and clear the next. Therefore, at easily accessible sites, it is always worth checking to see if the water is clear. The best summer visibility comes on a sunny day after a week of overcast weather.

Sometimes the only way to find good visibility in the late spring and early summer is to select a dive site deep enough that you can descend through the surface murkiness until the visibility improves. When diving in turbid water, use a compass; swim with your hands touching and extended forward to protect your head and face; and surface with a good reserve of air so that you can meet any emergency poor visibility might create.

One of the most beautiful dives I ever made was on a sunny day in May at Lookout Point in Howe Sound. Excessive Fraser River runoff and a healthy bloom of plankton had combined to make the surface almost opaque. There was only faceplate visibility until my buddy and I reached 50 feet (15 meters). Suddenly we were in a garden of fluffy white plumose anemones shimmering with phosphorescence. Spectacular! Like a night dive, only better, because it came as such a complete surprise. Is it any wonder I advocate diving year-round?

BULL KELP – Beauty or beast? If you have never been diving in kelp you should know something about it.

The large bull kelp is beautiful on its own as it streams above you like flags in the current. I love it just for that. Experienced North Pacific divers are lured to it for many other reasons too. For instance, it can help orient you. On the surface, bull kelp gives an indication of depth because in the Strait of Georgia it usually grows in less than 30 feet (9 meters) of water. Kelp shows you the direction the current is running. When it pops to the surface, the current is slowing down.

Under water, kelp gives a handhold in difficult current. In areas with lots of boats, if the kelp itself is not too thick to penetrate, it is a relatively traffic-free place to ascend.

Bull kelp on surface at slack water

It provides a rich habitat for marine life. You will often find crabs hiding under it and fish swimming through it. Urchins eat it as a favorite food. Kelp is interesting on its own, too. It is a seasonal plant which nearly dies off over the winter and grows again in spring and summer. It grows very rapidly, reportedly sometimes as much as 6 inches (15 centimeters) in a day. These facts are just a start. Interested divers can find a lot of fascinating information about kelp or marine algae.

It can be a hazard, though, if you are caught in it and then panic. When diving around bull kelp, be particularly careful at the surface. Kelp is easier to swim through under water. Enter the water by surface-diving down, feet first, to avoid entanglement. Always ascend with a reserve of air so that you can descend again, if necessary, and come up at another spot where the growth is not so thick. Bull kelp has a strong stem which is very difficult to break by hand. Wear a knife you can reach with either hand, so that if caught you can calmly cut your way free. I have never been caught in the kelp so that I had to cut my way free, but one time my buddy and I tried it to find out how difficult it would be. We discovered our knives cut the kelp like butter. But try it. Find out if your knife works. A few unprepared divers have drowned as a result of entanglement, and most of these drownings were on the surface. Do not avoid kelp because of its dangers, but use the many positive points which recommend it. Be careful when diving in it, and respect its strength.

CURRENTS AND RIPTIDES – The strongest tidal streams in the world occur in passages of the Strait of Georgia and Puget Sound. In some locations near islands and narrows there are tidal currents with massive kinetic energy – some race at the rate of 16 knots (30 kilometers/hour). No person can command this element, you must work with it. But you *can* glance at a chart and predict areas where current will be a serious consideration. And, where there is current there is also abundant marine life because the moving water provides food for many animals. It is well worth learning to dive safely in currents in order to enjoy the rich scenes that open to you:

1. Always ask local divers for advice about sites and times.

2. Wear a small volume mask. It is less likely than a large mask to be dislodged by the current.

3. Wear a whistle.

4. Learn to use your tide and current tables, charts and other tools and plan each dive carefully. Technical help enabling divers to determine *when to go* is burgeoning – more data, more devices are out there to help with currents.

Always think for yourself – do not rely on the expert in your crowd. Do not rely on the pickup boat, yet on some dives you must also have a pickup boat standing by. And do not rely on your charter operator to put you in at the right time. Every diver should learn to deal with currents and think for themselves on every dive. Ask your buddy to make a dive plan, too, then check to see if you have planned for the same time. Remember to account for daylight saving time when it is in effect. Many divers do not wear a dive watch because they calculate dive down-time using their dive computer. When diving high current sites of the North Pacific, it is also important to know the actual time. Wear a watch.

Every year divers stretch the limits – dare more, dive where bigger, more radical tidal currents flow. Many charter operators have learned to dive their "home" big-current sites safely, and they take divers there at the right time. When you dive a big-current site on complete slack, and on one of the best days of the year for it, it feels easy. It feels like a "piece of cake". It isn't. Many operators have great skill and local knowledge. Each diver should strive to acquire those skills. And divers should ask questions, too, plumb for all the information that's out there. Use everything you can.

Diving high-current sites is also becoming more possible because of the abundance of information and aids that are available – new current tables, computer programs to calculate current time and direction, as well as hand-held computers for the same purpose. Use one or more of the new tools, carefully – use what works for you. But whatever you do, do not become complacent about current.

5. When diving in an area subject to strong currents, a fairly safe rule for timing your dive is to get wet 30 minutes before slack tide, the period when the water is still and the tide is neither coming in nor going out. Remember that tides and currents do not always fit with the tables. Depend upon your common sense. Look at the water and sum up the situation visually before entering the water. For instance, at Sechelt Rapids be ready at the site 1 hour before slack, watching and waiting for the water to slow down. Then complete your dive shortly after the tide has turned.

6. When diving where the current is not too strong, you do not necessarily have to dive precisely on slack but somewhere near slack. Learn to crawl and rock climb: hold onto rocks and pull yourself along. Crawling up-current saves a lot of energy and air. Then when half of your air is gone, drift down-current until you have returned to your entry point. If caught in a stronger current than expected on a sandy bottom, you could "knife it". But this should be avoided if possible to protect marine life. Even holding onto rocks should be avoided because you are liable to damage the animals   and the bottom. Try not to disturb the marine life, nor even the rocks.

7. When diving in a location with very strong currents, such as Deception Pass between Fidalgo and Whidbey islands or Point Wilson Reef in Admiralty Inlet, plan to have a "live" boat – a vessel under power and not anchored – ready to pick up all divers, if necessary. Or, you can deliberately plan a "drift" dive as at Agate Passage or Tzoonie Narrows. A floating buoy with dive flag should mark the group of divers so that the following boat can follow easily and other boats can avoid the divers.

8. When diving from a boat in current, plan to descend at the anchor line and surface near the bow. Leave a floating line that is 200 feet (60 meters) long trailing behind. If you miss the boat you can catch onto the line. You travel just over 3 feet (1 meter) per second with a 2-knot (3¾-kilometer) per hour current. Thus 200 feet (60 meters) of line "buys" nearly one minute to swim across the current to reach the line. Attach a float or a plastic bottle to the end of the line or use a polypropylene line which floats.

When diving from a charter boat, one operator offers the following rule of thumb: "Never pay operator *before* going for a boat dive! Pay *after* he finds you and picks you up."

9. If caught in a rip current, an upwelling or downwelling do not try to swim against it. Swim across it and gradually work your way out.

10. Learn to cope with current and then discover some most rewarding diving.

Bull kelp flowing in direction current is moving

Finally, remember that all predictions are just that – only predictions. Whatever the source, do not accept current or tide information as infallible. No predictions are. Wind and barometric pressure can radically alter the time of the turn. According to the *Canadian Tide and Current Tables* published by the Canadian Hydrographic Service, "Currents are particularly sensitive to the effects of wind. The times of slack water can be advanced or retarded considerably by strong winds. In some instances, particularly if the following flood or ebb current is weak, the direction of current may not change and slack water may not occur."

When you reach the site check it out: look at the kelp, throw in a stick, float a bottle. If the current is not doing what you expected, trust what you see. Be prepared to watch and wait for the right moment to dive – if you have missed slack, call off the dive. And enjoy it another day.

BASIC SOURCES OF TIDE AND CURRENT INFORMATION FOR REGIONS IN THIS GUIDEBOOK ARE: the Canadian Hydrographic Service *Tide and Current Tables, Volume 5,* and the United States National Ocean Service (NOAA) *Tide Tables, West Coast of North and South America,* and *Tidal Current Tables, Pacific Coast of North America and Asia North* – all published annually.

A greater number of current tables are included in the Canadian tables than used to be. It has become possible to dive with a degree of confidence at wild current sites such as Sechelt Rapids and Race Rocks even though the "window of time" to dive is not great. The accuracy of the predictions at these sites is especially good since the dives are close to or at the current stations.

At most stations in the current tables you can expect slack within 15 minutes of their predictions 80% of the time. And since you can read Reference Station times straight from the current tables, it is easy to plan a dive near a Reference Station. However, after twenty-seven years of diving I still find it difficult to make conversions and predict slack at Secondary Stations using the basic tables. I find some of the aids out there helpful. One or more of the following modes of gaining current information could make it easier to plan your dive time.

• Books for More Information on Tides and Tidal Currents
Current and Tide Tables (published annually by Island Canoe, Inc.) covers Puget Sound, Deception Pass, the San Juans, the Gulf Islands and Strait of Juan de Fuca. It is an abridged version of the United States NOAA tables. Selected pages have been published and rewritten to make them easier to understand – only the tables needed for this region are included. Obtain at dive shops, marinas or outdoor stores.

And the following publications are an enormous help in waterways near small islands and convoluted inlets to give a concept of where the currents circle and eddy and do things different from simply flowing one direction when the tide floods and the other when it ebbs. Also useful in regions with straightforward ebb and flood flow.

Books and computer aids to help with information on current

Current Atlas: Juan de Fuca Strait to Strait of Georgia is a book of charts with arrows of varying thickness to indicate the direction and strength of current. These charts are based on theory using a numerical model. They are of limited value near the shore and in shallow areas, but could be useful for boat diving a mile or so (a few kilometers) from the shore at the outer sides of the Gulf and San Juan islands and Vancouver Island. These charts are easy for people with visual, rather than mathematical, orientation to relate to.

• Scope: From west of Race Rocks in Juan de Fuca Strait north through the Strait of Georgia to Discovery Passage at Campbell River, including the Gulf Islands and the San Juan Islands but not Howe Sound or Indian Arm. It must be used with either *Murray's Tables* or *Washburne's Tables*. The *Current Atlas* is purchased once, then you use it with new *Murray's* or *Washburne's* tables purchased annually.
• Where to obtain it: The *Current Atlas,* as well as *Washburne's* and *Murray's* tables, are available wherever nautical charts are sold and from Canadian Hydrographic Service, PO Box 6000, Sidney BC V8L 4B2, (604) 363-6358; fax (604) 363-6390.

Puget Sound Current Guide is a book of charts with arrows to indicate the direction of ebb and flood currents, and with notations of time corrections to make on current table daily predictions to determine slack water. These charts are based on observations. They are easy for people with visual, rather than mathematical, orientation to relate to.
• Scope: From Juan de Fuca Strait south to Olympia, Washington. Illustrates 103 current stations in Puget Sound.
• Expand its use: This book of maps can be used on its own or to complement the *Current Master* program.
Where to obtain it: Dive shops, marinas or contact Island Canoe, Inc., 3556 West Blakely Avenue NE, Bainbridge Island WA 98110, (206) 842-5997.

San Juan Current Guide: Including the Gulf Islands and Strait of Juan de Fuca is a book of charts with arrows to indicate the direction of ebb and flood currents, and with notations of time corrections to make on current table daily predictions to determine slack water. These charts are easy for people with visual, rather than mathematical, orientation to relate to.
• Scope: From Juan de Fuca Strait north to Dodd Narrows near Nanaimo in British Columbia. Illustrates more than 100 current stations.
• Expand its use: This book of maps can be used on its own or to complement the *Current Master* program.
• Where to obtain it: Dive shops, marinas or contact Island Canoe, Inc., 3556 West Blakely Avenue NE, Bainbridge Island WA 98110, (206) 842-5997.

Tidelog: Puget Sound Edition, daily tide graphics. A wonderful pair of waves shows the predicted high and low tides for Seattle for every day of the year. The waves give a very physical idea of the volume of tidal exchange for each day and even dip below the bottom line of the graph at minus tides. Below each wave, the time is given so divers can see when to expect high and low water. Beneath that, two lines mark the time of the predicted turn of the current at "The Narrows, north end" and "Admiralty Inlet, Bush Point". A mass of data including tides for Port Townsend, tide corrections for other locations, currents for Rosario Strait and Deception Pass, current corrections for other locations and a set of miniaturized Tidal Current Charts are in the back of the book. *Tidelog* is an excellent source of information for divers who want quick-and-easy but slight data as well as for divers who want a great many facts.

For added interest and fun, this popular book shows the state of the moon each day. I met a diver who uses *Tidelog* to record her dive time and experiences. Since it is apparent on the wave what the tide was supposed to be doing when she was diving, she gains a good record on which to base corrections, if required, for future dives at each site. *Tidelog* is issued annually – buy a new one each year. It is superb for people who relate to graphics.
• Scope: *Tidelog* contains information for all of the Washington dive sites in this guidebook.
• Where to obtain it: Dive shops or contact Pacific Publishers, PO Box 480, Bolinas CA 94924, (415) 868-2909.

Divers deliberately drifting Tzoonie Narrows, "live" boat *Anna V* following

On *Subsea Explorer*, waiting for slack in Admiralty Inlet

22

• Computer Aids for More Information on Tidal Currents
TideFinder is a hand-held tide and current computer. The big advantage of this instrument is its small size. *TideFinder* and its Operations Manual can be taken onto a boat easily – you do not need a notebook computer. You punch in the station name, the time you want the information for and it computes. Information about tides or currents, depending on which you ask for, is reported on a two-line digital display. Current computations you can obtain are: next ebb, next flood, next slack, next current, present current speed and direction of current. Tide computations you can obtain are: next high, next low, next minus, next tide and present tide height. *TideFinder* is suited to persons with an ability to relate to information displayed numerically instead of graphically.
• Scope: The west coast *TideFinder* covers the entire region of this guidebook. Though not all tide and current points are shown on the 62 maps in the Operations Manual, virtually all computable ones in the government tables are programmed in: presently 1,253 tide points and 882 current points from Mexico through Alaska are included and the number is growing.
• Where to obtain it: From marine electronic dealers or contact Conex Electro-Systems, Inc., 1602 Carolina Street, Bellingham WA 98226, (206) 734-4323.
The computer is programmed to calculate tides and currents through the year 2008. After that it can be updated.

TideView is a computer program (MS-Windows and Apple Macintosh). It puts information about tidal currents on the computer screen like a moving picture. You can pinpoint a spot where you plan to dive, and the exact time. Zoom in on the area and see the direction of currents and approximate strength of predicted currents – done with arrows with tails. More tails for greater current. It presents the same type of information as the *Current Atlas* but is more detailed, avoids the use of tables to select the chart of currents you require, and produces charts for any requested time. With *TideView,* you can also see and print graphs of tide predictions as well as current predictions. It comes with a refreshingly short manual of 14 pages, and can be used by both math-oriented persons and those who are visually-oriented.
• Scope: At the time of writing, from west of Race Rocks in the Strait of Juan de Fuca north to Texada Island in the Strait of Georgia. Its scope is increasing.
• Where to obtain it: Channel Consulting Ltd., 3-2020 Douglas Street, Victoria BC V8T 4L1, (604) 388-0800, 1-800-409-9909. The disk is sold like tables, one year at a time; after your initial purchase you can buy annual updates for one-third of the price.

Current Master program (MS-DOS) provides information on both tide heights and tidal currents. It is particularly useful for obtaining current predictions. Calculates duration of slack, too. The program eliminates the need to calculate for Secondary Stations – *Current Master* makes it easy to locate the nearest station where data for currents are available, then to obtain a printed summary of corrected data for that station. You can print out graphs of current speeds and tide heights. Useful for people who are not oriented to using charts and numbers and doing calculations but who are visually oriented. It is menu driven, easy to use – has a mouse interface.
One hitch: *Current Master* sometimes tells you it is not possible to predict slack at the place and time you request it and then you are left with no information. Always carry your basic tidal current table too.
• Scope: From Olympia, Washington, north through Puget Sound and Juan de Fuca Strait to Dodd Narrows near Nanaimo in British Columbia; covers over 300 locations. It must be used with the *Puget Sound Current Guide* or *San Juan Current Guide,* depending on dive site. Buy the map books once, the computer program each year.
• Where to obtain it: At dive shops or contact Island Canoe, Inc., 3556 West Blakely Avenue NE, Bainbridge Island WA 98110, (206) 842-5997.

BOATS AND LOG BOOMS – Thousands of boats also use the inland sea waters described in this guide. Areas where boat traffic is particularly heavy are noted in the detailed site descriptions, and you should be especially careful at these places. But remember, a boat could appear at any time over any site. Dive defensively:
1. Dive with a dive flag – it's required. And it helps. Use it but do not count on it to protect you.
2. When ascending, spiral and look up in order to see as much of the surface as possible, and look for boats.
3. Listen for boats. Where the bottom is featureless, dive with a compass and ascend close to the contour of the bottom all the way to shore. At other sites ascend near a rock face, up your boat or dive-flag anchor line or in a kelp bed, being careful not to become caught in the kelp. Larger vessels usually steer clear of kelp.
4. If you cannot ascend at a protected place, ascend with a reserve of air and if you hear a power boat, stay down until it passes. If you hear a really big ship, hang onto rocks or wedge yourself between boulders on the bottom.
5. When diving near log booms, ascend with a reserve of air so that if you arrive immediately under the log boom you will have time to descend and come up again at another place. Spiral, look up, and extend one arm above you as you ascend.

BROKEN FISHING LINE – Beware of broken bits of fishing line under water. It is very strong and difficult to see. Look for it where you know there are lots of fishermen and at rocky points near heavily populated areas. Carry a diver's knife; if you become entangled you can cut yourself free.

SURGE AND SURF – Since the scope of this guide is limited to inland sea and inlets protected from the open ocean, surge and surf are not factors to consider at the sites described.

MARINE LIFE – The color and variety of marine animals living in the Strait of Georgia and Puget Sound is astonishing. I carry an underwater light on every dive in order not to miss any of that color. The sea is teeming with life, all of it fascinating, and practically none of it dangerous to the diver.
   The greatest number of sea stars found in any one area of the world are here. North Pacific waters are unrivalled for colorful invertebrates – 5,000 species have been identified. Close to 400 species of fish live in the eastern North Pacific. Marine algae or kelps are abundant, as well. More than 640 species of marine algae have been recorded in British Columbia.
   At shallow sandy sites you will probably find large Dungeness crabs revealed only by a pair of eyes and a slight indentation in the bottom. Moon snails that look like something from another planet. And sometimes the bottom itself takes off like a flying carpet – starry flounders in flight!
   When diving deep look for yelloweye rockfish beneath ledges. You might find prawns – especially at night, or discover ancient ghostly clumps of cloud sponges with a small rockfish peeping from each tuberous appendage. No one knows how to gauge for sure, but some say a clump as tall as a man must be hundreds of years old. Some say thousands.
   Among rocky reefs you will find red Irish lords, kelp greenlings skittering away spookily into crevices, tiny grunt sculpins looking like precisely painted tropical fish. Lingcod sometimes grow to 30 or 40 pounds (14 or 18 kilograms) – and more – in the rocky current-swept depths. Or you might meet a 2,000-pound (900-kilogram) Steller sea lion. Large marine mammals abound: from dolphins to harbor seals, sea lions and killer whales. Gorgeous giant red nudibranchs, delicate as tissue paper, waft through the water near newly laid eggs cascading over rocky cliffs like an intricate lace shawl. Also many small nudibranchs live in these waters.

And the North Pacific is home to some of the world's largest octopuses. For many years octopuses had the reputation of being dangerous to divers, but this is myth. The octopus can be handled quite easily. If one grabs onto you, simply tickle it and it will release you and slip away. But if you touch one, be gentle. Octopuses are fragile and easily damaged as well as being much more frightened of you than you are of them.

What animals *are* potentially dangerous in North Pacific waters? The following creatures are sometimes considered dangerous, or simply bothersome, by divers:

• **Dogfish Sharks** – Dogfish are not known to attack people, but most divers leave the water when dogfish start circling in a pack.

• **Jellyfish** – More of a nuisance than a hazard, the red, brown, yellow and water jellyfish can leave a painful sting. If you have seen any jellyfish, you and your buddy should check one another for stinging tentacles before removing masks and gloves. Even after removing gear be cautious as the stingers stay active on your gear for hours. I have been told that urine is an antidote, also that canned milk neutralizes the sting. Jellyfish are seasonal and appear most often in fall and early winter.

• **Killer Whales** – Killer whales are not known to attack people, but most divers leave the water when killer whales appear. Again, some divers try to meet killer whales under water.

• **Lingcod** – Though not generally considered dangerous, the lingcod has a formidable set of teeth and has been known to attack divers. Males may be aggressive when guarding eggs during winter.

• **Ratfish** – The ratfish has a poisonous spine just in front of its dorsal fin. Avoid this spine. Once a ratfish bit my leg on a night dive. The only attack I have heard of, yet, but beware.

• **Sea Urchins** – Urchins have sharp spines and can cause nasty puncture wounds as well as damage dry suits. A couple of antidotes I have heard of are urine and meat tenderizer.

• **Seals and Sea Lions** – These animals are sometimes sought, sometimes avoided. One diver told me he saw a seal dislodge a diver's mask in play, and caused the diver to panic. Another told me of a friend whose daily dive companion is a seal. Sea lions may approach divers and some divers have reported injuries. Yet I include a write-up in *99 DIVES* with guidelines for a winter dive with Steller sea lions for those who choose it. Even in winter, do not dive close to haulouts, do not touch sea lions. And if you meet a bull in summer, watch out. It will be aggressive.

• **Sixgill Sharks** – Sixgills have not harmed people to date, but have been noted to be more aggressive at dawn and dusk. They are meat eaters and they have very large mouths with exceedingly sharp teeth. In spite of their sluggish appearance they can react with startling speed when annoyed. It is safer not to touch. Yet, again, I include a write-up in *99 DIVES* with guidelines for a summer dive with sixgill sharks.

• **Wolf-eels** – The wolf-eel with its very strong teeth and jaws can inflict a bad bite. These fish are not known to attack without provocation, and if you avoid sticking your hands into holes and crevices you will probably never tangle with one. Be wary but not dismayed if a wolf-eel lunges out of a cave at you. Many divers hand-feed wolf-eels causing them to approach divers.

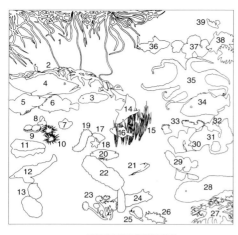

WHAT TO LOOK FOR

Rocky Reef
1. Bull kelp
2. Bottom kelp
3. Cabezon
4. Lingcod
5. Kelp greenling
6. Black rockfish
7. Red Irish lord
8. Swimming scallops
9. Abalones
10. Giant urchins
11. Rock scallop
12. Painted greenling
13. Chitons

Sand
14. Dogfish shark
15. Eelgrass
16. Seaperch
17. Striped seaperch
18. Leather star
19. Sea cucumber
20. Dungeness crab
21. Flounder
22. Sea pen
23. Plume worms
24. Orange peel nudibranch
25. Moon snail
26. Alabaster nudibranch

Rock Wall
27. Basket star
28. Wolf-eel
29. Chimney sponges
30. Grunt sculpin
31. Giant barnacles
32. Sailfin sculpin
33. Dahlia anemones
34. Copper rockfish
35. Octopus
36. Ratfish
37. Plumose anemones
38. Sunflower stars
39. Sea peaches

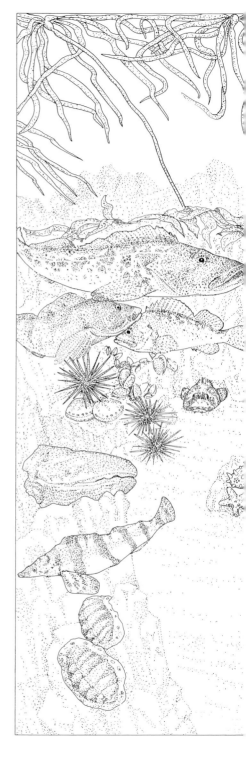

BOOKS ON FISH

Coastal Fishes of the Pacific Northwest by Andy Lamb and Phil Edgell, Harbour Publishing, Madeira Park BC, 1986.
(Brief facts on 174 species, easy to find. A drawing and a color photograph of every fish – fish silhouettes in table of contents. Index to common and scientific names.)

Pacific Coast Inshore Fishes by Daniel W. Gotshall, Sea Challengers, Monterey CA, 1989.
(User-friendly guide: covers 187 species with brief information including common and scientific names, features for identification, range and habitat; pictorial key to the fish families; 174 color photographs. Index to common and scientific names.)

Pacific Fishes of Canada, Bulletin 180 by J.L. Hart, Fisheries Research Board of Canada, Ottawa, 1973.
(Comprehensive descriptions of 325 fishes with a black-and-white drawing of every species, some color photographs. Index to common and scientific names.)

Probably More Than You Want to Know About the Fishes of the Pacific Coast by Robin Milton Love, Really Big Press, Santa Barbara CA, 1991.
(Full of facts you will find nowhere else, and it's fun! Illustrated with a drawing of each fish; common and scientific names index to the fishes.)

BOOKS ON A VARIETY OF MARINE LIFE

The Audubon Society Field Guide to North American Seashore Creatures by Norman A. Meinkoth, Alfred A. Knopf, New York, 1981.
(Pocket-sized identification guide for laypersons: filled with color photographs and well-organized data about invertebrates; a few diagrams.)

Beachwalker: Sea Life of the West Coast by Stefani Hewlett Paine, Douglas & McIntyre, Vancouver, 1992.
(Overall view for laypersons: includes fish, mammals, invertebrates. Black-and-white line drawings and photographs, some color.)

Between Pacific Tides by Edward F. Ricketts, Jack Calvin and Joel W. Hedgpeth, revised by David W. Phillips; Stanford University Press, Stanford CA, 1985.
(Scientific classic covering marine invertebrates, organized by habitat. Black-and-white photographs and drawings.)

Exploring the Seashore in British Columbia, Washington and Oregon by Gloria Snively, Gordon Soules Book Publishers, Vancouver, 1978.
(Guide for laypersons, organized by habitat: sea stars, crabs, kelp, anemones, sea birds and more. Well illustrated with line drawings; color photographs.)

Guide to Common Seaweeds of British Columbia, Handbook No. 27 by R.F. Scagel, British Columbia Provincial Museum, Victoria, 1972.
(Scientific but readable by anyone; no common names used. Information for each plant includes genus and species, description, habitat, distribution, and a line drawing; with index.)

Guide to Marine Invertebrates, Alaska to Baja California by Daniel W. Gotshall, Sea Challengers, Monterey CA, 1994.
(User-friendly guide covering 235 species of invertebrates and 18 tunicates. Each description includes common and scientific names, brief information about habitat, features for identification and a color photograph. Index to common names.)

Guide to the Western Seashore: Introductory Marinelife Guide to the Pacific Coast by Rick M. Harbo, Hancock House, Surrey BC, 1988.
(Photographic guide to invertebrates, fish, mammals and seaweeds. Brief descriptions along with 160 color photographs.)

Light's Manual: Intertidal Invertebrates of the Central California Coast edited by Ralph I. Smith and James T. Carlton, University of California Press, Berkeley CA, 1975.
(A scientific classic. Black-and-white drawings; index to scientific names.)

Northwest Shore Dives by Stephen Fischnaller, Bio-Marine Images, Edmonds WA, 1990.
(Drawings, photographs and a great deal of information about marine life as well as dive site descriptions in this volume which is primarily a dive guidebook for Washington. Index contains common and scientific names.)

Pacific Coast Nudibranchs: A Guide to the Opisthobranchs, Alaska to Baja California by David W. Behrens, Sea Challengers, Monterey CA, 1991.
(User-friendly comprehensive guide: covers 217 species with brief information including common and scientific names, features for identification, range and habitat; 228 color photographs.)

Seashore Life of the Northern Pacific Coast: An Illustrated Guide to Northern California, Oregon, Washington, and British Columbia by Eugene N. Kozloff, University of Washington Press, Seattle, 1983.
(Scientific information organized by habitat. Lots of color photographs. Index to common and scientific names.)

Tidepool & Reef: Marinelife Guide to the Pacific Northwest Coast by Rick M. Harbo, Hancock House, Surrey BC, 1980.
(Photographic guide to invertebrates, fish and seaweeds: 256 color photographs.)

PICTURE BOOK
The Emerald Sea by Dale Sanders (photographs) and Diane Swanson (text), Whitecap Books, North Vancouver BC, 1993.
(Elegant large-format book with fabulous color photographs of North Pacific marine life and a couple wrecks. Informally organized information about marine life; common and scientific names list. Index to common names.)

MARINE LIFE COURSES FOR SCUBA DIVERS
Andy Lamb's Marine Life Identification
3171 Huntleigh Crescent
North Vancouver BC V7H 1C9
(604) 929-4131

Marine Life Course for Scuba Divers
310-170 East 3rd Street
North Vancouver BC V7L 1E6
(604) 980-3406; fax (604) 980-2121

VIDEO CASSETTES
Sea Symphony by Lee Goldman, Visions of the Planet, Bellingham WA, 1994.
(Cool, green, kelp-forest scenes and brilliant close-ups of Pacific Northwest marine creatures in their natural habitat: stars of the show include giant octopuses, curious seals, orange sea pens, lingcod, sponges, wolf-eels, lion nudibranchs, rainbow sea stars and bowers of plumose anemones.)

The World Below Us by Andrew Bell, Abel Video Productions, Victoria, 1992.
(Steller sea lions, white-sided Pacific dolphins, an octopus, a giant silver nudibranch, a sea pen and more.)

DIVER TRAFFIC – Divers have become part of the marine life scene. Diving is a mainstream recreation now and there's good and bad in that. Lots of people to dive with. Lots of facilities. But diving etiquette on shore becomes more and more important. We need to be considerate when parking; be discreet when changing, not strip in the middle of the road before and after diving; take care not to trespass when walking to and from the water, and go quietly. When diving at night, it makes sense to avoid shining lights into the windows of private homes and to save wild parties for the wilds – enjoy quiet après-dive parties at beaches in the city.

And what about the effect of divers on the sea, the fish? Diver damage from dropping anchors on reefs and wrecks, kicking fragile cloud sponges, dragging equipment consoles on the bottom, snagging and breaking hydrocoral – it happens. Divers passing through can wreak havoc on the marine environment without the divers even being aware of it. Yet if we dive carefully we can look forward to returning again and again to pristine sites.

Also I believe we should look, not touch, and leave the sea and fish as we find them. Abalones and rock scallops are becoming scarce in British Columbia, particularly – perhaps due to commercial fisheries catches, perhaps due to sport divers. I still see many sport divers with spear guns in Washington and fish are noticeably scarce – recently I met a diver with a lance who said he was hunting octopuses. I have seen no spear guns in the past few years in British Columbia and I see lots of fish, yet many divers report fewer fish. I believe that if fish are decreasing in numbers, the growing number of hook-and-line fishermen and the growing number of seals might be the reason. They eat fish. In the past twenty years, the seal population has increased tenfold.

When creating artificial reefs we need to be careful that our additions do not harm the environment as we try to enhance it, and I do not believe in feeding fish as it alters their natural behavior. They become too trusting. Feeding a wolf-eel could result in the death of the animal. A friendly wolf-eel might lunge from its den looking for handouts, frighten a visiting diver and be killed.

When diving, we are favored guests in a special place. Let's not change that place, let's just go for a visit.

PUBLIC ACCESS – "You can't drive twenty minutes without reaching water in Washington," one dive buddy says.

Endless diving is at hand; access is only limited by our imagination. I hope readers of this guidebook will use it as a starting point, begin using these reference materials and then throw the guidebook away. Go out and find your own sites: use everything you can to learn where to gain access to the water. For a start, you can find new sites to dive from shore by looking for parks for access. Next learn about launching sites in each area, then use an inflatable or dive-kayak and there is no limit to where you can go. But go carefully and honor wildlife reserves.

See lists of publications in service information of each chapter with information on launch sites and facilities.

In Washington, whenever you see this official public access logo on a sign you may walk to the water.

Look for information on parks
• In British Columbia: federal or provincial parks, or forest service recreation sites.
• In Washington: federal, state, county or department of natural resources parks. And wherever you go, look for the official state public access sign that confirms access is permitted.

Look for information on launching ramps: Many launching ramps are listed in the service information of each chapter. In addition
• In British Columbia: Canadian Hydrographic Service small-craft charts and some other large scale ones show launching ramps with small black wedges.
• In Washington: many nautical charts show launching ramps.

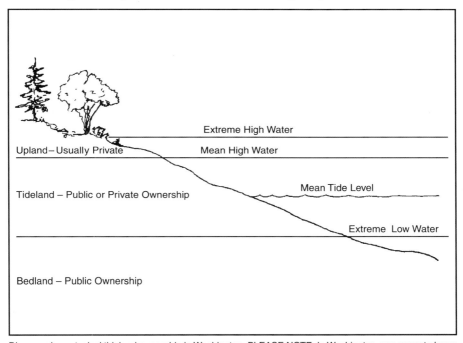

Diagram shows typical tideland ownership in Washington. PLEASE NOTE: In Washington, you cannot always land on the beach or even in shallow water. Privately owned property often extends below mean tide level to the extreme low-water mark.

Refer to lists of national wildlife refuge sites and ecological reserves so you do not inadvertently dive or land where it might be harmful to the marine life.
• For British Columbia: obtain a list of provincial ecological reserves from BC Parks, Planning and Conservation Services, 2nd Floor, 800 Johnson Street, Victoria BC V8V 1X4, (604) 387-5002; fax (604) 387-5757.
• For Washington: obtain a list of national wildlife refuge sites from San Juan Islands National Wildlife Refuge, 100 Brown Farm Road, Olympia WA 98506, (206) 753-9467.

To establish new official public access points
• In British Columbia: popular sites with entry across Crown land at road ends could be set aside as recreational reserves. To inquire, contact BC Lands, Ministry of Environment, Lands and Parks, Land Operations, Lower Mainland Region, Suite 401, 4603 Kingsway, Burnaby BC V5H 4M4, (604) 660-5500; fax (604) 660-5538.
• In Washington: refer to the *Shoreline Public Access Handbook* by James W. Scott. It contains a great deal of information about site planning, permit administrators' guidelines and how to proceed. Purchase from State of Washington Department of Ecology, Publications Department, PO Box 47600, Olympia WA 98504-7600, (206) 407-7472; fax (206) 407-6989.

KAYAK-DIVING – Going to the site using a "sit-on-top" dive-kayak as transportation is a wonderful way to extend the scope of where you can go diving. Use a dive-kayak to eliminate a difficult swim or to reach sites up to 2 to 3 nautical miles (4 to 5 kilometers) away. Or paddle close alongside the shore to reach a point or beach inaccessible by road. I believe every diver should try it out and consider making a dive-kayak a standard piece of their diving equipment.

Find someone to teach you the basics of diving with a dive-kayak or ask how to do it where you rent or buy a dive-kayak and remember that in both the United States and Canada every boat must be equipped with a personal flotation device (PFD) for each person on board. A guided excursion with an experienced kayak-diver is an ideal way to start. Then take it slowly.

The first time I used a dive-kayak my buddy and I paddled for 10 minutes across a short stretch of open water to a beach where it was easy to land and gear up. Next

At Rosario Beach, loading gear for Sares Head

dive I rolled off and got back on board in the shallows. Diving in open water looked like a giant step. I doubted I could climb back on, but soon found that part is easy. Once you are organized, it is also simple to roll off the kayak and get geared up in the water. First I hung a tether off my kayak to clip my weight belt to, but now have acquired a buoyancy compensator with weights in it. Makes the whole thing so easy.

The only limitations I have found with the single-person dive-kayaks I use is that the combined weight of diver plus gear must be no more than 250 to 300 pounds (115 to 135 kilograms). The dive-kayak will not float more weight. The only way to overcome that one is for a single diver to paddle a double kayak.

The second thing is that I cannot seem to avoid splashing water as I go – no problem for wet-suit divers. But on a hot day, dry-suit divers should stow their suits inside the dive-kayaks so the suits are dry to dive in and so they do not become overheated paddling to the site. If going to an open-water site or in winter, a dry-suit diver can put his or her suit halfway on and tuck the sleeves into the waist for paddling; then wriggle arms and head into the suit at the site. I've done it. But it is easier to put drip-rings on your paddle so you do not drip water into your lap. To me this messing about to keep my dry suit dry is worth it – a dive-kayak is freedom.

DIVING REGULATIONS AND SAFETY
Dive Flag Regulations in British Columbia
• Shore divers: when diving, fly your red-and-white diver-down flag from a float. It is required under the Canada Shipping Act. This diver-down flag is recognized throughout North America as marking an area where scuba diving is in progress.

• Boat divers: whenever divers are in the water, fly your red-and-white diver-down flag from a float on the water and fly your blue-and-white international Code Flag "A" – or Alpha flag – from the boat. The Alpha flag is required under the Canada Shipping Act. It is recognized throughout the world, and means "I have a diver down: keep well clear at slow speed."

Obtain the free *Safe Boating Guide* with details about dive flags from most marinas, any Coast Guard Station or from the Canadian Coast Guard, 800 Burrard Street, Suite 620, Vancouver BC V6Z 2J8. In Vancouver, telephone (604) 666-0146. In Victoria, telephone (604) 363-3879.

Dive Flag Regulations in Washington
• Shore divers: when diving, fly your red-and-white diver-down flag from a float. It is required by law in some counties and unless you know the regulations where you are, it is simpler always to fly it. This diver-down flag is recognized throughout North America as marking an area where scuba diving is in progress.

• Boat divers: fly your blue-and-white international Code Flag "A" – or Alpha flag – on all dives. The Alpha flag is required under the federal Regulations for the Prevention of Collisions also referred to by the short titles "The Collision Regulations" or "COL REGS" – or as "The Rules of the Road". The Alpha flag is a navigational signal indicating the vessel's restricted maneuverability and does not pertain to the diver. In addition, therefore, also fly your red-and-white diver-down flag from a float.

Obtain the free *Federal Requirements and Safety Tips for Recreational Boaters* booklet with details about use of the dive flag by boaters from most marinas and boat shops or obtain from the Commander, CCGD 13(B), US Coast Guard, 915 Second Avenue, Seattle WA 98174-1067. Send a self-addressed stamped envelope when requesting that the booklet be mailed to you.

Diving Safety in British Columbia and Washington
Divers Alert Network (DAN) is an international non-profit member-supported organization dedicated to diving safety. DAN's 24-hour diving emergency hotline number is listed at the top of the service information in each chapter of this guidebook.

Divers Alert Network (DAN)
Box 3823
Duke University Medical Center
Durham NC 27710
To join DAN: telephone 1-800-446-2671; or fax (919) 490-6630.

Membership in DAN provides
• 24-hour Diving Emergency Hotline (919) 684-8111
• Diving Medicine and Safety Infoline (919) 684-2948
• Assist America, a global emergency medical evacuation service
• Divers' medical insurance policy covering treatment expenses worldwide for any in-water diving or snorkeling accident, available to all residents of the United States and Canada
• *Alert Diver* bimonthly magazine
• Dan credit card, and more.

UNDERWATER PHOTOGRAPHY – "If you have a camera the very worst dive site is a good one," says one enthusiastic underwater photographer. Because of an awakening of ecological awareness and conservation, and because of improved cameras and housings, underwater video- and still-photography are becoming more and more popular. Some dive boats have video players on board so you can share your dive as soon as you surface. Now when the word "shoot" is used in diving, it connotes the idea of capturing a subject on film, rather than on the end of a spear.

What's different about underwater photography in the North Pacific sea? Winter is the best season for it because visibility is then at its best. Artificial light is usually required, as available light is almost always insufficient to produce good photographs. Endless subjects are at hand, particularly to photographers interested in close-up work, as there are so many colorful invertebrates in these waters. Even after years of photography, an enthusiast may find new subjects on every dive.

Underwater subjects are limited only by the imagination. One photographer specializes in photographing eyes of marine life as well as photographing subjects in the middle distance and the whole scene. The extreme close-up on the top left-hand side is the eye of a red Irish lord.

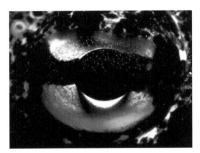
Eye of red Irish lord

Head of red Irish lord

Photographer captures the whole scene: a diver hovering close to the bottom at Edmonds Underwater Park, peering beneath plumose anemones at a red Irish lord.

34

Checking underwater camera before dive

MARINE LIFE CONSERVATION – In British Columbia you will be "one of the crowd" if you do not spearfish at popular sites and if you dive carefully to avoid damaging fragile marine life. For twenty years, divers have pressed for conservation.

Now, in 1994, for the first time government regulations are in place to completely protect two sites: Porteau Cove Marine Park and Whytecliff Park. Marine life may not be taken from these sites by any means – sport diving, sport fishing or commercial fishing. The areas are small. In addition, the regulations must be put in place anew each year. They could be reversed next year or the next. Nevertheless, this new government action makes 1994 a year for Canadian divers to remember. We have been hoping for this precedent for so long. These parks are the first locations just offshore from any coastline in British Columbia – or in Canada – to be fully protected.

In Washington, the history of parks goes way back: Edmonds became the first underwater park on the west coast in 1970. In 1993, Washington State Senate Bill 5332 was passed committing the state ". . . to conserve and protect unique marine resources of the state of Washington". To my knowledge, this new protection is not complete protection, but it is a wonderful start of involvement on the part of government to conserve marine life.

Conservation offers divers enormous challenge and can be an important uniting activity. Historically, conservation has been big with clubs. In future it could become an even more vital common interest – a great reason for divers to meet. Contact the following organizations:

The Marine Life Sanctuaries Society of British Columbia, PO Box 48299, Bentall Centre, Vancouver BC V7X 1A1, (604) 929-4131. The objective of the society is to protect areas of the British Columbia marine environment. An example of what they are doing: in 1994, the society staged the first annual "lingcod-egg-mass count" and all interested members took part.

Washington Scuba Alliance, 120 State Avenue NE #18, Olympia WA 98501-8212. This group promotes the study, protection, development and enhancement of the underwater environment – activities often are involved with artificial reef projects such as at Edmonds and the proposed Titlow Park Marine Preserve. The society appreciates written input from divers about where they want underwater parks.

SPEARFISHING AND SHELLFISH COLLECTING – I do not believe there is a place any longer for spearfishing at any dive site described in any diving guidebook. Scuba diving has become a mainstream recreation – too many people are doing it for it to be possible for any site to stay beautiful if each diver takes even just one empty shell.
• In British Columbia: Sport fishing regulations apply to collecting and spearfishing by scuba divers. At the time of writing, divers are required to obtain a license to take finned fish just as hook-and-line fishermen are. A license is not required to collect shellfish but regulations could change from year to year, and a closure on the taking of abalone by any means or from any site is in force at the time of writing. If you plan to visit remote or unusual sites and collect marine life for dinner in British Columbia, obtain a *British Columbia Tidal Waters Sport Fishing Guide* with current regulations, available free at sports stores.
• In Washington: Special sport fishing regulations apply to collecting and spearfishing by scuba divers. At the time of writing, divers in salt water may not take or fish for salmon, sturgeon, octopus or crabs with underwater spearfishing gear, and divers may not possess these fish. All license requirements related to bag limits, size, season and area restrictions for the taking of food fish and shellfish apply to divers, except that divers are limited to one lingcod per day during open season regardless of size. If you plan to visit remote or unusual sites and collect marine life for dinner in Washington, obtain a *Salmon, Shellfish, Bottomfish, Sport Fishing Guide* with current regulations, available free at sports stores.

Cautions Regarding Collecting Seafood: bivalve shellfish may be made unfit for people to eat by:

1. Feeding in waters polluted by sewage. Do not collect shellfish in highly populated areas.

2. Feeding on toxic organisms of the genus *Alexandrium* that produces a bloom commonly called "red tide". These microscopic one-celled animals may cause paralytic shellfish poisoning (PSP); high concentrations can cause illness or death. If shellfish come from red tide waters, cooking does not reduce their toxicity. The sea might take on a striking, reddish color when red tide is present or the water may be clear. Do not trust your own eyes on this one. Consult the local Fisheries Office for closed areas. Also look for posted notices and do not collect shellfish if you see a red tide sign. If you see no sign but suspect a problem, telephone.

• In British Columbia: Shellfish Infoline, recorded: (604) 666-3169.
• In Washington: Red Tide Hotline, recorded: 1-800-562-5632.

BOTTLE, CHINA AND JUNK COLLECTING – "I'm diving for history!" That is the exuberant way one diver describes his passionate pursuit of everyday relics of the past: bottles, cups and saucers, foot warmers, mining artifacts.

Try it. Diving for bottles opens a whole new world on land, stirs you to learn about pioneer days on Pacific shores, might become a wonderfully absorbing obsession! This diving specialty appeals to divers with the sleuth in them, appeals to those who like to explore, and may be lucrative for the discriminating collector. I love to explore but was still slow to catch onto the fun of diving for junk. Also, I soul searched and wondered if bottle collecting, too, is an unacceptable inclusion in a guidebook as I now believe collecting marine life to be. Are we destroying our heritage by taking old bottles buried in the muck? I think not. No one would ever have seen the bottles I found if I had not gone down to look: those bottles could not have been photographed on the ocean floor – they were buried in silt. Any things thrown overboard are not protected and are fair game. The only bottles and china you should not take are those within the vicinity of a shipwreck as they could be part of the wreck.

For years the general public has enjoyed the finding, trading, buying and selling of bottles on land – the fine arts department in the public library has countless books with bottle prices on their shelves. Despite the value placed on old bottles, they are not priceless. And bottles are not irreplaceable relics of a prehistoric civilization – diving for old bottles is not like digging in a midden nor are old bottles a limited resource. Enormous numbers of bottles are out there, and they are a fun, social trading commodity that got me reading history. Having thought about it hard, I happily allowed myself to become hooked.

To really get into "diving for dishes", I believe you must take each step dedicated artifact divers do. First, research in the library before diving. Next, have the fun or disappointment of the dive. Then research again after the dive to learn more about what you have found. For ideas to start you off, look for "bottle dives" in the index at the back of this book. When you have tried some of the known bottle sites, start finding your own. They are sure to be better, but use discretion and avoid locations near shipwrecks or offshore from land-based archaeological sites and middens. The process that worked to involve me in this diving specialty is as follows:

1. In the library: look at old maps, charts and photos, and read regional histories to locate former passenger-steamer wharves, logging camps and settlements. Many easy-to-read books are available about the Mosquito Fleet in Puget Sound. And many more books on Canadian maritime history. Union Steamships pioneered the waterways of British Columbia. It is to British Columbia what Hudson's Bay Company is to Canada. If you want to find old artifacts, learn where the Mosquito Fleet and Union Steamships called in.

It is helpful to see what a locale looked like in the old days. Photographs of old docks and wharves where the ships stopped are in some of these books, and some libraries have historic photograph files. The fine arts department of Vancouver Public Library has such a collection: it is well indexed, and most photos are dated. Buy or photocopy the old photographs and take them with you when you head out to dive.

2. At the site before diving: go to local museums, coffee shops and art galleries. Talk with people, and look for old photographs of terrain and buildings. Artifacts are often found at the base of a steep hill near an old dock; guess where objects might have rolled to. Sometimes old buildings and pilings of wharves are still there making it easy to locate where the action was. Look for any creeks that might flood in and deposit silt which would bury artifacts. Locations at least 100 yards (90 meters) away from such a creek are less likely to be silted over, especially crucial at shallow sites. Study your charts and compare them to what you see. Before diving, make a plan with your buddy about what you will do if vision is obscured. You are almost on your own when diving for junk as usually each diver stirs up so much silt.

3. In the water: take a light. Dive on the ebb, if possible, on days with an extreme tidal exchange. Usually best because the tide carries away the silt that you kick up. When at deeper sites that slope off rapidly on the chart, start deep and work your way up. At shallow sites, dive in a small area and gradually enlarge it. If looking for bottles thrown off a dock you can often find them in 30 to 40 feet (9 to 12 meters). Flat silty bottom is good for the determined collector who digs deep.

Fan the bottom gently with your hand to stir up silt and reveal hidden relics. If digging, wear gloves to protect yourself from broken glass. At open-water sites scan the tops of mounds. Once you've made some finds, visualize a trail and follow it.

Look for barnacles, the most obvious sign of age on china and bottles. Do an initial sort of your bottle finds while diving, and wash out as much silt as possible. Look for bottles with odd and unusual shapes and bottles with no threads for screw tops. Black shiny bottles may be old and rare and therefore most desirable. Look for bottles that do not have a seam running all the way up the neck. These are the hand-finished ones. If you find a bottle with a rough bit of glass called a "pontil" stuck to the bottom, you have found a really old collector's item. If delving for Union Steamship relics, look for logos on the china. Later you can date your finds because different logos were used at different times.

Once when diving for mining artifacts my buddy and I found a Mercedes-Benz. If you discover an unexpected item of that sort, wise to note the location and report it to the police. If you find fossils or a remarkable artifact that might be an ancient archaeological relic, do not disturb the site but note the location and report it to the appropriate government office in Washington or British Columbia on page 40.

4. At the site after diving: show-and-tell time when you and your buddy empty goodie bags and discuss what you've found is both fun and useful. You can have a closer look and put back what you decide you do not want. Or give it to your buddy. Or give it a local resident who has expressed interest in the history of the region.

5. At home after diving: clean your finds – If you want to. I sometimes prefer my finds complete with barnacles. If you choose to clean your bottles, china, crystal and other ceramics, one method is by soaking them in a 1:16 or 1:20 solution of muriatic acid and water. Set the objects in the mixture and cover. Take out occasionally and scrub. In two or three days your "pieces of history" should be clean. However, some bottle collectors say that acid damages really old glass.

6. Go back to the library: read about each object you found. Where does it belong in history? Where did it come from? When was it made? What is its value? Identify it.

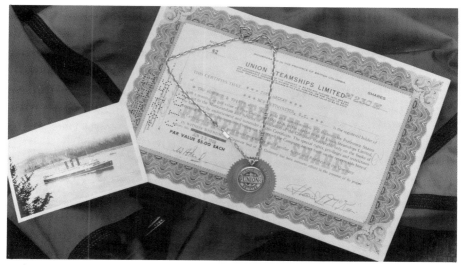

History weaves into the present: one bottle diver's memorabilia includes an old British Columbia Coastal Steamships photograph, an original Union Steamships Limited stock certificate and, on the certificate, a medallion made of the china logo from a Union steamship plate he found near Bowen Island. The logo was probably from the 1920s to 1940s.

• For More Information on Bottles

Bowen Island 1872-1972 by Irene Howard, Bowen Island Historians, Bowen Island BC, 1973.
(History of places where Terminal and Union steamships called in.)

Bottles in Canada: the collectors' guide to seeking, finding, dating, pricing and researching bottles by Doris and Peter Unitt, Clock House Publishing, Markham ON, 1972.
(Illustrations of more than 2,000 bottles; glossary and Canadian glass factories list.)

Diving for Northwest Relics: Identification and Dating of Bottles, Pottery and Marine Hardware by James Seeley White, Binford & Mort, Portland, 1979.
(Well illustrated.)

The Parks Canada Glass Glossary for the Description of Containers, Tableware, Flat Glass, and Closures by Olive Jones and Catherine Sullivan, Parks Canada, Ottawa, 1985.
(A system of recording data on glass artifacts is included. The book is illustrated with photographs and diagrams, one showing the parts of a bottle: bore, finish, lip, string rim, neck, shoulder, body, heel, resting point, push up, and base.)

Western Canadian Bottle Collecting, Volumes 1 and 2 by George Watson and Robert Skrill, The Westward Collector, Nanaimo BC, 1971 and 1973.
(Photographs of bottles and breweries; bottle prices; a directory of early breweries.)

Unitt's Canadian Price Guides to Antiques & Collectables (Books 12 through 15) by Peter Unitt and Anne Worrall, Fitzhenry & Whiteside, Markham ON, published from 1991 to 1993.
(Beer bottle photographs, breweries, prices. And fruit jars.)

ARCHAEOLOGICAL DIVING – Ancient relics and fossils are hidden beneath the seas. In 1992 a barbed harpoon point made of antler bone was found at Galiano Island. This tool is now being carbon-dated, it was probably crafted 6,800 years ago. Middens, petroglyphs and artifacts that were once on the surface of the earth are beneath the water today because sea level has risen as a result of the warm interglacial climatic period we are in now. Scuba diving makes these clues to the past available to researchers. Archaeological dive sites are becoming a major source of new evidence about prehistoric coastal plants, animals and people. At Galiano Island marine anthropologists worked with a staff of five and fifty volunteer field workers to excavate the harpoon. It was beneath 8 feet (2½ meters) of sand submerged in 10 to 20 feet (3 to 6 meters) of water, depending on tide height. Diving was documented on video cassettes. Casual visitors at the beach were offered on-site education about the sophisticated project. These two activities took this highly technical operation out of the experts-only realm and made it a vital, living event for everyone.

Opportunities for the thrill of discovery are limitless. At the time of writing, financial reward in Canada in the form of tax incentives, as well as sale to public institutions, are also possibilities, but that day may be passing. I am told by others that chances for remuneration are zilch – in any event, cultural treasures are priceless. In British Columbia, such objects as the harpoon point are protected under the provincial Heritage Conservation Act and under the federal Cultural Property Export and Import Act. In Washington, they are protected under the state Archaeological Sites and Resources Act. It is important that scuba divers become aware of and honor invaluable heritage material hidden beneath the sea.

The most important thing to do, if you make a find, is leave it where it is and contact the appropriate agency. They want to work with divers – archaeology could become a whole new purposeful recreational diving activity.

If you discover any old or new underwater shipwrecks, wrecked aircraft, artifacts or underwater fossils that are not well known, avoid any disturbance of the site, note the location and report your finds to the following agencies:

• In British Columbia: Director, Archaeology Branch, Ministry of Small Business, Tourism and Culture, 800 Johnson Street, 5th Floor, Victoria BC V8V 1X4, (604) 356-1045; fax (604) 387-4420. They are interested in any underwater fossils and relics, as well as any old wrecks with possible heritage value that are found in British Columbia that are not well known.

• In Washington: State Historic Preservation Officer, Office of Archaeology and Historic Preservation Department of Community, Trade and Economic Development, 11 West 21st Avenue, Olympia WA 98504, (206) 753-4011. They are interested in any underwater fossils and relics, as well as any shipwrecks and submerged aircraft with possible heritage value, that are found in Washington. If you wish to remove any fossil or artifact from any site, a permit may be required from this office and from the Department of Natural Resources (DNR).

If you wish to export any cultural material or finds from British Columbia to Washington or elsewhere, contact Movable Cultural Property Office, Department of Canadian Heritage, 300 Slater Street, Room 500, Ottawa ON K1A 0C8, (613) 990-4161. A permit is required for the export of all cultural property on the *Control List* which includes fossils, old arrowheads, airplane wrecks and other such finds – no permit required for objects less than 50 years old or made by a person still living.

If you wish to import cultural material into the United States, contact United States Customs Service, 1301 Constitution Avenue NW, Room 4345, Washington DC 20229, (202) 927-0440; fax (202) 927-0391 or (202) 927-6892. Import controls restricting transfer of cultural property might be in effect, so check. This control is in accordance with the Cultural Property Implementation Act of the UNESCO Convention and is to prevent pillage of invaluable heritage cultural property.

• For More Information on Archaeological Diving
Culture Department Library
Ministry of Small Business, Tourism and Culture
800 Johnson Street, Room 101
Victoria BC V8V 1X4
(604) 356-1440; fax (604) 356-7796
(This library contains archaeology reports and research material, including information about shipwrecks, fossils and ancient artifacts. The library is available for use by the public.)

WRECK DIVING – If you've ever seen the gleam in the eye of a diver who's discovered a wreck, you know what "wreck fever" means. I experienced that thrill of discovery when we found the wreck of the steamship *Ravalli* in Lowe Inlet off Grenville Channel in 1976. The surprise of seeing compacted salmon-can paper wrappers still intact from 1918 was unbeatable. Despite being under water for so long, the paper wrappers still had color on them and you could read the fine print.

Vast possibilities for exploration are available to insatiable wreck divers. A brochure of The Underwater Archaeological Society of British Columbia notes that more than 2,000 wrecks in 200 years are known to have sunk off the shores of British Columbia. Thousands of historic shipwrecks, both known and unknown, litter the North Pacific. Many have never been dived on. But even artificial reefs that have been created or sunk on purpose and well-known wrecks that have been dived on again and again provide a special diving interest or thrill. Heaps of ballast rocks are on the seabed as are bricks used as ballast in many ships sailing from England to Canada. Shipwrecks, "fake wrecks" and brick and rock ballast – all harbor quantities of marine life and have varied, fascinating histories. Wreck diving is exciting. It can also be dangerous. But like all other areas of diving, if you start slowly, build your experience and observe a few basic rules, wreck diving can be a safe and satisfying sport. Some suggestions and resources for wreck divers in Washington and British Columbia:

1. As always, dive with a buddy, and know your buddy very well. The two of you should review and practice "ditch-and-don" procedures and emergency ascents before diving on wrecks.

2. Start with easy wreck dives and progress gradually to more difficult ones. On all wreck dives, watch for cables and other appendages which you might snag your equipment on.

3. If diving on a wreck from a boat, be careful not to damage the wreck by dropping anchor on it. Mooring buoys are provided at some sites to protect the vessel below.

4. Be extremely wary of penetrating or entering the interior of any wreck. Be sure it is stable and is not going to collapse on you. Be particularly cautious when diving on a rotting timber vessel. Check surfaces in the way you check handholds when rock climbing to be sure they are solid. Take two good lights and use a return line to follow out if silt becomes stirred up or if both lights should fail. When entering, check the entry to be sure it will still be open when you are ready to exit.

Diving the 473-foot (144-meter) freighter *Vanlene* on the surf-washed west coast of Vancouver Island, my buddies and I entered the wreck and were startled to hear the door slam as the ship heaved in the surge. We were happy it did not latch when it slammed, we did get out – no problem. But that was good luck, not good planning. Surf conditions are not encountered in the region covered by this guidebook, I include this example just to say – plan carefully.

5. Always ascend with an adequate reserve of air in the event you encounter poor visibility, become caught on anything or must use a return line to find your way out.

6. Do not touch or disturb any underwater wrecks or artifacts unless you have applied for and have become a salvor or unless you are part of an official research team. Removing any artifacts from any shipwrecks is prohibited in Canada by the Canada Shipping Act, and in Washington by the Archaeological Sites and Resources Act.

7. If you discover any old or new underwater shipwrecks, wrecked aircraft or artifacts that are not well known, avoid any disturbance of the site, note the location and report your finds.

• In Washington report finds to

Commander
13th Coast Guard District (oan)
US Coast Guard
915 Second Avenue
Seattle WA 98174
(206) 220-7270
(Salvage laws in the USA require that you report the find of any shipwreck or wrecked aircraft that is not well known.)

Whatcom Maritime Historical Society
Underwater Archaeological Branch
PO Box 5157
Bellingham WA 98227-5157
(206) 647-8947; fax (206) 671-6572
(Purpose: to catalog, record, preserve and restore the past and present elements of our local maritime heritage.)

State Historic Preservation Officer
Office of Archaeology and Historic
  Preservation
Department of Community, Trade and Economic Development
111 West 21st Avenue
Olympia WA 98504
(206) 753-4011
(Shipwrecks and submerged aircraft, as well as other archaeological materials, are protected in Washington under the state Archaeological Sites and Resources Act. If you wish to remove any artifact from any site, a permit may be required from this office and from the Department of Natural Resources [DNR].)

• In British Columbia report finds to

Receiver of Wreck
Canadian Coast Guard
25 Huron Street
Victoria BC V8V 4V9
(604) 363-3303; fax (604) 363-0270
(Salvage laws in Canada require that you report the find of any shipwreck or wrecked aircraft that is not well known. Ask for the pamphlet A Guide to Reporting Wreck.*)*

Underwater Archaeological Society
  of British Columbia (UASBC)
c/o Vancouver Maritime Museum
1905 Ogden Avenue
Vancouver BC V6J 1A3
(This organization is dedicated to preserving and protecting all shipwrecks discovered in the waters of British Columbia.

UASBC Bulletin Board, IBM- or Macintosh-compatible PC, available to individuals and groups interested in diving: public messages about meetings equipment, diving issues. Users log on with PC, modem, and an ordinary telephone line. Pay only the long distance charges. Dial [604]525-5296)

• For More Information on Ships and Shipwrecks
COMPUTER DATA BASE LISTINGS
Automated Wreck and Obstruction Information System (AWOIS) (constantly updated), and the **User's Guide: Automated Wreck and Obstruction Information System (AWOIS)** booklet (usually updated annually) – both compiled by N/CG241, Station 6705, SSMC3, National Ocean Service (NOAA), 1315 East-West Highway, Silver Spring, MD 20910-3282, (301) 713-2702; fax (301) 713-4533.
(AWOIS is a database file with information on more than 9,500 wrecks in USA waters. Fees charged for every search.)

Marine Data Bulletin Board which is updated intermittently, compiled by National Ocean Service (NOAA), Hydrographic Technology Program, 1315 East-West Highway, Silver Spring MD 20910-3282, (301) 713-4574, available 24 hours a day.
(Information on wrecks; also indexes of aerial photographs, chart sales, tide gauge locations. Users log on with IBM-compatible PC, a modem, and an ordinary telephone line. Information is free via the bulletin board; pay only for the phone call.)

Shipwrecks! Washington State, Sets 1 and 2, compiled by Kent M. Barnard, Argonaut Resources, PO Box 743, Mukilteo WA 98275, telephone and fax (206) 355-6324, 1993.
(IBM-compatible database files: Set 1 covers 332 shipwrecks in Thurston, Pierce, Mason, King and Kitsap counties. Set 2 covers 227 wrecks in Jefferson, Snohomish, Island, Skagit and Whatcom counties, and wrecks in San Juan County. Details on known shipwrecks, directions to dive them, helpful to locate undiscovered wrecks.)

REGISTERS OF SHIPS
List of Ships, Volumes I and II, Ministry of Transport, Ottawa, published under various titles since 1874. Annual list.
(List of vessels on the register in Canada. Name of ship, material of hull, when built and length are some of the details provided.)

Lloyd's Register of Shipping, Lloyd's Register of Shipping, London, published from 1726 under various titles: *Lloyd's list; New Lloyd's list; Shipping gazette and Lloyd's list;* again as *Lloyd's list; Shipping and mercantile gazette; Lloyd's list;* then *Lloyd's Register of Shipping.* Published annually since 1778.
(Lists over 78,000 ships. Details included are ship's name, length, material of hull.)

Merchant Vessels of the United States, US Department of Transportation, US Coast Guard. Published annually since 1867, obtainable from Superintendent of Documents, US Government Printing Office, Washington DC.
(List of merchant ships: includes ship name, length, material of hull, year built.)

STORIES AND HISTORIES OF SHIPS
Canadian Pacific Afloat 1883-1968: A Short History and Fleet List by George Musk, Canadian Pacific, London, 1969.
(Canadian Pacific steamship history with illustrations and maps; contains information on the Granthall.*)*

Disaster Log of Ships by Jim Gibbs, Superior Publishing Co., Seattle, 1971.
(Covers shipwrecks in Washington and British Columbia. Fabulous illustrations.)

Echoes of the Whistle: An Illustrated History of the Union Steamship Company by Gerald Rushton, Douglas & McIntyre, Vancouver, 1980.
(Rich in photographs; useful to see locations where old docks were.)

Ferryboats: A Legend on Puget Sound by M.S. Kline and G.A. Bayless, Bayless Books, Seattle, 1983.
(A large-format story book and photographic record from the first ferry boat to publication; superbly indexed. Includes photos and a great deal of information on the Kehloken and Utopia.)

The H.W. McCurdy Marine History of the Pacific Northwest edited by Gordon Newell, The Superior Publishing Co., Seattle, 1966.
(A classic: this book is a companion volume to Lewis and Dryden's Marine History of the Northwest. Every one of its 706 pages is a very good read! The book is rich with photographs of ships and men, and superbly indexed. For an example of what is in it, read about the life of the 124-foot (38-meter) Mosquito Fleet steamer Utopia, in service from 1893 to 1929. This book covers the history of the growth and development of the maritime industry from 1895 to 1965.)

The H.W. McCurdy Marine History of the Pacific Northwest, 1966 to 1976 edited by Gordon Newell, The Superior Publishing Co., Seattle, 1977.
(A classic: this book follows up on the marine histories of Lewis and Dryden and H.W. McCurdy, again, with wonderful accounts and photographs of ships and men; well indexed. For an example of what is in it, see details on the large cargo vessel Vanlene which went aground in 1972. This book covers the growth and development of the maritime industry from 1966 to 1976.)

Lewis and Dryden's Marine History of the Pacific Northwest edited by E.W. Wright, The Lewis and Dryden Printing Company, Portland, 1895.
(A classic: detailed stories of ships and men, well illustrated and indexed. This 494-page review is a treasure, and you will be extremely lucky if you find it in a library. It covers the history of the growth and development of the maritime industry from the advent of the earliest navigators to 1895.)

Maritime Archaeology: New Studies in Archaeology by Keith Muckelroy, Cambridge University Press, Cambridge/London/New York/Melbourne, 1978.
(An overall view of shipwrecks around the world, including photographs of a shipwreck from the 4th century, and shipwrecks that were excavated instead of being dived on. It contains how-to tips on wreck diving, and is well illustrated with diagrams and photographs.)

More Shipwrecks of British Columbia by Fred Rogers, Douglas & McIntyre, Vancouver, 1992.
(Tales of shipwrecks and rescues – rich with detail. With indices of wrecks and captains. Also see Shipwrecks of British Columbia by the same author.)

Pacific Coastal Liners by Gordon Newell and Joe Williamson, Superior Publishing Co., Seattle, 1959.
(Designed for the reader's pleasure; another good read. Index of photographs.)

Pacific Steamboats by Gordon Newell, Superior Publishing Company, Seattle, 1958.
(Pictorial history of the Puget Sound Mosquito Fleet, including the Utopia. Photographic index.)

Pacific Tugboats by Gordon Newell and Joe Williamson, Superior Publishing Co., Seattle, 1957.
(A sampling of tugboats along with the human side of boating; drama, comedy, tragedy. Many photographs, well indexed.)

The Princess Story: A Century and a Half of West Coast Shipping by Norman R. Hacking and W. Kaye Lamb, Mitchell Press Ltd., Vancouver, 1974.
(History and photographs of the Princess ships and their Hudson's Bay and CPN company forerunners. The book covers from 1827 to 1974. Detailed fleet lists.)

Ships of the Inland Sea: The Story of The Puget Sound Steamboats by Gordon R. Newell, Binfords & Mort, Portland, 1951.
(Lively stories of the Mosquito Fleet. Contains a lengthy partial roster of ships from the 1800s to the modern Mosquito Fleet. Includes references to Kehloken *and* Utopia *and a description of the "Galloping Gertie" disaster.)*

Shipwrecks of British Columbia by Fred Rogers, Douglas & McIntyre, Vancouver, 1980.
(Adventurous stories of 100 wrecks and diving on them, with indices of wrecks and captains. Includes details of the Ravalli, Vanlene *and* Salvage Chief.*)*

Shipwrecks of the Pacific Coast by James A. Gibbs, Binfords and Mort, Portland, 1957.
(Stories of shipwrecks, with a chronological appendix list of all major shipwrecks on coastal, offshore and inland waters from 1500 to 1962.)

SOS North Pacific: Tales of Shipwrecks off the Washington, British Columbia and Alaska Coasts by Gordon R. Newell, Binfords & Mort, Portland, 1955.
(Covers Mosquito Fleet disasters – a very good read. A few drawings.)

Steamships and Motorships of the West Coast by Richard M. Benson, Superior Publishing Co., Seattle, 1968.
(A story in pictures and words about some famous and unusual motor-powered vessels including the SS Beaver, *first steamship to arrive in the North Pacific in 1836.)*

Vancouver's Undersea Heritage: Shipwrecks and Submerged Cultural Sites in Burrard Inlet and Howe Sound by David Leigh Stone, Underwater Archaeological Society of British Columbia, Vancouver, 1994.
(Details on 20 sites in the greater Vancouver area are in this book. Includes five site plans [Porteau Cove Marine Park and VT-100] and 21 photographs.)

Whistle Up the Inlet: The Union Steamship Story by Gerald A. Rushton, J.J. Douglas Ltd., Vancouver, 1974.
(History and photographs of the Union fleet, the men who sailed the ships, and the places where the ships called in: from 1889 to 1959.)

The Wreck Diver's Guide to Sailing Ship Artifacts of the 19th Century by David Leigh Stone, Underwater Archaeological Society of British Columbia, Vancouver, 1993.
(A unique addition to shipwreck literature: definitions, photographs and detailed drawings of what a sailing ship consists of, then the author breaks it down from ship to shipwreck.)

ARTIFICIAL REEFS – Preparing artificial reefs for diving is providing a fascinating new diving specialty for many recreational divers. Every year the reefs are becoming more sophisticated, more important.

Edmonds Underwater Park has unleashed the creative fancy of a myriad divers. The concrete-block-and-steel dinosaur at Edmonds is a far cry from the early days when most artificial reefs were made of heaps of tires. The sinking of the *G.B Church* and HMCS *Chaudiere* by the Artificial Reef Society of British Columbia demanded imagination, research, organization and dedication of another sort. Making the ships environmentally safe for sinking in the ocean by removing insulation, making them safe for diving by removing projections from them and providing openings for light, entry and exit are two challenges they met with these projects. Members of the society stress that artificial reef sites and materials be carefully evaluated and say artificial reefs should not be used as an excuse for dumping.

Fisheries personnel in Washington warn that artificial reefs must not become an excuse or justification for solid waste disposal in the marine environment. They are researching and brainstorming to gain more knowledge about appropriate habitats to attract specific marine life while not damaging the natural habitat. This research is an important professional specialty for marine biologists and all divers will want to think about it.

Diving the wonderful variety of artificial reefs is fun but artificial reefs are sometimes wrecks. Take the same precautions when diving them as when wreck diving, especially if entering the interior of a vessel.

• For More Information on Artificial Reefs

Washington State Department
  of Fisheries
PO Box 43135
Olympia WA 98504-3135
(206) 753-6600
Located at Natural Resources Building,
1111 Washington Street.

Artificial Reef Society
  of British Columbia
c/o The Vancouver Maritime Museum
1905 Ogden Avenue
Vancouver BC V6J 1A3

Video Cassette
Reefs of Steel: Artificial Reefs in British Columbia by Neil McDaniel and Gary Bridges, Wet Film Productions, Vancouver, 1992.
(Artificial reefs and wrecks in Porteau Cove Marine Park and wreck of G.B. Church.)

CLUBS AND ASSOCIATIONS
• In Washington: Recreational diving clubs are numerous and vital. They are united by the Washington Scuba Alliance which speaks with one voice for the sport. This vigorous group represents special diving interests as well as the interests of recreational divers (see page 36). Names of a few active clubs in Washington are Adventure Divers, Aquanuts, Atomic Ducks, Boeing Seahorses, Emerald Sea Dive Club, Kelp Crawlers, Kitsap Diving Association, Marker Buoys, Nor'west Divers, Pacific Northwest Dive Club, South Sound Divers and Tentacle Gang. For more names and information about clubs, ask at your local dive shop or contact the Washington Scuba Alliance, 120 State Avenue NE #18, Olympia WA 98501-8212, (206) 373-5367.

• In British Columbia: Every individual, every club and every diving business can take part in guiding the development of scuba diving. Membership in a council representing all sport and recreational scuba diving interests – commercial and individual – is available for a nominal fee, the cost of postage for the newsletter. Environment, safety, marketing/public relations and communications are the primary concerns. To become active in the council and for information about clubs in your region, contact Underwater Council of British Columbia, PO Box 5077, Main Post Office, Vancouver BC V6B 4A9. Obtain the council telephone number from your local dive shop.

Clubs for the purpose of diving and social events have been active in many communities for many years. New ones are formed all the time. Names of some old-timer clubs still meeting and diving in British Columbia are Aqua Soc, Aqua Addicts, Coquitlam Scuba Club, Deep Breathers, Nanaimo Dive Club, Pescaderos and Tide Rippers. Energetic societies of divers with special interests are also active – see under Conservation, Artificial Reefs and Wreck Diving. Another vital special interest group is an association for divers with disabilities.

Pacific Northwest Scuba Challenge Association – or Scuba Challenge – offers membership and diving activities to all divers. The association makes diving accessible to handicapped persons and promotes their integration into the community. This dynamic group offers scuba instruction, publishes a newsletter and sponsors dives. In addition, they go on day- and weekend-trips. More activities are demonstrations and slide presentations at rehabilitation centers and handicapped awareness events, distribution of video cassettes and materials regarding their activities to hospitals, schools and service clubs. Membership is open to able-bodied divers – ABs – as well as to divers with disabilities. For more information, contact Pacific Northwest Scuba Challenge Association, 4447 West 16th Avenue, Vancouver BC V6R 3E7, (604) 525 7149.

Wheelchair ramp at Mermaid Cove

NIGHT DIVING – If you've been disappointed in the marine life in an area, or by the diving in any way, or if you're just looking for an extra thrill – a new dimension – then try a night dive. In autumn, you'll see underwater fireworks.

Nothing else can match it for me. Many more animals come out at night. Some, like prawns, come up shallower and can be seen more easily then. And the old, familiar life takes on a new look. The eyes of ratfish glow like sapphires. When you switch off your light the smallest crab is magical in the fabulous phosphorescent night sea; orange sea pens shimmer neon green in the dark; and, if lucky, you might find an octopus – fantastic in the phosphorescence – coiling and uncoiling in a sparkle of light. Some practical notes on night diving:

1. Dive with a buddy you have dived with in the day, and stay right with your buddy.
2. Both divers carry an underwater light, but sometimes also try turning off both to savor the beauty of the phosphorescence.
3. Wear a chemical glow-tube light.
4. Use a compass.
5. Do not dive in currents at night in rocky areas, for the rocks come past too fast.
6. Surface with a reserve of air.
7. Leave a light on shore or on your boat, so you can find your way back.
8. Don't wait – do it now. Why not tonight?

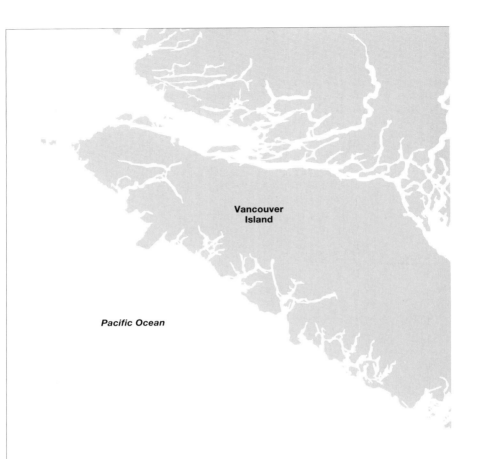

Vancouver
Island

Pacific Ocean

KEY TO CHAPTER MAPS

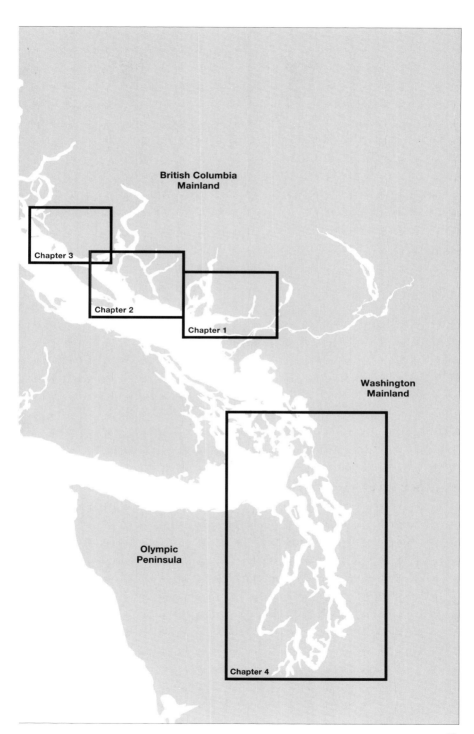

British Columbia
Mainland

Chapter 3

Chapter 2

Chapter 1

Washington
Mainland

Olympic
Peninsula

Chapter 4

Bottles from Mannion Bay, Bowen Island

Porteau Cove campground on Howe Sound

Moon jellyfish at wreck of *VT-100* in Indian Arm

CHAPTER 1
Vancouver, Howe Sound and Indian Arm

Girl in a Wet Suit off Stanley Park

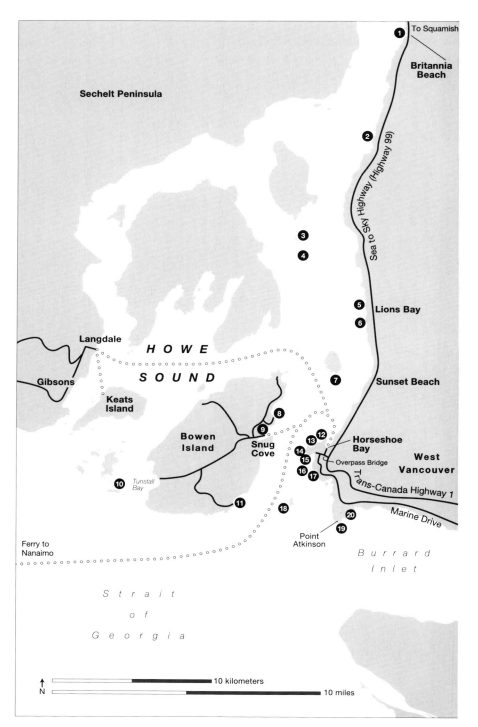

Sechelt Peninsula

To Squamish

Britannia
Beach

Sea to Sky Highway (Highway 99)

Lions Bay

Sunset Beach

H O W E
S O U N D

Langdale

Gibsons

Keats
Island

Horseshoe
Bay

West
Vancouver

Bowen
Island

Snug
Cove

Overpass Bridge

Tunstall
Bay

Trans-Canada Highway 1

Marine Drive

Ferry to
Nanaimo

Point
Atkinson

Burrard
Inlet

S t r a i t

o f

G e o r g i a

N

10 kilometers

10 miles

VANCOUVER, HOWE SOUND AND INDIAN ARM

Dives

1 Old Customs House
2 Porteau Cove Marine Park
3 Christie Islet
4 Pam Rocks
5 Lions Bay
6 Kelvin Grove
7 Bowyer Island
8 Millers Landing
9 Mannion Bay
10 Worlcombe Island
11 Seymour Bay
12 Copper Cove
13 Lookout Point
14 Whytecliff Park – Day Marker
15 Whytecliff Park – Whyte Islet
16 Bird Islet
17 Larsen Bay Park
18 Passage Island Reef
19 Lighthouse Park
20 Caulfeild Cove

21 West Cates Park
22 White Rock
23 Woodlands
24 Belcarra Bay
25 Whiskey Cove
26 Wreck of *VT-100*
27 Jug Island
28 Racoon Island
29 Twin Islands
30 Buntzen Power Plant
31 Silver Falls
32 Croker Island, Southeast Corner
33 Croker Island, Northwest Corner

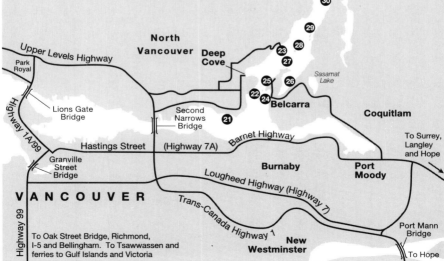

SERVICE INFORMATION *
Vancouver, Howe Sound and Indian Arm

Charts: Canadian Hydrographic Service
• 3311 Sunshine Coast–Vancouver Harbour to Desolation Sound (small-craft chart)
• L/C-3463 Strait of Georgia, Southern Portion
• 3481 Approaches to Vancouver Harbour
• 3494 Vancouver Harbour, Central Portion
• 3495 Vancouver Harbour, Eastern Portion
• L/C-3512 Strait of Georgia, Central Portion
• 3526 Howe Sound
• 3534 Plans–Howe Sound

Tide and Current Tables: Canadian Hydrographic Service *Tide and Current Table, Volume 5*

Diving Emergency Telephone Numbers
Dial 911: Say "I have a scuba diving emergency".

Vancouver Hospital & Health Services Centre: Dial (604) 875-4111 and say "I have a scuba diving emergency. I want the hyperbaric physician on call".

If medical personnel are unfamiliar with scuba diving emergencies, ask them to telephone DAN (Divers Alert Network): (919) 684-8111, then say "I have a scuba diving emergency".

Other Useful Numbers
Weather – Continuous Marine Broadcast (CMB) recorded, 24 hours; listen for weather in the Strait of Georgia or Howe Sound, telephone
    • At Vancouver: (604) 270-7411
Shellfish Infoline (red tide hotline), recorded: (604) 666-3169
Sportfishing Information Line, recorded: 1-800-663-9333

• Dive Shops
Vancouver
Adrenalin Sports
1512 Duranleau Street, Granville Island
Vancouver BC V6H 3S4
(604) 682-2881

Diver's World
1817 West 4th Avenue
Vancouver BC V6J 1M4
(604) 732-1344; fax (604) 273-0201

The Diving Locker
2745 West 4th Avenue
Vancouver BC V6K 1P9
(604) 736-2681; fax (604) 736-2320

Odyssey Diving Centre
2659 Kingsway
Vancouver BC V5R 5H4
(604) 430-1451; fax (604) 436-0139

UBC Aqua Society (Aqua Soc)
6138 SUB Boulevard
Student Union Building
University of British Columbia
Vancouver BC V6T 2A5
(604) 822-3329; fax (604) 822-6093

Richmond
Rowand's Reef
125-6080 Airport Road S
Richmond BC V7B 1B4
(604) 273-0704; fax (604) 273-7784

Squamish
G & S Scuba and Sports
40360 Tantalus Way, Highlands Mall
PO Box 2110
Squamish BC V0N 3G0
(604) 898-1575 – fax and telephone.

Greater Vancouver: North Shore

Aqua Sapiens Diving Ltd.
1386 Main Street
North Vancouver BC V7J 1C6
(604) 985-3483 – both fax and phone.

Capilano Divers Supply
1236 Marine Drive
North Vancouver BC V7P 1T2
(604) 986-0302; fax (604) 986-4646

Deep Cove Dive Shop
4342 Gallant Avenue
North Vancouver BC V7G 1K8
(604) 929-3116 or (604) 880-6340

The Wet Shop Diving & Watersports
    Centre Inc.
6371 Bruce Street, Horseshoe Bay
West Vancouver BC V7W 2G5
(604) 921-6371; fax (604) 433-0725

Greater Vancouver East: Coquitlam through Surrey to Langley

Cross Current Divers
14-2773 Barnet Highway
Coquitlam BC V3B 1C2
(604) 944-2780; fax (604) 944-2782

West Coast Scuba Centre
20-2755 Lougheed Highway
Port Coquitlam BC V3B 5Y9
(604) 942-4838; fax (604) 731-2802

Dive & Sea Sports
2-825 McBride Boulevard
New Westminster BC V3L 5B5
(604) 524-1188; fax (604) 525-3483

The Great Pacific Diving Company Ltd.
10020-152nd Street
Surrey BC V3R 8X8
(604) 583-1700; fax (604) 583-8508

Ocean Pro Divers
3189 King George Highway, Unit 2
Surrey BC V4P 1B8
(604) 538-5608; fax (604) 535-3695

Get Wet Adventures
20305 Fraser Highway
Langley BC V3A 4E8
(604) 530-1008; fax (604) 530-1828

Nautic Scuba
#22, 20460 Langley By-Pass
Langley BC V3A 5E7
(604) 533-9353

• Boat Rentals

Adventure Fitness Ltd.
1528 Duranleau Street
Granville Island
Vancouver BC V6H 3S4
(604) 687-1528
(Dive-kayak rentals. single kayaks for diver with gear. Also a double dive-kayak for two divers with gear.)

Empress Boat Sales and Rentals
7249 Curragh Avenue
Burnaby BC V5J 4W1
(604) 433-3985
(Car-top and trailerable boats for rent; also motors for rent.)

Gibsons Boat Rentals
PO Box 1018
Gibsons BC V0N 1V0
(604) 886-2628
(Boat rentals at Gibsons, Sechelt Peninsula.)

Sunset Marina Ltd.
34 Sunset Beach
West Vancouver BC V7W 2T7
(604) 921-7476
(Boat rentals from spring through fall. Launching year-round.)

• Launching for Howe Sound and Strait of Georgia

Horseshoe Bay

Sewell's Marina Ramp
6695 Nelson Avenue
West Vancouver BC V7W 2B2
(604) 921-3474; fax (604) 921-7027
(Launching at Horseshoe Bay; concrete ramp, good at tides greater than 2 feet [2/3 meter]. Restrooms in the park which is open year-round; telephone at gas station across street from ramp.)

Bowen Island

Tunstall Bay Public Ramp
Bowen Island, west side
(Launching over cobbled beach. No toilet, no telephone.)
    Located on the west side of Bowen: from Snug Cove, follow the signs for 5 miles (8 kilometers) to Tunstall Bay.

Sechelt Peninsula

Gibsons Marina
PO Box 1520
Gibsons BC V0N 1V0
(604) 886-8686
(Launching at Gibsons, Sechelt Peninsula: concrete ramp, good at all except extreme low tides. Restrooms and hot showers; telephones are next to marina office.)

• Launching for Indian Arm

North Vancouver

West Cates Park Public Ramp
Dollarton Highway
North Vancouver BC
(Launching only: asphalt ramp, good at all except extreme low tides. Restrooms and telephones next to the caretaker's home near totem pole at east end of park.)
    Located in North Vancouver – 3 miles (5 kilometers) east of Second Narrows Bridge; after entering the park, drive straight to the ramp.

Sea to Sky Highway

Sunset Marina Ltd.
34 Sunset Beach
West Vancouver BC V7W 2T7
(604) 921-7476
(Launching year-round; tarmac ramp, good at all tides. Boat rentals spring through fall. Restrooms at marina and telephone at top of ramp.)

Lions Bay Marina
60 Lions Bay Avenue, PO Box 262
Lions Bay BC V0N 2E0
(604) 921-7510
(Launching only; concrete ramp, good at all tides. Restrooms; telephone at marina office.)

Porteau Public Ramp
Porteau Cove Marine Park
Squamish Highway
(Launching only; concrete ramps, good at all tides. Restrooms across railway tracks at divers' change house; telephone at entrance to campground.)
    Located on the Sea to Sky Highway (Highway 99) north of Horseshoe Bay; Porteau Cove Marine Park is 15 miles (24 kilometers) north of Horseshoe Bay. It is 12 miles (19 kilometers) south of Squamish.

Port Moody

Rocky Point Park Public Ramp
Foot of Moody Street
Port Moody BC
(Launching only: concrete ramp, good at all tides. Restrooms across park are open April to October. Lots of pay parking space. Telephone next to parking area.)
    Located in the heart of Port Moody; follow the signs from the library on St. John's Street. Go down Moody Street to the water.

• Charter Boats and Charter Buses out of Vancouver, West Vancouver, North Vancouver and Port Moody

Charters to Indian Arm

Deep Cove Diver and *Baba*
Deep Cove Dive Shop
4342 Gallant Avenue
North Vancouver BC V7G 1K8
(604) 929-3116 or (604) 880-6340
(Day charters out of Deep Cove.)

Why Knot
CDNR Enterprises Inc.
#102-1190 Pacific Street
Coquitlam BC V3B 6Z2
(604) 944-6996 or (604) 258-5183
(Day charters out of loco to Indian Arm.)

Burrard Water Taxi
4224 East Pender Street
Burnaby BC V5C 2M3
(604) 293-1160
(Water taxi from Reed Point Marina in Port Moody to Indian Arm.)

Charters to Howe Sound and Indian Arm

Komokwa
Cross Current Divers
14-2773 Barnet Highway
Coquitlam BC V3B 1C2
(604) 944-2780; fax (604) 944-2782
(Day trips from Port Moody year-round to Indian Arm and Howe Sound. Summer liveaboards to Desolation Sound.)

Charters to a Variety of Destinations

Adrenalin Diver
Adrenalin Sports
1512 Duranleau Street, Granville Island
Vancouver BC V6H 3S4
(604) 682-2881
(One-day and weekend boat trips with land-based accommodation. Bus trips to Indian Arm, Sechelt, Powell River.)

Lady Goodiver
Lady Goodiver Charters
#381, PO Box 9060
Surrey BC V3T 5P8
(604) 220-7187
(Liveaboard custom charters to Port Hardy – pick up anywhere.)

Charters to Howe Sound

Adventure IV
Sea Going Adventures
231 Moray Street
Port Moody BC V3H 3T5
(604) 461-3186 or (604) 290-7667
(Day trips from Horseshoe Bay to Howe Sound. Wheelchair divers welcome.)

Apodaca and *Cormorant*
Cormorant Marine
Snug Cove
Bowen Island BC V0N 1G0
(604) 947-2243 or (604) 250-2630
(Day charters out of Horseshoe Bay to Howe Sound, Collingwood Channel.)

MV *Trick Deal* and Gus "The Bus"
Ocean Pro Divers
3189 King George Highway, Unit 2
Surrey BC V4P 1B8
(604) 538-5608; fax (604) 535-3695
(Day boat trips from Horseshoe Bay to Howe Sound and day trips on Gus "The Bus" out of Surrey to Whidbey Island and Sechelt for escorted shore diving.)

Arasheena
Arasheena Yacht Charters
3656 Blenheim Street
Vancouver BC V6L 2Y2
(604) 736-0938
(Charters out of Vancouver to Howe Sound, also the Gulf Islands.)

Oceaner
Diver's World
1817 West 4th Avenue
Vancouver BC V6J 1M4
(604) 732-1344; fax (604) 273-0201
(Day and liveaboard charters out of Vancouver, year-round.)

Shoal Searcher
Pacific Northwest Diving Adventures
122 West Kings Road
North Vancouver BC V7N 2L8
(604) 983-9454
(Weekend, week-long and longer liveaboards out of Vancouver. Wheelchair divers welcome.)

• More Information for Boat Divers and Kayak-Divers
Explore for new sites on your own; additional launching ramps, public beaches where you can land, and facilities are listed in the following publications:

Docks and Destinations by Peter Vassilopoulos, Seagraphic Publications, Vancouver, 1994. Available at bookstores. (Scope: Lists marina services, customer services and adjacent facilities, including hot showers, public telephones, launching ramps and entertainment. Illustrated with maps, photographs. From the San Juan Islands through Vancouver, Sunshine Coast and north to Desolation Sound and Port Hardy.)

Small Craft Guide, Volume 2: British Columbia, Boundary Bay to Cortes Island, Canadian Hydrographic Service, 1990. Available where nautical charts are sold. (Scope: Lists launching ramps and facilities.)

Southwestern British Columbia Recreational Atlas compiled by Informap in cooperation with British Columbia Ministry of Environment, Victoria, 1992. Available at bookstores. (Scope: Maps, lists of parks and facilities, wildlife reserves and viewing. Covers southwestern British Columbia coastline from southern border north beyond Desolation Sound and includes all of Vancouver Island.)

• More Dive Facilities

Breathing Air Systems
3311 Sophia Street, #2
Vancouver BC V5V 3T4
(604) 874-4168; fax (604) 873-3875
(Compressor rentals only – no air fills.)

Fraser Burrard Diving
12420 Vulcan Way
Richmond BC V6V 1J8
(604) 278-3323
(Compressor rentals only – no air fills.)

Divers West
1709 West 4th Avenue
Vancouver BC V6J 1M2
(604) 737-2822; toll-free in British
Columbia: 1-800-465-2822.
(Sell used diving equipment – no air fills.)

L & J Sport Diving
3-1771 East 2nd Avenue
West Vancouver BC V5N 1E3
(604) 251-7800; or (604) 671-5822
(Complete instruction facilities for people with disabilities.)

The Vancouver Area Diving Guide by Carl Trepanier contains details on more-or-less the same shore dives described in this chapter of *101 Dives* but from a slightly different viewpoint. It covers a total of 23 shore dives and a great many boat dives in Howe Sound and Indian Arm. While *101 Dives* covers 20 shore dives, 12 boat dives – 7 for kayak-divers – in the same area. To gain two views, refer to both guides.

• Ferry Information
British Columbia Ferry Corporation
Tsawwassen and Horseshoe Bay terminals
(604) 277-0277. Recorded schedules available 24 hours.
Toll-free in BC: 1-800-663-7600. Or (604) 669-1211 – both "live" – a person answers.
Telephoning from outside British Columbia: (604) 386-3431 "live".
(Ferries from Tsawwassen [south of Vancouver] to Swartz Bay [north of Victoria] and to the Gulf Islands; and from Tsawwassen to Departure Bay [Nanaimo]. And ferries from Horseshoe Bay to Departure Bay [Nanaimo], to Langdale [Sechelt Peninsula] and to Bowen Island.)

British Columbia Ferry Corporation
Langdale Ferry Terminal, Sechelt Peninsula
In Langdale, (604) 886-2242; in Vancouver, (604) 669-1211; toll-free in BC, 1-800-663-7600. *(Pedestrian ferries from Langdale to Keats Island.)*

• Tourist Information

Discover British Columbia
1117 Wharf Street
Victoria BC V8W 2Z2
1-800-663-6000: Toll-free throughout
Canada and the USA, including Hawaii
and parts of Alaska.

Vancouver Travel Infocentre
Plaza Level, Waterfront Centre
210-200 Burrard Street
Vancouver BC V6C 3L6
(604) 683-2000; fax (604) 682-6839

North Vancouver Travel Infocentre
131 East 2nd Street
North Vancouver BC V7L 1C2
(604) 987-4488; fax (604) 987-8272

Squamish Travel Infocentre
PO Box 1009
Squamish BC V0N 3G0
(604) 892-9244; fax (604) 892-2034

Vancouver Port Corporation Regulations: No sport diving is allowed between First and Second Narrows bridges or under them. When planning a dive in any other waters of Indian Arm or Vancouver Harbour west to Point Atkinson, telephone and obtain permission from the Harbour Master's Office. The telephone call is really just a routine. If there are no unusual circumstances in the harbour, permission to dive is granted easily.

The regulations are subject to change and may be altered as necessary. At the time of writing, provisional regulations for sport divers (By-Law A-1) require that you telephone the Vancouver Port Corporation office on a weekday at (604) 666-2405 and state the specifics of your dive plan request including:

1) Location of dive
2) Date and time
3) Duration of dive
4) Number of people diving
5) Contact person, who is not diving on this occasion, and telephone number.

In addition, divers are requested to fly the diver's flag at all times. Night diving from a boat must be from a lighted boat displaying an illuminated dive flag.

All persons sport diving in Vancouver Port Corporation waters from Indian Arm out to Point Atkinson light station should comply with Vancouver Port Corporation By-Law A-1. Anyone contravening the regulations runs the risk of being prosecuted and upon conviction of being fined up to $500.

How to Go: Highways, ferry boats and airplanes converge on Vancouver from all sides. Reach it by road on Trans-Canada Highway 1, Highway 99 or Highway 7. By ferry from Victoria or Nanaimo on Vancouver Island, or by ferry from the Sechelt Peninsula.

Arriving by road on the mainland, bridges are the keys to know where you are. Look at the map. Heading north on Highway 99 into Vancouver, know you are almost in the city when you cross Oak Street Bridge. Arriving from the Fraser Valley, notice when you cross Port Mann Bridge. If you plan to dive Indian Arm, be alert for the turnoff for some dives immediately across Port Mann. For others, immediately across Second Narrows Bridge. If diving at Howe Sound, keep going to Horseshoe Bay.

In the heart of the city, Lions Gate Bridge reaches from Stanley Park to North and West Vancouver. Before crossing, take a slow drive around Stanley Park to see the bronze statue of Girl in a Wet Suit. She sits on a rock in the harbour. Vancouver is surrounded by water. You can pick up a provincial road map on your way into town, and it will be easy to find your way around. Use the bridges.

* All of this service information is subject to change.

OLD CUSTOMS HOUSE
Shore Dive

Skill: All divers

Why go: Relics from the early 1900s, easy entry, no current to consider and a short swim make this a superb dive to try out gear and have fun searching for sunken "treasure".

We found mining artifacts, old bottles and old bricks – one probably manufactured on Anvil Island, perhaps as early as 1901 when the first brick plant was there. The brick had a raised anvil pattern on it. We were lured to the site because the possibility of finding a Union steamship china cup or plate is big. Union steamships called in at Britannia Beach from 1907 onward and it was an international customs house.

The Britannia Mine was founded in 1889 and started producing in 1904. At one time, it was one of the largest producing copper mines in Canada. The huge building on the mountain side was completed in 1923. It is a gravity-fed concentrator complex of unusual design, and was used until 1974 when the mine closed. In 1987, the concentrator complex was designated a national historic site.

We thought the artifacts we found had been thrown off the end of the dock to dispose of them when they were no longer useful because of impurities or cracks, pitched in the same spirit people today sometimes throw paper plates or beer cans into the sea, but most mining artifacts do not disintegrate rapidly. Crucibles and scorifiers are made of clay; cupels are made of bone-ash: these objects are for the purpose of purifying copper ore and assessing its value. We found an assayer's crucible, numerous cupels and two scorifiers, or roasting dishes.

Howe Sound is a deep fjord rimmed with high mountains on both sides. Flooding creeks periodically wash down the steep banks, and there have been floods at Britannia Beach. But the Old Customs House is probably far enough south from where Britannia Creek enters so that old artifacts have not been washed away.

Bottom and Depths: Thick silt. Drops steeply from base of pilings to a depth of 45 to 55 feet (14 to 17 meters). Then deeper.

Hazards: Silt. Dive on an ebbing tide that will carry away the silt your stir up. And before going down, make a plan with your buddy about what you will do if you lose one another because of poor visibility.

Telephones: • Across highway, immediately north of Old Customs House. • Across highway, ⅕ mile (⅓ kilometer) south of road exit from Old Customs House.

Facilities: Parking space for 10 or 12 cars. An art gallery with contemporary work is in the Old Customs House at the dive. The British Columbia Museum of Mining, chock-a-block with information and photographs of the old days, is across the road. Also cafés. Air fills nearby in Squamish, Horseshoe Bay and North Vancouver as well as throughout greater Vancouver.

Access: The Old Customs House dive is located on Howe Sound just off Sea to Sky Highway (Highway 99) in Britannia Beach. It is 7 miles (11 kilometers) south of Squamish and 20 miles (32 kilometers) north of Horseshoe Bay. Takes 30 minutes to reach it from Horseshoe Bay, 10 minutes from Squamish.

At Britannia Beach, turn off the highway when 300 yards (275 meters) south of the Old Customs House. Cross the railway tracks, and go north on a small dirt road. Just past the Customs House, turn left. Go through the gate, park and enter at the deteriorating launching ramp on the left-hand side. To search for artifacts, swim out to the end of the dock and prowl around the base of the pilings. The bottom is extremely silty and sheers off. To find artifacts, fan the silt to gently dislodge it.

Comments: After diving, you could visit The British Columbia Museum of Mining and tour the old mine.

Assayer's scorifier found below pilings

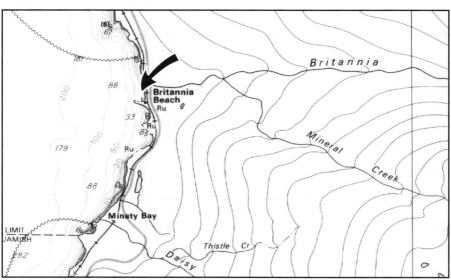

NOT TO BE USED FOR NAVIGATION: For information on obtaining navigational charts see page 318.
This is a portion of 3526.

1 Nautical Mile

PORTEAU COVE MARINE PARK
Shore Dive

Skill: All divers

Why go: Wrecks galore – easy-to-find sunken ships for divers with all levels of skill to explore.

The SS *Granthall* was a steamer tug, later powered with a diesel engine. This steel vessel is 95 feet (29 meters) long. It was built by the Canadian Pacific Railway in Montreal in 1928, cut into sections and shipped over land: first to Kootenay Lake where it hauled railway barges and carried passengers, then to Great Slave Lake, then to New Westminster. It was sunk at Porteau Cove in 1992. Shallow and easy to dive.

The *Centennial III* is a steel dredge tender, 33 feet (10 meters) long. It was scuttled at Porteau in 1991. Concrete blocks, pipe, slabs and columns, old tires, some steel H-beams and a ferroconcrete sailboat that is 45 feet (14 meters) long, also sunk in 1991, form the artificial reef close to the entry. Also shallow and easy to dive.

The *Nakaya* was a YMS-Class minesweeper in World War II. The wooden hull is 136 feet (41 meters) long. It was sunk at Porteau Cove in 1985. A long swim to it, and often current in this location, so check if the current will help you or make the dive difficult. It's deep – for intermediate and expert divers.

The park is often used for open-water certification dives. All artificial reef features of the park are in a boat-free zone reserved for divers. White buoys rim the protected area. It's a safe place to practice underwater navigation. The site is mostly current-free except for surface current when swimming to the *Nakaya*. Look for marine life, too. Galatheid crabs lurk in the shadows of the *Nakaya*. And divers have seen as many as six octopuses on one dive in the shallower part of the reef. Fun to find – but the wrecks are what most divers go for.

In 1981 Porteau Cove became the first underwater park in British Columbia. In 1994 the cove became a sanctuary – sightseeing only.

Bottom and Depths: Silty sand scattered with small rocks slopes gradually to the artificial reef. The *Granthall, Centennial III* and other features close to the entry range in depth from 30 to 50 feet (9 to 15 meters). The *Nakaya* rests on the bottom slightly skewed from northeast to southwest with the bow in 90 to 100 feet (27 to 30 meters), the stern in 60 to 70 feet (18 to 21 meters), depending on tide height.

Hazards: Silt, visibility, some current and the wrecks themselves. Often poor visibility in spring and summer because of Squamish River runoff, as well as plankton bloom. However, it is always worth checking to see if visibility is good. Beware of the wrecks becoming unstable – especially the *Nakaya.* Do not enter.

Telephones: • Porteau Cove Marine Park campground entrance. • Britannia Beach, 4 miles (7 kilometers) north.

Facilities: Changehouse for divers – lit at night. Hot showers, flush toilets. Map showing location of reefs and wrecks, and cold-water shower for washing gear at top of stairsteps to dive. Boat ramp. Waterfront campsites. Air fills in Horseshoe Bay, Squamish and throughout greater Vancouver. Dive-kayak rentals in Vancouver.

Access: Porteau Cove Marine Park is on Howe Sound beside Sea to Sky Highway (Highway 99) between Horseshoe Bay and Squamish. It is 20 minutes from Horseshoe Bay, the same from Squamish.

At Porteau Cove Marine Park, turn toward the water. The divers' changehouse with lots of room to park is on your left-hand side. Across the road and railway tracks, north of the launch ramp, you will see the map of park features beside concrete steps to the beach. Snorkel out to the buoy of your choice and go down – allow 20 minutes to snorkel to the *Nakaya*. Or, if you want the challenge, follow a compass heading from wreck to wreck.

To dive the *Nakaya:* Best to swim to it on the flooding tide, dive on slack and drift back with the ebb. The vessel is easy to find with a chain to follow down from the divers' float. At the time of writing, a penetration line is in place to follow through the wreck making it *feel* easy to dive. But beware. The hull is wood and disintegrating. Penetration is not advisable as the *Nakaya* could collapse on you.

Wheelchair access at launching ramp – however, at high tide most wheelchair divers "bum it" down the stairsteps rather than enter at the ramp which can be busy. Disabled divers can obtain permission to paddle a dive-kayak or other small boat from the launching ramp to the *Nakaya* float. Contact BC Parks, Garibaldi/Sunshine Coast District, Box 220, Brackendale BC V0N 1H0. Telephone (604) 898-3678; fax (604) 898-4171.

To get to Porteau Cove Marine Park
• From Horseshoe Bay, head north 15 miles (24 kilometers) on Highway 99. When you see an arched sign over a road on your left saying "Porteau Camp" slow down. Less than 1 mile (1½ kilometers) farther down the hill, turn left into Porteau Cove Marine Park.
• From Squamish at the head of Howe Sound go 12 miles (19 kilometers) south on Highway 99 and turn right into Porteau Cove Marine Park.

Comments: The park is so popular you're certain to meet other divers.

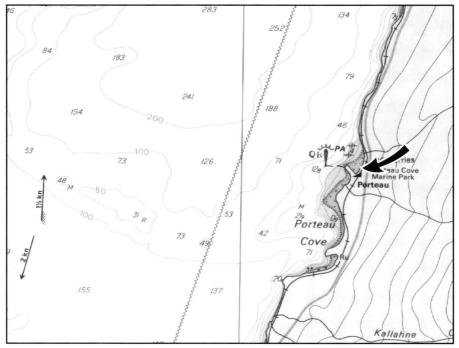

NOT TO BE USED FOR NAVIGATION: For information on obtaining navigational charts see page 318. This is a portion of 3526.

1 Nautical Mile

CHRISTIE ISLET
Boat Dive

Skill: All divers

Why go: Christie Islet, an ideal island to circle on one tank of air, provides some of the prettiest sightseeing in Howe Sound.

On one dive here we saw everything from a small swimming scallop to hermit crabs, spider crabs and dogfish. Sprays of pink-and-white striped dahlia anemones bloom along the wall. Huge white and purple tube-dwelling anemone tentacles pop out of the sand. Large orange and white plumose anemones are in profusion on the rocks. Lingcod and rockfish. You can go deep if you wish, but most of the life is shallow. Even cloud sponges and chimney sponges start at 50 to 60 feet (15 to 18 meters).

Once around the island gives you a fabulous cross-section of life.

Bottom and Depths: A sampling of almost every kind of sea floor: sloping sand, rock walls and huge boulders tumbled on top of each other. Small caves in 10 to 20 feet (3 to 6 meters) of water. The southeasterly side of the islet descends like a huge underwater mountain. Most of the life is in 40 to 50 feet (12 to 15 meters).

Hazards: Current, wind and broken fishing line. Boats and poor visibility, in summer, because of Squamish River runoff. Dive near the slack. Carry a knife. Listen for boats and ascend up the side of the islet, well out of the way of those boats.

Telephones: • Lions Bay Marina outside office. • Porteau Cove Marine Park campground entrance.

Facilities: None. Charters out of Vancouver, North Vancouver, West Vancouver, Port Moody, Coquitlam and New Westminster to Howe Sound. Launching at Horseshoe Bay and Sunset Beach in West Vancouver, in Lions Bay and Porteau Cove. Air fills throughout greater Vancouver, in North Vancouver, Horseshoe Bay and Squamish.

Access: Christie Islet is located in Howe Sound where Ramillies and Montague channels meet. It is ¾ nautical mile (1½ kilometers) south of Anvil Island, 7½ nautical miles (14 kilometers) north of Horseshoe Bay, and 4½ nautical miles (8 kilometers) southwest of Porteau Cove.

Charter out of Vancouver or Horseshoe Bay; launch at Lions Bay or Porteau Cove; or rent a boat or launch your own boat at Sunset Beach or Horseshoe Bay and go to Christie Islet. If windy, plan to leave a boat tender on the surface. The water can become choppy quickly at this exposed anchorage. When wind is from the south, anchorage is better at Christie Islet than at Pam Rocks. Anchor close-in at the northeast side in order to hit bottom and dive once around the islet.

Comments: Christie Islet is a Federal Migratory Bird Sanctuary. From May through July colonies of gulls and cormorants are nesting on Christie Islet. Do not land on the islet during this period because any disturbance could cause nest desertion.

Dogfish sharks

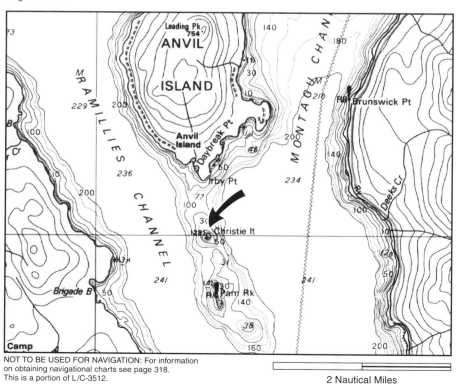

NOT TO BE USED FOR NAVIGATION: For information
on obtaining navigational charts see page 318.
This is a portion of L/C-3512.

2 Nautical Miles

PAM ROCKS
Boat Dive or Kayak Dive

Skill: All divers and snorkelers

Why go: Pam Rocks flaunts flamboyant displays of oversized life starting with the seals usually lying on the rocks.

Under water much of the life is oversized, too. Three-foot (1-meter) white plumose anemones, tube-dwelling anemones with 8-inch (20-centimeter) purple plumes, big sea peaches and transparent tunicates are all over the place. Orange dead man's finger sponges poke from the kelp-covered rocks in the shallows. You may see a rose star. In spring you'll see lots of nudibranchs. Fish life is not so big, but copper rockfish are abundant. Sometimes you'll see flounders, tiger rockfish, an octopus, lingcod and red Irish lords. Splendid cloud sponges start at 80 to 90 feet (24 to 27 meters).

But the big thrill at Pam Rocks comes when you've been in the water a long while and the seals have forgotten you're there. Sometimes you can come up and be part of their group.

Bottom and Depths: On the east side of the marker undulating rocky bottom, clean-swept by the current, ranges from 20 to 30 feet (6 to 9 meters) deep to a depth of 90 to 100 feet (27 to 30 meters). White sand between the rocks. In some places, deep canyon-like slots between the rocks.

Hazards: Current, wind, and broken fishing line. Boats and poor visibility in summer because of Squamish River runoff. Dive near the slack. Use your compass, be aware of your direction, and watch the current. Be particularly careful if you go down into the deep slots because the current can be strong. It is wise to leave a boat tender on the surface. Carry a knife. Listen for boats. If you hear a boat you can stay down until it passes. Kayak-divers should rest after diving before paddling back because of the possible danger of bringing on bends by overexertion after the dive.

Telephone: Lions Bay Marina, outside office.

Facilities: None. Charters out of Vancouver, North Vancouver, West Vancouver, Port Moody, Coquitlam and New Westminster to Howe Sound. Launching at Horseshoe Bay or Sunset Beach in West Vancouver, in Lions Bay and at Porteau Cove. Dive-kayak rentals in Vancouver.

Access: Pam Rocks are just over 1 nautical mile (2 kilometers) south of Anvil Island and 6½ nautical miles (12 kilometers) north of Horseshoe Bay where Ramillies and Montagu channels meet. The site is 5 nautical miles (9 kilometers) southwest of Porteau Cove; 3 nautical miles (6 kilometers) across open water from Lions Bay.

Charter out of Vancouver or Horseshoe Bay; launch your own boat at Lions Bay or Porteau Cove; launch a dive-kayak at Lions Bay; or rent a boat or launch your own boat at Sunset Beach or Horseshoe Bay and go north to Pam Rocks. On the surface the water can become choppy very quickly at this exposed site. It is an adventurous but possible paddle in a dive-kayak from Lions Bay. You must be very water-wise to do it. Pick a calm day to go, take marine flares, and do not try to cross back to Lions Bay if a "Squamish" wind from the north starts up while you are down. A difficult anchorage. Anchor southeast of the marker, between the two rocks, in 20 to 30 feet (6 to 9 meters).

Comments: Pam Rocks is a favorite site for underwater photographers in winter.

Diver looking around plumose anemones at "devilfish" peaks on head of giant octopus

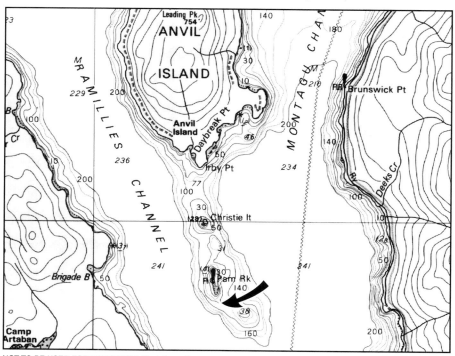

NOT TO BE USED FOR NAVIGATION: For information
on obtaining navigational charts see page 318.
This is a portion of L/C-3512.

2 Nautical Miles

LIONS BAY
Shore Dive

Skill: All divers

Why go: Super-easy access, short swim, a variety of marine life. Heading down, we saw blue-and-yellow striped seaperch and black perch schooling in the shallows. Blackeye gobies beneath the ledges. Quillback rockfish. Lingcod. Shrimp darting all over the place and three painted greenlings beside the riprap.

Chitons stick tight to the rocks. Big fat sunflower stars drape over them. Red dahlia anemones are deeper – they stand out. Each one like a many-petalled flower in the stark surroundings. We saw three feather stars. A few frilly white plumose anemones were poised on the rocks near the end of the point, while transparent tendrils of tube-dwelling anemones drifted delicately across the sand in the light current. On the way up, we saw the less mobile life in the shallows. Poked under ledges and saw heart tunicates on stalks. They look like purple- or maroon-colored upside-down tulips to me. And we saw a couple of large patches of brilliant orange encrusting sponge.

Bottom and Depths: The launching ramp leads into rocky but smooth shallows. On the right-hand side of the ramp, the silty sand gradually deepens to the end of a rectangular point. Beneath water, this land has been shored up with giant angular boulders or riprap. On the surface the entire area is 50 by 100 feet (15 by 30 meters) The riprap wall at the end of the point bottoms out to silty sand at 90 to 100 feet (27 to 30 meters). Above it, good rocky habitat all around the point with lots of holes, cracks and crevices for creatures to hide in.

Hazards: Boats, some current, transparent fishing line and wind in winter. Dive close alongside the riprap out of the way of boats and ascend up the side of the riprap, then swim back close to shore. Carry a knife for fishing line. Do not dive when a heavy northerly is blowing – even the riprap moves around in winter storms.

Telephone: Outside marina office, south end of the marina property.

Facilities: Restrooms at the marina and launching. Air fills in Horseshoe Bay, Squamish, North Vancouver and throughout greater Vancouver.

Access: Lions Bay is on Howe Sound in the village of Lions Bay. Reach it off Sea to Sky Highway (Highway 99) between Horseshoe Bay and Squamish. It is 10 minutes from Horseshoe Bay; 30 minutes from Squamish. Because the marina is heavily used for launching boats in summer, diving permitted only from October 15th through April 15th. A small fee for parking, launching and diving – a winter dive.

At the village of Lions Bay, turn off Highway 99 at the *northernmost* of the two exits to Lions Bay. Follow signs down Lions Bay Avenue to Lions Bay Marina: go across the railway tracks. Turn left and you will see the marina. Park near the launching ramp near the northern end of the marina property. A few rocks beside the ramp to sit on while gearing up. A super-easy entry at the launching ramp.

The bottom drops off quickly enough so you can easily become afloat; then swim a very short way out over the rocks and dive to a depth of 10 to 20 feet (3 to 6 meters). Turn right. And dive along the riprap wall – the big jumble of rocks that shore up the reclaimed rectangle of land. Go to whatever depth you are comfortable at. But throughout the dive stay close beside the riprap wall well out of the way of boats.

Wheelchair access exceptionally easy at this launching ramp entry.

Comments: Place-to-go for night diving in winter – telephone to arrange it.

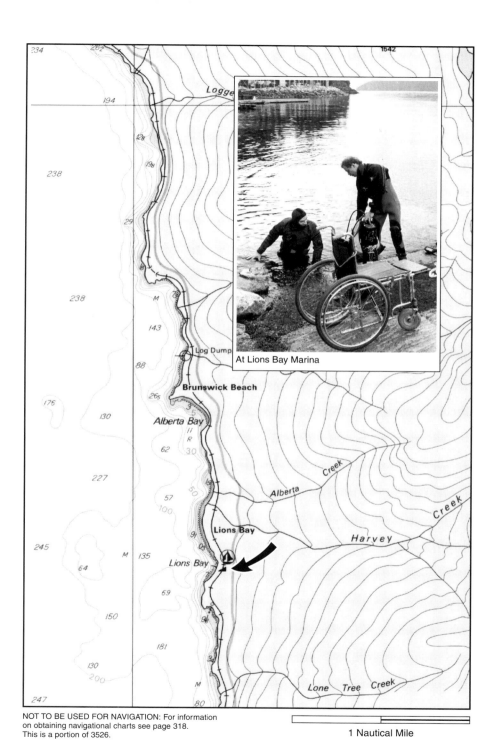

At Lions Bay Marina

NOT TO BE USED FOR NAVIGATION: For information
on obtaining navigational charts see page 318.
This is a portion of 3526.

1 Nautical Mile

KELVIN GROVE
Shore Dive or Kayak Dive

Tide Table: Point Atkinson

Skill: All divers

Why go: Octopuses, wolf-eels and red brotulas are resident at this site. That was enough to lure me. Two tanks are not enough.

Tank 1: Purple sea stars. Red slipper cucumbers. Orange burrowing cucumbers. A juvenile wolf-eel in a crack at 45 feet (14 meters) – it was peach colored. Pink dahlia anemones, tube-dwelling anemones, white plumose anemones. Quillback rockfish. A gray-and-maroon striped convict fish, or painted greenling. Sea lemons, an octopus in a deep indentation at 70 feet (21 meters). Two red brotulas in a crevice. A ratfish. And chimney sponges.

Tank 2: Sailfin sculpins. Alabaster nudibranchs. Sea cucumbers, brown and limp. Giant sunflower stars, white with orange spots. White burrowing cucumbers feathering between the cracks in the rocks. Two orange sea pens in the sand. One of the red brotulas, once again. And I had thought once in my life might never happen. This slim, sinuous brilliant fish is like a shiny red satin ribbon.

If you need more reasons: Easy entry. Easy to dive. I've been told there are grunt sculpins and I love to see them. Plus, it's a great beach for a picnic.

Bottom and Depths: The bottom slopes gently from the beach. Eelgrass in the bay. Vertical cracks and crevices for creatures to hide in along the rock wall, bottoming out to sand at 110 to 120 feet (34 to 37 meters) at the point. Also a wall to the south.

Hazards: Boats; sometimes poor visibility, in summer, because of Squamish River runoff. However, always worth checking to see if visibility is good. Listen for boats and ascend along the contours of the bottom all the way to the surface well out of the way of boats.

Telephones: • Lions Bay Marina, outside marina office. Go to Highway 99 and head north; take next exit (northernmost one) to Lions Bay and follow signs to the marina. • Grocery store in Lions Bay, outside. Go to Highway 99 and head north; take next exit (northernmost one) to Lions Bay and follow signs to the store.

Facilities: Restrooms at Lions Bay Beach Park. Dive-kayak rentals in Vancouver.

Access: Kelvin Grove is on Howe Sound in the village of Lions Bay. It is off Sea to Sky Highway (Highway 99) between Horseshoe Bay and Squamish: 10 minutes from Horseshoe Bay, 30 minutes from Squamish.

At Lions Bay, turn off Highway 99 toward the water into Kelvin Grove Road which is the *southernmost* of two exits to Lions Bay. Various roads go off Kelvin Grove Road to the right and left. To get to the beach, stay far left and curve down the hill. Cross the railway tracks and drop your gear at the head of the path to the water. Then return across the tracks and immediately turn right into the large parking lot. Walking to the dive, do not wear your hood when crossing the tracks. Small railway scooter cars race by and with a hood on you cannot hear them. This community beach park is signposted: "Members Only, Lions Bay Beach Park". Divers who don't live in Lions Bay have been going there for many years without problem. But if divers do not behave well or if the numbers of divers should overwhelm the beach to the detriment of Lions Bay residents, someone might ask you to prove you are a resident of Lions Bay or else leave.

The beach is not privately owned below high water mark – no beaches in British Columbia are. But the village of Lions Bay *does* own the path of 100 paces and the sixteen steps down to it, as well as the restrooms in the beach park. If entry through the beach park becomes prohibited, kayak-divers could paddle from Lions Bay Marina south for ¼ nautical mile (½ kilometer) to Kelvin Grove; land on the beach, gear up and dive. Gentle entry from the cobbled beach with silvered logs on it. Swim out over eelgrass and around to the point on your right.

Wheelchair divers who paddle dive-kayaks could access this one easily from Lions Bay.

Comments: Respect privately owned property: Observe parking regulations; keep a low profile; and behave considerately to maintain good relations.

Red brotula – at the time of writing, two of them resident at Kelvin Grove

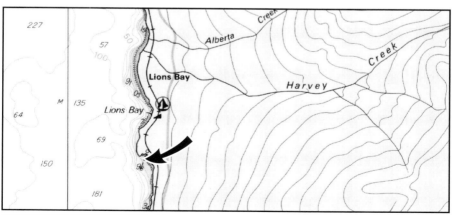

NOT TO BE USED FOR NAVIGATION: For information on obtaining navigational charts see page 318.
This is a portion of 3526.

1 Nautical Mile

BOWYER ISLAND
Kayak Dive or Boat Dive

Skill: All divers

Why go: An easy-to-dive reef with slots and crevices down the wall beneath it where octopuses and wolf-eels hide.

Swimming scallops, sea pens, red dahlia anemones, quillback rockfish, gum boot chitons, tube-dwelling anemones are at this site. We also saw the often-present, ever-glamorous white plumose anemones, a blood star, a giant silver nudibranch and lingcod, too. Lots of chimney sponges starting at 50 feet (15 meters). Feather stars are all over the wall.

Fun was had by all – when we dived, the charter captain had a rubber stamp of an octopus and a wolf-eel to put in the logbook of each diver who saw those creatures. My buddy and I got the octopus in our logs. But no wolf-eel for us that dive. However, we saw others down on the same site that night get the wolf-eel stamp in their logbooks. If you poke around, there's a good chance to see them.

A rich, safe site for open-water certification dives. Perfect for diving at night. And be sure to turn off your light, touch gently and see incredible neon-green phosphorescence ripple through the fronds of a sea pen.

Bottom and Depths: A rocky reef is at the southern tip of Bowyer Island. Sandy patches between the rocks. Over the edge of the reef, a wall goes down to however deep you want to go. The chart shows a ledge at 100 feet (30 meters) then plunges to 400 feet (120 meters). We went to 80 feet (24 meters).

Hazards: Boats and transparent fishing line. Listen for boats and ascend up the side of the island out of the way of boats, then swim out to your boat. Carry a knife.

Telephone: Horseshoe Bay waterfront gas station, across street from giant propeller and launching ramp.

Facilities: None at Bowyer Island. Charters out of Vancouver, North Vancouver, Horseshoe Bay, Port Moody, Coquitlam and New Westminster. Launching in Horseshoe Bay and off Sea to Sky Highway. Dive-kayak rentals in Vancouver. Air fills in Horseshoe Bay, Squamish, North Vancouver and throughout greater Vancouver.

Access: Bowyer Island is located in Howe Sound 2½ nautical miles (5 kilometers) north of Horseshoe Bay, 1 nautical mile (2 kilometers) west of Sunset Beach, and 2½ nautical miles (5 kilometers) southwest of Lions Bay.

Charter out of Vancouver or Horseshoe Bay; launch at Lions Bay; or rent a boat or dive-kayak or launch your own boat at Sunset Beach or Horseshoe Bay and go to Bowyer Island. Dive-kayakers could launch off the dock or ramp at Horseshoe Bay. The paddle takes 20 to 30 minutes. You must be water-wise if taking your own boat or dive-kayak to Bowyer, and have the sense not to paddle back if a "Squamish" wind – a wind from the north – comes up while you are down and blows down the inlet. Take marine flares.

Anchor at the southeast tip of Bowyer. If windy, leave a boat tender on the surface. The water can become choppy quickly at Bowyer Island, but the anchorage is well protected from northern Squamish winds.

Comments: Take a light for looking into cracks and crevices for those octopuses and wolf-eels.

Adventure IV picking up divers at reef, south end of Bowyer Island

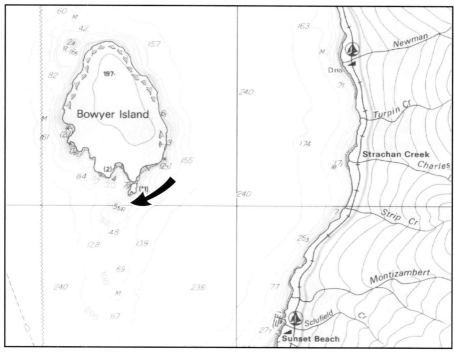

NOT TO BE USED FOR NAVIGATION: For information
on obtaining navigational charts see page 318.
This is a portion of 3526.

1 Nautical Mile

MILLERS LANDING
Shore Dive

Skill: All divers

Why go: Bouquets of white plumose anemones burgeon on top of the reef, cloud sponges billow below, and old bottles lie at the point on the right at Millers Landing. Union steamships called in here with the mailbags until 1900.

But what I'll never forget about Millers Landing is the sight of a dahlia anemone trying to eat a coon-striped shrimp. As we came around a rock, a lovely bright pink dahlia anemone held a 1½-inch (4-centimeter) shrimp with one of its tentacles and pulled the slender pink-and-black striped shrimp towards its flower-like mouth. The shrimp pulled back. The anemone pulled it forward again. The shrimp offered more and more resistance. Finally, the anemone let go and the shrimp swam just out of the anemone's grasp and stopped. A strange life-and-death struggle.

More dahlia anemones were on the stark rock, bright orange cup corals and tube worms. Octopuses hid in the rocks. I swished my light in a swath through a cloud of silvery fish. They swung, dancing with my light. Then we went over the drop-off into cloud sponges so beautiful that I didn't want to come up. Millers Landing makes me understand why cloud sponges are considered a speciality of Howe Sound.

Swimming back we saw sea pens, kelp greenlings, vermilion stars with turned up toes and small pale orange nudibranchs in the shallows.

Bottom and Depths: Rocky bottom, eelgrass, sand and silty white gravel slopes to the large rock reef 200 yards (185 meters) offshore in 40 to 50 feet (12 to 15 meters) of water. Beyond the reef, the bottom drops off sharply.

Hazards: Current, wind, and long walk to the dive. Small boats, in summer, and poor visibility caused by runoff from the Squamish and Fraser rivers, as well as plankton bloom. Some current around the point; dive the point on the slack. A "Squamish" wind can blow from the north and make entry and exit difficult. Listen for boats, start back before you are out of air, dive with a compass and navigate under water back to shore. After the dive, especially if you have been deep, first rest, then walk slowly up to your car to avoid overexertion which may increase risk of bends.

Telephones: • At Government Road and Miller Road • Snug Cove ferry landing.

Facilities: Roadside parking for four or five cars.

Access: Millers Landing is on Queen Charlotte Channel, east side of Bowen Island. It is a 15-minute ferry ride from Horseshoe Bay to Snug Cove on Bowen, then a 10-minute drive from Snug Cove to the dive.

At Bowen Island, drive 2 miles (3 kilometers) over good tarmac roads to the site. Coming off the ferry, pass the Country Store. Turn right at Miller Road when ⅓ mile (½ kilometer) off the ferry, and follow signs to Millers Landing. Just 1 mile (1½ kilometers) farther, the road turns left but you continue straight. Pass a turnoff to the left, then one to the right. Follow the arterial yellow line to a turnabout at the end of the road. Walk 200 yards (185 meters) down a narrow, fairly steep but well-graded trail and sloping steps to the beach. You might want to pack your gear down in two stages. Snorkel toward the rocks on your left. Just past the rocks, descend and follow a compass heading directly north to the reef.

Comments: Come and go quietly and respect private property so that the residents continue to welcome divers.

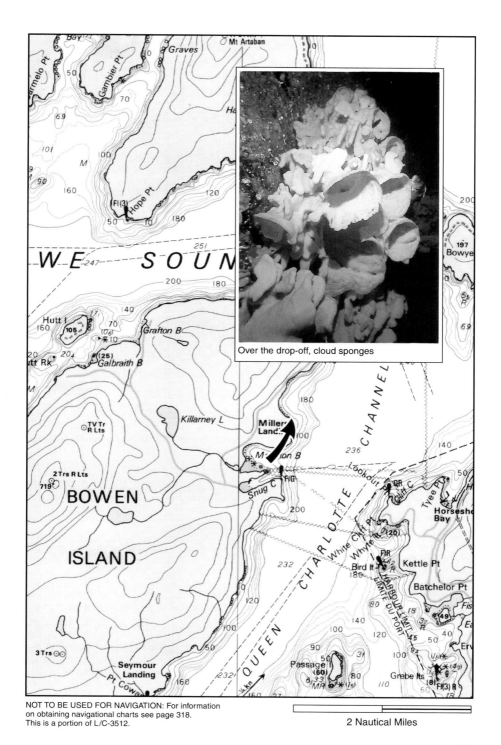

Over the drop-off, cloud sponges

NOT TO BE USED FOR NAVIGATION: For information on obtaining navigational charts see page 318. This is a portion of L/C-3512.

2 Nautical Miles

MANNION BAY
[DEEP BAY]
Shore Dive

Skill: All divers and snorkelers

Why go: Bottles new and old – thousands of them. Plus frequent sightings of small octopuses that live in the bottles. The dive is shallow, with easy entry and a short swim.

During one 60-minute exploratory dive my buddy and I found seven bottles that were "keepers" – at least they were keepers for a beginner like me. We had just reached a rich source – heaps of bottles – when it was time to come up. We found an embossed bottle from the Silver Springs Brewing Company, Victoria. I later identified it as being produced between 1908 and 1913. We found another bottle with Black Bear Brand on it, a dark green tapered one with an applied lip, two blue bottles with air bubbles in the glass, a dark amber one, and a Ginger Ale bottle, vintage 1940s or 50s. I'm still looking through bottle books. But from quick research after the dive, I would guess the tapered dark green bottle was probably made in the early 1900s.

Bottle dives start and end in the library. Before the dive I pored over history books for clues about where to go and what we might find. In 1889 a brick works was at the property we dived in front of. A year later Joseph Mannion built his home there. It was bought by Terminal Steamship Lines in 1900 to be a hotel and a Japanese gardener laid out the gardens. In 1920 the property was sold to Union Steamship Lines and they added cottages and a lodge. People used to row out from the cottages and dump their garbage. When you find a treasure-trove of bottles, you have probably happened onto the old resort dump.

Fascinating stuff. We did not find old dock pilings nor any Terminal or Union steamship china at Mannion Bay – not yet. But the potential is there. The potential is all around Bowen Island, as well as up the coast of British Columbia.

You can see the location of the old hotel and hotel float on Mannion Bay [Deep Bay] in the "Happy Isle" Historic Walking Tour brochure about Crippen Park. This brochure is provided by the Greater Vancouver Regional District (GVRD) parks department with the cooperation of the Bowen Island Historians. The dive is not in Crippen Park and, of course, the brochure does not mark the dive. But from the map in the brochure showing historic locations, you can figure out where to go.

The clues are on old maps and historic photographs as well as in history books. To gain information for this bottle dive and for future exploratory dives for bottles, china and other artifacts see pages 37 to 39.

This diving for history could become a wonderful obsession!

Bottom and Depths: Silty bottle-covered sand that slopes very gently to a depth of 45 to 60 feet (14 to 18 meters). We came across one slight seamount.

Hazards: Silt, small boats and water-skiers in summer. Weight yourself adequately so you can hover above bottom. Listen for boats; if you hear a boat, stay down until it passes. Allow time for a water-skier to pass as well.

Telephones: • At Government Road and Miller Road. • Snug Cove ferry landing.

Facilities: None at Mannion Bay; even roadside parking is very limited. At Snug Cove, restrooms in a concrete building on south side of Government Road just off the ferry. At Snug Cove, the restored Union Steamship Company Store, cafés and shops – many with a period flavor. No camping and no hotel on Bowen – Union Steamship Lines closed theirs in 1957. But some bed and breakfast places and cabins.

Access: Mannion Bay, formerly Deep Bay, is on the east side of Bowen Island. It is the first bay north of Snug Cove ferry landing. Travel 15 minutes by ferry from Horseshoe Bay to Bowen; then drive 1 mile (1½ kilometers) from Snug Cove to the dive. Safer to dive in winter when fewer boats coming and going in Mannion Bay.

At Snug Cove on Bowen, come off the ferry and almost immediately stop at the Union Steamship Company Store – it is on the right-hand side. Look in the rack outside. If the rack is stocked you will probably find the tourist brochure that describes the "Happy Isle Historic Walking Tour" and locates the old hotel and hotel float. Then go a short way on Government Road to Miller Road and turn right. Go on Miller Road to a junction with a church on the northeast corner. Turn right in front of the church, and at the "T" turn right again. From the ferry terminal to this point is only ½ mile (¾ kilometer). Then follow Melmore Road curving around. Pass Lenora Road. Come to another "T" and turn left. Turn right at the next road – it's steep. Drop your gear beside the water; return uphill and park at the roadside. Scramble over a few logs on the beach to the water.

Comments: The octopuses that often make their homes in bottles are not just a younger version of the larger *Octopus dofleini* which is the species we usually see in local waters. Look closely at the little smooth-skinned *Octopus rubescens*. This octopus is very red and its skin does not pebble up. We saw two on our dive at Bowen: one the size of my little finger; the second, the size of my hand.

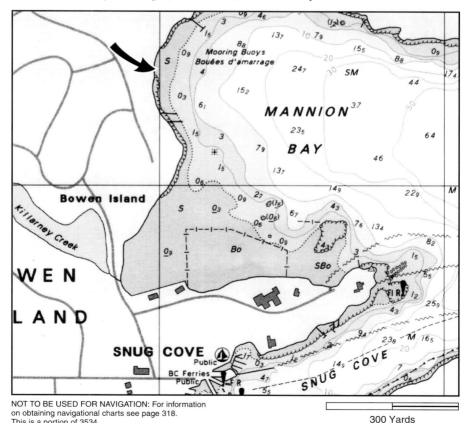

NOT TO BE USED FOR NAVIGATION: For information on obtaining navigational charts see page 318.
This is a portion of 3534.

300 Yards

WORLCOMBE ISLAND
Boat Dive

Tide Table: Point Atkinson

Skill: Intermediate and expert divers and snorkelers

Why go: It's a "holiday at home" for me to dive, then camp in the wilds so close to the city.
Worlcombe Island's great for photographers in fall and winter. It's the kind of place where you can take photographs all day. We not only saw a wide spectrum of marine life, but also found a small but old and attractive anchor. Other divers tell of fun scavenging for lead weights and flashers lost by fishermen. Old bottles, too – one beer bottle from a Victoria brewery. Variety is the keynote at Worlcombe.
Rockfish are so tame you can tickle their chins and they don't move. We saw crabs in the eelgrass, giant nudibranchs on the sand, cabezons and kelp greenlings. Cabezons are usually found over gravel bottom. Grind your teeth, or knock rocks together to attract cabezons. You might see a salmon in the kelp and eelgrass. Moving around to the rock wall you'll find trumpet sponges, tube worms, lots of small solitary cup corals, shrimp, and sometimes an octopus or a wolf-eel. We saw beautiful large dahlia anemones and a single swimming scallop. You might see a feather star. Cloud sponges and chimney sponges start at 60 feet (18 meters).

Bottom and Depths: The bottom varies. Eelgrass and sand in the small bay on the northeast shore. On the eastern tip, small rocks covered with bottom kelp are scattered over the sand. Around the corner on the southeastern side, a rock wall drops to a depth of 80 to 90 feet (24 to 27 meters). An even deeper drop on the south side.

Hazards: Current, wind, waves and broken fishing line. Small boats and poor visibility, in summer, because of Fraser River runoff. Dive on the slack. Carry a knife. Listen for boats and ascend along the bottom all the way to shore.

Telephone: Gibsons government wharf.

Facilities: None at privately owned Worlcombe Island. Plumper Cove Marine Park is in an apple orchard 4 nautical miles (7½ kilometers) away on Keats Island across from Gibsons Landing. The dock and anchorage are often crowded, but usually plenty of campsites are available at Plumper Cove where you will find running water, picnic tables and pit toilets. Charters out of Vancouver and Horseshoe Bay to Worlcombe. Car-top boat rentals in Vancouver. Air fills throughout greater Vancouver, in North Vancouver, Squamish and Horseshoe Bay.

Access: Worlcombe Island is in Collingwood Channel. It is 1 nautical mile (2 kilometers) west of Roger Curtis Point on the southwestern tip of Bowen Island; nearly 1½ nautical miles (3 kilometers) west of Tunstall Bay on Bowen Island; 3½ nautical miles (6½ kilometers) southeast of Gibsons; and 9 nautical miles (17 kilometers) southwest of Horseshoe Bay.
Charter out of Vancouver or Horseshoe Bay. Launch an inflatable or car-top boat at Tunstall Bay on Bowen or launch at Horseshoe Bay or Gibsons and go to Worlcombe Island. Worlcombe is very exposed. Be aware of wind and waves. If a strong west wind is blowing, you may have to leave someone in the boat, and you may not be able to anchor at all.
Anchor where it is most sheltered. In fine weather this shelter is usually on the north side. Just east of the marker on the northeast corner of the island there is a small bay conveniently near good diving. From here, dive around the southeastern tip of the island. At the end of your dive, look for bottles in the bay.

Comments: Worlcombe Island is just one of many sites where you can dive and camp nearby. Look at your charts and explore. There are fabulous cloud sponges in Howe Sound.

Tube worm, about three times life-size, feeding from current

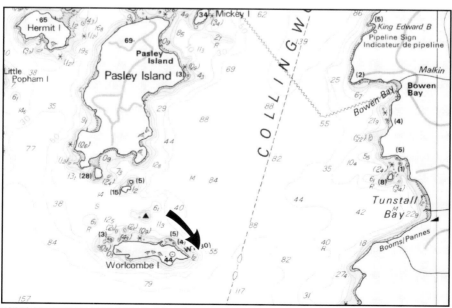

NOT TO BE USED FOR NAVIGATION: For information
on obtaining navigational charts see page 318.
This is a portion of 3526.

1 Nautical Mile

SEYMOUR BAY
Shore Dive

Skill: All divers and snorkelers

Why go: Seymour Bay is a low-key place where you don't have to do much planning to have a good dive. It's so pretty, both above and below water, that you should go when the sun is shining and plan to stay all day.

Most life is in 20 to 30 feet (6 to 9 meters). Swimming out over the sand we saw flounders, kelp greenlings and bright orange burrowing cucumbers flinging their fingers into the current. Sea peaches, tube worms and giant barnacles on the rock wall. Nudibranchs in the bottom kelp. An octopus curled up under a ledge in only 20 feet (6 meters) of water. Deeper, dahlia anemones flow from the wall. Occasional bursts of large orange plumose anemones are attached to isolated rocks on sloping white sand below the wall. Thousands of miniature sea pens feather the sand. Copper rockfish and some lingcod live at the point.

Heading back to shore or on your second dive, look in the bay for old bottles, and for plates and teacups with Union Steamship logos on them – in the 1920s commuters came daily by motor launch from Vancouver and Union steamships delivered mail to Seymour Bay.

Bottom and Depths: Rocks covered with bottom kelp are scattered around the end of the point, dropping off in gentle tiers to a smooth white sand bottom. Most life is around the rocks in 20 to 30 feet (6 to 9 meters).

Hazards: Some current and poor visibility, in summer, caused by Fraser River runoff, as well as plankton bloom. Dive on the slack on large tidal exchanges.

Telephones: • Near Snug Cove at Government Road and Miller Road. • Snug Cove ferry landing.

Facilities: None.

Access: Seymour Bay is at Bowen Island. It is a 15-minute ferry ride from Horseshoe Bay. Once on Bowen, it's a 20-minute drive over steep pot-holed roads, which might be impassable in winter, to Seymour Bay.

At Bowen Island drive 6 miles (10 kilometers) to Seymour Bay – half the distance is on roads in poor condition. At the junction that is ⅓ mile (½ kilometer) off the ferry, go straight. Follow the signs toward Tunstall Bay. Pass the school and bear left, following signs to Adams Road. When you have gone 2⅓ miles (3¾ kilometers), turn left into Cowan Road which is gravel. Follow this rough, steep road for 2 miles (3 kilometers) to a junction at a big tree. Turn left, following the signpost toward Arbutus Bay. When you reach another sign showing Arbutus Bay to the right, continue straight. Go ½ mile (¾ kilometer) farther to an old orchard overlooking the water. Just before the road turns to the left, there is room for one car to park. You could walk from here to check out the road – when I was last there you could drive 150 yards (140 meters) more to unload gear. From this place where you can drop gear, it is a steep scramble down a very rough trail for 125 yards (115 meters) to the beach. Then snorkel to the point on your right and descend.

Comments: Seymour Bay no longer has a dock or homes or other habitation. But the dive is good, you feel surrounded by history and the orchard is a beautiful peaceful place for a picnic. Take your garbage out and keep it beautiful. At the time of writing, this site is only for hardy adventurers willing to risk difficult roads and tote gear.

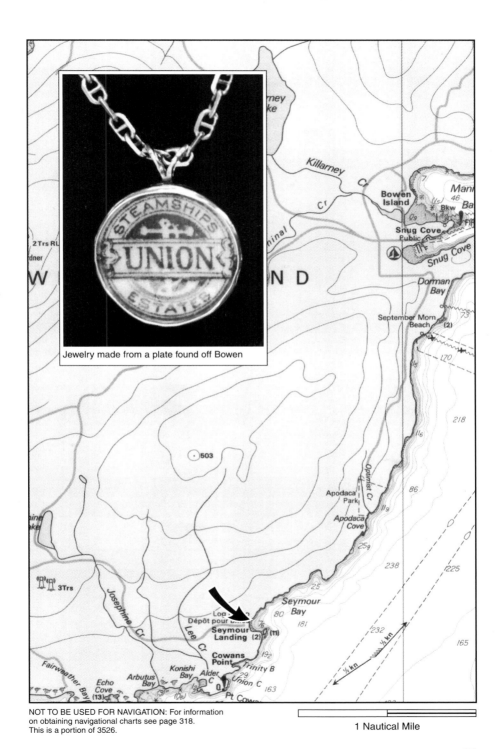

Jewelry made from a plate found off Bowen

NOT TO BE USED FOR NAVIGATION: For information
on obtaining navigational charts see page 318.
This is a portion of 3526.

1 Nautical Mile

81

COPPER COVE
Shore Dive

Tide Table: Point Atkinson

Skill: All divers and snorkelers

Why go: Because of the easy entry, Copper Cove is especially good for night diving enthusiasts.

If you're in the mood for a relaxed dive you'll enjoy the shallow rocky shores rimming the cove where you can see a variety of life. Bright orange dead man's finger sponges poke from the bottom kelp. Huge sunflower stars and masses of smaller ones cling to the rocks. Pale orange sea peaches and small brown and beige anemones cluster beneath the overhangs. Brown sea cucumbers, rockfish, barnacles, burrowing cucumbers and lingcod live along the rock-rimmed cove.

Night diving over the sand and eelgrass yields a whole new experience. We saw a variety of flatfish: a mottled sand dab, lemon sole and C-O sole. Interesting small fish: a whiting, a small white curled-up eelpout and a midshipman with golden eyes. And sculpins – a grunt sculpin, sailfin sculpins and a roughback sculpin, a small fish with an intricate dorsal fin that reminded me of a miniature lionfish. Spider crabs, prawns, hermit crabs, shrimp and lots of small ratfish come out on the sand at night.

And I love snorkeling back through the fabulous phosphorescent night sea.

Bottom and Depths: Rocks covered with bottom kelp rim Copper Cove bottoming out to smooth white sand at 20 to 30 feet (6 to 9 meters). The sand slopes gradually to whatever depth you might want to go. There are three deep rocky reefs just left of center of the cove, the first at 70 to 80 feet (21 to 24 meters). To find the reefs go to the point on your left and follow the bottom down to the right.

Hazards: Wind, and wash from the ferries. Poor visibility, in summer, because of Fraser/Squamish runoff. However, the water may be turbid one day and clear the next; worth checking. A "Squamish" wind from the north can blow up the surf making entry and exit difficult.

Telephone: Horseshoe Bay waterfront gas station, Bay Street and Royal Avenue. Across from big anchor on waterfront and across from Troll's Restaurant.

Facilities: None. Roadside parking very limited. Room for one or two cars. Be careful not to block driveways. Air fills at Horseshoe Bay and North Vancouver.

Access: Copper Cove is off Marine Drive above Horseshoe Bay. It is the first cove west of Horseshoe Bay ferry terminal – 15 minutes from Park Royal shopping center (just west of Lions Gate Bridge) in West Vancouver; 5 minutes from the Horseshoe Bay Overpass Bridge that is immediately west of Highway 99.

From the Overpass Bridge, go straight west on Marine Drive ½ mile (¾ kilometer) to Copper Cove Road. Turn right and go to the end of the road. Parking is limited: so unload gear, park and return to walk down the 41 concrete steps to the beach. Dive towards the point on your left.

To get to the Overpass Bridge above Horseshoe Bay, then to Copper Cove Road
• From Park Royal in West Vancouver (Highway 1A West/99 North), follow signs to Horseshoe Bay: go up Taylor Way, then left onto Upper Levels Highway (Highway 1 West/99 North). Go for 7 miles (11 kilometers) and follow signs to Whistler and Squamish, taking Exit 1. Immediately off Highway 1, turn left, crossing the Overpass Bridge. Continue straight to Copper Cove Road.
• From Horseshoe Bay ferry terminal: immediately off the ferry move to the Highway 99 lane. Follow signs to "Highway 99, Marine Drive and Horseshoe Bay", taking the

second Exit 0. After going under the Overpass Bridge and curving right uphill past the yield sign, turn left at Marine Drive and go straight to Copper Cove Road.
• From Horseshoe Bay in the village, head uphill on Nelson Avenue to Marine Drive. Turn right. Go west on Marine less than ½ mile (¾ kilometer) to Copper Cove Road.

Comments: Divers have not been welcomed here – let's change our image, park out of the way and come and go quietly.

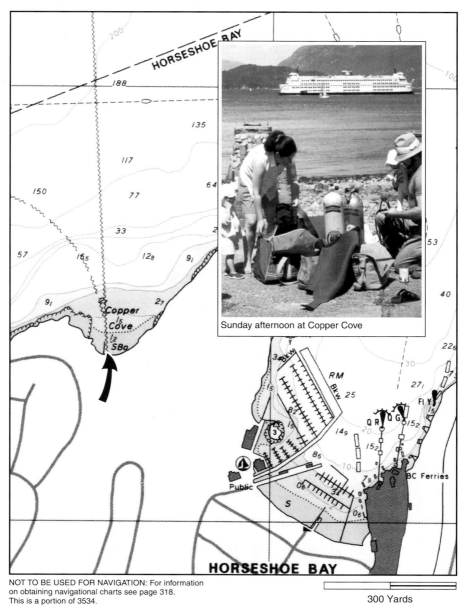

Sunday afternoon at Copper Cove

HORSESHOE BAY

NOT TO BE USED FOR NAVIGATION: For information on obtaining navigational charts see page 318.
This is a portion of 3534.

300 Yards

LOOKOUT POINT
Shore Dive

Skill: Intermediate and expert divers. All divers with guide.

Why go: Lookout Point, the western extreme of Cliff Cove, commonly called Telegraph Cove, is ideal for open-water certification dives, for photography, for night dives. Almost anything you can think of except spearfishing. It is part of Whytecliff Marine Park and Underwater Game Reserve.

So much life around Lookout Point that local divers keep coming back again and again. It's easy to choose your level and dive shallow or deep. When diving here I like to move down quickly to the second ledge at 50 to 60 feet (15 to 18 meters) where lovely clusters of white anemones are piled like mushroom caps on top of the rocks, spilling over into the valleys below. The walls are covered with small, anemone-like zoanthids. Octopuses live in the area. Lingcod, red Irish lords, urchins, rockfish, grunt sculpins, sea pens, ratfish, shrimp, sea peaches, hermit crabs and giant barnacles. Look for dogfish sharks and harbor seals.

Once on a night dive at Lookout Point I even saw a vermilion rockfish, a fish more commonly seen on the west coast of Vancouver Island. Deeper, you will see cloud sponges and small solitary cup corals.

Bottom and Depths: The point drops in rocky tiers. First a ledge at 30 to 40 feet (9 to 12 meters), another at 50 to 60 feet (15 to 18 meters); and another at 110 to 120 feet (34 to 37 meters). Bottom kelp covers broken rocks down to 30 to 40 feet (9 to 12 meters). Pockets of sand in the ledges.

Hazards: Current, broken fishing line, wash from the ferries, and small boats. Poor visibility in summer because of Fraser River runoff. The water may be turbid one day and clear the next; it is always worth checking it out. Visibility is best on a rising tide. Both flooding and ebbing tides can be overpowering. Dive near slack, especially on large tidal exchanges. Carry a knife. When ascending, and especially if you heard a ferry pass, watch out for logs being tossed about in the wash near shore. Listen for boats and ascend along the bottom all the way to shore.

Telephones: • Whytecliff Park, east of refreshment stand, by the tarmac path to beach. • Horseshoe Bay waterfront gas station, Bay Street and Royal Avenue.

Facilities: None. Roadside parking very limited. Be considerate of local residents. If parking is full, unload gear beside the path to Cliff Cove and park at the overload lot.

Access: Lookout Point juts into Queen Charlotte Channel near Horseshoe Bay. It is in Whytecliff Park. From Park Royal shopping center (just west of Lions Gate Bridge) in West Vancouver, 20 minutes; from the Overpass Bridge at Horseshoe Bay turnoff just west of Highway 99, 10 minutes.

From the Overpass Bridge at Highway 99, follow signs to Horseshoe Bay but at Nelson Avenue do not turn right to Horseshoe Bay – continue straight west on Marine Drive, following signs to Whytecliff Park. From the highway, it is 1½ miles (2½ kilometers) on narrow curving roads. At Whytecliff, follow the sign toward "Overload Parking". Take the upper road on your right; go ⅓ mile (½ kilometer) on Cliff Road. At the confluence of Cliff Road, Arbutus Road and Arbutus Place, look for a small sign on the right-hand side saying "Beach Access". A gravel path follows the telegraph line on your right down to Cliff Cove. It is 100 yards (90 meters) from road to beach; 35 stairsteps make access easy. At the beach you may have to climb over logs to reach the water. Snorkel to the point on your left and descend.

To get to the Overpass Bridge above Horseshoe Bay, then to Whytecliff Park
• From Park Royal in West Vancouver (Highway 1A West/99 North), follow signs to Horseshoe Bay: go up Taylor Way, then left onto Upper Levels Highway (Highway 1 West/99 North). Go for 7 miles (11 kilometers) and follow signs to Whistler and Squamish, taking Exit 1. Immediately off Highway 1, turn left, crossing the Overpass Bridge and continue straight on Marine Drive, following signs to Whytecliff Park.
• From Horseshoe Bay ferry terminal: immediately off the ferry move to the Highway 99 lane. Follow signs to "Highway 99, Marine Drive and Horseshoe Bay", taking the *second* Exit 0. After going under the Overpass Bridge and curving right uphill to Marine Drive, turn left and go straight west on Marine following signs to Whytecliff Park.
• From Horseshoe Bay in the village, head uphill on Nelson Avenue to Marine Drive. Turn right. Go west on Marine Drive following signs to Whytecliff Park.

Comments: Beautiful beach and beautiful dive. Whytecliff Park is closed to the harvest of marine life to a distance of 330 feet (100 meters) offshore.

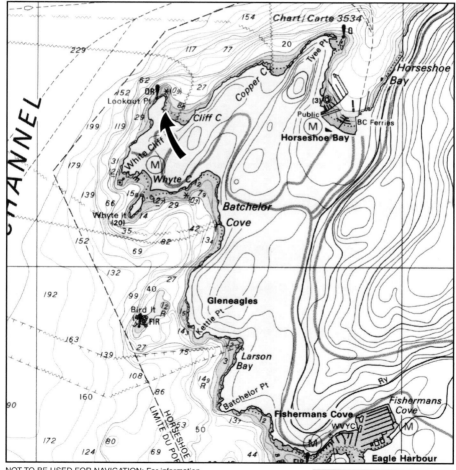

NOT TO BE USED FOR NAVIGATION: For information
on obtaining navigational charts see page 318.
This is a portion of 3481.

½ Nautical Mile

WHYTECLIFF PARK
DAY MARKER
Shore Dive

Skill: Intermediate and expert divers. All divers with guide.

Why go: Amazing to have this fabulous underwater world always waiting in its wildness. Incredible to think of this wild and wonderful seascape being right in the city. Even more unbelievable to expect that it will continue to be with us – forever, we hope, because spearfishing and removal of marine life are forbidden at Whytecliff Park Underwater Reserve.

The reef at the Day Marker is home for several marine animals that are so familiar to divers they're like old friends. Two octopuses are well known. Almost every time I dive here I meet one old grandfather lingcod. You'll see rockfish, red Irish lords, seaperch, sea pens, urchins, grunt sculpins and sea stars. Ratfish and sailfin sculpins, at night. Also on a night dive we saw a small stubby squid shimmer from blue to green to white like an opalescent teardrop pendant. Masses of white plumose anemones cascade down the sheer rock wall. At 80 feet (24 meters) fluffy white cloud sponges lure you further, lighting up the dark cliff below. And as you drop into the depths lit with these puffs of white you think that Whytecliff Park must have been named by divers.

The most seasoned diver will enjoy the rocky reef and fantastic drop-off past the Day Marker in Whytecliff Park.

Bottom and Depths: Rocky reef around the Day Marker, dropping off north of it. The wall plunges to 700 feet (200 meters).

Hazards: Depth, current and broken fishing line. Old cables from boat moorings if you swim out from the beach. Small boats and poor visibility, in summer, because of Fraser River runoff. However, if you dive deep you can get beneath it. There can be considerable surface current past the Day Marker and along the wall. On large tidal exchanges, dive near slack. Carry a knife. If caught in transparent fishing line you can cut your way free. Listen for boats and ascend up the rocks at the marker or along the wall all the way to the surface, well out of the way of boats.

Telephones: • Whytecliff Park, east of the refreshment stand, by tarmac path to beach. • Horseshoe Bay waterfront gas station, Bay Street and Royal Avenue.

Facilities: Large grassy area, picnic tables, playground and restrooms near the pavilion at the west end of the park. In summer, a refreshment stand, and just west of it, a freshwater tap to wash gear. A detailed Whytecliff Marine Park Dive Site Map of the entire park, including Lookout Point, can be purchased from dive shops or from West Vancouver Municipal Hall, Parks and Recreation Department, 750 17th Street, West Vancouver BC V7V 3T3, (604) 922-1211.

Access: The Day Marker – and The Cut – at Whytecliff Park are on Queen Charlotte Channel near Horseshoe Bay. The site is 20 minutes from Park Royal shopping center (west of Lions Gate Bridge) in West Vancouver; and it is 10 minutes from the Overpass Bridge at Horseshoe Bay turnoff just west of Highway 99.

From the Overpass Bridge at Highway 99, follow signs to Horseshoe Bay but at Nelson Avenue do not turn right to Horseshoe Bay – continue straight past the firehall going west on Marine Drive and follow signs to Whytecliff Park. From the highway, it is 1½ miles (2½ kilometers). At Whytecliff, drive completely around the park to the refreshment stand. A variety of rock steps and tarmac paths go from the refreshment stand to the beach – at high tide each path is about 100 paces to the water. From the beach, swim out close beside the shore on the right. Go 100 yards (90 meters) to the point and the Day Marker that marks the reef. Continue a short way northwest past the reef to the drop-off.

The Day Marker and The Cut can still be reached by way of steep steps and a path down the narrow ravine to The Cut. This entry is at the west end of the park, and east of the pavilion. You can climb down to the sea and go straight to the Day Marker, or turn right and dive the sheer wall. Since the path can be very slippery when wet, most people are glad now to be able to use one of the easier access points to the beach, followed by a short swim to the wall.

To get to the Overpass Bridge above Horseshoe Bay, then to Whytecliff Park
• From Park Royal in West Vancouver (Highway 1A West/99 North), follow signs to Horseshoe Bay: go up Taylor Way, then left onto Upper Levels Highway (Highway 1 West/99 North). Go 7 miles (11 kilometers) and follow signs to Squamish, taking Exit 1. Immediately off Highway 1, turn left, crossing the Overpass Bridge and continue straight on Marine Drive, following signs to Whytecliff Park.
• From Horseshoe Bay ferry terminal: immediately off the ferry, move to the Highway 99 lane. Follow signs to "Highway 99, Marine Drive and Horseshoe Bay", taking the *second* Exit 0. After going under the Overpass Bridge and curving right uphill to Marine Drive, turn left and go straight west on Marine, following signs to Whytecliff Park.
• From Horseshoe Bay in the village, head uphill on Nelson Avenue to Marine Drive. Turn right. Go west on Marine Drive, following signs to Whytecliff Park.

Comments: Great place to meet divers.

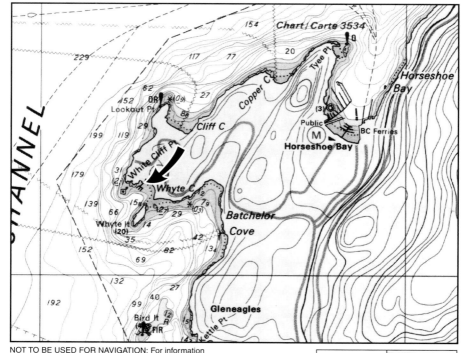

NOT TO BE USED FOR NAVIGATION: For information
on obtaining navigational charts see page 318.
This is a portion of 3481.

½ Nautical Mile

WHYTECLIFF PARK
WHYTE ISLET
Shore Dive

Skill: All divers and snorkelers

Why go: Whyte Islet is a popular open-water certification site within Whytecliff Park Underwater Reserve where you can easily skin dive to see flounders and crabs, or enjoy a shallow dive.

Whyte Islet's smooth rock walls give homes to a variety of marine animals. You'll see lots of little things: calcareous tube worms attached to shallow rocks, sea lemons, leather stars and purple sea stars. Sea cucumbers all over the bottom. You're sure to see orange plumose anemones tilting their ruffled fronds to the current. You might see an octopus. A couple of lingcod are usually cruising around the islet. Look for dogfish sharks and, on almost every night dive, resident seals come buzzing by. I've even seen a feather star at Whyte Islet.

Bottom and Depths: Eelgrass and sand in 10 to 20 feet (3 to 6 meters) of water on your right. A rock groin, which dries on most low tides, leads out to Whyte Islet. Beside the islet a smooth rock wall drops to sand at 10 to 20 feet (3 to 6 meters), sloping gradually to a depth of 50 to 60 feet (15 to 18 meters) at the tip of Whyte Islet.

Hazards: Small boats and poor visibility, in spring and summer. Some current. Large cables protruding from the rocks. Wear extra weight, listen for boats and ascend close along the bottom all the way to shore. Current can be quite strong at the tip of Whyte Islet. If you feel current, stay under water and pull yourself along on the rocks, and watch for the cables.

Telephones: • Whytecliff Park, east of the refreshment stand, by tarmac path to beach. • Horseshoe Bay waterfront gas station, Bay Street and Royal Avenue.

Facilities: Whytecliff Park has a large grassy area, picnic tables, children's playground and restrooms open year-round. In summer, a refreshment stand, and a few steps away, a freshwater tap to wash gear. Changerooms near the rock groin are open most of the year. If planning a special mid-winter dive you could request that the changerooms be opened for it. Write to Recreation Manager, West Vancouver Parks and Recreation Department, 750 17th Street, West Vancouver BC V7V 3T3, (604) 922-1211.

Access: Whyte Islet at Whytecliff Park is on Queen Charlotte Channel near Horseshoe Bay. It is 20 minutes from Park Royal shopping center (west of Lions Gate Bridge) in West Vancouver; 10 minutes from the Overpass Bridge at Horseshoe Bay turnoff just west of Highway 99.

From the Overpass Bridge at Highway 99, follow signs to Horseshoe Bay but at Nelson Avenue do not turn right to Horseshoe Bay – continue straight past the firehall and go west on Marine Drive, following signs to Whytecliff Park. From the highway, 1½ miles (2½ kilometers). At Whytecliff, drive completely around the park to the refreshment stand. Walk down an easily inclined tarmac path and steps on the left-hand side to the water.

To get to the Overpass Bridge above Horseshoe Bay, then to Whytecliff Park
• From Park Royal in West Vancouver (Highway 1A West/99 North), follow signs to Horseshoe Bay: go up Taylor Way, then left onto Upper Levels Highway (Highway 1 West/99 North). Go 7 miles (11 kilometers) and follow signs to Squamish, taking Exit 1. Immediately off Highway 1, turn left, crossing the Overpass Bridge and continue

straight on Marine Drive, following signs to Whytecliff Park.

• From Horseshoe Bay ferry terminal: immediately off the ferry move to the Highway 99 lane. Follow signs to "Highway 99, Marine Drive and Horseshoe Bay", taking the *second* Exit 0. After going under the Overpass Bridge and curving right uphill past the yield sign to Marine Drive, turn left and go straight west on Marine, following signs to Whytecliff Park.

• From Horseshoe Bay in the village, head uphill on Nelson Avenue to Marine Drive. Turn right. Go west on Marine Drive, following signs to Whytecliff Park.

Comments: Spearfishing and removal of underwater specimens are forbidden in Whytecliff Park Underwater Reserve.

Whyte Islet on left, Day Marker around point on right

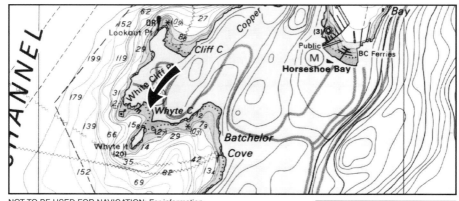

NOT TO BE USED FOR NAVIGATION: For information on obtaining navigational charts see page 318. This is a portion of 3481.

½ Nautical Mile

BIRD ISLET
Kayak Dive or Boat Dive

Skill: Intermediate and expert divers

Why go: Anemones are the highlight. Huge white plumose anemones cluster on top of the rocks and billow between the crevices and beneath the overhangs. Delicate pink snakelock anemones and calcareous tube worms are on the walls, transparent tube-dwelling anemones in the sand.

Green urchins, nudibranchs, swimming scallops, and bright yellow knobby encrusting sponges are more marine animals you might see at Bird Islet. It is in town, but feels like wilderness.

Also look for lead cannonball weights to salvage at this popular fishing site.

Bottom and Depths: The rounded rock of Bird Islet bottoms out to sand at 20 to 30 feet (6 to 9 meters) at the north end. The rock walls are smooth – not much to hold onto. Deeper, south of the islet, the walls are undercut and riddled with slits, caverns and hiding places. The islet is deceptive. An underwater plateau runs southward to the marker. Diving on a low tide, we reached a depth of 70 feet (21 meters).

Hazards: Boats, current and transparent fishing line – but most of all the deceptive shape of the islet, combined with the presence of small boats near the marker. Fishing boats and sailboats – remember, the latter are silent – are often present. Use a compass. Dive out and back, and do not ascend in the open water. Plan your dive to return to the islet where you can ascend close to the wall all the way to the surface. Dive on or near slack. Carry a knife. If caught in fishing line, you can cut your way free.

Telephones: • Whytecliff Park, by tarmac path to beach at Whyte Islet. • Horseshoe Bay waterfront gas station, Bay Street and Royal Avenue.

Facilities: None at Bird Islet. Air fills in Horseshoe Bay, North Vancouver and throughout greater Vancouver. Dive-kayak rentals in Vancouver. Car-top and trailerable boats and motors for rent in Burnaby. Launching ramp in Horseshoe Bay.

Access: Bird Islet is in Queen Charlotte Channel ½ nautical mile (1 kilometer) south of Whytecliff Park, and west of the golf course at Gleneagles. It is 2½ nautical miles (5 kilometers) from Horseshoe Bay.

Charter or launch at Horseshoe Bay, or go by dive-kayak. Boats can anchor at the south end of the islet. Dive out and back on the west side – do not try to circle the island. Use your compass.

Kayak-divers will find a narrow cove at the southeast side of the islet where it is easy to gear up and leave your boat. You have a choice of three launching points – all reached by Marine Drive. Then paddle 10 to 20 minutes.
• Whytecliff Park is the easiest place to launch because a great deal of parking space is available – even then, go early, especially on weekends. There are both stairsteps and a graduated tarmac path to the beach (see directions to Whytecliff on page 88).
• Larsen Bay Park is the closest point to paddle from but you must walk 200 yards (185 meters) down a steep, wooded path to the beach (see directions to Larsen Bay on page 92).
• Batchelor Cove, at the foot of Dufferin Avenue, is the access with the least distance to carry gear. Sixteen stairsteps go to the beach. At high tide, you're there. At low tide, 36 paces to the water across cobbled beach. The difficulty is that no parking space is available at the end of the road. However, you could drop gear, then park part way up the hill. To reach Batchelor Cove, turn left down Dufferin when just past

Copper Cove Road and go ⅓ mile (½ kilometer) to the water (see directions to Copper Cove Road on page 82).

Comments: Excellent place for a first-kayak dive, as the paddle is short and you can gear up in the shallows or on the rocks. Then dive.

Bird Islet

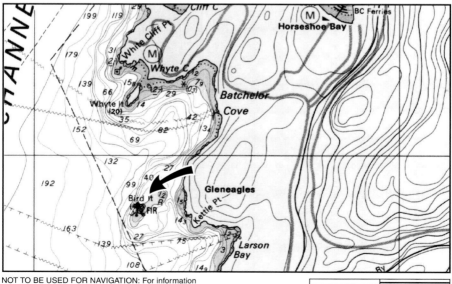

NOT TO BE USED FOR NAVIGATION: For information
on obtaining navigational charts see page 318.
This is a portion of 3481.

½ Nautical Mile

LARSEN BAY PARK
Shore Dive

Tide Table: Point Atkinson

Skill: All divers and snorkelers

Why go: Larsen Bay – often called Blink Bonnie – is as nice as its nickname.

An ideal place for a pleasant shallow dive and family picnic. Small broken rock heaped at the bottom of the walls rimming the bay is covered with beautiful patches of purple-satiny kelp and scraps of emerald green kelp. I've come nose-to-nose with a number of small lingcod, lots of rockfish, kelp greenlings and hundreds of spooky little blackeye gobies hanging in niches in the wall. And nearly trampled uncountable numbers of flounders beneath my fins. Look for sea peaches, urchins, decorator crabs, sea lemons, silvery herring in summer, schools of sand lances on cloudy days or at night, occasional plumose anemones, masses of purple stars and sun stars. There's a shy octopus in residence, too, in a deep crack beneath the small private jetty on your right. Look for it, but leave it for others to enjoy at this popular, open-water certification site. Look for Dungeness crabs in the eelgrass in the bay. Hermit crabs on the silty sand.

Basically this dive is a good shallow one, but you can go deep and into sponges if you swim far out over the sand. Prawns come up onto the sand at night. And I saw a snake prickleback for the first time while night diving at Larsen Bay Park.

Bottom and Depths: Rock walls rim the bay which bottoms out to flat sand at 20 to 30 feet (6 to 9 meters). Broadleaf bottom kelp too.

Hazards: Boats and poor visibility in summer. Listen for boats; use a compass and navigate back to shore staying close to the bottom all the way. Because of silt, visibility is seldom good at Larsen Bay and in spring and early summer the water can become particularly murky with Fraser River runoff. However, the water may be turbid one day and clear the next, so it is always worth checking to see if visibility is good.

Telephones: • Gleneagles Golf Course, beside the Professional Shop, from Gleneagles Drive, go ⅓ mile (½ kilometer) north on Marine Drive and turn left. • Fishermans Cove, Thunderbird Marina at top of ramp at wharf, ¾ mile (1⅓ kilometers) south on Marine Drive.

Facilities: Small pocket park, crescent of beach, pit toilets, and parking for ten cars.

Access: Larsen Bay is near Horseshoe Bay. It is 15 minutes from Park Royal shopping center (west of Lions Gate Bridge) in West Vancouver; 5 minutes from the Overpass Bridge that is immediately west of Highway 99 at the Horseshoe Bay turnoff.

From the Overpass Bridge, immediately west of the bridge turn left down Marine Drive. Go south for ¾ mile (1⅓ kilometers) to Gleneagles Drive with a sign "To Blink Bonnie". A bus shelter is on the right. Turn right toward the water on Gleneagles and wind down it nearly ½ mile (¾ kilometer) to the end of the road. You will see Gleneagles Golf Course on your right and a tennis court on your left. Park, suit up and go down the steps and steep, wooded path; walk 200 yards (185 meters) to the beach. Snorkel to the point on your right and go down.

To get to the Overpass Bridge above Horseshoe Bay, then Gleneagles Drive
• From Park Royal in West Vancouver (Highway 1A West/99 North), follow signs to Horseshoe Bay: go up Taylor Way, then left onto Upper Levels Highway (Highway 1 West/99 North). Go 7 miles (11 kilometers) and follow signs to Squamish, taking Exit 1. Immediately off Highway 1, turn left, crossing the Overpass Bridge and immediately turn left down Marine Drive.

• From Horseshoe Bay ferry terminal: immediately off the ferry move to the Highway 99 lane. Follow signs to "Highway 99, Marine Drive and Horseshoe Bay", taking the *second* Exit 0. After going under the Overpass Bridge and curving right uphill, do not continue uphill past the "yield" sign – turn left downhill onto Marine Drive.
• From Horseshoe Bay in the village, head uphill on Nelson Avenue to Marine Drive. Turn left. Go east on Marine Drive for ⅕ mile (⅓ kilometer) and just before the Overpass Bridge turn right, still on Marine Drive, and go south to Gleneagles Drive.

Comments: Come and go quietly so that local residents will continue to welcome divers at Larsen Bay.

School of sand lances

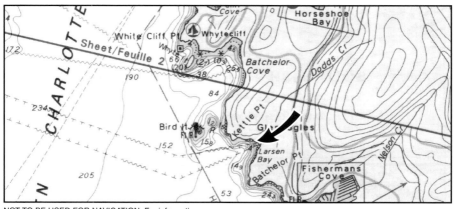

NOT TO BE USED FOR NAVIGATION: For information on obtaining navigational charts see page 318. This is a portion of 3311.

1 Nautical Mile

PASSAGE ISLAND REEF
Boat Dive

Tide Table: Point Atkinson

Skill: Expert divers. Guided intermediates with anchor line to descend on.

Why go: Passage Island Reef is a magnificent underwater mountain for sightseeing.

Rising to within 20 to 30 feet (6 to 9 meters) of the surface, this large mound covered with boulders lies in current-swept Queen Charlotte Channel. All of the water flowing between Bowen Island and West Vancouver pours over this large reef which snags nutrients to feed the fish.

Diving here you drop onto piles of white plumose anemones tumbling one over the other like a gigantic feather bed. I was tempted to lie in it and luxuriate in the fluffy white fronds. Moving down the side of the huge mound we saw lingcod lying on their chins, looking out of dark seams in the rock. Each nook and cranny conceals another large fish or octopus. Transparent sea squirts hang from boulders like clusters of plastic grapes. Sea cucumbers, calcareous tube worms, burrowing cucumbers, sunflower stars and urchins are on the reef.

Skirting the southern end of the reef, we swam through a field of sea pens into a ghostly garden of tall, slim white sea whips.

Bottom and Depths: The reef rises like a huge mound scattered with boulders. Sloping muddy bottom surrounds the base of the reef at 50 to 60 feet (15 to 18 meters). The top of the reef is always 20 to 30 feet (6 to 9 meters) below the surface.

Hazards: Current, small boats and wind. Poor visibility, in summer, because of Fraser River runoff. Dive on the slack, especially on large tidal exchanges. Listen for boats and ascend on your anchor line well out of the way of small boats. Visibility best in fall and winter, and on an ebbing tide.

Telephone: Fishermans Cove, Thunderbird Marina at top of ramp from the water.

Facilities: None. Charters out of Vancouver, North Vancouver, West Vancouver, Port Moody, Coquitlam and New Westminster. Launching at West Vancouver, Horseshoe Bay and Lions Bay. Air fills in Horseshoe Bay, North Vancouver, Squamish and throughout greater Vancouver.

Access: Passage Island Reef is in Queen Charlotte Channel between Point Atkinson and Bowen Island; it is ¼ nautical mile (½ kilometer) west of the southern tip of Passage Island.

Charter out of Vancouver or Horseshoe Bay and go to Passage Island Reef. Or rent a boat or launch your own boat at Horseshoe Bay and go 4 nautical miles (7 kilometers) around to Passage Island Reef. Wind from almost any direction can make anchoring impossible at this very exposed site. Go on a calm day.

To find the reef, go out from Passage Island: head south down the west side of it and as soon as you see Point Atkinson lighthouse between Passage Island and the islet at its southern tip, go west. Then use your depth sounder or plumb with a lead line until you find the reef.

Comments: If you can find it, Passage Island Reef is intriguing.

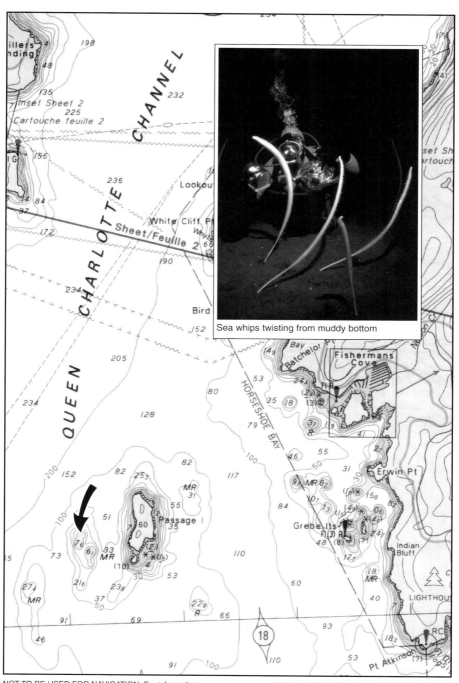

Sea whips twisting from muddy bottom

NOT TO BE USED FOR NAVIGATION: For information
on obtaining navigational charts see page 318.
This is a portion of 3311.

1 Nautical Mile

LIGHTHOUSE PARK
Shore Dive or Kayak Dive

Current Table: Second Narrows

Skill: Intermediate and expert divers

Why go: Lighthouse Park has the wildest underwater seascape and the most fantastic variety of marine life in the Vancouver area.

One dive at Lighthouse Park reveals an incredible amount of life. Large, gray warty cabezons and delicate shimmering kelp greenlings live side-by-side. Beautiful sea pens burrow in pools of sand between ledges covered with purple and pink sea stars. Schools of black rockfish swim past. Copper rockfish and lingcod live along the wall. We saw a huge octopus hiding under a ledge, little hairy lithode crabs, and small bryozoans that look like pale pink Christmas trees. Boulders smothered with orange anemones so thick that you can't see the rock. One-inch (2½-centimeter) slipper cucumbers flame from the wall next to 5-inch (13-centimeter) orange trumpet sponges and giant barnacles. Crevices overflowing with large white plumose anemones slice the dark slope. Cloud sponges start at 65 feet (20 meters). There are green and red urchins, dahlia anemones and red Irish lords at Lighthouse Park.

It's the richest dive in Vancouver. But the people who know it intimately say the marine life is noticeably declining – even here. Please leave your spear guns at home.

Bottom and Depths: Flat sand scattered with rocks and brown bottom kelp gently tiers off, then drops in dramatic ledges with huge boulders poised at the edge. Light silt over all.

Hazards: Current, wind and broken fishing line. Small boats, poor visibility, in summer, because of Fraser River runoff; and the dangers of overheating and exhaustion hiking between the parking lot and the site. Dive on slack using current tables for Second Narrows. Even though not seeming logical, it works. Enter 15 or 20 minutes before the turn of the tide. Do not dive at Lighthouse Park if a strong west wind blows up surf. Carry a knife. Listen for boats and ascend close to the bottom all the way to shore. Divers hiking to the site and kayak-divers should allow plenty of time to reach it for slack. Then rest before heading back, because of the possible danger of bringing on bends by overexertion after diving.

Telephones: • Marine Drive and The Dale shopping center; it is ⅕ mile (⅓ kilometer) east of Marine Drive and Beacon Lane. • Cypress Park shopping center, 1½ miles (2½ kilometers) east on Marine Drive.

Facilities: Lighthouse Park is large and forested with 9 miles (14 kilometers) of trails, a sign-posted circular nature walk, and wild, rocky beaches for picnics. Restrooms and large parking area year-round. In summer, occasional nature walks as well as access to the Phyl Munday Nature Room. For information, telephone Lighthouse Park at (604) 922-5408 or (604) 925-1071. Dive-kayak rentals in Vancouver.

Access: Lighthouse Park is at Point Atkinson which is the entrance to Burrard Inlet. It is off Marine Drive in West Vancouver between Park Royal shopping center (west of Lions Gate Bridge) and Horseshoe Bay: 15 minutes from Park Royal, 10 minutes from Horseshoe Bay.

At the 4900 block Marine Drive, turn into Beacon Lane and drive to the parking area at the end of it. Vehicle access is not permitted beyond this point except by special permission. From the parking lot, it is still ½ mile (¾ kilometer) down well-graded road to some park buildings. Then climb down one of the steep, treacherous rocky paths to a small bay east of the lighthouse.

Divers who walk it should allow at least an hour to carry gear to the water and to get geared up ready to dive. Do not suit up at the parking lot or you will be too warm before getting wet.

Groups may apply for permission to drive one vehicle with all of their gear to a point 100 yards (90 meters) from the water. The divers could then return to park the vehicle, and then walk c mile (¾ kilometer) to the site. Apply for permission to dive three weeks in advance. If permission is granted you will be given a key to open the gate and a letter to show you are permitted at the site. Apply in writing to Recreation Manager, West Vancouver Parks and Recreation Department, 750 17th Street, West Vancouver BC V7V 3T3. Telephone on weekdays from 8:30 a.m. to 4:00 p.m. (604) 922-1211.

Kayak-divers could drive to Caulfeild Cove (see directions to Caulfeild Cove on next page), paddle ¾ nautical mile (1½ kilometers) around to Lighthouse Park, land and dive from the shore. And wheelchair divers who paddle dive-kayaks could launch from the float at Caulfeild.

To get to Marine Drive and Beacon Lane
• From Park Royal in West Vancouver, go west on Marine Drive for 6 miles (10 kilometers) and turn left into Beacon Lane.
• From Horseshoe Bay ferry terminal: immediately off the ferry move to the Highway 99 lane. Follow signs to "Highway 99, Marine Drive and Horseshoe Bay", taking the *second* Exit 0. After going under the bridge and curving right uphill, do not continue uphill past the "yield" sign – turn left downhill onto Marine Drive. Go southeast on Marine Drive for 3 miles (5 kilometers) to Beacon Lane.
• From Horseshoe Bay in the village, head uphill on Nelson Avenue to Marine Drive. Turn left. Go ⅕ mile (⅓ kilometer) and turn right. Go southeast for 3 miles (5 kilometers) on Marine Drive to Beacon Lane.

Comments: Lighthouse Park is great for a family outing – and a great dive!
Permission required from Harbour Master's Office to dive at Lighthouse Park.

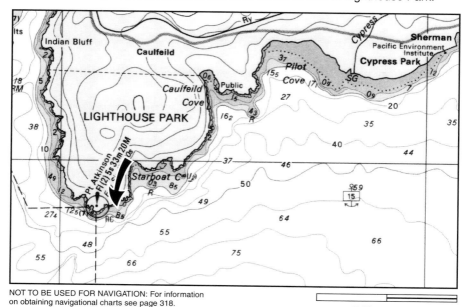

NOT TO BE USED FOR NAVIGATION: For information on obtaining navigational charts see page 318.
This is a portion of 3481.

½ Nautical Mile

CAULFEILD COVE
Shore Dive

Skill: All divers

Why go: Caulfeild Cove attracts divers because it's a source of bottles – new and old.

First settled as a large private estate in 1899, there were no roads from West Vancouver to Caulfeild until Marine Drive was built in 1915. Ships called in frequently. Bottles and other things have been falling overboard for almost a century. Today there is still a float at Caulfeild Cove in the same spot as the original one. Old-time residents reminiscing about beach parties at Caulfeild recall valuable losses like diamond rings. The bottom is muddy and hides things well. You can always hope you will turn up something that's been buried for years.

While diving here we saw flounders and Dungeness crabs disappearing in a cloud of "dust". Hermit crabs, blood stars and an occasional delicate nudibranch.

But the site is best for bottles.

Bottom and Depths: Near the float the bottom is muddy and 15 to 25 feet (5 to 8 meters) deep, sloping to 35 to 45 feet (11 to 14 meters) at the mouth of the cove. Eelgrass, near shore.

Hazards: Poor visibility, shallow depths and boats, especially on summer weekends. Keep just off the bottom so that you do not stir up silt unnecessarily. Wear extra weight. Listen for boats and ascend with a reserve of air; if you hear a boat you can stay down until it passes.

Telephones: • Marine Drive and The Dale shopping center – when leaving Caulfeild, do not turn back. The road is one way. Continue from Caulfeild Cove along The Dale; from the float, go ⅓ mile (½ kilometer) to the shopping center at Marine Drive. • Cypress Park shopping center, 1 mile (1½ kilometers) east on Marine Drive.

Facilities: Government float. Roadside parking, grassy pockets of park between rocky points connected with walking trails. Restrooms, in summer, next to waterfront trail east of roadside parking at Dogwood Lane and Pilot House Road. Nice park land and beach for a picnic.

Access: Caulfeild Cove is off Marine Drive in West Vancouver between Park Royal shopping center (west of Lions Gate Bridge) and Horseshoe Bay: 15 minutes from Park Royal, 10 minutes from Horseshoe Bay.

At the 4600 block Marine Drive, head southwest down Picadilly South. At Pilot House Road, turn left; the road becomes one way. Pilot House Road winds for ⅓ mile (½ kilometer) alongside the waterfront park to the wharf and float at Caulfeild Cove. Park at the roadside and walk down a short footpath to the water. When wet the trails can be slippery. Wheelchair access down the ramp to the float.

To get to Marine Drive and Picadilly South
• From Park Royal in West Vancouver, go west on Marine Drive for 5½ miles (9 kilometers) and veer left into Picadilly South.
• From Horseshoe Bay ferry terminal: immediately off the ferry move to the Highway 99 lane. Follow signs to "Highway 99, Marine Drive and Horseshoe Bay", taking the *second* Exit 0. After going under the bridge and curving right uphill, do not continue uphill past the "yield" sign – turn left downhill onto Marine Drive. Go southeast on Marine Drive for 3½ miles (6 kilometers) to Picadilly South. Turn sharply right.

• From Horseshoe Bay in the village, head uphill on Nelson Avenue to Marine Drive. Turn left and go ⅕ mile (⅓ kilometer). Turn right, still on Marine Drive, and go southeast for 3½ miles (6 kilometers) to Picadilly South. Turn sharply right.

Comments: Easy access and entry make this a good dive for new divers, especially in winter when fewer boats are on the water.

Permission required from Harbour Master's Office to dive at Caulfeild Cove.

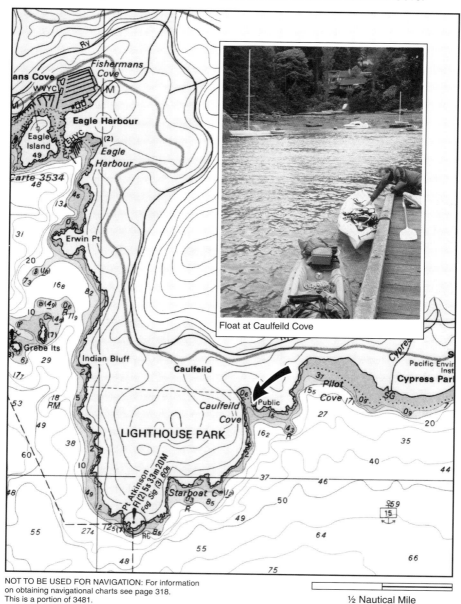

Float at Caulfeild Cove

NOT TO BE USED FOR NAVIGATION: For information on obtaining navigational charts see page 318.
This is a portion of 3481.

½ Nautical Mile

WEST CATES PARK
Shore Dive

Skill: Intermediate and expert divers

Why go: Cates Park is close to the city. I still can't believe it's so easy to go out for a short dive on a rocky reef – a quick visit to another country!

Red rock crabs live on the reef. Dungeness crabs live around it. As we swam out through vast plains of bright orange sea pens we saw little snails scrambling all around. Snake pricklebacks, Oregon tritons and flounders are everywhere, too. And you might see grunt sculpins. Cates Park provides a pleasant morning or afternoon of sightseeing diving and might provide a very unusual experience. The "Lions of the Sea", often referred to as hooded nudibranchs, have been seen at this site. Look for them in winter.

Bottom and Depths: Rocky reef, 200 yards (185 meters) southeast of the wharf. It is 10 to 20 feet (3 to 6 meters) deep. Eelgrass around the reef. Silty sand, stretches from shore to the reef.

Hazards: Boats, poor visibility, shallow depths and some current. Be careful of hordes of small boats on summer weekends. For best visibility, dive one hour before low slack. It is shallow. Wear extra weight and use a compass so that you can stay on the bottom for the duration of your dive.

Telephone: Beside restrooms, east end of Cates Park.

Facilities: Large grassy area, picnic tables, large parking lot, wharf and launching ramp. Restrooms next to caretaker's home at east end of the park near the totem pole are open year-round. Fresh water to wash equipment, in summer only; the tap is opposite Malcolm Lowry Trail, also at the east end of park. Air fills throughout greater Vancouver, in North Vancouver and Deep Cove.

Access: Cates Park is where Second Narrows turns north into Indian Arm. It is on the *west* side of Indian Arm at Roche Point in North Vancouver – 10 minutes off Trans-Canada Highway 1 from Second Narrows Bridge (north end).

At the north end of Second Narrows Bridge, head east on Main Street across the Seymour River. Continue straight, following signs toward Deep Cove. Go for 3 miles (5 kilometers) on Dollarton Highway to Cates Park. Park near the wharf west of Roche Point. Suit up, and enter here. The reef is 200 yards (185 meters) offshore southeast of the launching ramp.

Wheelchair access at gently sloping ramp. Safer in winter because of fewer boats.

To get to Second Narrows Bridge (north end)
• From Highway 1 West, heading *north* across Second Narrows Bridge, move to the right-hand lane. Take Exit 23B. Follow signs toward Deep Cove.
• From Highway 1 East, go through West Vancouver and North Vancouver but *do not cross* Second Narrows Bridge. Take Exit 23A. Turn left onto Main Street, and go straight, following signs toward Deep Cove.

Comments: The park is great for a family picnic or for larger groups year-round. This ramp-side dive is safer in winter when fewer boats are on the water, but many open-water certification dives take place at East Cates Park – place-to-go in summer.

Permission required from Harbour Master's Office to dive at Cates Park. Telephone weekdays (604) 666-2405.

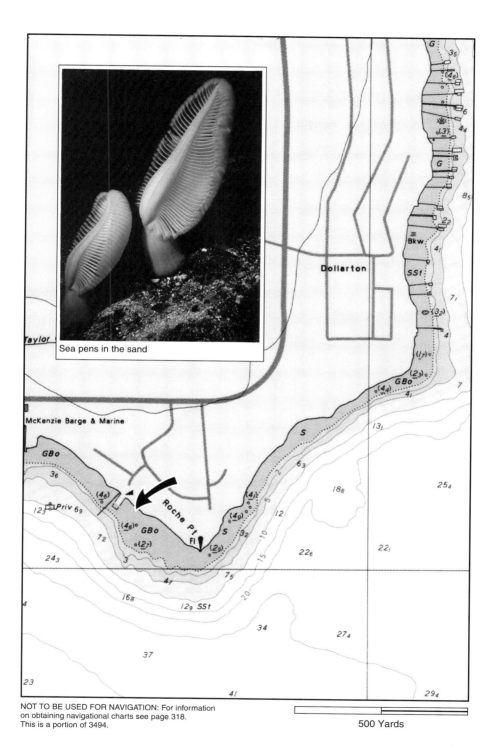

Sea pens in the sand

McKenzie Barge & Marine

Taylor

Dollarton

Roche Pt

NOT TO BE USED FOR NAVIGATION: For information
on obtaining navigational charts see page 318.
This is a portion of 3494.

500 Yards

101

WHITE ROCK
[STRATHCONA]
Shore Dive

Skill: All divers and snorkelers

Why go: White Rock, commonly called Strathcona, combines sandy-bottom life and high-current life all on one dive.

Diving on the inside of White Rock you'll see flounders, Dungeness crabs, Oregon tritons, alabaster nudibranchs and masses of sea cucumbers on the sand and hiding in the bottom kelp. Sometimes all you can see of a flounder are its eyes projecting above the sand. On the outside current-swept channel we saw large purple stars plastered to the wall. Giant barnacles, plumose anemones, small tube worms. You can see chitons and bright orange burrowing cucumbers. Rockfish hang by the wall. Orange sea pens and transparent filaments of tube-dwelling anemones feather the flat sand in the channel beyond White Rock.

Bottom and Depths: Broken rock covered with bottom kelp is scattered around the base of the island. Along the channel side the rock wall falls to a depth of 50 to 60 feet (15 to 18 meters), bottoming out to flat sand in the channel. Sand and eelgrass in the bay between the shore and White Rock.

Hazards: Current. Red jellyfish, in the fall. Dive on the slack. If you have seen any red jellyfish, check for stinging tentacles before removing masks and gloves.

Telephone: Dollar Shopping Centre on Dollarton Highway; it is ⅓ mile (½ kilometer) south of Strathcona Road and Deep Cove Road junction. Go straight south: Deep Cove Road becomes Dollarton Highway.

Facilities: Public wharf. Air fills in North Vancouver and Deep Cove.

Access: White Rock, or Strathcona, is on the *west* side of Indian Arm near Second Narrows. It is in North Vancouver, 4 miles (7 kilometers) east of Second Narrows Bridge off Trans-Canada Highway 1. From Second Narrows Bridge, 15 minutes to the dive.

At Mount Seymour Parkway, go east 3¾ miles (6 kilometers). Turn left onto Deep Cove Road; then right into Strathcona Road, the first road on the right. Go for ⅓ mile (½ kilometer) to the water where two or three cars may park by the government wharf. Do not jump off the wharf unless it is a very high tide, as the beach beneath it dries at low tide. Snorkel 100 yards (90 meters) to White Rock, go down and dive right around it.

To get to Mount Seymour Parkway
• On Highway 1 West: heading *north* across Second Narrows Bridge, move to the right-hand lane. Immediately across the bridge, take Exit 23B. Cross the Seymour River and follow signs to Mount Seymour Park. Turn left onto Riverside Drive, then right onto Mount Seymour Parkway.
• On Highway 1 East: from Horseshoe Bay, West Vancouver and North Vancouver, go east on Highway 1 but *do not cross* Second Narrows Bridge. Take Exit 22. Follow signs to Mount Seymour Park and go onto Mount Seymour Parkway.

Comments: Many private residences around this little cove and no place for a picnic. Good for the dive only. Then go to Cates Park or the park at Deep Cove.

Permission required from Harbour Master's Office to dive at White Rock. Telephone (604) 666-2405.

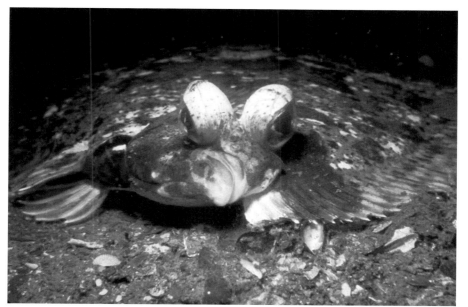

Flounder in shallows blending with the bottom

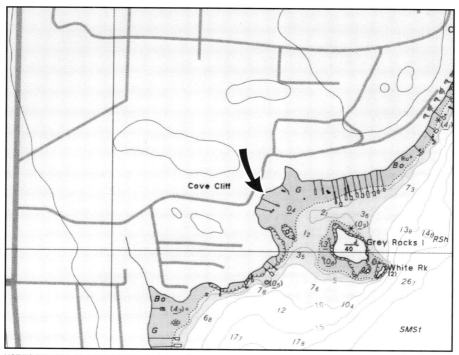

Cove Cliff

Grey Rocks I

White Rk

NOT TO BE USED FOR NAVIGATION: For information
on obtaining navigational charts see page 318.
This is a portion of 3495.

500 Yards

WOODLANDS
Shore Dive

Tide Table: Vancouver

Skill: All divers

Why go: Woodlands provides opportunity for a deep dive or a shallow dive at the one site. As the name suggests, there's a real wilderness feeling both above and below water.

Look for hairy lithode crabs which are not seen everywhere but are quite often present in this part of Indian Arm. Lots of decorator crabs and rockfish on the wall. Flounders on the flat sand. And an unequalled cascade of Johnnie Walker whiskey bottles kept me speculating for months about the kind of party once held at Woodlands!

Perhaps some old bottles here, too.

Bottom and Depths: Hard sand, 20 to 30 feet (6 to 9 meters) deep, slopes from the wharf to the island. At the marker and around to the left, a rock wall drops off to a depth of 110 to 120 feet (34 to 37 meters). A cascade of small broken rock and rubble is down it.

Hazards: Boats, especially in summer. Red jellyfish, in the fall. Poor visibility. Listen for boats and if you hear a boat, stay down until it passes. Extremely important to use a dive flag at this site. Use a compass and ascend close to the bottom all the way to shore. If you have seen any red jellyfish, you and your buddy should check one another for stinging tentacles before removing your masks and gloves. For the best visibility dive on an outgoing tide.

Telephone: Mount Seymour Parkway and Mount Seymour Road, at shopping center on northeast corner.

Facilities: Limited parking space at site. Air fills in Deep Cove and North Vancouver.

Access: Woodlands is on the *west* side of Indian Arm in a remote corner of North Vancouver. It is 7 miles (11 kilometers) from the north end of the Second Narrows Bridge. From Highway 1 to the dive takes 20 minutes.

At Mount Seymour Parkway in North Vancouver go east 2 miles (3 kilometers) to Mount Seymour Road at a traffic light; a shopping mall is on the left-hand side. Turn left toward Mount Seymour Park. Go for ½ mile (¾ kilometer). Just before the park gates, turn right into Indian River Drive. Again go ½ mile (¾ kilometer); at the "Woodlands" sign, turn left up Indian River Crescent. Pass a few homes, then drive through the woods on this narrow, winding road. It is partly gravel and becomes steep. Then go 3 miles (5 kilometers) to a "Stop" sign. You have to park here, but first drive downhill to unload gear. From the unloading zone to the wharf is 50 feet (15 meters).

For a deep dive, swim from the wharf to the marker on Lone Rock Point, descend and work your way around the wall to your left. For a shallow dive stay in the bay. But this is unsafe on a sunny summer weekend when boats are coming and going. Shallow dives at Woodlands are advisable only on a weekday in winter. Before you jump in, look at the ladder on the wharf to see where to climb out. It is on the inside of the wharf facing toward shore.

To get to Mount Seymour Parkway in North Vancouver
• On Highway 1 West: heading *north* across Second Narrows Bridge, move to the right-hand lane. Immediately across the bridge, take Exit 23B. Cross the Seymour River and follow signs to Mount Seymour Park. Turn left onto Riverside Drive, then right onto Mount Seymour Parkway.

• On Highway 1 East: from Horseshoe Bay, West Vancouver and North Vancouver, go east on Highway 1 but *do not cross* Second Narrows Bridge. Take Exit 22. Follow signs to Mount Seymour Park and go onto Mount Seymour Parkway.

Comments: Good for the dive only. Even though in the wilds, private property surrounds the wharf and there is no place for a picnic. Local residents resent divers who are thoughtless about parking, and who do not stay under water when diving and boats are around. Watch these two points and improve our image in order that divers will be welcomed at Woodlands.

Permission required from Harbour Master's Office to dive at Woodlands. Telephone weekdays (604) 666-2405.

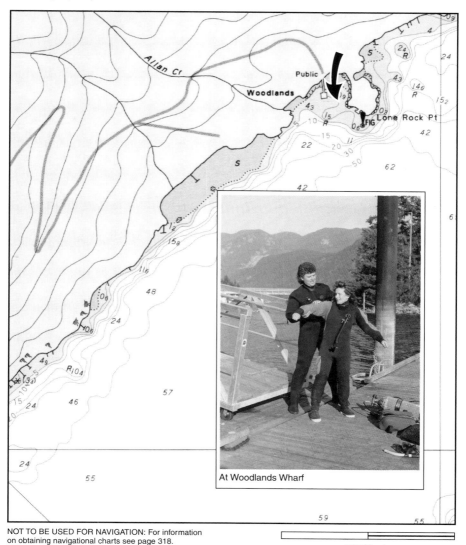

At Woodlands Wharf

NOT TO BE USED FOR NAVIGATION: For information on obtaining navigational charts see page 318. This is a portion of 3495.

500 Yards

BELCARRA BAY
Shore Dive

Skill: All divers and snorkelers

Why go: Easy sightseeing, easy fun. At Belcarra Bay there's a small rocky reef for sightseeing, with the easiest possible entry and the shortest possible swim. The area is small, but picturesque. Sunflower stars, purple sea stars, orange and white plumose anemones. Chitons and calcareous tube worms cling to the rocks. Tube worms beneath the wharf. You might see rockfish, too. Flatfish on the sand and sculpins. Nudibranchs – even lion nudibranchs, also called hooded nudibranchs, have been seen here, perched, wafting like ghosts on the kelp.

Look for a hermit crab inhabiting a borrowed home – usually a triton shell. Scan the eelgrass and silty sand around the reef for Dungeness and red rock crabs. Look for nothing but a slight indentation in the sand and a pair of eyes. Because crabs bury themselves, they are difficult to see. When you spot one, look but don't take. No wildlife removal allowed at this park. Leave even the empty shells for hermit crabs to move into.

Bottom and Depths: Sandy, muddy bottom slopes gently to 40 feet (12 meters). Look for crabs in 15 to 30 feet (5 to 9 meters) of water in the eelgrass immediately in front of the wharf and to your left. The mini-reef which is 20 to 30 feet (6 to 9 meters) deep is at right angles to the end of the wharf, 20 to 30 feet (6 to 9 meters) north. Giant sea pens are in 25 to 35 feet (8 to 11 meters) of water near the day marker, 300 yards (275 meters) south of the wharf.

Hazards: Small boat traffic, especially in summer, and poor visibility. Red jellyfish, in the fall. Listen for boats; if you hear a boat, stay down until it passes. Also look up before ascending, to avoid the boats of crab fishermen. Visibility is best in winter, but at all times of year try not to stir up the silt. If you have seen any red jellyfish, you and your buddy should check one another for stinging tentacles before removing your masks and gloves.

Telephone: Belcarra Park beside refreshment stand.

Facilities: Large grassy area, parking, picnic tables and wharf. Restrooms are open year-round, the refreshment stand in summer only. Air fills throughout greater Vancouver including Coquitlam, Port Coquitlam, New Westminster, Surrey and Langley.

Access: Belcarra Bay is on the *east* side of Indian Arm. It is in Belcarra Park and is reached by way of Port Moody off Highway 7A. It takes 35 minutes from Second Narrows Bridge to the dive; 25 minutes from Port Mann Bridge.

In Port Moody, turn off Highway 7A. Go north to Ioco Road and follow signs to Ioco, Bedwell Bay and Belcarra. From Highway 7A turnoff, go 7 miles (11 kilometers) to Belcarra Picnic Area. Go on Ioco Road to First Avenue – it is 3 miles (5 kilometers). Turn right. First Avenue becomes Bedwell Bay Road; continue on it. Do not turn right to White Pine Beach in Belcarra Park – from White Pine turnoff, continue 2½ miles (4 kilometers) more along Bedwell Bay Road. Just past the entry to Belcarra Picnic Area is Midden Road. You could drop gear at the gate at the end of Midden Road, then return to park at the picnic area. Easy entry over sand or from the wharf. Entry to the water from the wharf is wheelchair accessible.

To get to Port Moody
• From downtown Vancouver, go east on Hastings Street (Highway 7A) for 4 miles (7 kilometers) to Highway 1. When across Highway 1, continue 3 miles (5 kilometers)

more on Hastings to Inlet Drive. Bear left on Inlet which becomes Barnet Highway, still Highway 7A, and go to Port Moody. At St. John's Street, turn left and continue through Port Moody to signs to Ioco Road. Turn left.
• From North Vancouver (Highway 1 East): head *south* on Second Narrows Bridge, and move to the "Hastings Street 7A Bridgeway Street" lane. Take Exit 26 and follow signs to Hastings Street East. Head east through Burnaby on Hastings (Highway 7A) for 3 miles (5 kilometers) to Inlet Drive. Bear left on Inlet Drive which becomes Barnet Highway (Highway 7A) and go to Port Moody. At St. John's Street, turn left and continue through Port Moody to signs to Ioco Road. Turn left.
• From Highway 1 in Fraser Valley: take Exit 44 at *north* end of Port Mann Bridge. Go *east* on Highway 7 (Lougheed Highway) for 4 miles (7 kilometers) to Port Coquitlam. Turn left onto Barnet Highway (Highway 7A) and go 1¼ miles (2 kilometers) to Port Moody. Turn right following signs to Ioco Road.

Comments: Please observe park hours which vary in different seasons. A permit must be obtained for after-hours diving. Simply plan it and apply at least two weeks before your dive: Greater Vancouver Regional District (GVRD) Parks Department, 4330 Kingsway, Burnaby BC V5H 4G8. Telephone weekdays (604) 432-6352.

Permission required from Harbour Master's Office to dive at Belcarra Park. Telephone weekdays (604) 666-2405.

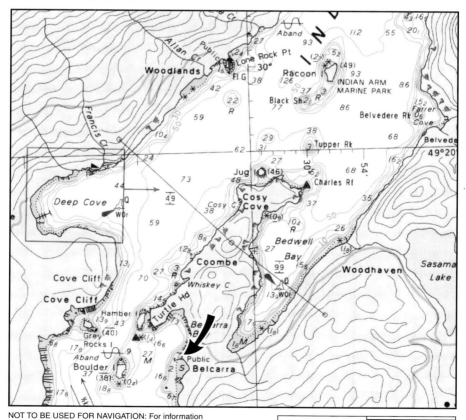

NOT TO BE USED FOR NAVIGATION: For information on obtaining navigational charts see page 318.
This is a portion of 3311.

1 Nautical Mile

WHISKEY COVE
Shore Dive

Tide Table: Vancouver

Skill: All divers

Why go: Whiskey Cove is a great lazy-day dive. The combination of an easy entry, short swim and shallow dive reward you with a wide variety of life. It will stay that way, as no removal of wildlife is allowed at this park.

You'll see striped seaperch, rockfish and small lingcod. The fingers of bright orange burrowing cucumbers creep out of crevices. A rock face covered with transparent tunicates and tube worms. When diving here I stopped to look at them. Some tube worms waited until my finger was only 1 inch (2½ centimeters) away before retracting. Then we cruised around past a wall covered with sea stars. A lovely sight — almost like cutout paper snowflakes, but in dark tones instead of white.

There's life on the sand, as well. Oregon tritons, Dungeness crabs and small snails scurry about. Suddenly the sea floor moves. It's a flounder before you. A field of sea pens stretches into Indian Arm.

Bottom and Depths: The bay is rimmed with rocky walls, bottoming out to silty white sand at 30 to 40 feet (9 to 12 meters). The wall on the right is undercut with small crevices and caves. A field of tall sea pens is in 40 to 50 feet (12 to 15 meters) of water straight out from the wall — these sea pens are 1-foot (⅓-meter) high.

Hazards: Small boats and some current. Red jellyfish, in the fall. Listen for boats and ascend up the wall. If you feel any current pull yourself along the wall. If you have seen jellyfish, check for stinging tentacles before removing masks and gloves.

Telephone: Belcarra Park Picnic Area by the refreshment stand. Go ½ mile (¾ kilometer) back to Bedwell Bay Road, turn left. Then right into the picnic area.

Facilities: Parking for three or four cars.

Access: Whiskey Cove is on the *east* side of Indian Arm. It is in Belcarra Park and is reached by way of Port Moody off Highway 7A. It takes 5 minutes from Second Narrows Bridge to the dive; 25 minutes from Port Mann Bridge.

In Port Moody, turn off Highway 7A. Go north to loco Road and follow signs to loco, Bedwell Bay and Belcarra. From Highway 7A turnoff, go 7 miles (11 kilometers) to Whiskey Cove. Go on loco Road to First Avenue — it is 3 miles (5 kilometers). Turn right. First Avenue becomes Bedwell Bay Road; go to the end of Bedwell Bay Road. Pass the entry to Belcarra Picnic Area. Turn right, still on Bedwell Bay Road, and go ½ mile (¾ kilometer) more to a parking area with room for three or four cars. It is just before Whiskey Cove Lane. Walk down a trail — 100 paces through the woods to the small log-covered crescent of beach. Snorkel to the left or the rock wall on the right of Whiskey Cove.

To get to Port Moody
• From downtown Vancouver, go east on Hastings Street (Highway 7A) for 4 miles (7 kilometers) to Trans-Canada Highway 1. Across Highway 1, continue 3 miles (5 kilometers) more on Hastings to Inlet Drive. Bear left on Inlet which becomes Barnet Highway, still Highway 7A, and go to Port Moody. At St. John's Street, turn left and continue through Port Moody to signs to loco Road. Turn left.
• From North Vancouver (Trans-Canada Highway 1 East): heading *south* on Second Narrows Bridge, move to the "Hasting Street 7A Bridgeway Street" lane. Take Exit 26 and follow signs to Hastings Street East. Head east through Burnaby on Hastings (Highway 7A) for 3 miles (5 kilometers) to Inlet Drive. Bear left on Inlet Drive which

becomes Barnet Highway (Highway 7A) and go to Port Moody. At St. John's Street, turn left and continue through Port Moody to signs to Ioco Road. Turn left.

• From Highway 1 in Fraser Valley: take Exit 44 at *north* end of Port Mann Bridge. Go *east* on Highway 7 (Lougheed Highway) for 4 miles (7 kilometers) to Port Coquitlam. Turn left onto Barnet Highway (Highway 7A) and go 1 mile (1½ kilometers) to Port Moody. Turn right following signs to Ioco Road.

Comments: Please observe park hours which vary in different seasons. A permit must be obtained for after-hours diving. Simply plan it and apply at least two weeks before your dive: Greater Vancouver Regional District (GVRD) Parks Department, 4330 Kingsway, Burnaby BC V5H 4G8. Telephone weekdays (604) 432-6352.

Permission required from Harbour Master's Office to dive at Whiskey Cove in Belcarra Park. Telephone weekdays (604) 666-2405.

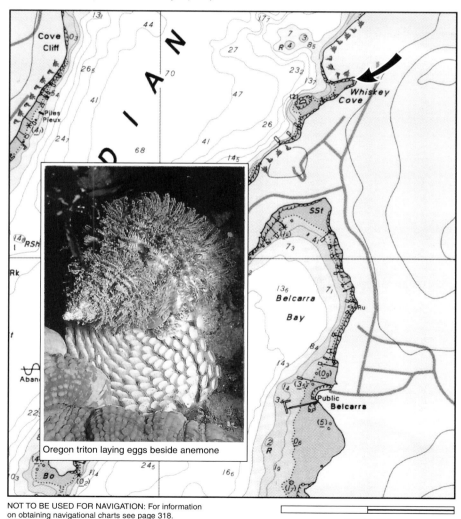

Oregon triton laying eggs beside anemone

NOT TO BE USED FOR NAVIGATION: For information
on obtaining navigational charts see page 318.
This is a portion of 3495.

500 Yards

WRECK OF VT-100
Shore Dive

Skill: All divers

Why go: Shallow, close to shore, and obviously in the shape of a ship – much of this 136-foot (41-meter) wooden hull and steel superstructure remains intact. A forward gun platform, which once held the 3½-inch (90-millimeter) cannon, is plainly visible.

The *VT-100* is great for a first wreck dive, a natural for practicing compass navigation, a favorite of divers for years. And, to add to the fascination, this old wreck has recently acquired a new identity. Until 1983 the vessel was known as Canadian minesweeper HMCS *Cranbrook*. Then a local diver discovered it to be the wreck of an American Yard Class Minesweeper (YMS) built during World War II. After the war, the vessel was brought to Bedwell Bay where it was being made into a wood-chip barge, and it was redesignated as the *Vancouver Tugboat-100* – the *VT-100*. In 1956 vandals started a fire on board and the *VT-100* burned to the water line and sank.

Diving the wreck we also saw lacy white nudibranchs tipped with blue, spider crabs, calcareous tube worms, white and orange plumose anemones. Seaperch, pile perch and rockfish, large and small, congregating inside the hull as though contained in a fishbowl. Swimming back to shore over sandy bottom crawling with Dungeness crabs, snails and flounders, galaxies of moon jellyfish billowed around us like a whole miniature universe under water.

Bottom and Depths: The *VT-100* lies on gently sloping, muddy bottom. The bow is in 55 to 65 feet (17 to 20 meters) of water at the south end, the stern in 42 to 52 feet (13 to 16 meters) at the north end.

Hazards: The wreck itself, small boats and poor visibility. Water-skiers, in summer. Red jellyfish, in the fall. The wreck is intact – but crumbling dangerously – and should not be entered even by the most experienced wreck divers. Listen for boats; if you hear a boat, stay down until it passes. Allow time for a water-skier to pass, as well. Or use a compass and navigate to shore under water. Try not to stir up the silt. If you have seen any red jellyfish, you and your buddy should check one another for stinging tentacles before removing masks and gloves.

Telephone: At Belcarra Park, refreshment stand. Return to Bedwell Bay Road, and go 1 mile (1½ kilometers) farther west, and turn left into Belcarra Park picnic area.

Facilities: None at the site. Even roadside parking is very limited. Picnic sites and restrooms 1 mile (1½ kilometers) west on Bedwell Bay Road at Belcarra Bay picnic area; also 1½ miles (2½ kilometers) east at White Pine Beach on Sasamat Lake.

Access: The wreck of the *VT-100* is in Bedwell Bay, *east* side of Indian Arm, in the village of Belcarra and is reached by way of Port Moody off Highway 7A. It takes 35 minutes from Second Narrows Bridge; 25 minutes from Port Mann Bridge.

In Port Moody, turn off Highway 7A. Go north to Ioco Road and follow signs toward Ioco, Bedwell Bay and Belcarra picnic area. From Highway 7A turnoff, go for 6 miles (10 kilometers), passing White Pine Beach at Sasamat Lake, to Kelly Avenue. Turn right on Kelly and wind down a short way towards the water. At Kelly Avenue and Marine Avenue turn sharply left and go 200 yards (185 meters). Park by the roadside, but well off the road, just past a "No Parking" sign near steps to a wharf. Walk down one of the short steep trails to the rocky beach – 27 paces to the water. Do not trespass on wharves and boathouses. All are privately owned property constructed on leased water-lots. Respect also any new "No Parking" signs.

Enter and swim toward the point, follow a 330-degree compass bearing. One hundred yards (90 meters) offshore you should come to the *VT-100* lying north to south.
• Tatlow Trail, a well-graded path and stone steps to the rocky beach, starting at Marine Avenue and Watson Road, is a new access to the water. To reach it, turn right at the end of Kelly and go 200 yards (185 meters) to the end of Marine Avenue. From there, 50 paces to the water. You could paddle a dive-kayak from the foot of Tatlow Trail, or swim back to the entry described above, then out to the wreck.
• Kayak-divers could launch here, cross the bay and dive the Bedwell Bay mystery wreck and *Western Dispatcher.* More details on these wrecks, and a site plan of the *VT-100,* are in *Vancouver's Undersea Heritage,* a book published by UASBC.

To get to Port Moody
• From downtown Vancouver, go east on Hastings Street (Highway 7A) for 4 miles (7 kilometers) to Highway 1. Across Highway 1, continue 3 miles (5 kilometers) more on Hastings to Inlet Drive. Bear left on Inlet which becomes Barnet Highway, still Highway 7A, and go to Port Moody. At St. John's Street, turn left and continue through Port Moody to signs to loco Road. Turn left.
• From North Vancouver (Highway 1 East): head *south* on Second Narrows Bridge, and move to the "Hasting Street 7A Bridgeway Street" lane. Take Exit 26 and follow signs to Hastings Street East. Head east through Burnaby on Hastings Street for 3 miles (5 kilometers) to Inlet Drive. Bear left on Inlet Drive which becomes Barnet Highway (Highway 7A) and go to Port Moody. At St. John's Street, turn left and continue through Port Moody to signs to loco Road. Turn left.
• From Highway 1 in the Fraser Valley: take Exit 44 at the *north* end of Port Mann Bridge. Go *east* on Highway 7 (Lougheed Highway) for 4 miles (7 kilometers) to Port Coquitlam. Turn left onto Barnet Highway (Highway 7A) and go 1 mile (1½ kilometers) to Port Moody. Turn right, following signs to loco Road.

Comments: Come and go quietly and be considerate about where you park. Private property is all around Bedwell Bay. Let's keep ourselves in good grace at this popular open-water training site.

Permission required from the Harbour Master's Office to dive at Bedwell Bay. Telephone weekdays (604) 666-2405.

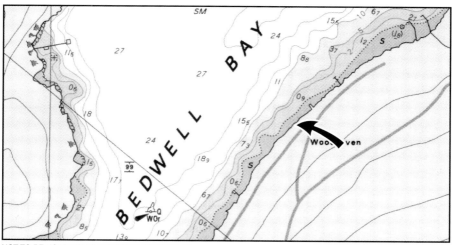

NOT TO BE USED FOR NAVIGATION: For information on obtaining navigational charts see page 318.
This is a portion of 3495.

500 Yards

JUG ISLAND
Kayak Dive or Boat Dive

Skill: All divers and snorkelers

Why go: "Crab City" is all you can call it! Red rock crabs hide amongst the rocks around the island. In fall and winter, female Dungeness crabs, bulging with bright red eggs, are 8 inches (20 centimeters) apart all down the entire silty slope.
   This breeding ground for crabs is a phenomenon to see. But don't take any of them. Let them breed and continue to populate Indian Arm. No removal of wildlife at this park; come here for sightseeing. Anemones, sea lemons, sea stars and some rockfish hover around the rocky shores of the island. Flounders cover the sand.

Bottom and Depths: Rocky bottom with some lettuce kelp surrounds Jug Island and slopes gradually to silty sand. A small shallow reef, 10 to 15 feet (3 to 5 meters) deep, where small boats might go aground on a low tide lies between the beach and Jug Island. This is good snorkeling. From 20 to 25 feet (6 to 8 meters) on down, the gentle slope becomes very silty and suitable for crabs to hide.

Hazards: Boats. Water-skiers in summer. Red jellyfish, in the fall. On sunny summer weekends speedboats pulling water-skiers dash around near Jug Island, but there is a 5-knot (9-kilometer/hour) speed limit between the mainland and Jug Island so that is the best place to swim across. You probably will not encounter water-skiers there. However, since the site is so shallow boats are real hazards. Wear extra weight. Listen for boats; if you hear a boat, stay on the bottom until it passes. If diving the out-side of the island and you hear a boat, wait long enough for a water-skier to pass, too. If you have seen red jellyfish, check for stinging tentacles before removing masks and gloves.

Telephones: • Belcarra Park, beside refreshment stand. • Deep Cove, above government dock at foot of Gallant Avenue.

Facilities: None at Jug Island. Pit toilet at the beach on the peninsula south of Jug Is-land. Launching in North Vancouver and Port Moody. Charters out of Vancouver, North Vancouver and Port Moody. Water taxi out of Reed Point in Port Moody. Dive-kayak rentals in Vancouver.

Access: Jug Island is in Belcarra Park and is near the center of the south end of In-dian Arm. It is like a piece broken off the peninsula which forms Bedwell Bay. Jug Is-land is 1½ nautical miles (3 kilometers) east of Deep Cove, and 3 nautical miles (6 kilometers) northeast of Cates Park. It is less than 1 nautical mile (2 kilometers) north of Whiskey Cove where you could launch a kayak.
   Rent a dive-kayak and paddle from Whiskey Cove to Jug Island (see Whiskey Cove on page 108); take a rental boat and launch it or launch your own boat at North Vancouver or Port Moody; charter out of Vancouver, North Vancouver or Port Moody; or take a water taxi from Port Moody – 20 minutes to the dive.
   Anchor near the island or land on the small sandy beach on the mainland just south of Jug Island and snorkel 100 yards (90 meters) to the rocky point on the east end of the island. From here descend and swim east towards the point of mainland on your right. You'll soon be in the city of crabs.

Comments: Lovely little sandy beach for a picnic opposite Jug Island, but often it's in the shade in winter and crowded on summer weekends. The best time for a dive and picnic is on a sunny fall day during the week.

Permission required from Harbour Master's Office to dive at Jug Island. Telephone weekdays (604) 666-2405.

Dungeness crab

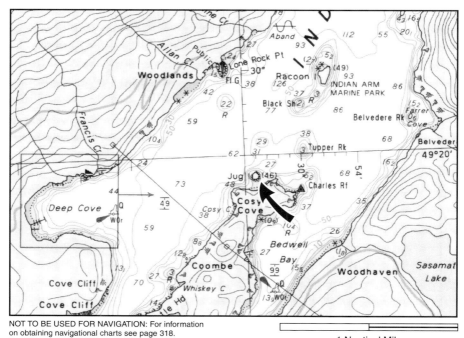

NOT TO BE USED FOR NAVIGATION: For information
on obtaining navigational charts see page 318.
This is a portion of 3311.

1 Nautical Mile

Skill: All divers and snorkelers

Why go: Racoon Island is a picturesque undersea garden – ideal for open-water certification dives as well as photography – and it drops off, too. A variety of both sand and rock dwellers live here.

The first time I dived at Racoon Island we anchored over the white gravel bottom. As we jumped in a pair of harbor seals were playing, but they disappeared rapidly. We were soon into picturesque terrain with a rocky reef on either side. Gorgeous white and orange plumose anemones that are 1- and 2-feet (⅓- and ⅔-meter) tall cluster on top of each reef. We saw a few rockfish, one decorator crab, and a variety of other crabs. We looked over the edge of the dark drop-off and turned back towards the sand.

Snails scurried away. Tube worms snapped in. We saw egg cases of moon snails, Oregon tritons and flounders. Millions of minute transparent fairy shrimp. Back at shore, beautiful little colorful anemones fill the tide pools.

Racoon Island is a good experience. I'll go back anytime.

Bottom and Depths: Two rocky reefs undulating from 30 to 40 feet (9 to 12 meters) deep parallel the northern shore. At the eastern end of the reefs, a sheer drop-off to 275 feet (84 meters). One of the darkest drop-offs I've seen. It stopped us at 80 feet (24 meters). At the western end of the reefs, eelgrass and coarse white broken-shell bottom.

Hazards: Boats, including silent sailboats, more numerous since Racoon became notable as part of Indian Arm Marine Park. Red jellyfish, in the fall. Use a compass and ascend up the side of the island or spiral and look up as you ascend. If you have seen any red jellyfish, you and your buddy should check one another for stinging tentacles before removing your masks and gloves. Kayak-divers who dive deep should rest before paddling back to avoid bringing on bends by overexertion after the dive.

Telephone: Deep Cove, above government dock at foot of Gallant Avenue.

Facilities: None at Racoon Island. But nearby at Twin Islands you will find camping, a pit toilet and walking trails. Air fills are available throughout greater Vancouver at Coquitlam, Port Coquitlam, New Westminster, Surrey, Langley, North Vancouver and Deep Cove.

Access: Racoon Island is in Indian Arm Marine Park near the southern end of Indian Arm, 2 nautical miles (4 kilometers) northeast of Deep Cove, 3 nautical miles (6 kilometers) northeast of Cates Park in North Vancouver.

Charter out of Vancouver, North Vancouver or Port Moody; take a water taxi from Reed Point in Port Moody – 25 minutes to the dive. Take a rental boat and launch it at North Vancouver or launch your own dive-kayak or boat at Deep Cove and go to Racoon Island. Anchor near the northwest shore, just north of the widest bulge of the island, in 30 to 40 feet (9 to 12 meters) of water. Or land on the island and enter from the pebble beach. Swim straight north and down to the two rocky reefs.

Comments: On the way home, another good dive, I'm told, at Tupper Rock.

Permission required from Harbour Master's Office to dive at Racoon Island. Telephone weekdays (604) 666-2405.

Looking north up Indian Arm toward Racoon Island

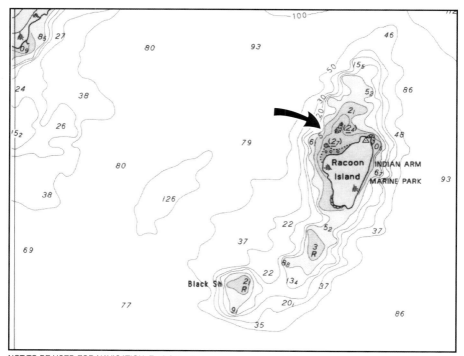

NOT TO BE USED FOR NAVIGATION: For information
on obtaining navigational charts see page 318.
This is a portion of 3495.

500 Yards

TWIN ISLANDS
Boat Dive

Tide Table: Vancouver

Skill: All divers and snorkelers

Why go: Twin Islands is particularly interesting in winter because it's a breeding ground for both crabs and lingcod. Also the place one of our local divers found a new species of chiton now named after him, *Tonicella goertsoni*.

And many more creatures are here. Gorgeous gardens of orange and white plumose anemones – so common in our waters but at all times beautiful – grace the southern end. I gasp with delight when I see them clustered on the rocks. We saw large pink dahlia anemones, small white nudibranchs with orange tips and heaps of Oregon tritons with yellowish rice-shaped eggs. Lots of shrimp and rockfish, a hairy chiton and a brown buffalo sculpin. Our dive was capped by the sight of two lingcod, one finning eggs, and by the sight of masses of crabs red and round with eggs.

A rich winter's day.

Bottom and Depths: At the wharf the silty sand bottom, scattered with crabs, is 20 to 30 feet (6 to 9 meters) deep. Towards the southern tip the bottom is covered with loose rock, dropping gradually to a depth of 40 to 50 feet (12 to 15 meters). Boulders are scattered about. At the north tip of the islands there is little marine life, but plenty of interesting rock formations.

Hazards: Boats. Red jellyfish, in the fall. Ascend up the side of the island out of the way of boats. If you have seen any red jellyfish, you and your buddy should check one another for stinging tentacles before removing your masks and gloves.

Telephone: Deep Cove, above government dock at foot of Gallant Avenue.

Facilities: Space to pitch your tent, a pit toilet, trails, a dinghy dock and ramp at Twin Islands. If you have your own boat, you could plan to camp and dive a couple of times here or move on to Racoon or Jug islands. Launching in North Vancouver and Port Moody. Air fills throughout greater Vancouver: at Coquitlam, Port Coquitlam, New Westminster, Surrey, Langley, North Vancouver and Deep Cove.

Access: Twin Islands is in Indian Arm Marine Park a quarter of the way up Indian Arm. It is 2 nautical miles (4 kilometers) northeast of Deep Cove and 4 nautical miles (7 kilometers) northeast of Cates Park in North Vancouver.

Take a water taxi from Reed Point in Port Moody. Take a dive-kayak and launch it at Deep Cove in North Vancouver; or launch your own boat or a rental boat at North Vancouver or Port Moody. Or charter: a variety of charters available out of Ioco, Port Moody and Deep Cove. Anchor near the dock on the east side of Big Twin, the northern island. Enter here and dive south towards the tip of the southern island.

Comments: You might find an anchor too – a great many boats come here.

Permission required from Harbour Master's Office to dive at Twin Islands. Telephone weekdays (604) 666-2405.

Why Knot landing divers at Twin Islands dock

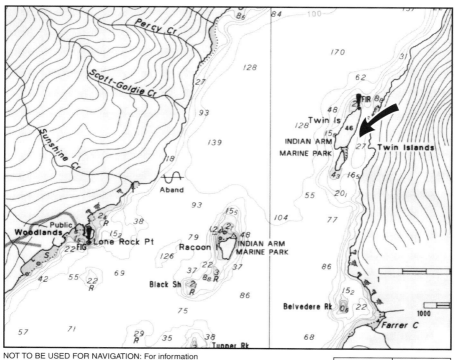

NOT TO BE USED FOR NAVIGATION: For information
on obtaining navigational charts see page 318.
This is a portion of 3495.

½ Nautical Mile

BUNTZEN POWER PLANT

Boat Dive

Skill: Intermediate and expert divers

Why go: Beautiful rock formations plummet to a depth of 110 to 120 feet (34 to 37 meters). The wall by Buntzen Power Plant is renowned as *the* drop-off of Indian Arm.

As we dived through the shallows, schools of bright blue and yellow seaperch glinted in the sun. Millions of moon jellyfish throbbed through the water. Then there were no more. Spindly spider crabs and hairy lithode crabs – two specialties of Indian Arm – were clinging to the smooth rock wall. Little else. It felt barren. We saw a few scattered rockfish. At 80 feet (24 meters), a pale white blenny. Suddenly, a red jellyfish streaming tentacles that were 10-feet (3-meters) long. Beautiful! And bright slipper cucumbers decorating the dark wall sweeping down . . . down . . . down . . . to yelloweye rockfish deep along the wall.

Bottom and Depths: Broken rock covered with lettuce kelp gives way immediately to sheer rock wall with loose gravel spilling over it. Beautiful rock formations drop to a depth of 110 to 120 feet (34 to 37 meters). Slightly farther out it drops 90, then over 300, then over 600 feet (27, 90, 180 meters).

Hazards: Extreme depth and tail-race from the dam. Red jellyfish, in the fall. At any time, day or night, the power plant gates might be opened without warning and a huge volume of water discharged between the dock and dive site. The discharge is above the surface and it is extremely turbulent. Because the gates are remotely controlled, divers will not be warned even when flying their diver's flag. Do not swim under water past the gates. Snorkel past. If you have seen any jellyfish, check for stinging tentacles before removing your masks and gloves.

Telephone: Deep Cove, above government dock at foot of Gallant Avenue.

Facilities: The dock and the land by the powerhouse are owned by BC Hydro and Power Authority. As long as we leave the property as we find it and use it at our own risk, BC Hydro will continue to allow divers to use the area. Launching in North Vancouver and Port Moody. Charters out of Vancouver, North Vancouver and in Port Moody. Water taxi out of Reed Point in Port Moody. Air fills are available throughout greater Vancouver: at Coquitlam, Port Coquitlam, New Westminster, Surrey, Langley, North Vancouver and Deep Cove.

Access: Buntzen Power Plant is halfway up the east side of Indian Arm. It is 4 nautical miles (7 kilometers) northeast of Deep Cove and 5 nautical miles (9 kilometers) northeast of Cates Park in North Vancouver; 9 nautical miles (17 kilometers) northeast of Reed Point in Port Moody.

Charter, take a water taxi, or take a rental boat and launch it or launch your own boat and go to Buntzen. Tie up by the big concrete power station, referred to by BC Hydro as Buntzen Number Two. There is another power plant slightly north, but Buntzen Number Two is the first one on your right as you go up Indian Arm. From the dock, snorkel north around the corner to the right and go down.

Comments: Buntzen is brightest in the afternoon. For a morning dive. you might try Best Point or Silver Falls – or look at the chart and explore a new site on the west side of Indian Arm.

Permission required from Harbour Master's Office to dive at Buntzen Power Plant. Telephone weekdays (604) 666-2405.

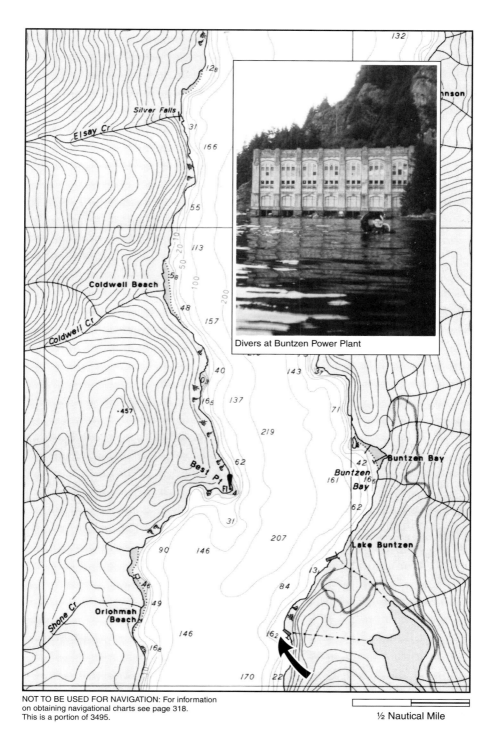

132

nson

Silver Falls

Elsay Cr

31

166

55

113

Coldwell Beach

48

Coldwell Cr

157

40

·457

165

137

219

71

Best Pt

62

Fl 4

Buntzen Bay

42

Buntzen
Bay

161

165

62

31

207

Lake Buntzen

90

146

13

84

Shone Cr

49

Orlohmah
Beach

146

162

168

170

22

Divers at Buntzen Power Plant

NOT TO BE USED FOR NAVIGATION: For information
on obtaining navigational charts see page 318.
This is a portion of 3495.

½ Nautical Mile

SILVER FALLS
Boat Dive

Tide Table: Vancouver

Skill: All divers

Why go: If, some morning, you want to dive over a drop-off go up Indian Arm to Silver Falls.

Silver Falls is on the west side of Indian Arm and morning sun shines through the water. As you descend through the shallows you'll see lots and lots of tube worms. Schools of seaperch range through the lettuce-kelp covered area to 20 to 30 feet (6 to 9 meters). From there the bottom rolls down almost immediately into dark depths. An occasional boulder sits on the side of the steep slope. Crimson slipper cucumbers stick to the rocks. Quillback rockfish and pale gobies hide in the crevices. Look for the weird hairy lithode crabs often seen in Indian Arm.

When diving at Silver Falls I saw my first ctenophores, or sea gooseberries. They look like free-floating walnuts with tails. A "first sighting" always marks a place, and makes it special for me.

Bottom and Depths: Small broken rocks covered with bottom kelp down to a depth of 20 to 30 feet (6 to 9 meters). Then smooth silt-covered rock, a steep roll downward. An occasional big boulder perched on the edge of the drop-off.

Hazards: Depth. Red jellyfish, in the fall. If you have seen any red jellyfish, you and your buddy should check one another for stinging tentacles before removing your masks and gloves.

Telephone: Deep Cove, at government dock.

Facilities: None at Silver Falls. Small rocky beach. Land your boat and picnic after your dive at the rocky beach north of Silver Falls. Launching in North Vancouver at Cates Park and in Port Moody at Rocky Point Park. Day charters out of Deep Cove, Ioco and Port Moody. Water taxi out of Reed Point in Port Moody. Air fills throughout greater Vancouver: at Coquitlam, Port Coquitlam, New Westminster, Surrey, Langley, North Vancouver and Deep Cove.

Access: Silver Falls is three quarters of the way up the west shore of Indian Arm. It is 5½ nautical miles (10 kilometers) northeast of Deep Cove and 7½ nautical miles (14 kilometers) northeast of Cates Park.

From Port Moody a water taxi goes to Silver Falls in 30 minutes. Take a water taxi, a charter, rent a boat or launch your own boat at Cates Park or Rocky Point Park. A small rocky beach where there used to be a loading conveyor, 200 yards (185 meters) north of Silver Falls, is a good place to land your boat. Descend and dive south towards Silver Falls.

Comments: From Silver Falls look across at a groove down the mountain from Buntzen Lake to the Buntzen Power Plant. That groove was made when the Buntzen Beasty – our coastal Ogopogo – slid into Indian Arm.

Permission required from Harbour Master's Office to dive at Silver Falls. Telephone weekdays (604) 666-2405.

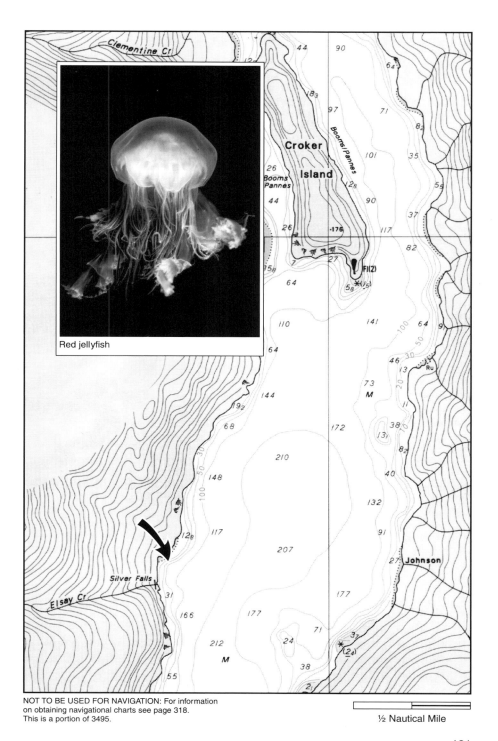

Clementine Cr

Croker Island

Booms Pannes

Booms Pannes

Red jellyfish

Fl(2)

M

Ru

Silver Falls

Elsay Cr

Johnson

M

NOT TO BE USED FOR NAVIGATION: For information
on obtaining navigational charts see page 318.
This is a portion of 3495.

½ Nautical Mile

CROKER ISLAND, SOUTHEAST CORNER
Boat Dive

Tide Table: Vancouver

Skill: All divers and snorkelers

Why go: "Paradise" one experienced diver calls this area, maybe because you can find almost anything you can name somewhere around Croker Island.

Clumps of anemones and sea stars overflow the south point. We saw small dahlia anemones, chitons, green urchins, painted greenlings and burrowing cucumbers. Lingcod and rockfish haunt the ledges and the overhangs shelving down the western side under the bay. As you move around the tip to the eastern side below the light, the water is thick with small shrimp. Tarantula-like hairy lithode crabs hang by a leg from the sheer smooth cliff that plunges 100 feet (30 meters).

There's no way that one tank is enough at Croker. You might try the northeast corner for your second dive.

Bottom and Depths: At the southwestern tip of Croker beautiful rock formations, large overhangs, caves and ledges drop to 100 feet (30 meters) and more, to whatever level you choose. On the southeastern side, a sheer cliff plunges for 100 feet (30 meters). Because little current stirs up the silt, in winter visibility ranges up to 100 feet (30 meters) all around the island.

Hazards: Boats in summer. Red jellyfish, in the fall. Listen for boats and keep close to the bottom all the way to shore. If you have seen any red jellyfish, you and your buddy should check one another for stinging tentacles before removing your masks and gloves.

Telephone: Deep Cove, above government dock at foot of Gallant Avenue.

Facilities: None at uninhabited Croker Island. If the tide is out, maybe room for a picnic on the rocks by the light. Launching in North Vancouver and Port Moody. Charters out of Ioco, Deep Cove and Port Moody. Water taxi out of Reed Point in Port Moody. Air fills throughout greater Vancouver: at Coquitlam, Port Coquitlam, New Westminster, Surrey, Langley, North Vancouver and Deep Cove.

Access: Croker Island is at the head of Indian Arm. It is 7 nautical miles (13 kilometers) northeast of Deep Cove, 9 nautical miles (17 kilometers) northeast of Cates Park, and 13 nautical miles (24 kilometers) north of Reed Point.

Charter, take a water taxi, take a rental boat and launch it or launch your own boat at North Vancouver or Reed Point and go to the top of Indian Arm to Croker. A good place to start your dive is at the south tip of the island. Anchor west of the light in the bay on the southwest side.

Comments: Excellent for photography in winter when visibility is best.

Permission required from Harbour Master's Office to dive at Croker Island. Telephone weekdays (604) 666-2405.

From Croker Island Light, looking south down Indian Arm

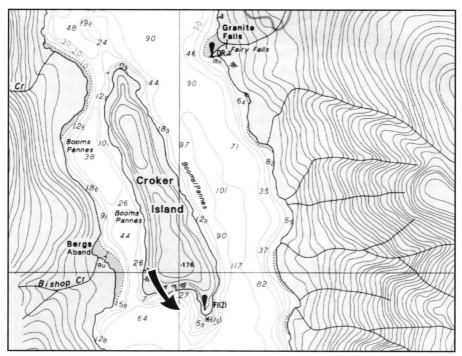

NOT TO BE USED FOR NAVIGATION: For information
on obtaining navigational charts see page 318.
This is a portion of 3495.

½ Nautical Mile

CROKER ISLAND, NORTHWEST CORNER
Boat Dive

Tide Table: Vancouver

Skill: All divers and snorkelers

Why go: Emerald green water like I've seen nowhere else in British Columbia was here at the northwest corner of Croker – on a sunny day in late September! I was lured to this dive because I was told there were swimming scallops. We saw one swimming scallop, but what hooked me was the visibility and the drop-off.

Dark and deep and green. Curvaceous rock formations, as if sculpted by current, ripple the steep wall. We saw four big lingcod, spider crabs, big fat hairy lithode crabs, a crescent gunnel, a sturgeon poacher, and crimson slipper cucumbers, also called creeping pedal cucumbers – they look like red lace. Plumose anemones brighten the scene from 20 to 40 feet (6 to 12 meters). Going deep is okay, because safety stops on the way up are interesting.

In the shallows in the bay, we saw a sand dab with a shrimp in its mouth. Lots more shrimp, too. Lots of cucumbers, two white nudibranchs with brown spots and stacks of little rockfish and silvery perch.

At the northern end of Croker you'll see beautiful variety again. Masses of cucumbers, stars, small barnacles, tube worms, seaperch, kelp greenlings and an occasional octopus and grunt sculpin. A forest of sea whips. Huge schools of herring and salmon grilse sometimes, too.

Bottom and Depths: Rocky with pockets of sand in the bay, plenty of area in the shallows at 15 to 25 feet (5 to 8 meters). On the northwestern side, a ledge at 65 to 75 feet (20 to 23 meters); then the wall sheers off deeper than we wanted to go – to a depth of 130 to 140 feet (40 to 43 meters). On the northern tip rocky bottom undulates to a depth of 60 to 70 feet (18 to 21 meters). Good also for snorkeling here. On the northeastern side, another drop-off to nowhere – to a depth of 165 to 175 feet (50 to 53 meters) on the chart.

Hazards: Depth. Boats in summer. Red jellyfish, in the fall. Listen for boats and keep close to the bottom all the way to the surface. If you have seen any red jellyfish, check for stinging tentacles before removing masks and gloves.

Telephone: Deep Cove, above government dock at foot of Gallant Avenue.

Facilities: None at uninhabited Croker Island. Launching in North Vancouver and Port Moody. Charters and water taxi out of Port Moody. Charters out of Ioco and Deep Cove. Air fills throughout greater Vancouver.

Access: This dive is at the head of Indian Arm. It is 8 nautical miles (15 kilometers) northeast of Deep Cove and 10 nautical miles (19 kilometers) northeast of Cates Park in North Vancouver; and 14 nautical miles (26 kilometers) north of Reed Point in Port Moody.

Charter, take a water taxi, take a rental boat and launch it or launch your own boat at North Vancouver or Rocky Point and go to the top of Indian Arm to Croker Island. From Reed Point you could reach Croker in 35 minutes by water taxi. The dive is at the northwest tip of the island. Anchor in the small cove south of the point.

Comments: Indian Arm is usually calm winter and summer. After diving, one diver water-skied home.

Permission required from Harbour Master's Office to dive at Croker Island. Telephone weekdays (604) 666-2405.

Sturgeon poacher

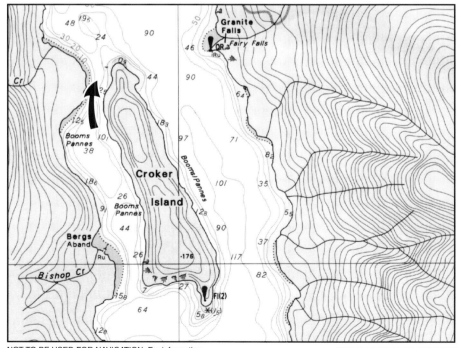

NOT TO BE USED FOR NAVIGATION: For information
on obtaining navigational charts see page 318.
This is a portion of 3495.

½ Nautical Mile

125

Sheltered cove at White Islets

Baiune out of Pender Harbour

Through kelp at Sutton Islets into Skookumchuck Narrows

CHAPTER 2
Sechelt Peninsula

Sechelt Rapids, looking north to Sutton Islets

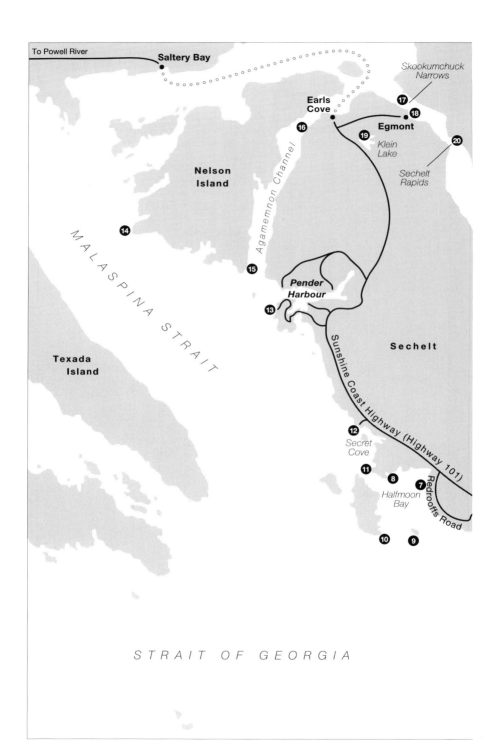

To Powell River

Saltery Bay

Skookumchuck Narrows

Earls Cove

17

18

16

19 **Egmont**

Klein Lake

20

Nelson Island

Sechelt Rapids

14

Agamemnon Channel

15

Pender Harbour

13

Sechelt

M A L A S P I N A   S T R A I T

Texada Island

Sunshine Coast Highway (Highway 101)

12

Secret Cove

11

8

7

Halfmoon Bay

Redrooffs Road

10

9

S T R A I T   O F   G E O R G I A

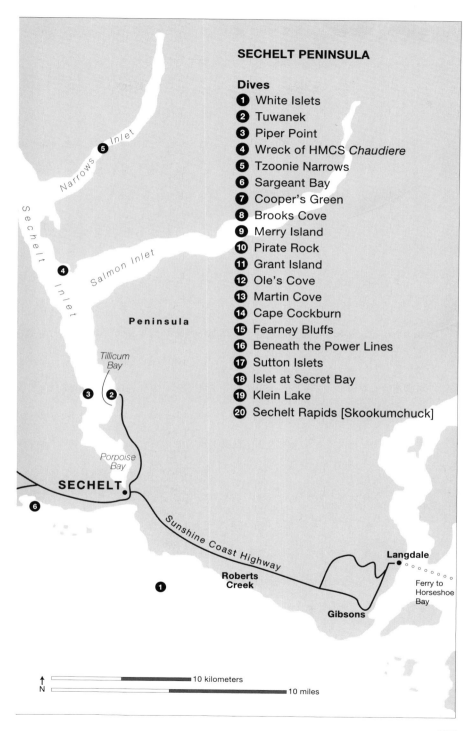

SECHELT PENINSULA

Dives

1. White Islets
2. Tuwanek
3. Piper Point
4. Wreck of HMCS *Chaudiere*
5. Tzoonie Narrows
6. Sargeant Bay
7. Cooper's Green
8. Brooks Cove
9. Merry Island
10. Pirate Rock
11. Grant Island
12. Ole's Cove
13. Martin Cove
14. Cape Cockburn
15. Fearney Bluffs
16. Beneath the Power Lines
17. Sutton Islets
18. Islet at Secret Bay
19. Klein Lake
20. Sechelt Rapids [Skookumchuck]

Narrows Inlet

Sechelt Inlet

Salmon Inlet

Peninsula

Tillicum Bay

Porpoise Bay

SECHELT

Sunshine Coast Highway

Roberts Creek

Langdale

Ferry to Horseshoe Bay

Gibsons

↑
N

10 kilometers

10 miles

SERVICE INFORMATION *
Sechelt Peninsula

Charts: Canadian Hydrographic Service
- 3311 Sunshine Coast–Vancouver Harbour to Desolation Sound (small-craft chart)
- 3312 Jervis Inlet & Desolation Sound (navigation atlas and cruising guide)
- L/C-3512 Strait of Georgia, Central Portion
- 3514 Jervis Inlet
- 3535 Plans–Malaspina Strait

Tide and Current Tables: Canadian Hydrographic Service
Tide and Current Table, Volume 5

Diving Emergency Telephone Numbers
Dial 911: Say "I have a scuba diving emergency".

Vancouver Hospital & Health Sciences Centre: Dial (604) 875-4111 and say "I have a scuba diving emergency. I want the hyperbaric physician on call".

If medical personnel are unfamiliar with scuba diving emergencies, ask them to telephone DAN (Divers Alert Network): (919) 684-8111, then say "I have a scuba diving emergency".

Other Useful Numbers
Weather – Continuous Marine Broadcast (CMB) recorded, 24 hours; listen for weather in the Strait of Georgia, telephone
- At Comox: (604) 339-0748
- At Vancouver: (604) 270-7411

Shellfish Infoline (red tide hotline), recorded: (604) 666-3169
Sportfishing Information Line, recorded: 1-800-663-9333

• Dive Shops in Sechelt

Tidalwave Diving Co.
Wharf Road (north end)
Sechelt Inlet (PO Box 2569)
Sechelt BC V0N 3A0
(604) 885-3328; fax 885-9538
Radiotelephone, Channel 9
(Waterfront and roadside air fills.)

Seasport Scuba
5567 Dolphin Street
PO Box 2668
Sechelt BC V0N 3A0.
(604) 885-9830 – fax and telephone.

• Resort Air Stations

Sechelt Inlet
Porpoise Bay Charters
Located at 7629 Sechelt Inlet Drive
Tuwanek; see address next page.
(604) 885-5950
Toll-free in Canada: 1-800-665-3483
(Waterfront and roadside air fills.)

Secret Cove
Georgia Strait Diving Charters
RR1, Jolly Roger Site, C-51
Halfmooon Bay BC V0N 1Y0
(604) 885-3388 or (604) 230-2587;
fax (604) 885-7564
(Waterfront and roadside air fills.)

Pender Harbour
Lowe's Resort
PO Box 153
Madeira Park BC V0N 2H0
(604) 883-2456; fax (604) 883-2474

Egmont
Egmont Marina Resort
General Delivery, Egmont BC V0N 1N0
(604) 883-2298

SECHELT INLET, SOUTH END
• Boat Charters

Anna I, Anna II, Anna III, Anna IV, Anna V
Porpoise Bay Charters
7629 Sechelt Inlet Drive, Tuwanek
RR 1, Kelsey's Site, C-18
Sechelt BC V0N 3A0
(604) 885-5950
Toll-free in Canada: 1-800-665-3483
(Charters out of Tuwanek. Also dive packages that include air, charters, hot tub, and waterfront accommodation with meals or self-contained guest house. Wheelchair divers welcome.)

Chaudiere Shuttle
Chaudiere Reef Dive Tours & Charters
PO Box 2442
Sechelt BC V0N 3A0
(604) 885-4420; fax (604) 885-4128
(Charters out of Tillicum Bay with inflatable tenders; also inflatable rentals and charters.)

Inlet Predator
A & A Marine
RR 1, S-15, C-59
Madeira Park BC V0N 2H0
(604) 883-9659
(Charters out of Porpoise Bay. Wheelchair divers welcome.)

MV *Karelia*
Halfmoon Bay Charters
PO Box 1546
Sechelt BC V0N 3A0
(604) 885-5111 or (604) 230-8527
(Charters out of Porpoise Bay; also rent trailerable boat with motor.)

MacKenzie Sea Services Ltd.
5718 Anchor Road
PO Box 1670
Sechelt BC V0N 3A0
(604) 885-7851; fax (604) 885-7164
(Charters out of Porpoise Bay.)

Snowcrest
Northwest Charters
31928 Casper Court
Clearbrook BC V2T 2J7
(604) 853-0540
(Charters out of Porpoise Bay with an Inflatable tender.)

Tzoonie
Tzoonie Outdoor Adventures
5644 Cowrie Street
PO Box 157
Sechelt BC V0N 3A0
(604) 885-9802
(Day and overnight charters out of Porpoise Bay. Overnight trips include camping and hot tub in Narrows Inlet.)

• Boat Rentals and Launching
Chaudiere Zodiac Rentals
PO Box 2442
Sechelt BC V0N 3A0
(604) 885-4420; fax (604) 885-4128
(Inflatable rentals at Tillicum Bay; also charters with inflatable tenders.)

Tillicum Bay Marina Inc., located off East Porpoise Bay Road, Sechelt Inlet
General Delivery
Roberts Creek BC V0N 2W0
(604) 885-2100
(Launching for a fee at Tillicum Bay, Sechelt Inlet: concrete ramp, good at all tides for small boats only. Pit toilets; telephone outside marina office.)

Porpoise Bay Public Ramp
Wharf Road (north end), next to government wharf
Sechelt BC
(Launching at the head of Sechelt Inlet: concrete ramp, good at all except extreme low tides. Toilet at wharf. Telephone inside at pub next to ramp; outdoor telephone in the center of Sechelt, northwest corner from the traffic light.)

From Sunshine Coast Highway 101: turn right at the traffic light in the center of the town of Sechelt and go ⅔ mile (1 kilometer) to foot of Wharf Road.

SECHELT INLET, NORTH END
For Sechelt Inlet, Skookumchuck Narrows and Agamemnon Channel

• Boat Charters

Arctic Courier and *Shaman II*
Egmont Marina Resort
General Delivery
Egmont BC VON 1N0
(604) 883-2298
(Day charters, boat rentals and water taxi to sites. Also launching, restrooms, hot showers, bunkhouse, cabins, camping, pub. Wheelchair divers welcome.)

MV *Skeena*
Blue Horizon Charters
#9, 558 Cardero Street
Vancouver BC V6G 2W6
(604) 681-2849
(Liveaboard charters out of Egmont.)

• Boat Rentals

Bathgate's Store & Marina
General Delivery, located beside government wharf
Egmont BC VON 1N0
(604) 883-2222
(Boat rentals – also water taxi. Restrooms with hot showers; telephone outside store.)

Egmont Marina Resort
General Delivery
Egmont BC VON 1N0
(604) 883-2298
(Boat rentals. Also air fills, launching, charters, water taxi to sites, hot showers, bunkhouse, cabins, camping, pub.)

• Boat Launching
Egmont Marina Resort
General Delivery, Egmont BC VON 1N0
(604) 883-2298
(Launching north of Egmont for Skookumchuck Narrows and Agamemnon Channel; dirt and gravel ramp, good at all tides. Restrooms; telephone outside Backeddy Pub.)

Egmont Public Ramp
Egmont BC
(Launching in Egmont at Skookumchuck Narrows: tarmac ramp, good at high tides only. Restrooms and telephone nearby at Bathgate's Marina.)
Just before reaching the government wharf, turn north into Maple Road. Turn right into Bradwynne Road and immediately right again down ramp.

STRAIT OF GEORGIA AND AGAMEMNON CHANNEL

• Boat Charters
out of Secret Cove

Blackfish
Blackfish Charters
RR 2, S-26, C-16
Gibsons BC VON 1V0
(604) 885-7977
(Charters out of Secret Cove .)

Seaborne 99
Georgia Strait Diving Charters
RR 1, Jolly Roger Site, C-51
Halfmoon Bay BC VON 1Y0
(604) 885-3388; fax (604) 885-7564
(Charters out of Secret Cove; dive packages that include "condo" and meals. Wheelchair divers welcome.)

• Boat Charters
out of Pender Harbour

Baiune
Sunshine Coast Tours
4289 Orca Road, RR 1, S-9, C-1
Garden Bay BC VON 1S0
(604) 883-2280; fax (604) 883-2352
Toll-free in BC, Alberta and throughout the USA: 1-800-870-9055
(Day charters out of Pender Harbour; other ports for groups, by arrangement. Full packages available for individuals.)

Madeira Marina
PO Box 189
Madeira Park BC VON 2H0
(604) 883-2266
(Water taxi out of Pender Harbour to dive sites, but not diving from boat.)

STRAIT OF GEORGIA, MALASPINA STRAIT AND AGAMEMNON CHANNEL
• Boat Rentals at Gibsons, Secret Cove and Pender Harbour

Gibsons Boat Rentals
PO Box 1018
Gibsons BC V0N 1V0
(604) 886-2628
(Boat rentals at Gibsons.)

Halfmoon Bay Charters
PO Box 1546
Sechelt BC V0N 3A0
(604) 885-5111 or (604) 230-8527
(Trailerable boat rental with motor; also charters out of Porpoise Bay.)

Coho Fishing Adventures
104 East 49th Avenue
Vancouver BC V5W 2G2
(604) 324-8214
In USA, telephone 1-800-663-8755
(Boat rentals and guided charters out of Secret Cove.)

Lowe's Resort
PO Box 153
Madeira Park BC V0N 2H0
(604) 883-2456; fax (604) 883-2474
(Boat rentals at Pender Harbour.)

Duncan Cove Resort
4686 Sinclair Bay Road
RR 1, S-15, C-13
Garden Bay BC V0N 1S0
(604) 883-2424; fax (604) 883-2414
(Boat rentals at Pender Harbour. Also launching.)

Fisherman's Resort & Marina
PO Box 68
Garden Bay BC V0N 1S0
(604) 883-2336
(Boat rentals at Pender Harbour. Also launching.)

• Launching at Gibsons, Sechelt, Halfmoon Bay and Pender Harbour
Gibsons Marina
PO Box 1520
Gibsons BC V0N 1V0
(604) 886-8686
(Launching at Gibsons for Strait of Georgia: concrete ramp, good at all except extreme low tides. Restrooms and hot showers; telephones next to marina office.)

Selma Park Ramp
Highway 101
Selma Park BC
(Launching at Selma Park for Strait of Georgia: concrete ramp, good at medium to high tides. Toilet. Parking space. Telephone in Sechelt on right-hand side of highway. The telephone is nearly 1 mile [1½ kilometers] north on Highway 101.)
Located south of town of Sechelt off Sunshine Coast Highway 101
• Heading north on Sunshine Coast Highway 101: from Wilson Creek, go 2½ miles (4 kilometers) to the launching ramp turnoff sign at Selma Park.
• Heading south on Sunshine Coast Highway 101: from the town of Sechelt go 1 mile (1½ kilometers) south to the launching ramp turnoff sign at Selma Park.
    Access to the ramp is across privately owned land and the owners point out that you use the ramp at your own risk. At the time of writing, the ramp is available at no cost to the public.

Cooper's Green Public Ramp
Foot of Fisherman's Road, off Redrooffs Road
Halfmoon Bay BC
(Launching at Halfmoon Bay for Strait of Georgia: concrete ramp, good at all except extreme low tides. Restrooms in summer; telephone outside restrooms.)
Located north of town of Sechelt off Sunshine Coast Highway 101
• Heading north on Sunshine Coast Highway 101: when you are 4 miles (7 kilometers) take Redrooffs Road. Go north on Redrooffs for 5½ miles (9 kilometers) to

Fisherman's Road and turn right downhill to the water.

• Heading south on Sunshine Coast Highway 101: take Redrooffs Road when nearly 1 mile (1½ kilometers) south of the turnoff to Smugglers Cove Provincial Park. Go south on Redrooffs Road for 1 mile (1½ kilometers) to Fisherman's and to the water.

Madeira Marina
Madeira Park Road
PO Box 189, Madeira Park BC V0N 2H0
(604) 883-2266
(Launching at Pender Harbour: concrete ramp, good at all tides; also water taxi to dive sites, but not diving from boat. No restrooms but pit toilet in summer at adjacent park. Telephone outside marina office.)

Madeira Park Public Ramp
Foot of Madeira Park Road
Madeira Park BC
(Launching at Pender Harbour: concrete ramp, good at medium and high tides only. Pit toilets in summer at adjacent park. Flush toilets in summer across Madeira Park Road at Pender Harbour Infocentre. Telephone on dock.)
To reach it, turn off Highway 101 at Madeira Park and go through the business district: the ramp is at the end of Madeira Park Road across from the Elementary School.

Duncan Cove Resort
4686 Sinclair Bay Road
RR 1, S-15, C-13
Garden Bay BC V0N 1S0.
(604) 883-2424; fax (604) 883-2414
(Launching at Pender Harbour: concrete ramp, good at all except extreme low tides. Also boat rentals. Restrooms; telephone outside marina office.)

Fisherman's Resort & Marina
PO Box 68
Garden Bay BC V0N 1S0
(604) 883-2336
(Launching at Pender Harbour: tarmac ramp, good at all except extreme low tides; also boat rentals. No public restrooms; telephone outside marina office.)

Irvines Landing Marina & Pub
RR 1, S-10, C-9
Garden Bay BC V0N 1S0
(604) 883-2296 or (604) 883-1145
(Launching at mouth of Pender Harbour: asphalt ramp, good at all except extreme low tides. Also pub, hot showers, camping, accommodations. Restrooms; telephone across road from ramp.)

• **More Information for Boat Divers and Kayak-Divers**
Explore for new sites on your own; additional launching ramps, public beaches where you can land, and facilities are listed in the following publications:

Docks and Destinations by Peter Vassilopoulos, Seagraphic Publications, Vancouver, 1994. Available at bookstores. (Scope: Lists marina services, customer services and adjacent facilities, including hot showers, public telephones, launching ramps and entertainment. Illustrated with maps, photographs. From the San Juan Islands through Vancouver, Sunshine Coast and north to Desolation Sound and Port Hardy.)

Small Craft Guide, Volume 2: British Columbia, Boundary Bay to Cortes Island, Canadian Hydrographic Service, 1990. Available where nautical charts are sold. (Scope: Lists launching ramps and facilities.)

Southwestern British Columbia Recreational Atlas compiled by Informap in cooperation with British Columbia Ministry of Environment, Victoria, 1992. Available at bookstores. (Scope: Maps, lists of parks and facilities, wildlife reserves and viewing. Covers southwestern British Columbia coastline from southern border north beyond Desolation Sound and includes all of Vancouver Island.)

• More Dive Facilities
Mako Lodge Adventures, located in Roberts Creek
1086-B Orange Road, above Highway 101
RR 2, S-12, C-4, Gibsons BC V0N 1V0
(604) 886-7704 – both fax and telephone.
(Dive packages include air fills, charters and lodge – air fills for lodge guests only. Charters to Sechelt Inlet and Sunshine Coast. Wheelchair divers welcome.)

• Ferry Information
British Columbia Ferry Corporation
Langdale Terminal
Gibsons BC
Toll-free in BC: 1-800-663-7600. Or (604) 886-2242.
Telephoning from outside British Columbia, (604) 386-3431.
(Ferries from Langdale to Horseshoe Bay [West Vancouver].)

British Columbia Ferry Corporation
Earls Cove Terminal
Earls Cove BC
Toll-free in BC: 1-800-663-7600. Or (604) 883-2515.
Telephoning from outside British Columbia, (604) 386-3431.
(Ferries across Jervis Inlet from Earls Cove to Saltery Bay.)

• Tourist Information
Discover British Columbia
1117 Wharf Street
Victoria BC V8W 2Z2
1-800-663-6000: Toll-free throughout Canada and the USA, including Hawaii and parts of Alaska.

Pender Harbour Travel Infocentre
12911 Madeira Park Road
PO Box 265
Madeira Park BC V0N 2H0
(604) 883-2561
(Summer only.)

Sechelt Travel Infocentre
5555 Highway 101, PO Box 360
Sechelt BC V0N 3A0
(604) 885-3100; fax (604) 885-9538

Gibsons Travel Infocentre
668 Sunnycrest Road, PO Box 1190
Gibsons BC V0N 1V0
(604) 886-2325; fax (604) 886-2379

How to Go: Sechelt Peninsula is connected to the mainland of British Columbia by 1,100 yards (1,000 meters) of land. It's "water country" – getting there is half the fun.

The southern tip of Sechelt is a quick-trip-away from Horseshoe Bay in West Vancouver – 40 minutes by ferry. The northern tip of Sechelt is a leisurely-trip-away from Vancouver Island: two ferry boat rides plus driving. The ferry from Comox to Powell River takes 1¼ hours; next drive 30 minutes to Saltery Bay; then ride the ferry for 50 minutes to Earls Cove at north end of Sechelt.

* All of this service information is subject to change.

Skill: Intermediate and expert divers

Why go: Wilderness above and below water. Blue sky, white rock and green depths where fish are a specialty – we saw at least forty medium-sized lingcod on one summer dive. This site is a lingcod breeding ground. Quillback rockfish line the vertical crevices in the rock, noses up, as if in formation. Lots of kelp greenlings cruise in the open. We saw tiger rockfish hiding in deep, dark crevices.

Anemones, sea stars, chimney and cloud sponges are spaced out on the stark rock as if on display. Snakelock anemones, also called crimson anemones, fling long, fleshy flamboyant red fingers into the current. Also white snakelocks. Christmas anemones cling to the rock with brilliant mottled red and green stalks. Peach-colored carnivorous anemones are on the rock. Isolated plumose anemones, orange ones and white. Red urchins and green ones. You might find an octopus or two. Tube worms are under ledges. Transparent tube-dwelling anemones and sea pens are on the sand. We saw purple sea stars, slime stars, blood stars, a rose star and tiny yellow stars. Sea lemons, a frilly orange and white nudibranch. Plus a special treat – a first-time sighting for me – two mating pairs of box crabs.

You might meet a harbor seal. At the end of our dive as we headed up over the shell bottom, a seal swooped around us, repeatedly came within 5 to 10 feet (1½ to 3 meters) and seemed to want to play. We hung around in 5 feet (1½ meters) for a long time. It was hard to leave the water because of the lure of the friendly seal.

Bottom and Depths: White shell and gravel bottom gently but quickly slopes off to smooth, dark rock creased with vertical crevices. The rock wall rolls down into darkness, bottoms out to sand at 105 to 115 feet (32 to 35 meters), depending on tide height. South of it, a boulder field; more gravel and clam shells at the southern tip.

Hazards: Current, small boats and poor visibility near shore from bird droppings that wash off the islets. Danger of overexertion after the dive for kayak-divers who dive deep. Dive on slack. Current is reasonably unpredictable at this site. When windy, current is probably more predictable on larger exchanges when the tidal movement overrides the effect of winds. Kayak-divers should take a rest before paddling back to avoid the possibility of bringing on bends by overexertion after the dive.

Telephones: • Roberts Creek store, 2 miles (3 kilometers) east at other end of Beach Road. • Highway 101 opposite Roberts Creek campground entrance: return up Flume Road to Highway 101, turn left and go ¾ mile (1⅓ kilometers).

Facilities: None at White Islets. Picnic tables and pit toilets at Roberts Creek picnic site on Beach Road at foot of Flume Road.

Access: White Islets are in the Strait of Georgia southeast of Sechelt and immediately south of Wilson Creek. Exposure to westerly and southeasterly winds could make access difficult – pick a calm day.

Go by boat to the narrow cove on the north side of the larger White Islet near its western end and anchor or land. Snorkel a short way out from the protected cove and dive toward the point to the east.

Charter out of the town of Sechelt or Halfmoon Bay; or launch your own boat at Selma Park Ramp just south of Sechelt and go 3 nautical miles (6 kilometers) to the White Islets. Anchoring is difficult for larger boats because of the sand bottom; you might need a boat tender.

Kayak-divers: launch at west end of Beach Road where there is space for three or four cars to park. Carry across 30 to 50 yards (27 to 46 meters) of sand and cobble beach, depending on tide height, and paddle 1½ nautical miles (3 kilometers) to the White Islets. It takes 25 to 30 minutes. Land in the narrow cove, which is a sandy beach at low tides, and gear up. The cove is sheltered from most winds and is a good place to leave your dive-kayak.

To get to west end of Beach Road
• Heading north on Highway 101, go nearly ½ mile (¾ kilometer) past Roberts Creek Road to Flume Road. Turn left and go 1 mile (1½ kilometers) on Flume to Beach Road. Turn right. Go ½ mile (¾ kilometer) to the end of Beach Road.
• Heading south on Highway 101, when south of the town of Sechelt and ¾ mile (1⅓ kilometers) past Roberts Creek Provincial Park campground turn right into Flume Road. Go for 1 mile (1½ kilometers) on Flume to Beach Road. Turn right. Go ½ mile (¾ kilometer) to the end of Beach Road.

Comments: On a calm day, a dive-kayak is perfect for exploring the coves of the White Islets.

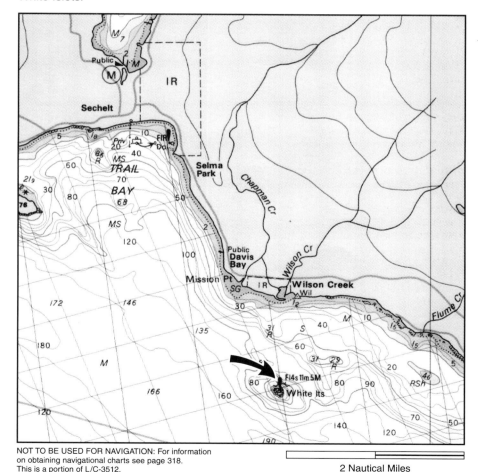

NOT TO BE USED FOR NAVIGATION: For information on obtaining navigational charts see page 318.
This is a portion of L/C-3512.

2 Nautical Miles

TUWANEK
Shore Dive

Tide Table: Point Atkinson

Skill: All divers and snorkelers

Why go: The shallow waters around three small islands at Tuwanek are like a large aquarium. It's beautiful for first open-water dives. Beautiful for fish. Beautiful for available light photography.

Small fish are everywhere. You'll see schools of black-and-white striped pile perch. Lots of reddish pink and yellow-tinged rockfish apparently totally unafraid. I touched one with my light. Delicate yellow-and-blue striped seaperch school everywhere in the sunny shallows. Hundreds of tube-snouts, too. You're bound to see maroon-and-gray vertically striped painted greenlings, sometimes called convict fish. Lots of these very territorial and colorful 4- to 5-inch (10- to 13-centimeter) convict fish live here. They'll probably try to chase- you from their particular portion of the sea.

Many other creatures at Tuwanek, as well. Red hydroids – or heart tunicates – that look like little tulips cling to the rocks. Sea lemons and alabaster nudibranchs eat bottom kelp. Angular orange dead man's finger sponges twist out of the rocks. A small crab menaced me from under a leaf of kelp. Sea peaches and transparent sea squirts hang like grapes from the wall.

Sun shines through the shallow water and lights it all.

Bottom and Depths: Shallow undulating rocky bottom encircles the islands. When swimming out, don't give up. Keep going past the log-dump debris covering the bottom near shore. Large rocks and boulders are tumbled in 25 to 30 feet (8 to 9 meters) of water at the south end of the island directly out from the point, making marvelous hiding places for all kinds of life. At 50 to 75 feet (15 to 23 meters) the bottom turns to silty sand. South of the point near the creek the bottom drops off swiftly to muddy bottom, scattered with a series of logs fallen to look like pick-up-sticks.

Hazards: Small boats in summer. Listen for boats and ascend along the contours of the bottom all the way to shore.

Telephones: • Tillicum Bay Marina, at end of Naylor Road; do not go down Tillicum Bay Road. From Tuwanek, go for 1 mile (1½ kilometers) back toward Sechelt to the turnoff to the marina at Naylor Road. • At Porpoise Bay Park: go 3½ miles (6 kilometers) back toward Sechelt to the turnoff to Porpoise Bay Park. Telephone is at the park entrance.

Facilities: Cobbled beach for a picnic at Tuwanek. No restrooms or pit toilets at Tuwanek, so if you wear contact lenses, wash your hands and put lenses in on the ferry or at a restaurant stop before you reach the site. Camping year-round 3½ miles (6 kilometers) back at Porpoise Bay Provincial Park with picnic tables, pit toilets and fire rings; hot showers in summer. Air fills at Tuwanek and Sechelt.

Access: Tuwanek is north of the town of Sechelt on the protected waters of Sechelt Inlet. It is a 10-minute drive out of Sechelt. Sechelt is 35 minutes from the Langdale ferry and 55 minutes from Earls Cove.

In Sechelt, follow signs toward Porpoise Bay Provincial Park: go north on Wharf Road to Porpoise Bay Road. Turn right and go 6 miles (10 kilometers) on Porpoise Bay Road along the east side of the inlet. Pass turnoffs to Porpoise Bay Provincial Park and Tillicum Bay. You are nearly there when you see a small carved wooden sign saying "Tuwanek". Continue ⅓ mile (½ kilometer) to where the road comes close to the water. One or two cars can park at the side of the road. You'll see lots of overturned dinghies on the beach. Swim to the island. Wheelchair accessible at high tide for those who can get across 10 feet (3 meters) of sand. High tide is best.

Comments: Come and go quietly in small groups – no noise pollution. Leave this beautiful beach as clean as we find it so the people of Tuwanek will welcome divers.

Dead man's finger sponges

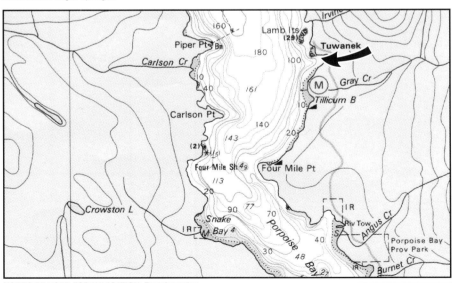

NOT TO BE USED FOR NAVIGATION: For information on obtaining navigational charts see page 318. This is a portion of L/C-3512.

2 Nautical Miles

PIPER POINT
Kayak Dive or Boat Dive

Skill: All divers

Why go: Piper Point has a totally wild and unexploited feeling – yet so easy to dive.
There is no current in this part of Sechelt Inlet and the deep waters of the inlet seem crystal clear year-round. Visibility is excellent – sometimes 20 to 50 feet (6 to 15 meters) in summer. Even more in winter. You experience a marvelous sensation of spaciousness when everything that's happening can be seen.

When I dived here I saw things I've seen nowhere else: a sea star consuming a sea pen; another sea star eating a clam; and a pair of wolf-eels under the edge of a rock that looked as large as a house. Orange and white anemones and sponges shaped like little castles are scattered on top of the rock. Seaperch and rockfish hang like mobiles in the water all around.

Going up we saw a sleek ratfish. And a school of herring swept past, making a silvery glint.

Bottom and Depths: Rocky bottom with some bull kelp drops quickly to a wide ledge at 60 to 70 feet (18 to 21 meters) – depending on tide height, where the big boulder lies. Over the edge of this ledge it's almost bottomless – 525 feet (160 meters) on the chart. Steep sides are typical of much of Sechelt Inlet.

Hazards: Depth, bull kelp and possible danger of overexertion by kayak-divers. Watch your depth. You tend to go deeper when the water is clear. Carry a knife. Kayak-divers who have dived deep should rest before paddling back. Strenuous exercise after diving may increase the risk of bends.

Telephones: • Tillicum Marina Resort, Tillicum Bay. • Lighthouse Pub, beside government wharf at Porpoise Bay in Sechelt.

Facilities: Wilderness camping at Piper Point. Launching at Tillicum Bay. Camping with picnic tables, pit toilets and fire rings; in summer, camping with hot showers at Porpoise Bay Provincial Park. Dive-kayak rentals available in Vancouver. Charters out of Tillicum Bay, Porpoise Bay and Tuwanek. Air fills at Tuwanek and in the town of Sechelt.

Access: Piper Point is located on the west side of Sechelt Inlet halfway between Porpoise Bay and Salmon Inlet. It is in Sechelt Inlets Provincial Recreation Area.

Charter or launch at Porpoise Bay in the town of Sechelt and go 4 nautical miles (7 kilometers) to Piper Point. Or you could launch at the end of Naylor Road at Tillicum Bay or hand-launch over the sand at Tuwanek and go 2 nautical miles (4 kilometers) across the water to it. At Piper Point, anchor in the bull kelp just south of the point. Go down and work your way southwest.

Kayak-divers could cross Sechelt Inlet, cautiously, when weather is calm and dive from shore at Piper Point. Wheelchair divers who paddle dive-kayaks could launch at Tillicum Bay ramp.

Comments: "Shelter from the sea" is the meaning of the Indian word for Sechelt. When the wind is blowing in the Strait of Georgia, Sechelt Inlet is the place to dive.

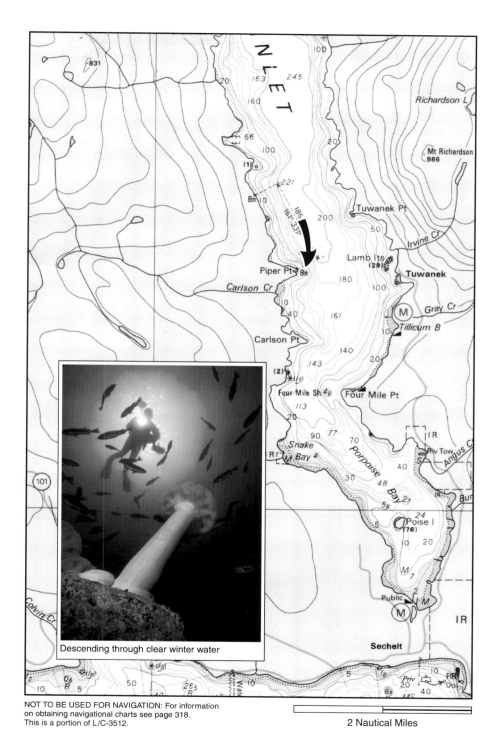

Descending through clear winter water

NOT TO BE USED FOR NAVIGATION: For information
on obtaining navigational charts see page 318.
This is a portion of L/C-3512.

2 Nautical Miles

WRECK OF HMCS CHAUDIERE
Boat Dive

Tide Table: Point Atkinson
Add 3 hours to high slack
Add 2 hours to low slack

Skill: Expert divers for wreck penetration. Intermediate divers for wreck exterior dives.

Why go: The "Everest of Wreck Diving" – an apt description applied to the *Chaudiere* immediately after sinking. It must be the best "fake wreck" in the world. This warship is mammoth. Easy to find. Awesome! It is pale military gray – spooky when you descend on the great big ghostly hull in clear winter water.

A superb vessel to use when teaching wreck diving – the *Chaudiere* offers endless potential for penetration by wreck divers. But make no mistake, exploration is a challenge. The *Chaudiere* is deep and complex – with 67 rooms on the four decks open for diving. Lots of equipment remains on board to photograph and play with. Look for radar equipment with knobs to turn at the "ops" (operations) level below the bridge; a bathtub, toilet and sink in the Captain's quarters. Fax machine with levers to switch in the "com" (communications) shack on the next level down where the wardroom is. Ovens with working doors in the galley on the "Burma Road" level that has 42 rooms. This deck is at the bottom of the ship and is the deepest one open to divers. The first day the *Chaudiere* was down, divers crawled into the gun turret at the top of the ship, and swam through the ward room. Penetration of at least one of those 67 rooms – all lying on their side, is almost irresistible. That's the danger. Yet intermediate divers who choose *not* to go inside will find it fascinating, and easy, to prowl around outside. You can traverse the length of the vessel pulling yourself along on the rails.

Marine life, too. Glassy tunicates and orange plumose anemones surround the stern where the vessel came to rest on the ocean floor. The second day the ship was beneath the sea, divers saw shrimp, a gunnel and sculpins sheltering inside the hull, a feather star in the officers' mess. Six months later, feather duster worms, quillback and yelloweye rockfish, lingcod, prawns, millions of crystal tunicates and many more creatures were living on it and in it.

Shaped like a great big canoe – the hull is tall and slim. It is 65 feet (20 meters) high, with a beam of 45 feet (14 meters) and is 366 feet (112 meters) long. On the day of sinking, December 5, 1992, it became the largest artificial reef on the west coast of North America – third largest in the world.

Bottom and Depths: The *Chaudiere* lies on its port side, bow pointing south. At high tide, depth at the top of the hull at the stern is 60 feet (18 meters); at the bow, 100 feet (30 meters). The stern rests on gently sloping rock bottom at 90 feet (27 meters) at high tide. Beneath the bow, 145 feet (44 meters) on the chart.

Hazards: Depth, the temptation to explore, and some surface current. The wreck is vast. Just diving the length of the ship on the outside of it, you could easily stay down too long. If entering the wreck, beware of disorientation because of its sheer size, its position on its side, and the great number of rooms. It is easy to be lured farther and farther into the hull. Make a dive plan; be aware of time. Only expert wreck divers trained in penetration and with full information about the *Chaudiere* should enter. Ascend at one of the marker-buoy chains where you can make a safety stop out of the way of boats and under control, if current. Pay attention to surface current, and go down to get out of it.

Telephones: At Egmont: • Bathgate's Marina, above government wharf. • Backeddy Pub at Egmont Marina, north of Egmont. At Sechelt Inlet, south end: • Tillicum Marina Resort, Tillicum Bay. • Lighthouse Pub (inside), beside the government wharf at Porpoise Bay in the town of Sechelt.

Facilities: Primitive camping at nearby Kunechin Islets, part of Sechelt Inlets Provincial Recreation Area. And a variety of offerings are available from dive shops, resorts and charter operators to get divers to the *Chaudiere*. Dive packages with land-based accommodation are available – stay at a dive lodge and go. Rent a trailerable boat. Rent an inflatable. Take a day charter or liveaboard charter. Yours to choose.

Access: The wreck of HMCS *Chaudiere* is in Sechelt Inlet in the bay north of Kunechin Point. It is 9 nautical miles (17 kilometers) north of the town of Sechelt, the same distance south of Egmont. Approach the *Chaudiere* from the north or south.

Charter or launch out of Tillicum Bay or Porpoise Bay – both at the *south* end of Sechelt Inlet. Tillicum Bay is part-way up the inlet and cuts the travel time on the water by one-third. Or charter or launch out of Egmont which is *north* of Sechelt Inlet and go south to the *Chaudiere* off Kunechin Point. In the bay north of Kunechin Point, 220 yards (200 meters) offshore, a yellow buoy marks the stern of the *Chaudiere*. A second yellow buoy marks the stack amidship. A third yellow buoy marks the bow. No motor traffic is permitted between these yellow caution marker buoys and do not tie onto them. It is a federal offense to make fast to a marker or tamper with any aid to navigation. Mooring buoys might be there to tie onto.

For your first dive, you could explore half the length of the vessel. Start at the bow in deeper water, follow the rail to amidships and ascend up the chain. Your second dive, you could go down the stern chain, explore from there to amidships and go up that chain again. And you haven't even started – two dives are not enough!

To get to the bay north of Kunechin Point
• From Tillicum Bay or Porpoise Bay, go *north* up Sechelt Inlet. The first opening you pass is Salmon Inlet on your right-hand side. Immediately north of it, again on the right-hand side, you pass the Kunechin Islets; then you are at Kunechin Point.
• From Egmont, go *south* through Sechelt Rapids [Skookumchuck] – plan your passage through Sechelt Rapids in advance. Refer to the current table for Sechelt Rapids. You might need slack, depending on the speed of your vessel. Currents up to 16 knots (30 kilometers/hour) race through this narrows. Once through Skookumchuck, pass the mouth of Narrows Inlet on your left-hand side and continue south to Salmon Inlet. Kunechin Point is on the left-hand side immediately north of the mouth of Salmon Inlet. If you reach the Kunechin Islets you have gone too far.

Comments: More information regarding the ship obtainable from local dive shops.

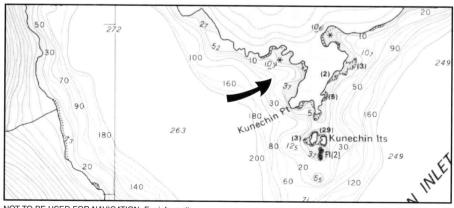

NOT TO BE USED FOR NAVIGATION: For information
on obtaining navigational charts see page 318.
This is a portion of 3312.

1 Nautical Mile

TZOONIE NARROWS
Boat Dive

Current Table: Sechelt Rapids
Add 10 minutes

Skill: Intermediate and expert divers. All divers with guide.

Why go: Remote, protected, perfect "intro" to drift diving. On a slow cruise through we saw large clusters of tiny almond-shaped lampshells – millions of them! Leafy hornmouth whelks heaped on one another. A forest of short-stemmed brown kelp ribbons. Tube-dwelling anemones. A sea lemon. Two large lingcod, kelp greenlings, silvery pile perch, striped seaperch, and quillback, blue and black rockfish. Big rock scallops. Feather stars, giant barnacles, orange solitary cup corals, white encrusting sponges, cemented tube worms that look like popcorn balls, and bands of small white plumose anemones. The bottom feels bright. You might see a wolf-eel which sometimes comes out in the open. When my buddy tickled a brown Irish lord on eggs, then pointed out an 8-inch (20-centimeter) long decorated warbonnet with a spike on its head, my day was made.

Charter boats even drift this site at night. It would be difficult to get lost: Tzoonie Narrows is 50 yards (46 meters) wide at its narrowest point. Safe, too, because of less boat traffic than at most narrows and because it is protected from wind. We dashed up from Sechelt to dive Tzoonie during a December snowstorm on a day when all power on Sechelt Peninsula (and much in Vancouver) was knocked out by wind, snow and ice. The dive was not affected. The boat trip *was* a bit cold and bumpy, but hot chocolate back at the pub while rehashing the dive and we were warm again.

Bottom and Depths: Boulders and kelp. Maximum depth, 50 to 60 feet (15 to 18 meters).

Hazards: Current and boats. Maximum current, 4 knots (7½ kilometers/hour). Diving, stay close to the bottom or wall; ascend at the side, out of the way of boats.

Telephones: At Egmont: • Bathgate's Marina above government wharf. • Backeddy Pub, Egmont Marina, north of Egmont. At Sechelt Inlet, south end: • Tillicum Marina Resort, Tillicum Bay. • Lighthouse Pub, beside government wharf at Porpoise Bay in town of Sechelt.

Facilities: Rustic camping at the adjacent Sechelt Inlets Provincial Recreation Area on northeast side of Narrows; pit toilets and places to pitch tents.

Access: Tzoonie Narrows is halfway up Narrows Inlet, a finger of water that branches off Sechelt Inlet. Tzoonie is 19 nautical miles (35 kilometers) from Porpoise Bay in the town of Sechelt, and 11 nautical miles (20 kilometers) from Egmont. To go from deeper to shallower water, plan to drift through on the ebb.

Charter or launch out of Porpoise Bay or Tillicum Bay in Sechelt Inlet (south end) or out of Egmont in Skookumchuck Narrows (north of Sechelt Inlet) and go to Narrows Inlet. At Narrows Inlet, go northeast to Tzoonie Narrows and through it. Enter the water on the southern side of Tzoonie. Drift through on an ebbing current with a "live" boat following.

To get to Narrows Inlet by boat
• From Porpoise Bay or Tillicum Bay go *north* through Sechelt Inlet to Narrows Inlet and Tzoonie. The distance is greater than approaching from Egmont, but the approach is easier to plan from Porpoise Bay as no rapids must be considered.
• From Egmont, go *south* through Sechelt Rapids [Skookumchuck] – plan your passage through Sechelt Rapids in advance. Refer to the current table for Sechelt

Rapids. You might need slack, depending on the speed of your vessel. Currents up to 16 knots (30 kilometers/hour) race through this narrows.

Comments: Winter or summer it's great. At night, remember to take a light-stick as well as an underwater light.

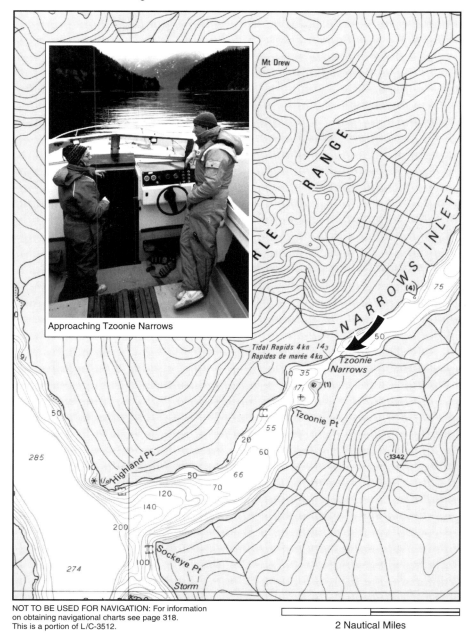

Approaching Tzoonie Narrows

2 Nautical Miles

NOT TO BE USED FOR NAVIGATION: For information
on obtaining navigational charts see page 318.
This is a portion of L/C-3512.

SARGEANT BAY
Shore Dive

Skill: All divers and snorkelers

Why go: Easy entry, easy dive in a beautiful location, lots to discover diving. We saw purple sea stars, giant sunflower stars, tiny white stars plastered on the wall like cutouts. Filmy white anemones beneath a dark overhang. Transparent sea squirts. Purple tube worms. I saw a long striped fish – it looked like a small candy cane, slip between the rocks. We saw brown cucumbers, a bright orange cucumber, a decorator crab with no decoration. Alabaster nudibranchs. Young nudibranchs on the way – we saw a ribbon egg mass of a sea lemon, which always reminds me of an apple peel, as well as a cluster of nudibranch eggs like strings of small seed pearls heaped in a jewel box .

We glimpsed a sailfin sculpin hiding in a vertical crease of the wall. Lots of little fish swimming in the shallows – the sun was out. It felt like tropical waters.

Bottom and Depths: Rock wall with creases, slits and overhangs. Boulders at the point. The wall drops to a depth of 20 to 30 feet (6 to 9 meters), depending on tide height, with smooth sand at its base.

Hazards: Shallow depth and silty sand. Easiest entry and diving at high tides. Weight yourself so you can stay down, but hover above bottom so you do not stir up silt.

Telephones: • Wakefield Inn; outside; go 3 miles (5 kilometers) south on Redrooffs and Highway 101. • Cooper's Green; go 4 miles (7 kilometers) north.

Facilities: Grassy park, sandy beach – lots of space for a picnic. Wheelchair-accessible toilet. Room for 10 or 12 cars to park at Sargeant Bay. Camping nearby at Porpoise Bay Provincial Park. Air fills in the town of Sechelt and at Secret Cove.

Access: Sargeant Bay is on the Strait of Georgia in Sargeant Bay Provincial Park which is on Redroofs Road (south end). Redroofs cuts off of Sunshine Coast Highway 101 between the town of Sechelt and Halfmoon Bay. Allow 45 minutes from Langdale ferry, 55 minutes from Earls Cove to reach it. At Sargeant Bay, walk to the far end of the beach. It takes 5 minutes. Enter across the gently sloping sand and dive or snorkel beside the rock wall on the left-hand side of the bay.

Clubs and other groups who dive at the park may avoid that long walk with gear and drop it at the entry point. Vehicle access to the beach berm is possible by advance arrangement. To request a key for vehicle access to the berm, contact BC Parks on weekdays from 9 a.m. to 4 p.m. at Porpoise Bay Provincial Park, PO Box 644, Sechelt BC V0N 3A0, telephone (604)885-9019.

The dive is wheelchair accessible at large high tides and with vehicle access to the beach berm. High tide leaves 6 feet (2 meters) of sand to cross.

To get to Redroofs Road and Sargeant Bay
• From Langdale, Gibsons and Sechelt, head north on Highway 101: go for 4 miles (7 kilometers) beyond the town of Sechelt and veer left into Redroofs Road. Drive along Redroofs 1 mile (1½ kilometers) to a sign at Sargeant Bay Provincial Park.
• From Earls Cove and Pender Harbour, go south on Highway 101: when ½ mile (¾ kilometer) past the turnoff to Smuggler Cove Provincial Park at Brooks Road, leave the highway and bear right. Go down Redroofs Road. Wind along Redroofs past Cooper's Green. From the highway, it is 5 miles (8 kilometers) to the turnoff to Sargeant Bay Provincial Park.

Comments: Bird watching as well as sea life at Sargeant Bay. Wetland enhancement of fish and bird habitat in the park.

Sea lemon and its eggs like an apple peel

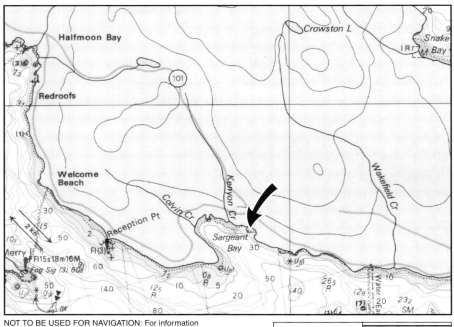

NOT TO BE USED FOR NAVIGATION: For information
on obtaining navigational charts see page 318.
This is a portion of L/C-3512.

2 Nautical Miles

COOPER'S GREEN
Shore Dive

Skill: All divers and snorkelers

Why go: Nice and easy entry and swim. Pleasant park for a picnic after diving.

Marine life? Look for a wolf-eel, an octopus, huge white plumose anemones. We saw sunflower stars, blood stars, a vermilion star, sea pens, sea peaches and sea cucumbers. Orange dead man's finger sponges and even a vase sponge. Delicate white petals of a nudibranch, a few kelp greenlings and a 1-foot (⅓-meter) lingcod. Lettuce kelp and clams in the shallows.

An excellent place for a first dive with a new diving partner or to check out gear. It's shallow. On the outside of the rock, no deeper than 60 feet (18 meters). No current here, so you can dive anytime day or night but go carefully: the site is next to a launching ramp. Safest in winter.

Bottom and Depths: Slopes gently. Around the rock, it bottoms out to coarse sand and pebble bottom at 50 to 60 feet (15 to 18 meters), depending on tide height.

Hazards: Boats – lots of them in summer, and there could be poor visibility because of silt. Log booms are sometimes tied to the rock. Best as a winter dive. Always fly a dive flag at this multi-purpose site – if you do not have one, you can rent a diver's flag and float. Listen for boats, and ascend on the west or south side of the rock and close to it. Then snorkel to shore. If you dive when a log boom is tied up to the rock, be aware of it. If the water becomes dark, head out from beneath the boom to the light. Try to stay off the bottom, so you do not stir up silt.

Telephones: • Cooper's Green, outside by the beach house. • Halfmoon Bay store.

Facilities: Picnic tables, restrooms in summer, and lots of room to spread out at Cooper's Green. Keep the groundskeeper happy by not wearing your wet suit or dry suit into the restrooms, and by taking care not to track mud and gravel into them.

Access: Cooper's Green is on Halfmoon Bay, Strait of Georgia side of Sechelt Peninsula. It is on Redrooffs Road (north end). Redrooffs cuts off of Sunshine Coast Highway 101 between Sechelt and Halfmoon Bay – the dive is midway on the peninsula between Langdale and Earls Cove. Allow 1 hour from each ferry to reach it.

At Cooper's Green, dive or snorkel out to the rock on the left-hand side of the ramp and rock as you face the water. The diving area is marked. Dive around the south end of the rock and the ocean side of it, staying down out of the way of boats.

To get to Redrooffs Road and Cooper's Green
• From Langdale, Gibsons and Sechelt head north on Highway 101: go for 4 miles (7 kilometers) beyond the town of Sechelt and veer left into Redrooffs Road. Drive along Redrooffs for 5 miles (8 kilometers) to Cooper's Green. Go past it up the hill to Fisherman's Road, turn left and go down Fisherman's Road to drop gear. Then return for roadside parking on Redrooffs at Cooper's Green.
• From Egmont and Pender Harbour, go south on Highway 101: just past the turnoff to Smuggler Cove Provincial Park at Brooks Road, bear right down Redrooffs Road. Go 1¼ miles (2 kilometers) to Fisherman's Road – it is at the top of the hill. Drive down Fisherman's to the launching ramp and drop gear, then return to Redrooffs and head south downhill for roadside parking at Cooper's Green.

Comments: Nice and easy – "life's a beach" at this pretty park. But please note: no air compressors allowed at the park and keep your dog on a leash.

Easy access at Cooper's Green

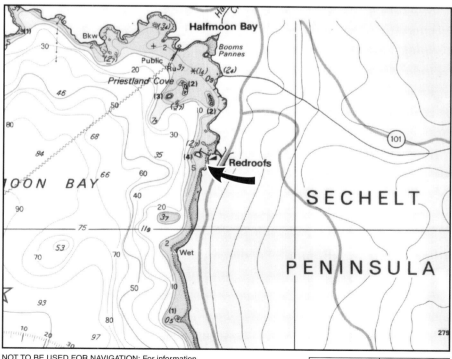

NOT TO BE USED FOR NAVIGATION: For information
on obtaining navigational charts see page 318.
This is a portion of 3535.

½ Nautical Mile

BROOKS COVE
Kayak Dive or Shore Dive

Table: Point Atkinson

Skill: All divers and snorkelers

Why go: There's a lot of good diving in the Secret Cove area – but mostly from boats. If you have no boat and you still want to dive, here's one place you can go. The price: one very long swim or else paddle a dive-kayak to it.

What will you get for your efforts? If you go far enough you'll come to a rock wall dropping to a depth of 80 to 90 feet (24 to 27 meters). You'll see lingcod, rockfish, greenlings and sponges. Octopuses in crevices. Wolf-eels, if you look hard. But save your air till you arrive at the site.

Swim on the surface right around to the second point on your left. The water is usually clear at Brooks Cove with visibility up to 80 feet (24 meters) in winter. If swimming, you don't have to go down to see what's there. While snorkeling out and while still in the shallows, we saw nudibranchs, small crabs, anchovies and perch. Slightly deeper we saw ratfish, dogfish, some medium-sized lingcod and countless schools of other smaller fish. All this before we started our dive.

And then down to the sponges.

Bottom and Depths: In the bay, mud and eelgrass slope gently out to depth of 20 to 30 feet (6 to 9 meters), depending on tide height. At the point 350 yards (320 meters) around the corner on your left, the wall drops 80 to 90 feet (24 to 27 meters).

Hazards: Current and long swim. Dive on slack. For very fit divers or kayak-divers.

Telephones: • General store, near government wharf at Halfmoon Bay, inside. Go south on Highway 101, bear right on Redrooffs and almost immediately turn right to foot of Mintie Road. • Cooper's Green, outside by the beach house. Continue south along Redrooffs Road for 1¼ miles (2 kilometers) past Mintie Road to it.

Facilities: Room for four or five cars to park at Brooks Cove. It is just past the parking lot for Smuggler Cove Provincial Park which is a walk-in or boat-in park – you cannot drive to it. After the dive, you could walk to Smuggler Cove or, if you've got a dive-kayak, you could paddle to Smuggler Cove and explore for new dives. It is a prime area for primitive camping and boat diving. Dive-kayak rentals in Vancouver.

Access: Brooks Cove is in Halfmoon Bay on the Strait of Georgia side of Sechelt Peninsula. It is off Sunshine Coast Highway 101 between Sechelt and Halfmoon Bay – the dive is midway on the peninsula between Langdale and Earls Cove. Allow just over 1 hour from either ferry to reach it.

At Brooks Road, follow signs to Smuggler Cove Provincial Park. Drive for 2 miles (3 kilometers) to the sea. Homes are on both sides of Brooks Cove. Enter the water only a few steps from the road end over the rocky log-strewn beach. Then a very long swim. I warn you: It is 350 yards (320 meters) around the corner on your left before you arrive at the wall.

To get to Brooks Cove Road
• From Langdale, Gibsons and Sechelt, head north on Highway 101: Go 10 miles (16 kilometers) beyond the town of Sechelt. When ⅔ mile (1 kilometer) past the north end of Redrooffs Road, you will see a sign to Smuggler Cove Provincial Park. Turn left into Brooks Road.
• From Egmont and Pender Harbour, go south on Highway 101: When 2 miles (3 kilometers) past the Buccaneer Bay turnoff, look for the Smuggler Cove Provincial Park sign at Brooks Road. Turn right.

Comments: Great beach for a small fire and supper after the dive.

From April 15th through October 15th, if the weather is extremely hot and dry, telephone the Sunshine Coast District Office of the Ministry of Forests at (604) 485-0700, and ask if beach fire permit required.

Lingcod, approachable where not hunted

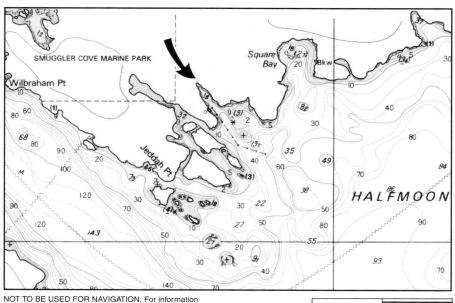

NOT TO BE USED FOR NAVIGATION: For information
on obtaining navigational charts see page 318.
This is a portion of 3535.

½ Nautical Mile

MERRY ISLAND
Boat Dive

Skill: Intermediate and expert divers

Why go: For some the scattered remains of the *Salvage Chief* and the two wrecks, *Linda-K* and *Carla-N,* are the big attractions at Merry Island. For others the lead fishing weights, the octopus that regularly suns itself on the 10-foot (3-meter) reef, or the wall thick with red dahlia anemones that drops down at the southeast end.
    The steel-hulled *Salvage Chief* was stranded here in 1925. The *Linda-K* and *Carla-N* in 1962. All three have been dived on a lot, but a wreck always excites the imagination. Who stayed on the ship to the end? What did they do on the *Salvage Chief* when it was picked up by a swell, crashed onto the reef, and holed?
    Merry Island glows in my memory as the place with the best visibility I've experienced anywhere outside of the tropics. And I dived here on a day in May when most other places in the Strait of Georgia were blotted out by river runoff. Visibility sometimes does deteriorate because of plankton bloom in summer, but this seems one of the last areas to be affected.
    Wrecks, anemones and excellent visibility for photography are all part of the dive at Merry Island.

Bottom and Depths: The reef is large broken rocks with bull kelp. It dries at very low tides and can be 10 feet (3 meters) deep on high tides. Heading southeast, the slope is gradual to a depth of 50 to 60 feet (15 to 18 meters), depending on tide height. Then the rock wall drops off sharply.

Hazards: Current, wind and bull kelp. Dive on the slack. Carry a knife.

Telephones: • Merry Island Lighthouse radiotelephone. • Cooper's Green, outside by the beach house. • General store, near government wharf Halfmoon Bay, inside.

Facilities: None at Merry Island. Air fills at town of Sechelt; Madeira Park, Pender Harbour; and Secret Cove. Launching at Halfmoon Bay, trailerable boat rentals and inflatable rentals in Sechelt, charters and boat rentals at Secret Cove. A beautiful wilderness campsite at Smuggler Cove at the northeast end of Welcome Passage. No drinking water, but pit toilets and a place to pitch your tent at Smuggler Cove.

Access: Merry Island is in the southern end of Welcome Passage on the Strait of Georgia side of Sechelt Peninsula. Allow 55 minutes from Langdale and 40 minutes from Earls Cove ferry terminal to drive along Sunshine Coast Highway 101 to Secret Cove or Halfmoon Bay. Wind from almost any direction can be a problem at this very exposed site. If going in a small vessel, pick a calm day.
    Charter out of Sechelt and go north. Or charter, rent or launch out of Secret Cove or Halfmoon Bay and head south. From Secret Cove, go for 4 nautical miles (7 kilometers). From Halfmoon Bay, go 3 nautical miles (6 kilometers) to Merry Island. The reef is at the southern side of Merry Island. Be careful as you approach, especially on low tides. The reef dries at 2-foot (⅔-meter) tides.
    To find the reef, line yourself up on the intersection of two lines. One line runs from the south tip of Merry Island to the Merry Island Light; the other from the south tip of the island just south of Merry Island to Reception Point Light. At the pinnacle of the reef the *Salvage Chief* was holed. Scraps of all three wrecks have been found just to the north of this pinnacle.

Comments: Look for cormorant nests and harbor seals on Merry Island.

Merry Island Lighthouse from Franklin Island

NOT TO BE USED FOR NAVIGATION: For Information
on obtaining navigational charts see page 318.
This is a portion of 3535

½ Nautical Mile

153

PIRATE ROCK
Boat Dive

Tide Table: Point Atkinson
Add 10 minutes

Skill: Expert divers

Why go: Pirate Rock sits "king-of-the-castle" on top of a series of irregular ledges, boulders, and arches. Anchor heaven. It's one of the most dramatic pinnacles of rock I've dived.

And there's more than an average amount of life around it. Quillback rockfish – smallish to medium-sized – crowd the cracks of the rocks. Tube worms, sea peaches and plumose anemones hold tight under the overhangs. Sea pens tilt out of pools of sand between the ledges. Greenlings hide in the bottom kelp. Lingcod move in and out of the shadows.

Deeper, ratfish slide past big gray immobile chimney sponges. A wolf-eel hides in a hole under the rocks, while snakelock anemones, thick like fringe on a Spanish shawl, test the current with sticky fingers. And cloud sponges that are 1-foot (⅓-meter) wide float below like fluffy summer clouds in a beautiful reverse world.

Look for anchors.

Bottom and Depths: Bull kelp is attached to irregular rocky bottom around Pirate Rock that is 20 to 30 feet (6 to 9 meters) deep, depending on tide height. Ledges, overhangs and arches which you can swim through surround the rock. The arches are formed by boulders tumbled one over the other. The north side drops off quickly. Narrow ledges tier down to 10 to 20 feet (3 to 6 meters), to 60 and 80 feet (18 and 24 meters) and on.

Hazards: Current and wind. Small fishing boats, bull kelp and broken fishing line. Dive on slack. Even then it is difficult. Currents come in streaks on the surface. One streak from Welcome Pass side. Then dead water. Then another streak of current from the west side of Thormanby Island. A pickup boat is advisable. Pirate Rock is popular with salmon fishermen. Be especially careful of small-boat traffic in salmon fishing season. Because the bottom undulates irregularly it is difficult to find your anchor line or to ascend along the rock all the way to the surface. Listen for boats and ascend cautiously; if you hear a boat you can stay down until it passes. Carry a knife.

Telephones: • Merry Island Lighthouse radiotelephone. • Cooper's Green, outside by the beach house. • General store, near government wharf at Halfmoon Bay, inside.

Facilities: None at Pirate Rock. Charters, launching and boat rentals – including inflatable and trailerable boats – at Sechelt, Halfmoon Bay and Secret Cove. Waterfront air fills at Secret Cove. A wilderness provincial park at Smuggler Cove at the northeast end of Welcome Passage. No drinking water, but you will find pit toilets and a place to pitch your tent at Smuggler Cove.

Access: Pirate Rock is ¼ nautical mile (½ kilometer) off the southeast tip of South Thormanby Island near Welcome Passage beside Sechelt Peninsula. Allow 55 minutes from Langdale and 40 minutes from Earls Cove to drive Highway 101 to Secret Cove or Halfmoon Bay.

Charter out of Sechelt and head north. Or charter, rent or launch at Halfmoon Bay or Secret Cove and head south. From Halfmoon Bay go 3 nautical miles (6 kilometers) southwest or 4 nautical miles (7 kilometers) south of Secret Cove. Anchor anywhere around the rock, but do not tie onto the marker. It is a federal offense to make fast to a marker or tamper with any aid to navigation. Anchor carefully. In winter, south wind might blow you onto the rocks.

Comments: One of the warmest sandy swimming beaches in British Columbia is only 3 nautical miles (6 kilometers) north of Pirate Rock between the Thormanby Islands at Buccaneer Bay.

From South Thormanby, off to nearby Pirate Rock

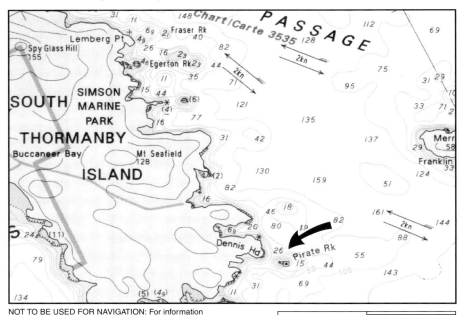

NOT TO BE USED FOR NAVIGATION: For information on obtaining navigational charts see page 318.
This is a portion of 3311.

1 Nautical Mile

GRANT ISLAND
Boat Dive

Skill: Intermediate and expert divers. All divers with guide.

Why go: Grant Island Light marks the narrowest point, the deepest drop-off and the place in Welcome Passage where you will find the most of everything. Familiar creatures – masses of quillback rockfish, giant barnacles at the point, lots of ratfish cruising beside the current-swept bottomless wall. And a great variety of unusual marine animals.

We saw hard pink hydrocoral and small dwarf gorgonian coral – it is bright red. Both were "firsts" for me on that dive. You might see Puget Sound king crabs. While the sponges are magnificent: we saw chimney sponges, trumpet sponges and vase sponges – one that looked like a giant lily.

Bottom and Depths: Bull kelp. And bottom kelp on the rocky bottom north of the lighthouse, close to shore. It is 50 to 60 feet (15 to 18 meters) deep. South towards the point, the rock wall drops almost straight down. Over 475 feet (145 meters) on the chart.

Hazards: Current, rough water, boats, and bull kelp. Dive on the slack. Choose a calm day. Listen for boats and ascend up the wall, well out of the way of those boats. Carry a knife for kelp.

Telephones: • Merry Island Lighthouse radiotelephone. • General store, near government wharf Halfmoon Bay, inside.

Facilities: None at Grant Island. Air fills at the town of Sechelt, at Secret Cove, Egmont and Madeira Park, Pender Harbour. Charters, rentals and launching ramps at Secret Cove, Halfmoon Bay and Sechelt – even inflatable charters. A beautiful wilderness provincial park is ¼ mile (½ kilometer) away at Smuggler Cove. No drinking water, but pit toilets at Smuggler Cove – plus a place to pitch your tent. It's some of the best camping and diving available in British Columbia.

Access: Grant Island is at the north end of Welcome Passage. It is 3 nautical miles (6 kilometers) northwest of Halfmoon Bay. Allow 40 minutes from Earls Cove and 55 minutes from Langdale ferry terminal to drive Highway 101 to Halfmoon Bay.

Charter out of Secret Cove, Halfmoon Bay, or Sechelt or rent or launch at Halfmoon Bay or Sechelt and go to Grant Island. Anchor north of the lighthouse around the corner out of Welcome Passage. Dive towards the light.

Comments: Worth diving here just to see the unusual pink hydrocoral and red gorgonian corals. They start at about 80 feet (24 meters). But because they're only 4 or 5 inches (10 or 13 centimeters) tall, you must look closely to find them in this vast seascape.

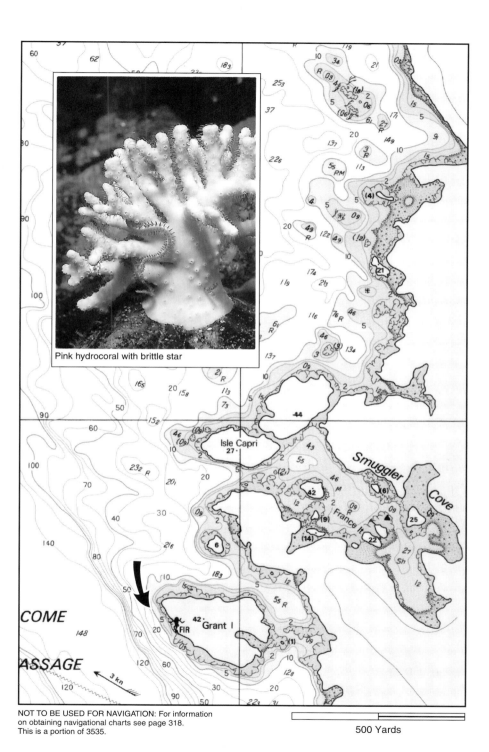

Pink hydrocoral with brittle star

NOT TO BE USED FOR NAVIGATION: For information
on obtaining navigational charts see page 318.
This is a portion of 3535.

500 Yards

OLE'S COVE
Shore Dive

Skill: All divers

Why go: If you want a plain old-fashioned reef – no frills, nothing special, just a good reef – Ole's Cove is it.

From the surface little indicates a reef. Some bull kelp, but it's difficult to see, especially at high tide. You have to go on trust. The easiest way to find the reef is to set your compass and swim under water straight out from shore.

You'll see moon jellyfish and sea stars in the eelgrass. Shrimp, miniature sea pens and tube-dwelling anemones feathering the sandy shallows. At the rocky reef, 200 to 300 feet (60 to 90 meters) offshore, we saw crabs in the bottom kelp, boulders covered with red anemones, white encrusting sponge, transparent sea squirts, and small orange sponges. Striped seaperch and pile perch school around the rocks. You'll see rockfish, kelp greenlings, painted greenlings, lingcod and dogfish.

A typical reef and a satisfying dive.

Bottom and Depths: Sand and eelgrass slope gradually from shore to 25 feet (8 meters) deep. Rocky reef starts 200 to 300 feet (60 to 90 meters) offshore and undulates easily down. Some boulders, bottom kelp and bull kelp. Depending on tide height, the reef bottoms out to sand at a depth of 50 to 60 feet (15 to 18 meters).

Hazards: Boats and bull kelp, especially in summer. Listen for boats; if you hear one, stay down until it passes. Or better yet – follow your compass back to shore under water.

Telephone: Lord Jim's Resort Hotel, inside but available 24 hours. Look for telephone signpost south of the office. Go up three stairsteps, turn left and go into hall. The telephone is on the right-hand side.

Facilities: None at Ole's Cove. Air fills at Sechelt, Egmont, Secret Cove and at Madeira Park, Pender Harbour.

Access: Ole's Cove is north of Welcome Passage in Malaspina Strait. It is north of Secret Cove off Sunshine Coast Highway 101. The turnoff is at Mercer Road. Allow 1 hour from Landgale, and 40 minutes from Earls Cove to reach it.

From Highway 101, turn into Mercer Road. From the highway, less than ⅔ mile (1 kilometer) to the dive. Go to Ole's Cove Road. Turn right. Go up the hill, and immediately turn right again into Backhouse Road. Follow Backhouse Road winding around through the woods. Drive for ⅓ mile (½ kilometer) to where the road dips down near the water. Room for two or three cars to park at the roadside. Between two homes, you will see a mailbox. Behind it, natural stone steps and a short gravel path to the cove. Since the bottom does not deepen quickly, set your compass and follow it straight out from shore to find the reef.

To get to Mercer Road
• From Sechelt, go north on Highway 101. When 1½ miles (2½ kilometers) past the Buccaneer Bay turnoff, look for Lord Jim's Resort sign at Mercer Road.
• From Pender Harbour, go south on Highway 101. When 5½ miles (9 kilometers) past Francis Peninsula Road, look for Lord Jim's sign at Mercer Road.

Comments: A good afternoon's dive when the sun has warmed the rocks.

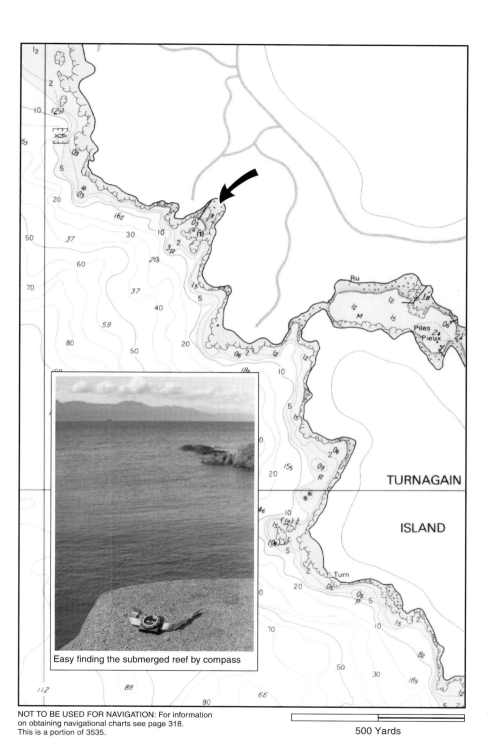

Easy finding the submerged reef by compass

TURNAGAIN

ISLAND

Ru

Piles
Pieux

Turn

NOT TO BE USED FOR NAVIGATION: For information
on obtaining navigational charts see page 318.
This is a portion of 3535.

500 Yards

MARTIN COVE
Shore Dive

Skill: All divers

Why go: If you want a quick uncomplicated dive with a wilderness feeling beneath the water, try this quiet cove south of Pender Harbour.

You'll see flounders, Oregon tritons and sea stars on the sandy floor. Look for moon snails as well. Along rocky walls rimming both sides of the cove we found beautiful small green anemones contrasting with very red rocks in the shallows; purple crabs scurrying about; and purple stars sticking on the rocks. Millions of almost-transparent blackeye gobies dart all about. Pipefish, pile perch and striped seaperch glint in the sun. Rockfish hang along the wall. Deeper we saw sea peaches, dahlia anemones and lingcod.

Chimney sponges at 60 feet (18 meters) and you're in the wilderness.

Bottom and Depths: The cove is rimmed with rock walls dropping to sand bottom which slopes to deep water. Some boulders along the wall.

Hazards: Wind could blow into the bay. Fatigue, if lured too far by the chimney sponges. Watch your time.

Telephones: • Beaver Island Grocery, which is on Francis Peninsula Road, 2 miles (3 kilometers) back toward highway. • Francis Peninsula Road and Highway 101.

Facilities: None, except in summer, a crescent of beach for a picnic. Homes rim the cove. Use toilet facilities before you arrive. Air fills, camping, accommodations, boat charters, boat rentals, and launching at nearby Pender Harbour.

Access: Martin Cove is in Malaspina Strait south of Pender Harbour. It is off Francis Peninsula Road, the southernmost of three access roads to the Pender Harbour area. From Langdale, go north on Sunshine Coast Highway 101 for 1 hour to Francis Peninsula Road. From Earls Cove, go south 25 minutes to it.

From Highway 101, turn onto Francis Peninsula Road and go west for 4 miles (7 kilometers) to Martin Cove. On the way, cross a small bridge at Bargain Narrows onto Beaver Island. Past this bridge, the road winds all over the place. Keep on the main road to Martin Road. If you reach the end of the road, you have gone ⅓ mile (½ kilometer) too far. Park at the roadside, just past Martin Road, and walk 100 paces down a well-worn path through the woods to the beach. Entry is easy.

To get to Francis Peninsula Road
• From Langdale and Sechelt, go north on Highway 101. Past Halfmoon Bay and 5½ miles (9 kilometers) past Lord Jim's turnoff, turn left into Francis Peninsula Road.
• From Earls Cove, go south on Highway 101. When you are ⅔ mile (1 kilometer) past Madeira Park turn right into Francis Peninsula Road.

Comments: An exceptionally easy and totally pleasant dive.

Lined chiton clinging to rock

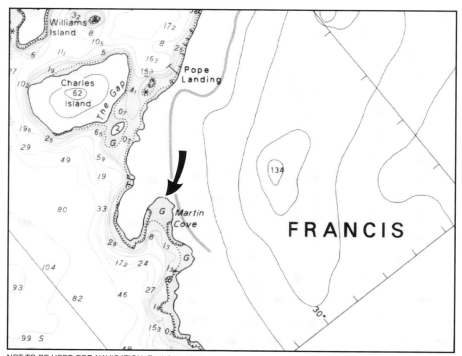

NOT TO BE USED FOR NAVIGATION: For information
on obtaining navigational charts see page 318.
This is a portion of 3311.

500 Yards

CAPE COCKBURN
Boat Dive

Skill: Intermediate and expert divers and snorkelers. All divers with guide.

Why go: Tumbling in terraces, the clean-swept rocks and gravel of Cape Cockburn sheer off into deep waters like something at the end of an ancient glacier. A different dive.

At first you look around, but see little life. We saw simply smooth-carved rock ledges stairstepping down, clean undercut overhangs, and not much else. Look again. Shine your light. Stark, dark grooves slicing vertically down the smooth rock are full of pastel life. They are brimming with pink and pale green anemones so thick you can't see the rock. Under a ledge at only 25 feet (8 meters) we saw a sunburst of yellow cloud sponge. Small orange cloud sponges nearby. Alabaster nudibranchs gleaming white on white and petal-like pale orange nudibranchs with white tips – both only a couple of inches (centimeters) long – are isolated islands of delicate beauty on the vast rock fall.

Deeper, velvety-red snakelock anemones hang from the clean rock wall like exquisite flowers reaching velvet fingers into the current. Deeper still, large chimney sponges. Then darkness.

At this extreme western tip of Cape Cockburn alternate sweeps of smooth rock and sand slope into the dramatic dark of Malaspina Strait.

Bottom and Depths: Smooth rocks, ledges and overhangs slope rapidly to 850 feet (260 meters). South of the cape the rocks drop in ledges and terraces, as well. These are the really different dives.

For a more usual shallow reef with boulders, bull kelp, rockfish, lingcod and more life altogether, dive immediately below the light.

Hazards: Current. Dive on the slack.

Telephone: Irvines Landing, Pender Harbour.

Facilities: None at uninhabited Cape Cockburn. Air fills, boat charters, rentals, and launching, camping and accommodations at Egmont and Pender Harbour.

Access: Cape Cockburn is on Malaspina Strait at the westernmost extreme of Nelson Island, 7 nautical miles (13 kilometers) northwest of Pender Harbour.

Charter, rent or launch at Pender Harbour, go 7 nautical miles (13 kilometers) north to Cape Cockburn, anchor or tie up on the shore, and go down.

Comments: Magnificent spot to sit and sun on the rocks.

Cape Cockburn

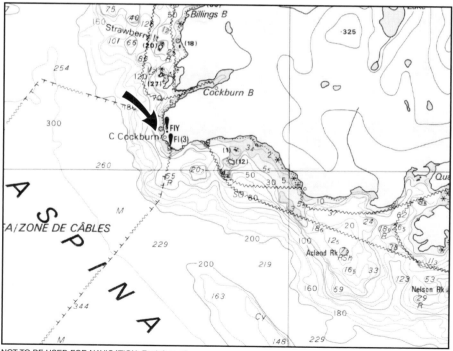

NOT TO BE USED FOR NAVIGATION: For information
on obtaining navigational charts see page 318.
This is a portion of L/C-3512.

2 Nautical Miles

FEARNEY BLUFFS
Boat Dive

Skill: Expert divers, guided intermediate divers and snorkelers

Why go: Divers always rave about one thing at Fearney – the massive cloud sponges!

Fearney is the most fabulous wall, with the most glorious cloud sponges. Chimney sponges, too. The granite wall drops straight down: deep, deep, deep. The feeling of space is incredible. Back off the wall to see the whole scene and so you do not damage the delicate sponges. Come close, carefully, to look at smaller creatures. We saw flaming red slipper cucumbers. Staghorn bryozoans that look like hard coral. At 100 feet (30 meters), several small branching dwarf gorgonian corals. They were 6 inches (15 centimeters) tall and bright red. *Paragorgia arborea,* another species of red gorgonian coral is also found at this site. Large fans of these red gorgonians, some 3 feet (1 meter) high, live at depths of 165 feet (50 meters) and deeper in Agamemnon Channel – beyond sport-diving limits. This gorgonian coral occurs in few sites in the world, maybe nowhere else.

We also saw tiny green urchins, red dahlia anemones, transparent sea squirts, orange cup corals and yellow ones. Tiger, quillback and yelloweye rockfish, a couple of lingcod. Giant barnacles, rock scallops, feather stars on the wall. Moon jellyfish in the open water. A silvery cloud of herring. Stopping in the shallows is a pleasure, too, with heaps of purple sea stars, crabs, seaperch and maroon-and-gray striped painted greenlings which I love for their color. For their markings.

It is beautiful all the way. But somehow nothing really matters at Fearney Bluffs except the red coral. The white puffs of cloud sponge. The wall.

Bottom and Depths: A wall. Smooth granite plunges to 280 feet (86 meters) with undercuts in places. Narrow rocky ledges for safety stops at 10 to 20 feet (3 to 6 meters) close alongside the wall.

Hazards: Current, with some swirly water on large tidal exchanges. Dive on slack.

Telephone: Irvines Landing, mouth of Pender Harbour.

Facilities: A magnificent spot to sit and sun on the rocks after diving. Air fills, boat charters, boat rentals, water taxi and launching; hot showers, camping and accommodations at Pender Harbour and Egmont.

Access: Fearney Bluffs are located at the south end of Agamemnon Channel almost in Malaspina Strait. The site is 2 nautical miles (4 kilometers) northwest of Pender Harbour – you will see the bluffs for a long way when you approach from this direction. The dive is 12 nautical miles (22 kilometers) from Egmont; go northwest then south through Agamemnon Channel to Fearney Bluffs.

Charter, take a water taxi, rent a boat or take your own boat. Launch at Pender Harbour or Egmont and go to Fearney. The bluff above water mirrors what is below. Famous last words but I'll risk it – you can't miss the bluff. Fearney is exposed to southeast wind; pick a calm day. It is too deep to anchor and better not to anchor anyway as you might damage the cloud sponges. Dive from a "live" boat. Or tie up at the wall – lots of cables to tie onto.

Comments: Take a light to pick up color on the dive.

Gearing up at Fearney Bluffs

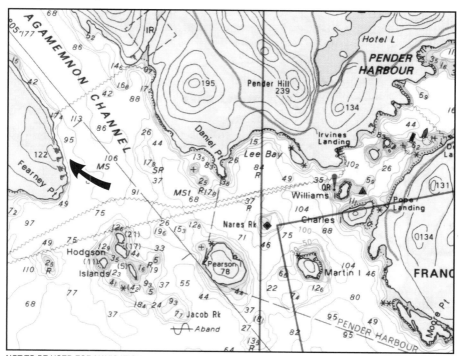

NOT TO BE USED FOR NAVIGATION: For information
on obtaining navigational charts see page 318.
This is a portion of 3311.

1 Nautical Mile

BENEATH THE POWER LINES
Boat Dive

Skill: Expert divers and guided intermediates over the wall. All divers and snorkelers on ledge.

Why go: Sponges! Glistening like spun ivory, tentacles of cloud sponges twist from the stark, dark wall beneath the power lines – some as large as 3 feet (1 meter) wide. They reach out and down. Many are shiny yellow. Look for chimney sponges too.

As at Fearney Bluffs, this sponge site is also well known for the large fans of red gorgonians up to 3 feet (1 meter) high that live at depths of 165 feet (50 meters) and deeper. I did not see any fans beneath the power lines as I limited my maximum depth to 125 feet (38 meters) – stayed within sport-diving limits. We enjoyed a slow cruise along the wall. And there's another whole dive to enjoy in the shallows.

While I think of Agamemnon as being great for those who "think deep", this site is also a wonderful dive for mixed groups because of the life on the ledge. Pile perch and sculpins are everywhere. Look for sea lemons, painted greenlings in the kelp, tube-worms, bryozoans, sea peaches and encrusting sponges on the rocks.

Bottom and Depths: Rocky, shallow bottom in cove. Brown bottom kelp covers the rocks. Bull kelp, especially in summer. From the cove, the bottom rolls gently down to a sharp lip, or ledge, at 60 to 70 feet (18 to 21 meters) – depending on tide height – where the drop-off plunges. Accordion-like lines on the chart show the series of ledges in rapid succession – a dramatic plunge into Agamemnon Channel.

Hazards: Depth, wind, minimal current and some bull kelp, in summer. If anchoring and it is windy, look at wind direction and consider surface current it will create. Dive near slack. Consider wind when planning the direction of your dive. Do not dive on the ebb if wind is pushing the water in the same direction. Make a dive plan for depth as well, and carry it out – these depths are so alluring. Carry a knife for kelp.

Telephones: • Outside ferry terminal at Earls Cove, 1½ nautical mile (2¾ kilometers) northeast. • At Egmont Marina, outside the Backeddy Pub, 4 nautical miles (7 kilometers) northeast around corner in Skookumchuck Narrows.

Facilities: None in Agamemnon Channel. Charters and launching at Egmont and Pender Harbour.

Access: Beneath the Power Lines site is at the northern end of Agamemnon Channel on the eastern shore. It is 4 nautical miles (7 kilometers) southwest around the corner from the marina at Egmont, and 9 nautical miles (17 kilometers) north of Pender Harbour.

Charter or launch at Egmont or Pender Harbour, go to the power lines and anchor in the cove opposite Caldwell Island in Agamemnon Channel. Boats with a tender could do a slow drift along the wall.

Comments: Agamemnon Channel – for divers who think deep.

Cloud sponge in Agamemnon Channel

NOT TO BE USED FOR NAVIGATION: For information
on obtaining navigational charts see page 318.
This is a portion of L/C 3512.

2 Nautical Miles

SUTTON ISLETS
Kayak Dive or Boat Dive

Skill: Intermediate and expert divers. All divers with guide.

Why go: Dive into the famous – or infamous – Skookumchuck Narrows. And you could make it in ten minutes by dive-kayak from your campsite or cabin at Egmont Marina to this varied, rich site.
Tiger rockfish flash their orange and black stripes beneath the ledges, swimming scallops clap up from the bottom. Lots of them here. We saw heaps of crab shells, leavings of octopuses. And the nooks and crannies down the rocky ledges of the Sutton Islets are perfect places for wolf-eels to lurk. Bright green lettuce kelp, brown bottom kelp, and bull kelp provide hiding places for urchins, crabs and pile perch. Sea stars decorate the rocks. At the base of the rocky wall, look for mauve hydrocoral.
After the dive, there are convenient cold-water taps for washing gear. Coin-operated hot showers. Food, fireplace, and sometimes live music in the Backeddy Pub.

Bottom and Depths: The rocky shore cascades down with easy-to-stop-at ledges. One at 80 to 90 feet (24 to 27 meters), depending on tide height. Bull kelp, especially in summer. Lots of lettuce kelp and brown bottom kelp.

Hazards: Current, boats, bull kelp. Dive on slack; the window of time to dive is small. The back eddies are unpredictable. Charter boats often do it as a drift dive. Only expert divers with a great deal of current experience should dive this without a "live" boat. If traveling by dive-kayak, pick a day with a tidal exchange of 5 feet (1½ meters) or less and dive precisely on slack so that you can get back to your kayak. Ascending, listen for boats – many speedboats pass through the channel and go into the marina. Do not ascend through open water: use the kelp as a protected place and hug the contours of the bottom all the way to the surface at the island. Carry a knife for kelp.

Telephone: Egmont Marina, outside Backeddy Pub.

Facilities: None at the Sutton Islets. At the marina on the western shore, air fills, water taxi, boat rentals, charter boats, launching, restrooms, coin-operated hot showers. Cold-water taps for washing gear. Cabins, camping and bunkhouse – bring your sleeping bag. Also restaurant and pub. Also charters out of Pender Harbour. Dive-kayak rentals in Vancouver.

Access: The Sutton Islets are in Skookumchuck Narrows north of Egmont. The dive is less than ½ nautical mile (1 kilometer) offshore from the Egmont side of the channel, and is a 10-minute paddle.
Go by charter, water taxi or rental boat, launch your own boat or go by dive-kayak. The closest point to go from by dive-kayak is Egmont Marina. It is less than ½ nautical mile (1 kilometer) to the channel side of the southernmost of the Sutton Islets, and is a 10-minute paddle. Or you could rent a boat at Egmont or paddle ¾ nautical mile (1½ kilometers) from the public ramp at Egmont to the site. We paddled out to a small cove on the channel side to gear up. We dived on a high tide at the turn to ebb and worked southward toward the marker for the first half of the dive. Then when almost half our air was gone we drifted almost back to the cove with the current – there was a small back eddy in the cove that slowed us down when we reached it.

Comments: More good diving nearby at the northern Sutton Islet, also easily reachable by dive-kayak. Walter, the wolf-eel, used to reside in a den on its western side.

Launching dive-kayaks, Sutton Islets at distant marker

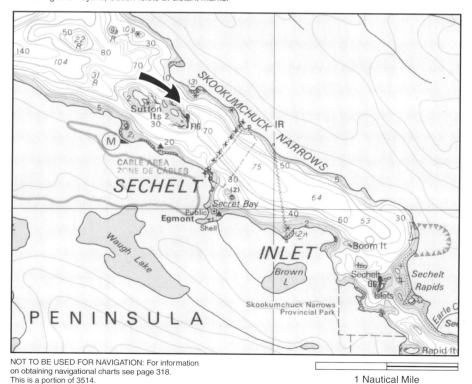

NOT TO BE USED FOR NAVIGATION: For information
on obtaining navigational charts see page 318.
This is a portion of 3514.

1 Nautical Mile

ISLET AT SECRET BAY
Shore Dive or Kayak Dive

Current Table: Sechelt Rapids
Subtract 10 minutes

Skill: Intermediate and expert divers

Why go: Only a few sites where you can dive from shore and see swimming scallops. Egmont is one of them. That's what lured me here – millions of swimming scallops.

A circuit of the islet reveals many other things, as well. Beautiful red tube worms in the shallows. Gum boot chitons, alabaster nudibranchs, sea lemons, shrimp and bright orange branches of dead man's finger sponges. Deeper in the kelp, greenlings are all over the place. Sea peaches and transparent sea squirts cling to the wall. Brilliant red-and-black striped tiger rockfish hide under ledges. Swimming scallops dot the bottom everywhere, raining up around you when your shadow passes over them. A real treat.

Bottom and Depths: Rocky bottom undulates down quickly all around the islet. Bull kelp and lots of bottom kelp from 20 to 40 feet (6 to 12 meters). Some big rocks, crevices and overhangs. Then the wall drops abruptly, leveling off to silty sand at 75 to 85 feet (23 to 26 meters). Swimming scallops all over the bottom on the channel side of the island.

Hazards: Current, boats, long swim and bull kelp. Dive near the slack. Listen for boats and stay close to the side of the islet all the way to the surface. Save some energy for the swim back, especially if the current starts up. Carry a knife for kelp.

Telephones: • Bathgate's Store & Marina, outside. • Egmont Marina, outside the Backeddy Pub. It is 1 mile (1½ kilometers) north on Maple Road.

Facilities: Restrooms and hot showers during store hours. Water taxi and boat rentals. Launching ramp close-by at foot of Bradwynne Road. Air fills and charters nearby, too. Dive-kayak rentals in Vancouver.

Access: The islet is in the center of the entrance to Secret Bay at Skookumchuck Narrows, top of the Sunshine Coast. The dive is 15 minutes off Sunshine Coast Highway 101 at Egmont. The Egmont Road turnoff is immediately south of Earls Cove. From Langdale, 1½ hours to Egmont Road.

At Egmont Road, follow signs toward Skookumchuck Narrows Provincial Park. The road twists and turns. Just past the park you reach the government wharf at Egmont. Drop your gear beside the wharf and return up the hill. Room for three or four cars to park at the left-hand side. You need about 15 minutes to swim from the dock to the islet.

Kayak-divers can launch from the public ramp. Just before reaching the government wharf, turn north into Maple Road. Turn right again into Bradwynne Road and immediately right down the ramp. Wheelchair access at this public ramp; but no level place to park close beside the ramp.

To get to Egmont Road
• From Langdale, drive north on Highway 101 to Egmont Road, which is 13 miles (21 kilometers) past the Madeira Park turnoff at Pender Harbour. When you see signs to Skookumchuck Narrows Provincial Park, turn right into Egmont Road.
• From Earls Cove, go ⅔ mile (1 kilometer) and turn left into Egmont Road.

Comments: Divers are welcomed at Egmont.

Swimming scallops

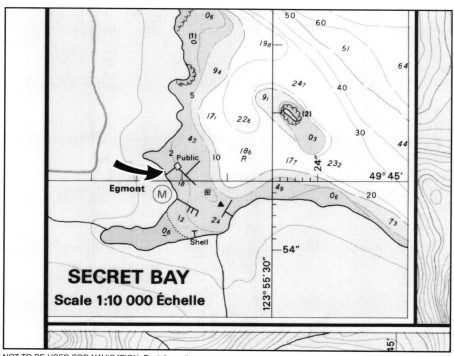

SECRET BAY

Scale 1:10 000 Échelle

NOT TO BE USED FOR NAVIGATION: For information
on obtaining navigational charts see page 318.
This is a portion of 3312.

500 Yards

KLEIN LAKE
Shore Dive

Tide Table: None, non-tidal freshwater lake

Skill: Intermediate and expert divers

Why go: Super-easy night dive site at your campsite, super-easy way to rinse salt water off gear, different life under the water.

Klein Lake offered a surprise. We went for a night dive looking for freshwater crayfish – crawdads I called them as a kid. But we found salamanders, bright orange, slipping up from the silt without disturbing it, swimming in the open water, then slipping into the silt again. They were 2 to 6 inches (5 to 15 centimeters) long, had four feet and a long flat tail. They looked smooth and sleek. They are probably rough-skinned newts, the most common tailed amphibians in British Columbia, according to biologists we talked with later, though they did not look rough to us. In addition, their coloration is supposed to be orange on the underside, brown to reddish brown on top. We saw only orange. I wonder! Upon reading, the habits of the animals we saw did not totally fit any description we could find. One thing is known. You might find them in many ponds and small lakes. But seeing them might be limited to the aquatic phase of their life in May and June. Another book said males become smooth skinned and orange color in winter when breeding. So much to learn.

I see the possibility of a new challenge out there: new species to discover and describe; a whole world of biological knowledge to be enlarged upon by divers observing the life-style of salamanders and newts, amphibians who live a double life. One life on land, one beneath the water.

Bottom and Depths: Gradually deepens from log-clogged shoreline to who knows how deep in the middle of the lake.

Hazards: Silt. The silt in this lake was arm-length deep. Weight yourself carefully so you can hover above the bottom.

Telephone: Earls Cove ferry terminal, 4 miles (7 kilometers) from the dive. Return to Egmont Road, then Highway 101 and head north.

Facilities: Klein Lake Recreation Site offers spacious, private, treed campsites, with picnic tables, pit toilets and fire rings. Camp a few steps from the dive entry and come up from a night dive to cook dinner over a campfire.

Access: Klein Lake is off Egmont Road – the dive is 15 minutes off Sunshine Coast Highway 101 near the top of Sechelt Peninsula. Egmont Road is 5 minutes south of Earls Cove. From Langdale, 1½ hours north to Egmont Road.

At Egmont Road, follow signs toward Skookumchuck Narrows Provincial Park. Go 1 mile (1½ kilometers) and turn right into North Lake Forest Service Road. Go along this gravel road for 1¼ miles (2 kilometers). Past North Lake at a fork in the road, turn right and continue ⅔ mile (1 kilometer) to Klein Lake Recreation Site. At the fork in the road here, again go right and continue ½ mile (¾ kilometer) to a campsite beside the lake. This one is ideal, but if already occupied, many more campsites beside the lake.

To get to Egmont Road
• From Langdale, drive north on Highway 101 to Egmont Road. Egmont Road is 13 miles (21 kilometers) past the Madeira Park turnoff at Pender Harbour. When you see signs to Skookumchuck Narrows Provincial Park, turn right into Egmont Road.
• From Earls Cove, go ⅔ mile (1 kilometer) and turn left into Egmont Road.

Comments: Water so clear. If you do not stir it up – it feels like you can see forever.

Waiting for dark at Klein Lake

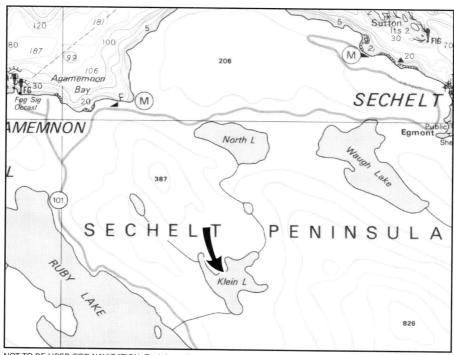

NOT TO BE USED FOR NAVIGATION: For information
on obtaining navigational charts see page 318.
This is a portion of 3514.

1 Nautical Mile

SECHELT RAPIDS
[SKOOKUMCHUCK]
Boat Dive

Skill: Expert divers. Intermediate divers with guide.

Why go: Winter and summer, the hottest spot to dive in British Columbia has to be Sechelt tidal rapids. The ocean floor is like a brilliant flower garden of the sea.

Sechelt Rapids – known locally as the Skookumchuck – is the fastest-flowing tidal rapids in the world. And destined to become a mecca for world divers. The Skookumchuck is surf-washed from top to bottom. It churns. Four times every day with every turn of the tide. This eggbeater action nurtures an intriguing array of marine creatures. Many of the invertebrates look like they are from the shallows, but at Skookumchuck the "shallow" life lives deep. The marine scene here – even at 100 feet (30 meters) – looks to me like a west-coast tidepool more than anything else.

The Skookumchuck is in constant motion. At the same time, diving the Skookumchuck is a slow motion flight into a field of wildflowers: pink, powder blue, and mint-green anemones blowing in the wind. Or an informal garden: these delicate flowers of the sea are heaped like blossoms in a flamboyant Renoir painting. Or a formal garden: we see pebble patterns, Japanese style, on the ocean floor. White encrusting sponge covers the rocks, lighting up the depths with reflected sunlight. Yellow encrusting sponge covers the remaining boulders and jagged rocks that are not bright white or pale pastel. Tiny orange cup corals polka dot whatever surface is left to cling to.

On the way up we see two orange-and-black-striped tiger rockfish beneath a dark ledge, a brown Irish lord, tube worms, purple urchins, giant barnacles, a school of black rockfish, kelp greenlings flashing past. You might see a Puget Sound king crab. An octopus. Purple sea stars, as always, are heaped in the shallows. While blue sea stars – from deep to shallow – splay their knobby fingers throughout this exotic undersea garden.

It's rich. Potentially dangerous. Worth planning for.

Bottom and Depths: Huge boulders spill in heaps into a gorge to the bright sandy bottom at 100 to 110 feet (30 to 34 meters).

Hazards: Current, upwellings, and downwellings: 15- to 16-knot (28- to 30-kilometer/hour) currents sometimes race through Skookumchuck. At slack tides when divers go, a great many boats pass through the narrows, too. One inlet resident coaches boat captains through. Stories of a 50-foot (15-meter) fishing boat flipping in the Skookumchuck are rampant at the pub. I've heard that Skookum Island trembles with large tidal exchanges – *not* the day to go.

Dive on a day when it is likely you can dive under control – even then you *must* have a pickup boat. No diver's flag will help you if you pop up unexpectedly beneath a boat – you do not have to fly through these rapids willy-nilly and out of control. Pick your dive time carefully. Winter is best when tidal exchanges are smaller and less boat traffic – visibility is better, too. Your first time, go with a charter operator who knows Skookumchuck, dive with a reliable buddy you know well. And enjoy.

Telephones: • At Egmont: Outside Bathgate's Marina, above the government wharf. • Outside Backeddy Pub at Egmont Marina, north of Egmont. • At Sechelt Inlet: Tillicum Marina Resort, Tillicum Bay. • Lighthouse Pub, beside government wharf at Porpoise Bay in town of Sechelt.

Facilities: Wilderness camping beside Skookumchuck. Air fills, boat charters and rentals, launching, camping, hot showers, cafés and pubs at Egmont and Sechelt.

Access: Sechelt Rapids is at the northern entry to Sechelt Inlet. It is 17 nautical miles (31 kilometers) north of Porpoise Bay, 1½ nautical miles (3 kilometers) south of Egmont.

Charter, rent or launch at Porpoise Bay or Egmont. Choose a day when maximum current speed on both sides of slack (ebb or flood) is less than 5 knots (9 kilometers/hour). Be ready 30 minutes before predicted slack – it is probably the time to dive. But as always at a high-current site, be there ahead of time ready to go since the currents do not always perform as predicted.

To dive the gorge on a flood, go to the northwest tip of the islet on the east side of the islets that are north of Sechelt Rapids. To dive the gorge on the ebb, enter at the opposite end of it. (See the map on page 128 and the arrows on the nautical chart on this page.) Watch and wait for the current to slow down; roll off the boat and head down. Leave a boat tender *experienced with Sechelt Rapids* ready to pick you up. When the current turns and gathers speed, time to end your dive.

To get to Sechelt Rapids
• From Porpoise Bay, go north: you will pass Salmon Inlet and Narrows Inlet. You are almost there when you pass Skookum Island and then Rapid Islet on the left-hand side. Speedboat Pass is between two of the northernmost of the Sechelt Islets in Sechelt Rapids. It is between the islet in the center and the islet east of it.
• From Egmont, go south: the first islets you reach are the Sechelt Islets. Speedboat Pass is between the islet in the center and the islet to the east of it.

Comments: Before diving Sechelt Rapids, if you have time, hike to Roland Point at Skookumchuck Narrows Provincial Park to see the spectacle of the rapids from shore. The footpath heads south from Egmont Road immediately west of Egmont. Room for two or three cars to park beside a map of the trail. Check the current table for Sechelt Rapids and plan to arrive at maximum flow. Allow 45 minutes to walk to Roland Point. Another 45 minutes to return.

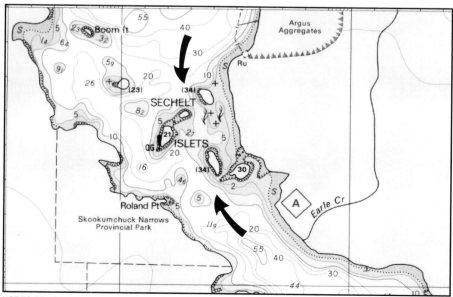

NOT TO BE USED FOR NAVIGATION: For information
on obtaining navigational charts see page 318.
This is a portion of 3514.

½ Nautical Mile

Gardens of anemones

A rose star

Off to Iron Mines by water taxi from Lund

By single and double kayaks to dive wreck of *Adventurer*

CHAPTER 3
Powell River and North

Pink snakelock anenomes in Jervis Inlet

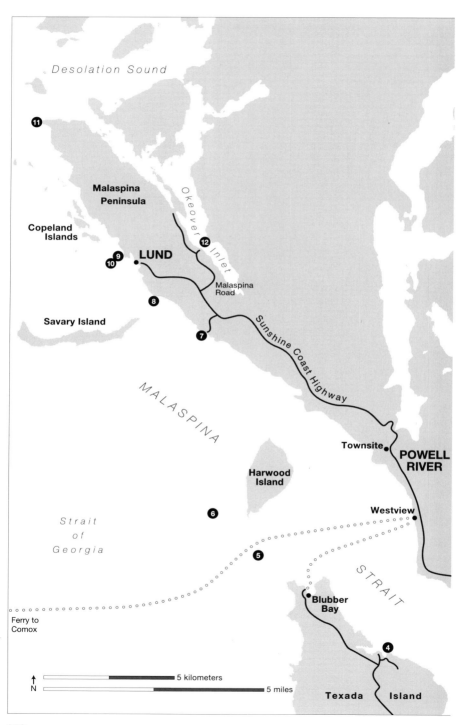

Desolation Sound

Malaspina
Peninsula

Copeland
Islands

LUND

Okeover Inlet

Malaspina
Road

Savary Island

Sunshine Coast Highway

MALASPINA

Strait
of
Georgia

Harwood
Island

Townsite

POWELL
RIVER

Westview

STRAIT

Ferry to
Comox

Blubber
Bay

5 kilometers

N

5 miles

Texada   Island

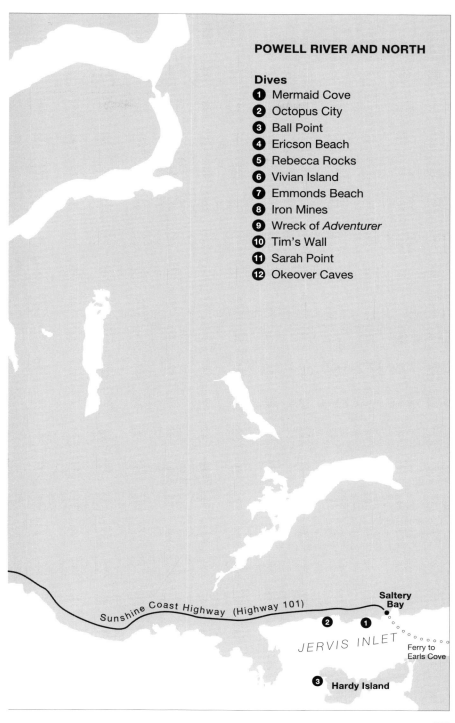

POWELL RIVER AND NORTH

Dives
1. Mermaid Cove
2. Octopus City
3. Ball Point
4. Ericson Beach
5. Rebecca Rocks
6. Vivian Island
7. Emmonds Beach
8. Iron Mines
9. Wreck of *Adventurer*
10. Tim's Wall
11. Sarah Point
12. Okeover Caves

Saltery Bay

Sunshine Coast Highway (Highway 101)

JERVIS INLET

Ferry to Earls Cove

Hardy Island

SERVICE INFORMATION *
Powell River and North

Charts: Canadian Hydrographic Service
- 3311 Sunshine Coast–Vancouver Harbour to Desolation Sound (small-craft chart)
- 3312 Jervis Inlet and Desolation Sound (navigation atlas and cruising guide)
- L/C-3512 Strait of Georgia, Central Portion
- L/C-3513 Strait of Georgia, Northern Portion
- 3514 Jervis Inlet
- 3536 Plans–Strait of Georgia
- 3538 Desolation Sound and Sutil Channel
- 3555 Plans–Vicinity of Redonda Islands and Loughborough Inlet
- 3559 Malaspina Inlet, Okeover Inlet and Lancelot Inlet

Tide and Current Tables: Canadian Hydrographic Service
Tide and Current Table, Volume 5 and *Volume 6*

Diving Emergency Telephone Numbers
Dial 911: Say "I have a scuba diving emergency".

Vancouver Hospital & Health Sciences Centre: Dial (604) 875-4111 and say "I have a scuba diving emergency. I want the hyperbaric physician on call".

If medical personnel are unfamiliar with scuba diving emergencies, ask them to telephone DAN (Divers Alert Network): (919) 684-8111, then say "I have a scuba diving emergency".

Other Useful Numbers

Weather – Continuous Marine Broadcast (CMB) recorded, 24 hours; listen for weather in the Strait of Georgia, telephone
- At Comox: (604) 339-0748

Shellfish Infoline (red tide hotline), recorded: (604) 666-3169
Sportfishing Information Line, recorded: 1-800-663-9333

• Dive Shops
Westview
Emerald Sea Diving Adventures
4675 Marine Avenue
Powell River BC V8A 2L2
(604) 485-7637; fax (604) 485-7647
(Guiding for shore dives and boat dives.)

Lund
Good Diving & Kayaking
Lund Hotel
PO Box 47
Lund BC V0N 2G0
(604) 483-3223 – both fax and telephone. Telephone to arrange for reception of fax.
(Waterfront and roadside air fills; also guiding, dive packages with accommodation and dive-kayak rentals.)

• Air Station
Westview
Pacific Northwest Diving Adventures
Located at Beach Gardens Resort
7074 Westminster Avenue
Powell River
Mailing address: 122 West Kings Road
North Vancouver BC V7N 2L8
(604) 485-0916; telephone to arrange for air fills.
(Waterfront and roadside air fills. Also boat dives.)

• Boat Charters and Rentals
Out of Westview for Malaspina Strait and Strait of Georgia

Champagne Lady and *Shoal Searcher*
Pacific Northwest Diving Adventures
Located at Beach Gardens Resort
7074 Westminster Avenue
Powell River
Mailing address: 122 West Kings Road
North Vancouver BC V7N 2L8
Powell River: (604) 485-0916
Campbell River: (604) 935-6711
Vancouver: (604) 983-9454
(Day, weekend, week-long and longer liveaboard charters out of Westview, Vancouver and Campbell River. Also a land-based option at Cortes Island. Wheelchair divers welcome.)

Aqua-Knotts III
Powell River Divers
4351 Marine Avenue
Powell River BC V8A 2J9
(604) 485-4526
(Charters out of Westview.)

Sun Runner
Emerald Sea Diving Adventures
4675 Marine Avenue
Powell River BC V8A 2L2
(604) 485-7637; fax (604) 485-7647
(Day charters out of Westview and other points, as the boat is trailerable.)

Out of Lund for Malaspina Strait and Strait of Georgia and out of Okeover Inlet

Clam Raker
Mystery Reef Charters
RR 2, Malaspina Road, C-7
Lund BC V0N 2G0
(604) 483-9906
(Charters out of Lund and Okeover Inlet to Desolation Sound.)

Dave's Boat Rental
PO Box 61
Lund BC V0N 2G0
(604) 483-3667 and 483-3484
(Boat rentals summer only, May to end of September.)

Good Diving & Kayaking
Lund Hotel
PO Box 47
Lund BC V0N 2G0
(604) 483-3223 – both fax and telephone. Telephone to arrange for reception of fax.
(Dive-kayak rentals: single kayaks, one diver with gear. Also a double kayak for two divers with gear. And packages.)

Lund Water Taxi Ltd.
General Delivery
Lund BC V0N 2G0
(604) 483-9749
(Water taxi out of Lund, book in advance.)

Major Rock
Gateway Charters
General Delivery
Lund BC V0N 2G0
(604) 483-4820
(Charters out of Lund: they range from Texada to Desolation Sound, Okeover Inlet and beyond. Custom dive packages using your choice of accommodation: the local hotel, rustic campground, your own RV or a bed and breakfast.)

Sea Days
Stan's Service
3480 Marine Avenue
Powell River BC V8A 2H4
(604) 485-2144
(Charters out of Okeover Inlet.)

Out of Vancouver Island for Strait of Georgia

My Joan
Sail Pacific Yacht Charters
PO Box 1555
Comox BC V9N 8A2
(604) 339-7850 or 336-2150
(Liveaboard sail/dive charters out of Comox to Vivian, Mitlenatch, Denman, Hornby islands and Sunshine Coast.)

• Boat Launching

At Saltery Bay for Jervis Inlet
Saltery Bay Picnic Site Ramp
(Launching for Jervis Inlet. Good, medium to high tides; accommodate boats up to 30 feet [9 meters] at high tide. Pit toilets. Telephone at ferry terminal.)

Off Highway 101, 2 miles (3 kilometers) past Saltery Bay ferry terminal, and 19 miles (30 kilometers) southeast of Powell River and Westview.

At Westview for Malaspina Strait
Municipal North Harbour Ramp
Foot of Courtenay Street, north end of ferry terminal, Westview (Powell River)
(Concrete ramp on the Strait of Georgia; good at all tides. Telephone and restrooms at south end of ferry terminal .)

At Texada Island for Strait of Georgia
Shelter Point Park Public Ramps
Texada Island, west side
(Concrete launching ramps, one protected with a westerly wind, the second protected with a southeasterly wind. Good at all times except extreme low tides. Year-round camping and pit toilets, telephone at concession stand. Fast food and flush toilets in summer.)

From Blubber Bay, 30 minutes to Shelter Point. Follow signs to Gillies Bay. Just past Gillies Bay, turn right at Shelter Point Road. The park and the two ramps are at the end of it.

Texada Boat Club Ramp
Sturt Bay [Marble Bay]
Texada Island, northeast side
(Concrete ramp. Good at medium to high tides. Limited parking space. No toilets at ramp; telephone outside Texada Island Inn.)

From Blubber Bay, follow signs to Van Anda – takes 15 minutes. At Van Anda, go past the Texada Island Inn, down the hill and bear left onto Marble Bay Road. At the junction, turn right onto Sellentin Street and continue straight. At a three-way fork in the road, Sellentin turns right but you keep going straight on the middle road. At the time of writing, a gray house is at the fork and the middle road is gravel – this road goes to the ramp.

At Lund for Malaspina Strait
Lund Public Ramp
End of Highway 101 North
(Concrete ramp, good at tides of 2 feet [2/3 meter] and greater: launching for Thulin Passage and Malaspina Strait. Telephone, restrooms, café a few steps away at Lund Hotel.)

At north end of Highway 101: go 19 miles (30 kilometers) north of Powell River to the end of the road at Lund.

Dinner Rock Ramp
Dinner Rock Recreation Site
Off Highway 101
(Dirt ramp: launching for car-top boats at Strait of Georgia. Carry over 30 feet [9 meters] of log-strewn cobble beach to the water. Wheelchair accessible pit toilet and camping at launch site. Telephone on Highway 101 outside hotel at Lund. Go to the highway and head north for 5 miles [8 kilometers].)

When 30 minutes north of Powell River, turn left onto Dinner Rock Road, a steep dirt road, open May to October. The turnoff is immediately southeast of an Okeover Arm Provincial Park sign at the roadside and 7 miles (11 kilometers) north of Sliammon. From Highway 101, nearly 1 mile (1½ kilometers) to the water. The road is closed in winter.

At Head of Okeover Inlet
Okeover Inlet Public Ramp
Off Malaspina Road
Malaspina Peninsula
(Gravel and concrete ramp: good for boats up to 20 feet [6 meters]. Best at mid-tides of 7 to 8 feet [2 to 2½ meters]; it is difficult to pull forward at high tides. The concrete part of the ramp is exposed at low tides, the gravel part at higher tides. Telephone on float; pit toilets at nearby Okeover Arm Provincial Park campground.)

Off Highway 101, 30 minutes north of Powell River. Past Sliammon look for signs to Okeover Arm Provincial Park. Turn right into Malaspina Road. Go north for 2⅓ miles (3¾ kilometers) to the head of Okeover Inlet, commonly known as Okeover Arm.

• More Information for Boat Divers and Kayak-Divers
Explore for new sites on your own; additional launching ramps, public beaches where you can land, and facilities are listed in the following publications:

Docks and Destinations by Peter Vassilopoulos, Seagraphic Publications, Vancouver, 1994. Available at bookstores. (Scope: Lists marina services, customer services and adjacent facilities, including hot showers, public telephones, launching ramps and entertainment. Illustrated with maps, photographs. From the San Juan Islands through Vancouver, Sunshine Coast and north to Desolation Sound and Port Hardy.)

Small Craft Guide, Volume 2: British Columbia, Boundary Bay to Cortes Island, Canadian Hydrographic Service, 1990. Available where nautical charts are sold. (Scope: Lists launching ramps and facilities.)

Southwestern British Columbia Recreational Atlas compiled by Informap in cooperation with British Columbia Ministry of Environment, Victoria, 1992. Available at bookstores. (Scope: Maps, lists of parks and facilities, wildlife reserves and viewing. Covers southwestern British Columbia coastline from southern border north beyond Desolation Sound and includes all of Vancouver Island.)

• Ferry Information
British Columbia Ferry Corporation
Westview Terminal
4465 Willingdon Avenue
Powell River BC V8A 2M7
Toll-free in BC: 1-800-663-7600. Or
(604) 485-2943.
Telephoning from outside British
Columbia: (604) 386-3431.
(Ferries from Westview to Comox on Vancouver Island; also from Westview to Texada Island.)

British Columbia Ferry Corporation
Saltery Bay Terminal
Saltery Bay BC
Toll-free in BC: 1-800-663-7600. Or
(604) 487-9333.
Telephoning from outside British
Columbia: (604) 386-3431.
(Ferries across Jervis Inlet from Saltery Bay to Earls Cove.)

• Tourist Information
Discover British Columbia
1117 Wharf Street
Victoria BC V8W 2Z2
1-800-663-6000: Toll-free throughout
Canada and the USA, including Hawaii
and parts of Alaska.

Powell River Travel Infocentre
4690 Marine Avenue
Powell River BC V8A 2L1
(604) 485-4701; fax (604) 485-2822

How to go: Powell River is on the mainland of British Columbia but you must take a ferry to get there.
• From Vancouver, go to Horseshoe Bay and take a 40-minute ferry ride to Langdale on the Sechelt Peninsula. Drive for 1¼ hours to Earls Cove and take a 50-minute ferry ride to Saltery Bay. Drive half an hour to Westview which is really the center of Powell River.
• From Sechelt Peninsula, go from Earls Cove to Saltery Bay on the ferry – takes 50 minutes. Then drive to Westview and Powell River in half an hour.
• From Vancouver Island, go to Courtenay; then follow signs to Little River ferry terminal at Comox. Take a 1¼-hour ferry ride to Westview and Powell River.

* All of this service information is subject to change.

MERMAID COVE
Shore Dive

Skill: All divers and snorkelers

Why go: To meet a mermaid in the underwater valley at Mermaid Cove. Her hand reaches out. At first sight, it is almost as if to fend you off – then her gesture invites you to the green depths.

When I first saw the mermaid statue, a rockfish was in her hair, like a comb holding it back. We circled cautiously. Her tail rests lightly beside a rock, and she looks startled as if she might swim away. If there were nothing else to see, the timid mermaid would be enough, but look, too, for the nearby resident octopus. Also timid. Other sights at Mermaid Cove include dozens of blackeye gobies in the bottom kelp in the shallows. We saw many kelp crabs, orange dead man's finger sponges, sculpins, rockfish and lingcod; a garden of anemones – dahlia, snakelock and plumose, and you might find bottles.

To dive deep, roll over the edge of the drop-off on your right. Once over the prickly green urchins, you are into the never-never land of big chimney sponges curving down the steep slope like huge pipes. Ratfish, shimmering blue and silver, soar slowly beneath you, lazily rippling their pectoral fins. You may see a red-and-black flash as a tiger rockfish dashes into a crevice. Decorator crabs. And white puffs of cloud sponges below. Deeper, yelloweye rockfish.

The elegant bronze mermaid stands 9 feet (2¾ meters) tall. Beneath the water she looks even larger. The marine life, too, seems bigger than life at Mermaid Cove. The romantic idea of the underwater mermaid statue was conceived by Jodi Willoughby when her husband, Jim, provided a wet suit for the model of sculptor Elek Imredy. In 1970 Imredy created the bronze statue of Girl in a Wet Suit that is on a rock off Stanley Park in Vancouver. From that time, the Willoughbys spearheaded the mermaid project, and many divers pitched in to collect money for it. Nineteen years later Jodi's dream was realized. The mermaid statue was completed by scuba diver/sculptor Simon Morris and ceremoniously sunk at Saltery Bay in 1989.

Bottom and Depths: Rocky bottom covered with lettuce kelp is in the valley leading to where the mermaid is at 50 to 60 feet (15 to 18 meters), depending on tide height. West of the mermaid, smooth rock undulates to a drop-off 150 feet (46 meters) offshore. Crevices are along the wall. A compass is useful to guide you back over the undulating bottom.

Hazards: Boats and poor visibility in summer. Listen for boats: ascend up the marker buoy chain and then snorkel to shore. Or navigate to shore, staying close to the bottom all the way, well out of the way of boats.

Telephone: At Saltery Bay roadside, 300 yards (275 meters) uphill from ferry terminal.

Facilities: Changerooms, cold-water showers for divers to wash gear, wheelchair-accessible toilet and picnic table. Campsites, pit toilets and fire rings at campground at Mermaid Cove; lots of big trees around each campsite clearing. Boat launching at Saltery Bay picnic site, 1¼ miles (2 kilometers) up Highway 101 toward Powell River.

Access: Mermaid Cove is at Saltery Bay Provincial Park on Jervis Inlet near Powell River and is reached by Sunshine Coast Highway 101. Divers arriving by boat should take care not to drop anchor on the mermaid sculpture which is close-by the floating dive flag and inshore from it.

From Highway 101, turn into Saltery Bay campground. Go to the Mermaid Cove sign that says "No Parking Beyond This Point". Drive to the water, where only handicapped persons are allowed to park, and drop gear. Easy entry down the path and zigzag concrete ramp. Because the ramp stops short of the water at lower tides, wheelchair access only with tides of 10 feet (3 meters) and greater. To see the mermaid, follow the shallow canyon out from shore. Or swim to the dive flag and go down. Dive the left wall face to see anemones and look for old bottles; the right face to see sponges.

To get to Saltery Bay Provincial Park campground
• From Saltery Bay ferry landing, go on Highway 101 for ⅔ mile (1 kilometer).
• From Powell River, drive south on 101 for 30 minutes to the campground.

Comments: You might want to see *The Emerald Sea: The Emerald Princess* video showing the sculptor at Mermaid Cove and the mermaid sinking into the sea. It is available in Powell River.

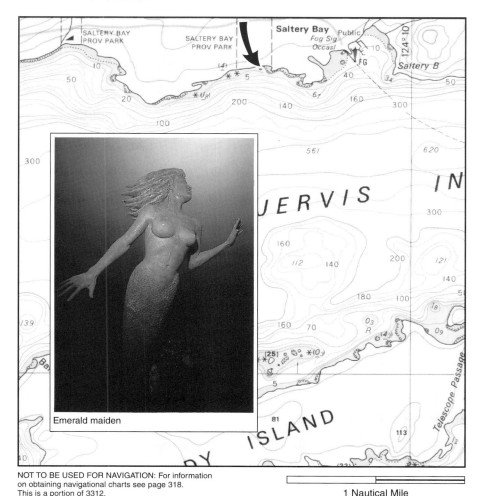

Emerald maiden

NOT TO BE USED FOR NAVIGATION: For information
on obtaining navigational charts see page 318.
This is a portion of 3312.

1 Nautical Mile

OCTOPUS CITY
Shore Dive

Skill: All divers

Why go: For easy access, a wreck to look for, to explore the spacey boulder garden called Octopus City. And it's a great night dive with lots of ratfish – hundreds of them.
  During the day, we saw two ratfish, flounders rippling over the bottom. A hermit crab tumbling and rolling to escape us. A red rock crab. A purple crab. We saw two octopuses, each hiding beneath a separate boulder, ready to reach out to catch a crab on the sand. Sea pens, dinner-plate-sized sea stars and tube-dwelling anemones are also on the sand. Sparsely scattered orange and white plumose anemones tilt from the tops of the widely spaced boulders. We saw deep purple tube worms, tiny white nudibranchs, peach-colored nudibranchs, delicate alabaster nudibranchs, quillback rockfish and a few lingcod. Seaperch, schools of juvenile rockfish, blackeye gobies and egg cases of moon snails in the eelgrass. At the wreck, many small fish. Night or day, take a light – to see shy octopuses hiding beneath the boulders.
  Octopus City is a good place to check out new gear, a new diving buddy or simply enjoy an uncomplicated dive. But just look and do not take – locally honored as a marine life reserve.

Bottom and Depths: Silty sand, then cobble bottom and eelgrass slopes gently from shore to the white sand. Big-leafed, brown bottom kelp is around the large rocks close to shore. Bright white sand surrounds the widely scattered boulders that range from 60 to 80 feet (18 to 24 meters) deep. The wreck is at 50 to 60 feet (15 to 18 meters).

Hazards: Boats and poor visibility in summer. Listen for boats and use your compass. If you hear a boat, navigate to shore and then snorkel back to the exit point.

Telephone: Saltery Bay, 300 yards (275 meters) from ferry terminal at roadside.

Facilities: Freshwater pump for divers to wash gear, wheelchair-accessible pit toilet, lots of parking space and picnic tables. Air fills in Westview.

Access: Octopus City is in Jervis Inlet near Powell River. It is at Saltery Bay Provincial Park picnic site on Sunshine Coast Highway 101.
  At Saltery Bay picnic site, easy entry down a trail with salmonberries beside it. From the north end of the parking lot, walk 150 paces down the trail. From the end of the trail, cross the rocks. You can sight on Ball Point, or follow a 190-degree compass bearing to an underwater cable. Then follow the cable out to the boulders. From the boulder at the end of the cable, head southeast to the wreck; then through the eelgrass to the ramp. Or, in summer, safer to return to the trail.
  Wheelchair divers could enter at the concrete launching ramp and swim toward the point on the right – it is 300 yards (275 meters) – or go by dive-kayak. When nearing the point, look for the end of the trail, land the kayak, dive and look for the cable.

To get to Saltery Bay picnic site
• From Saltery Bay ferry landing, go on Highway 101 for 2 miles (3 kilometers) to the picnic site.
• From Powell River heading south on Highway 101, drive for 30 minutes. Go 19 miles (30 kilometers) to the picnic site. If you reach the campsite, you've gone too far.

Comments: In winter, watch for Steller sea lions. They come from Scotch Fir Point to explore.

Ratfish

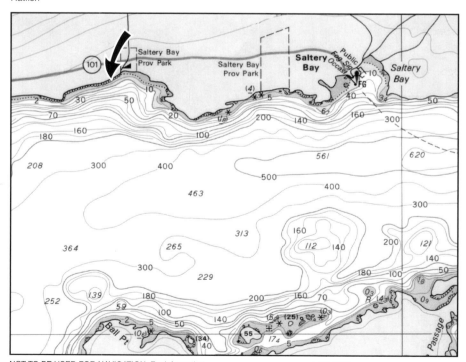

NOT TO BE USED FOR NAVIGATION: For information
on obtaining navigational charts see page 318.
This is a portion of 3514.

1 Nautical Mile

BALL POINT
Kayak Dive or Boat Dive

Skill: All divers

Why go: Cloud sponges – the most fabulous I've seen anywhere – burgeon orange and yellow and white down the steep slopes of Ball Point at Hardy Island.

Pale green and golden bottom kelp decorates the shallows in gossamer folds veiling tube worms, seaperch, alabaster nudibranchs, sea lemons, painted greenlings, sea cucumbers, blackeye gobies and kelp greenlings. We saw seals and rock scallops. Lots of lingcod, juvenile yelloweye rockfish, dahlia anemones, tiger rockfish, some chimney sponges and great puffs of cloud sponges like huge rain clouds in a prairie sunset sky.

Life is in zones. Lots of marine animals in the kelp to 40 feet (12 meters). From 40 to 60 feet (12 to 18 meters), not much to see except red-and-pink striped dahlia anemones. And then sponge, sponge, sponge . . .

If you like cloud sponges – you'll love Ball Point!

Bottom and Depths: Rocky bottom covered with kelp falls away in irregular ledges to a depth of 30 to 40 feet (9 to 12 meters), depending on tide height. Then a steep rock wall slopes down.

Hazards: Some current, small boats, broken fishing line, depth and the possibility of overexertion after diving. Dive near the slack. Listen for boats and ascend close to the bottom all the way to shore, well out of the way of those boats. Carry a knife. Kayak-divers who dive deep should rest before paddling back to avoid overexertion which may increase risk of bends.

Telephone: Saltery Bay, 300 yards (275 meters) uphill from ferry terminal at roadside.

Facilities: Beautiful place for a wilderness picnic on the rocks at Ball Point. Picnic tables, pit toilets and launching ramp at Saltery Bay picnic site. Tenting at Saltery Bay campground. Air fills in Westview.

Access: Ball Point is on the Jervis Inlet side of Hardy Island. From Saltery Bay ramp go 2 nautical miles (4 kilometers) south to Hardy Island. A small cove just south of Ball Point is convenient for anchoring or beaching your boat.

Comments: I went there because of the enthusiastic description of another diver: "Fantastic! It would take three big barrels to hold one sponge!"

Giant cloud sponges

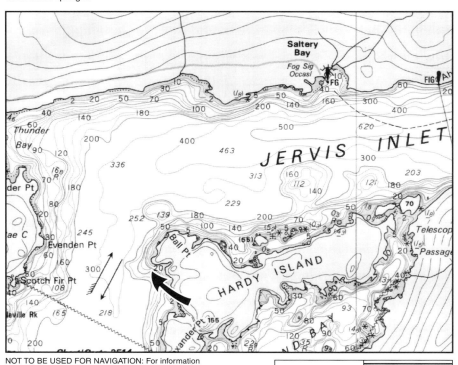

NOT TO BE USED FOR NAVIGATION: For information
on obtaining navigational charts see page 318.
This is a portion of L/C-3512.

2 Nautical Miles

ERICSON BEACH
Shore Dive

Skill: All divers and snorkelers in cove. Intermediate and expert divers deeper.

Why go: Ericson Beach is perfect for a picnic, easy to reach, good for night diving. And the scene is photogenic above and below water. At least four octopuses in residence, an avenue of anemones, troops of small fish in Van Anda Cove.

At Octopus City we find one octopus at home, three dens littered with the leavings of crab. But the occupants are out to lunch. From there we go to the Avenue of Anemones along the submerged power cable that leads away from Octopus City and toward the shore north of the wharf. Orange and white plumose anemones, pink snakelock anemones and swimming scallops crowd the cable. The eyes of scallops clinging to the cable gleam as if lit by electric current. The scallops do not swim but hang on tight to the cable. We wonder if a magnetic corona surrounds it.

Beside the cable, we see orange sea pens, clusters of big gray chimney sponges, tiny white nudibranchs, a lingcod, chitons like oval-shaped buttons, lacy white tube-dwelling anemones. Green bottom kelp brightens it all, with small fish swimming in and out of wisps of gauze-like brown kelp in this ever-so-easy-to-reach cove at Ericson Beach.

Bottom and Depths: In the cove, gently sloping cobbled bottom to the silty sand. Rocky bottom with silt gradually deepens to a depth of 90 to 100 feet (27 to 30 meters) at Octopus City, depending on tide height. The cable slopes up from Octopus City and levels out at 50 to 60 feet (15 to 18 meters) beyond the end of the wharf.

Hazards: Boats, poor visibility and depth. Listen for boats, especially if poor visibility, and ascend cautiously. When a westerly wind is blowing, the water clears up giving visibility of 80 to 100 feet (24 to 30 meters). When a southeasterly is blowing, visibility drops to a range of 40 to 50 feet (12 to 15 meters) or less.

Telephone: Texada Island Inn, outside.

Facilities: None. No dive facilities at Texada, but camping at Shelter Point.

Access: Ericson Beach is on Van Anda Cove at Texada Island. Take the car ferry from Westview to Blubber Bay on Texada, 35 minutes.

From Blubber Bay, drive 15 minutes to the dive. Go to a "T" junction. Gillies Bay and Shelter Point are to the right. You turn left to Van Anda and follow the main road with the yellow line. Go downhill. At the junction immediately past the firehall, stay right and go through town. Go 330 feet (100 meters) past the wharf to a small, rough public access road. Space for one or two cars to park a few steps from the water at Ericson Beach where new divers and snorkelers can poke around among the rocks toward the point. Also lots to see in Van Anda Cove – especially fish.

Intermediate and expert divers could follow a compass bearing from Ericson Beach to the Avenue of Anemones on the suspended cable or to Octopus City.
• To Octopus City: follow a 300- to 330-degree compass bearing to the cable running along the bottom. Or snorkel part way or all the way to the point – but to find Octopus City be sure to stay left of the point until you reach the cable. At the cable, turn right. Follow the cable a short way to the mounds of boulders at Octopus City.
• To the Avenue of Anemones: swim out from Ericson Beach past the point. Dive down and continue on the 300- to 330-degree compass bearing to the suspended cable. When you reach it, turn left and follow the cable as it gradually slopes up and levels off at 50 to 60 feet (15 to 18 meters). If you follow the cable throughout your

dive, you will probably surface beyond the end of the wharf. You could exit at the wharf or swim back to the beach.

Comments: Lots more diving at Texada – I am lured to kayak-dive from Shelter Point, Strait of Georgia side of the island. Dick Island is close-by.

Ericson Beach

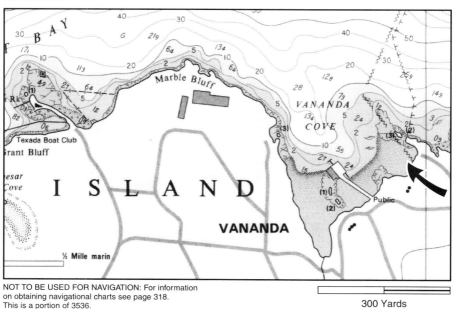

NOT TO BE USED FOR NAVIGATION: For information
on obtaining navigational charts see page 318.
This is a portion of 3536.

300 Yards

REBECCA ROCKS
Boat Dive

Skill: All divers and snorkelers

Why go: Even a dark stormy day feels sunny and bright under water at the beautiful reef undulating around Rebecca Rocks.

It's full of all the life a reef should have: lacy white nudibranchs, bright pink limpets, sea lemons, blue and orange sea stars and alabaster nudibranchs. We saw sea cucumbers and rock scallops. Lots of fish, too. Kelp greenlings everywhere. Lingcod, rock greenlings and millions of very small rockfish. A dogfish in the distance. Often harbor seals present at Rebecca Rocks to snorkel and dive with.

At the south edge of the reef you can drop into sponge country – but to me Rebecca Rocks is most beautiful for the large area of shallow reef swarming with life.

Bottom and Depths: Rocky reef undulates from 30 to 50 feet (9 to 15 meters) deep, depending on tide height. Ledges, overhangs and some bull kelp. Deep on the south side.

Hazards: Wind, current, boats, broken fishing line and deceptively undulating bottom. Dive on the slack. Listen for boats and ascend cautiously; if you hear a boat, stay down until it passes. Carry a knife. Use a compass and watch the current to determine your position so you do not stray too far from your boat.

Telephone: Blubber Bay, Texada Island, beside post office.

Facilities: None. Air fills and charters at Westview and Lund. Charters also out of Comox and Courtenay on Vancouver Island.

Access: The Rebecca Rocks site is 1 nautical mile (2 kilometers) northwest of Texada Island in Algerine Passage, and it is 5 nautical miles (9 kilometers) west of Westview and Powell River. It is very exposed to wind from all directions. Pick a calm day. Charter out of Westview or Lund on the Sunshine Coast; out of Comox on Vancouver Island; or launch at Texada Island or Westview and go to Rebecca Rocks. Anchor, do not tie onto the marker. It is a federal offense to make fast to a marker or tamper with any aid to navigation. Dive anywhere around Rebecca Rocks; choose your location depending upon current direction.

Comments: Rebecca Rocks is a sensitive habitat and local divers honor all waters within ¼ nautical mile (½ kilometer) of it as a reserve. Do not harvest any marine life. A satisfying dive for sightseers and photographers.

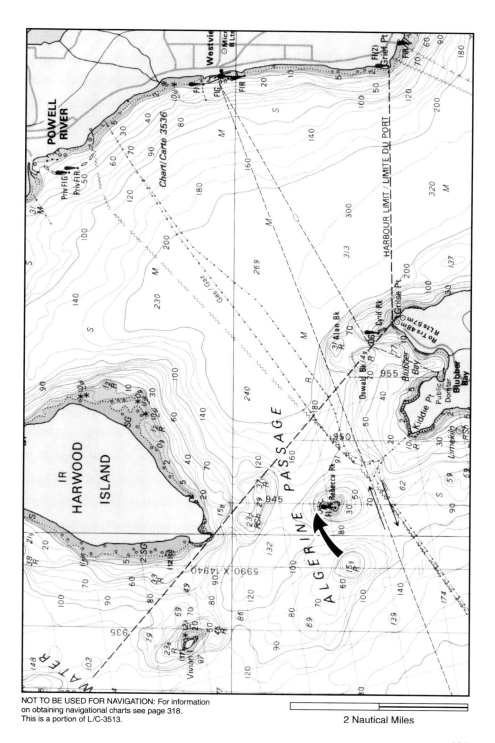

NOT TO BE USED FOR NAVIGATION: For information
on obtaining navigational charts see page 318.
This is a portion of L/C-3513.

2 Nautical Miles

VIVIAN ISLAND
Boat Dive

Skill: Intermediate and expert divers on wall. All divers and snorkelers in shallows.

Why go: Vivian Island is an exceptional three-in-one dive, including a few scraps of wreck in medium depth; a sheer sponge-covered wall dropping off to a depth of 115 to 125 feet (35 to 38 meters), depending on tide height; and abalones, rock scallops and huge limpets in the shallows.

Harbor seals are often at Vivian – fun for snorkelers. The wreck of the *Shamrock,* a 76-foot (23-meter) tug built in Vancouver in 1887, is scattered down the southeast wall within reach of shallow divers. It crashed on the rocks in a fog in December 1926. Sport divers found the remains in 1973. Not much to see today: the shape of a ship is gone but bricks from the boilers might be seen in a depth of 40 to 50 feet (12 to 15 meters). Some say a propeller and parts of a boiler are still down there.

What happened to the anchor and chain winch machinery that have not been recovered? Are they hidden at the bottom of the wall? If you see any of these parts of the steam tug and its equipment, leave them on the bottom for others to enjoy – but make good mental notes and inform the Underwater Archaeological Society of British Columbia of the location of your finds. The society is interested in hearing from divers regarding all shipwrecks and artifacts.

Drifting down the wall, the gorgeous variety of sponges pushed away all thoughts of the *Shamrock.* Lots of lemon yellow cloud sponges. Some orange. Many fluffy white ones. Vase sponges, too. Snakelock anemone tentacles flow from the wall. I saw the orange-and-white stripes of a juvenile yelloweye rockfish hiding in a sponge. Another hanging near the wall. Lots of quillback rockfish.

It's a richly decorated wall – fabulous both going down and coming up. So much to see in the shallows – in the land of urchins, rock scallops, and abalones. You could easily use two tanks of air or more at this site. With 100-foot (30-meter) visibility in winter, it is a photographer's paradise.

Bottom and Depths: Rocky bottom with some boulders at 20 to 30 feet (6 to 9 meters) slopes off quickly to a depth of 40 to 50 feet (12 to 15 meters) and the edge of the creviced wall. Sheer wall drops straight down to a depth of 115 to 125 feet (35 to 38 meters), depending on tide height. Clean white sand at the base of the wall.

Hazards: Wind, current, boats, depth and broken fishing line. Dive near the slack. Listen for boats. Carry a knife.

Telephone: Blubber Bay, Texada Island, beside post office.

Facilities: None at this uninhabited island. Air fills and charters at Westview and Lund. Charters also out of Comox and Courtenay on Vancouver Island.

Access: Vivian Island is at the southern end of Shearwater Passage, 8 nautical miles (15 kilometers) west of Westview and 1 nautical mile (2 kilometers) west of the southern tip of Harwood Island. Vivian Island is exposed to winds from all directions. Pick a calm day. Charter out of Westview or Lund on the Sunshine Coast; out of Comox on Vancouver Island; or launch at Texada Island or Westview. Anchor near the southeast corner of the island in 40 to 50 feet (12 to 15 meters) of water and go down.

Comments: Vivian Island is a sensitive habitat and local divers honor all waters within ½ nautical mile (1 kilometer) of it as a reserve. Do not harvest any marine life.

After diving, row ashore and explore cactus-covered Vivian Island, but be careful not to disturb nesting gulls.

Curious seal in shallows

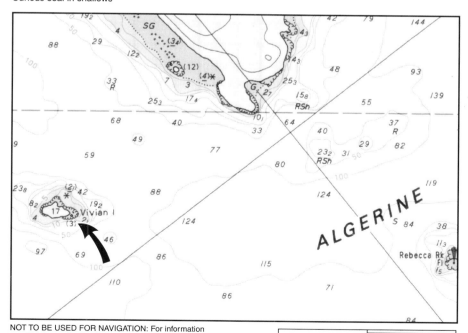

NOT TO BE USED FOR NAVIGATION: For information on obtaining navigational charts see page 318.
This is a portion of 3311.

1 Nautical Mile

EMMONDS BEACH
Shore Dive

Skill: All divers

Why go: Emmonds Beach is good for a quick, quiet dive anytime day or night – no crowds at the site. You can see life typically found both on sand and on rock walls. You can dive shallow or deep.

Swimming over the sand we saw wispy tube-dwelling anemones, sculpins, hermit crabs, flounders and shiners. Masses of rockfish hanging around the rock. Over the rock and down the wall we saw sunflower stars, mustard-yellow trumpet sponges, tiger rockfish, lacy white burrowing cucumbers and several lingcod.

Access is easy over a narrow pebble beach. The swim is a moderate one to the place where the bottom drops off quickly. At low tide it is easier: a large rock that dries at 8-foot (2½-meter) tides is 100 yards (90 meters) offshore. The drop-off is just the other side of this rock. The rock is nicknamed Magoo Rock after the shortsighted cartoon character from the 1950s, because often it is difficult or impossible to see. When I dived at Emmonds Beach, because Magoo Rock was not visible, we set our compasses, swam out over slowly sloping sand till we reached the rock. Then we swam up and over and down the other side where we dropped onto narrow ledges stairstepping steeply down to small cloud sponges at 70 to 80 feet (21 to 24 meters). We also saw the inevitable emerald-eyed ratfish hovering by the wall.

Ratfish and cloud sponges – almost always part of the deep Powell River area underwater scene.

Bottom and Depths: Smooth sand slopes to a depth of 30 to 40 feet (9 to 12 meters) at the base of Magoo Rock. The top of the rock dries at 8-foot (2½-meter) tides. Beyond the rock, the creviced wall drops away in steep, narrow ledges.

Hazards: Boats and poor visibility, in summer. Small boats are moored immediately over the dive site. Listen for boats: If the tide is low, ascend up the side of the rock and swim to shore on the surface. If the tide is high, best to navigate back to shore with a compass.

Telephones: • Sliammon, beside Highway 101; it is 5 miles (8 kilometers) south of Emmonds Road and Highway 101 junction. • Outside Lund Hotel, at the roadside 4½ miles (7½ kilometers) north of Emmonds Road and Highway 101 junction.

Facilities: Pleasant place for a picnic; a very civilized feeling on this cobbled crescent of beach encircled by homes. Parking for one car. Air fills at Lund and Westview.

Access: Emmonds Beach is on Malaspina Strait near Shearwater Passage. It is north of Powell River near Lund, and is ½ mile (¾ kilometer) off Highway 101 at the end of Emmonds Road.

Go down Emmonds Road which is unpaved. When you see the water straight ahead, do not turn right. Go straight to the end of the road. Walk down a short path to the beach and swim straight out toward Magoo Rock. If it is not visible, set your compass on a 150-degree heading toward Vivian Island which is 6 nautical miles (11 kilometers) away or toward the right of the tip of Harwood Island. Swim straight out 100 yards (90 meters) before going down. Descend and continue swimming on a straight line under water. Go over the rock and down the wall.

To get to Emmonds Road
• From Powell River, go north following signs to Sliammon and Lund; 25 minutes past Powell River, look for Emmonds Road. It is past Sliammon and just past a Craig

Road sign that is in a sharp curve in the highway. At Emmonds Road you will see a small road sign and a large sign to Gustafson's. Veer left into Emmonds Road.
• From Lund, go 4 miles (7 kilometers) south; 10 minutes to Emmonds Road.

Comments: The waters around Magoo Rock are honored by local divers as a reserve – no taking of any marine life.

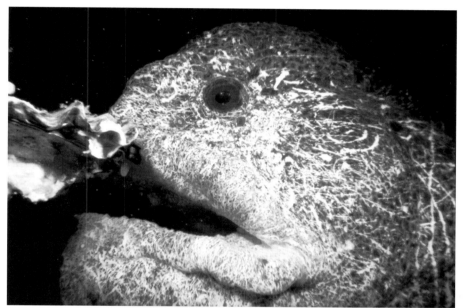

Wolf-eel eating oyster at Magoo Rock

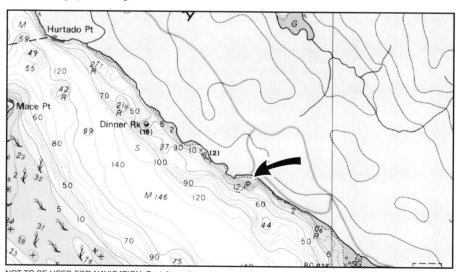

NOT TO BE USED FOR NAVIGATION: For information on obtaining navigational charts see page 318.
This is a portion of L/C-3513.

2 Nautical Miles

IRON MINES
Kayak Dive or Boat Dive

Skill: Expert divers. Intermediate divers with pickup boat.

Why go: Dramatic splashes of red and white are down the sheer wall. Did Cezanne paint this dark rock dappled with light, or Van Gogh throw his paints at it?

Giant cloud sponges plunge in an endless cascade. These cloud sponges at Iron Mines are whiter than any I've seen before – made still whiter by red anemones massed around them. Red snakelocks undulate in the slow flow. We drift past, cruise effortlessly. We see a tiny grunt sculpin, acorn barnacles, leather stars, giant red urchins. You might also see galatheid crabs, brittle stars, nudibranchs, tiger rockfish, Puget Sound king crabs, black rockfish at the point. My buddy looks out from the wall, and points as a minuscule squid scoots past. On the wall, we see seamed tennis ball sponges, flabby yellow sponges and hard pink hydrocoral like scrunched up baby's fingers. Gray chimney sponges curve out and upwards like ancient lead pipes.

The water is crystal clear. I look down – it's bottomless. Look up – see coppery red arbutus trees twisting from the cliffs above Iron Mines.

Bottom and Depths: Rock wall sheers to 500 feet (150 meters) on the chart. Rich marine life from the surface to 100 feet (30 meters) and more.

Hazards: Depth, some current and boats. If travelling by dive-kayak, consider that overexertion after the dive may increase the risk of bends. Dive the depth you are comfortable at, marine life all the way. If diving with no pickup boat, dive on slack and be aware of current direction – it can vary at different depths. Kayak-divers should rest after deep dives before paddling back. All divers *listen* and *look for* boats – boat traffic to Desolation Sound is extremely heavy in late summer and ocean kayaks move silently. When ascending, spiral and hug the wall all the way to the surface.

Telephone: Lund Hotel, at roadside.

Facilities: None at Iron Mines. Air fills and charters at Westview and Lund. Dive-kayak rentals, water taxi, charters, launching and a grocery store at Lund. Also a café, pub and restaurant – all on the water. Camping and car-top launching at nearby Dinner Rock Recreation Site.

Access: The Iron Mines dive is beneath the north face of Hurtado Point in Malaspina Strait, 1½ nautical miles (3 kilometers) southeast of Lund – 5 minutes by water taxi to the dive, 20 or 30 minutes paddling a dive-kayak on flat water. It is 1 nautical mile (2 kilometers) north of Dinner Rock. For less wind on the water, go in the morning.

Charter, take a water taxi, paddle a dive-kayak or launch your own boat at Lund and head south. Or paddle a dive-kayak north from Dinner Rock. If going by dive-kayak from Lund, it is easier to paddle to Iron Mines with the ebb and paddle back with the flood. Look ahead. Past the second point heading south, you will see small depressions and caves in the cliffs with waterfalls spilling over some of them but Iron Mines cannot be seen from the water.

At *low tides* you might secure an inflatable to heaps of rocks beside the wall or tie a dive-kayak onto the rocks; expect wash from passing boats. Diving from a larger boat you will need a boat tender because it is too deep to anchor. Current is gentle but varies at different levels, especially when windy. With a pickup boat, part of the pleasure of this dive is doing it as a gentle drift.

If diving from an inflatable or dive-kayak and no boat tender, dive on slack. Notice current direction at various levels, work upcurrent during the dive and ascend clinging to the wall. Then drift or pull yourself back to your boat. Wheelchair divers who paddle dive-kayaks will find easy access at the ramp and the float at Lund.

Because of the high bluff, dive at noon or after for maximum sunlight.

Comments: The caves in the cliff that divers call Iron Mines were never a mine. They were test-tunnels used for samples; the mine is just south of the holes. This mine was the first Crown-granted mine claim in the area after Lund was settled in 1899. The mine was operated until 1906 – not for iron but for copper, gold and silver. Stories are told that after the mine closed the tunnels provided a hiding place for pirate treasure: a ship's bell, ship's wheel, portholes, a crystal jug and china taken from *Cottage City* when it was stranded at Willow Point south of Campbell River in 1911. It is said a spelunker found the treasure at Iron Mines in 1946.

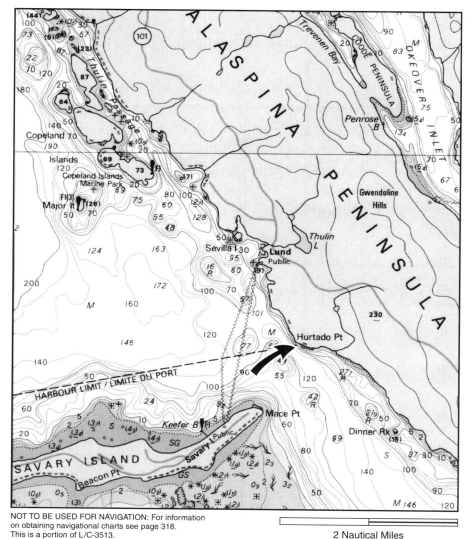

NOT TO BE USED FOR NAVIGATION: For information on obtaining navigational charts see page 318. This is a portion of L/C-3513.

2 Nautical Miles

WRECK OF ADVENTURER
Kayak Dive or Boat Dive
(Shore Dive, but access privately owned)

Tide Table: Point Atkinson
Add 10 minutes

Skill: All divers

Why go: To dive the *Adventurer* and *North Star* wrecks. To explore a shallow kelp-covered wall with nooks and crannies and critters hiding in it.

Painted greenlings, lingcod, kelp greenlings and clouds of herring cruise in the kelp, seaperch are around the wrecks, tube-snouts swim jerkily through the shallows. Sea pens, silver nudibranchs and tube-dwelling anemones are in the sand on the way to the wrecks. The fish boat *North Star* is 30 feet (9 meters) long, shallow, intact and lies precariously on its side, looks ready to slide. The *Adventurer* stands upright. It was 86 feet (26 meters) long but has been down 25 years and is crumbling. Dive them soon!

Past the wrecks, it's also a rich dive. The kelp curtain at the Little Wall hides sea lemons and alabaster nudibranchs, coils of nudibranch eggs like apple peel, flaming red slipper cucumbers, white cucumbers, chimney sponges. Sea stars and big fat brown cucumbers are beneath the kelp on the bottom. We saw a juvenile wolf-eel in the open – there must be more hiding in the many tiny slit ledges. We laughed when we came to a heap of toilets at the north end of Little Wall, probably placed by divers with a sense of humor who wanted to give people a surprise in this beautiful setting.

Bottom and Depths: Broken rock with bottom kelp slopes quickly to the top of the *North Star* at 20 to 30 feet (6 to 9 meters), depending on tide height. The *Adventurer* stands upright on a ledge at 60 to 70 feet (18 to 21 meters). Sand between ledges, some boulders and light silt over all. The Little Wall is covered with big, broadleafed brown kelp, bottoms out to sand at 50 to 60 feet (15 to 18 meters) with narrow under-cut ledges.

Hazards: Boats and the wrecks themselves. Boat traffic to popular cruising sites north of Lund is extremely heavy in summer. And remember that ocean kayaks move silently. *Listen* and *look for* boats as you ascend. Hug the contours of the bottom all the way to the surface well out of the way of those boats. Do not penetrate the wrecks and stay clear of the steep slope below *North Star.*

Telephone: Lund Hotel, at roadside.

Facilities: None at the site. Air fills, launching ramps and charters at Lund and Westview. Water taxi and dive-kayak rentals at Lund.

Access: The *Adventurer* is at the southern end of Thulin Passage, top of the Strait of Georgia. It is 1 nautical mile (2 kilometers) northwest of Lund on the Malaspina Peninsula side of the passage. Descending steep steps from Norland Road off Finn Bay Road has been the usual mode of reaching it but the land is privately owned.

Charter out of Lund or Westview. Or take a water taxi, launch a boat or paddle a dive-kayak from Lund. Head northwest 1 nautical mile (2 kilometers) to the first cove on the right-hand side around the point past Finn Bay. Look for two dive flags painted on the rocks that help locate the wrecks. Line up those flags with the tip of Savary Island and swim from the south end of the rocky cove to the wrecks – start down right away. Follow a 210- to 215-degree compass bearing. Go out 40 feet (12 meters) to the *North Star* poised on a steep wall. Explore it, then continue on the same line over a boulder to the *Adventurer.*

To get to the Little Wall from the *Adventurer,* head north. Explore the base of the wall at 50 to 60 feet (15 to 18 meters). Swim back and forth up the wall to the surface.

The *Adventurer* site is exposed to southeast winds – thus the many wrecks. Go in good weather.

• Kayak-divers can paddle to the *Adventurer* in 15 or 20 minutes. Kayak-divers and divers with an inflatable could land on the rocks and gear up. Beware of wash from Desolation Sound boat traffic. Wheelchair access good at ramp and float at Lund.

• Divers with larger boats could anchor north of the wrecks but take care not to drop anchor on them. Again, beware of wash.

Comments: Locally honored as a reserve – do not take or disturb any marine life.

Off rocks to *Adventurer*

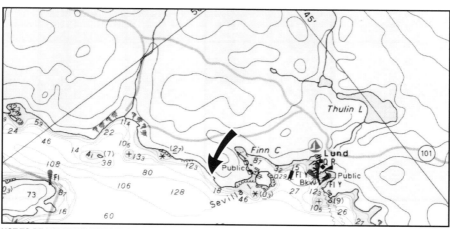

NOT TO BE USED FOR NAVIGATION: For information
on obtaining navigational charts see page 318.
This is a portion of 3311.

1 Nautical Mile

TIM'S WALL
Kayak Dive or Boat Dive
(Shore Dive, but access privately owned)

Tide Table: Point Atkinson
Add 10 minutes

Skill: Intermediate and expert divers

Why go: Not only to dive the *Adventurer* and *North Star* wrecks written up in the previous dive but also to dive Tim's Wall. At Tim's Wall you might see tiger rockfish, ratfish, yelloweye rockfish, dogfish, king crabs. And you *will* see sponges.
　　Swim quickly to the wrecks and past them: plan to visit them on the way up. Going to the wrecks, you will see sea pens, giant nudibranchs and tube-dwelling anemones in the sand. Painted greenlings, lingcod, kelp greenlings and clouds of herring are in the kelp; seaperch are around the wrecks. The fish boat *North Star* lies precariously on its side on a steep slope, looks ready to slide. The *Adventurer* stands upright.
　　Past the wrecks, the sponges at Tim's Wall.

Bottom and Depths: Broken rock with bottom kelp slopes quickly to the top of the *North Star* at 20 to 30 feet (6 to 9 meters), depending on tide height. The *Adventurer* stands upright on a ledge at 60 to 70 feet (18 to 21 meters). Sand is between the ledges, some boulders and light silt over all. Tim's Wall starts at 90 to 100 feet (27 to 30 meters) and drops straight down.

Hazards: Boats, the wrecks themselves, the possibility of overexertion after diving. Boat traffic to popular cruising sites north of Lund is extremely heavy sin summer. Ocean kayaks move silently. *Listen* and *look for* boats as you ascend and hug the contours of the bottom all the way to the surface, well out of the way of those boats. As mentioned in the previous dive, do not penetrate the wrecks and stay clear of the steep slope below *North Star.* Kayak-divers who dive deep as well as divers climbing the steep hill should rest before heading back to avoid overexertion which may increase risk of bends.

Telephone: Lund Hotel, at roadside.

Facilities: None at the site. Air fills, launching ramps and charters at Lund and Westview. Water taxi and dive-kayak rentals at Lund.

Access: Tim's Wall is at the southern end of Thulin Passage, top of the Strait of Georgia. It is 1 nautical mile (2 kilometers) northwest of Lund on the Malaspina Peninsula side of the passage. Descending steep steps from Norland Road off Finn Bay Road has been the usual mode of reaching it but the land is privately owned.
　　Charter out of Lund or Westview. Or take a water taxi, launch a boat or paddle a dive-kayak from Lund. Head northwest 1 nautical mile (2 kilometers) to the first cove on the right-hand side around the point past Finn Bay. Look for two dive flags painted on the rocks that help locate the wrecks. Line up those flags with the tip of Savary Island and swim from the south end of the rocky cove to the wrecks – start down right away. Follow a 210- to 215-degree compass bearing. Go out 40 feet (12 meters) to the *North Star* poised on a steep wall; then continue on the same line over a boulder to the *Adventurer.*
　　To get to Tim's Wall, continue on the line you took from shore to the wrecks. Swim over gently sloping sand and a sandy mound. Keep going. Follow a valley of sand down to the right and then curve left around to the wall. Dive south on the wall.

　　The site is exposed to southeast winds – thus the many wrecks. Go in good weather.
• Kayak-divers can paddle from Lund to the site in 15 or 20 minutes. Divers with

kayaks or an inflatable could land on the rocks and gear up. Beware of wash from Desolation Sound boat traffic. Wheelchair access good at ramp and float at Lund.
• Divers with larger boats could anchor north of the wrecks but take care not to drop anchor on them. Again, beware of wash.

Comments: Locally honored as a reserve – do not take or disturb any marine life.

Feather star

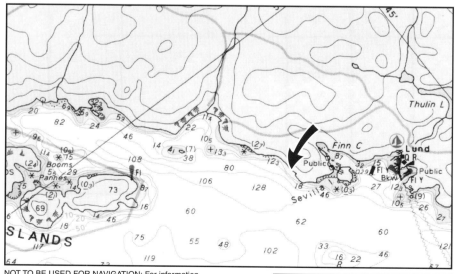

NOT TO BE USED FOR NAVIGATION: For information
on obtaining navigational charts see page 318.
This is a portion of 3311.

1 Nautical Mile

SARAH POINT
Boat Dive

Tide Table: Point Atkinson
Add 10 minutes

Skill: Intermediate and expert divers

Why go: Sarah Point is at the top of Malaspina Peninsula, the northernmost inhabited mainland coast connected by road and ferry to southwestern British Columbia. It's wilderness. It drops quickly. And I like that.

Stark is the word to describe Sarah Point. Angular rocks drop away quickly. Large and beautiful dahlia anemones reach sticky red fingers into the current flowing past the dark rock wall. Big chimney sponges start at 60 feet (18 meters). Cloud sponges, just over the lip of the narrow ledge at 80 feet (24 meters). At 100 feet (30 meters), cloud sponges are magnificent.

When I dived at Sarah Point large fish were noticeably absent. Perhaps because it was summer, the surface waters were warm and the fish had gone deep. But we did see numerous small rockfish, some kelp greenlings, sea pens in the sand on the narrow ledges, and nudibranchs in the kelp.

Bottom and Depths: Angular broken rock covered with bottom kelp slopes quickly to 30 feet (9 meters). Some boulders. Narrow ledges drop in steep stairsteps down, down and down. And silt over all.

Hazards: Boats, current and broken fishing line. Small boat traffic is extremely heavy in late summer at this popular salmon-fishing site. Listen for boats and ascend hugging the contours of the slope all the way to the surface, well out of the way of those boats. Dive near the slack. Carry a knife. If caught in transparent fishing line you can cut your way free.

Telephone: Lund Hotel, at roadside.

Facilities: None at this wilderness point. Air fills, dive-kayak rentals, charters, launching ramp, café and grocery store at Lund. Rustic camping with pit toilet and a place to pitch your tent at the provincial marine park on the southernmost of the Copeland Islands.

Access: Sarah Point is at the top of Malaspina Peninsula at the southern entrance to Desolation Sound. It is 6 nautical miles (11 kilometers) beyond Lund, the end of the road going north. Charter out of Lund or Westview or launch at Lund and follow the coast 6 nautical miles (11 kilometers) northwest through Thulin Passage. Anchor or land in a small cove just south of Sarah Point and go down.

Comments: Unlimited diving and snorkeling around the moss-covered Copeland Islands and at Major Islet – both less than 2 nautical miles (4 kilometers) from Lund. Wolf-eels, more wrecks and harbor seals year-round; sea lions in winter. I have followed a wolf-eel while snorkeling. You could camp and dive from your kayak all summer and never run out of new sites.

Shoal Searcher heading to Desolation Sound

NOT TO BE USED FOR NAVIGATION: For information
on obtaining navigational charts see page 318.
This is a portion of 3538.

1 Nautical Mile

OKEOVER CAVES
Kayak Dive or Boat Dive

Tide Table: Campbell River
Add 45 minutes

Skill: Intermediate and expert divers

Why go: You want to see caves, or see a feather star swim; the wind is blowing hard making the water rough on the west side of Malaspina Peninsula; or maybe you just love a fabulous wall. Go to Okeover Inlet.

Orange and white plumose anemones decorate the overhangs and cuts as you plunge to the first cave. We don't see much else until we've gone into the biggest, deepest cave. Then we look around: see a field of feather stars, a single swimming scallop, sea cucumbers and a lingcod that is probably 12 to 15 pounds (5 to 7 kilograms). We see crimson snakelock anemones. A rose star. Red and green Christmas anemones. Shallower, moon jellyfish, hermit crabs, magenta heart tunicates. A small alabaster nudibranch. Sighting a tiny grunt sculpin, our caves dive feels complete.

Brittle stars, long slinky sea worms, orange encrusting sponges and strange mussels also live in the incredibly still waters at Okeover Inlet.

Bottom and Depths: A sheer rock wall drops off. The deeper cave is at 90 to 100 feet (27 to 30 meters), depending on tide height. It is 30 feet (9 meters) wide, 8 feet (2½ meters) high and goes in for 15 feet (5 meters). The second cave is at a depth of 55 to 65 feet (17 to 20 meters). It is 20 feet (6 meters) wide, 8 feet (2½ meters) high and goes in for 8 feet (2½ meters). North of the dive flag, beneath the huge bluff, big boulders drop off steeply in huge giant steps. Dive as shallow or deep as you want to.

Hazards: Silt year-round, transparent fishing line, boats and poor visibility from plankton bloom, in summer. Enter the caves carefully and do not kick up silt. Carry a knife. Listen for boats and ascend close to the wall all the way to the surface.

Telephone: Okeover Inlet government dock.

Facilities: None. Launching ramp off Malaspina Road – the ramp is good for small boats only. Camping with picnic tables, pit toilets and fire rings at nearby Okeover Arm Park. Air fills at Westview and Lund. Dive-kayak rentals and charters at Lund.

Access: The Okeover Caves site is on the east side of Okeover Inlet, commonly known as Okeover Arm, near Lund. The usual launch point for the dive is at Malaspina Peninsula, 30 minutes north of Powell River.

Charter at Okeover Inlet, take a water taxi or head across the inlet in your own boat from the ramp at Malaspina Road. A dive-kayak would do it. Go to the black rock bluff on the opposite shore – less than 1 nautical mile (2 kilometers) to a large indentation where a dive flag is painted on the rock. The deeper cave is below it and south.

Anchor in the indentation south of the dive flag. You can land on the flat rock, suit up and swim around to the north side of it. Drop straight over the wall: At 70 to 80 feet (21 to 24 meters) when you reach a bulge, kick away from the wall and out over it so you don't stir up silt. Beneath the bulge, you will see a big dark hole – the larger cave. When you enter be careful not to kick up silt. To find the second cave, work your way up through boulders at the north side of the wall. Imagine where the dive flag was painted on the rock and go toward it. The second cave is beneath the flag at 55 to 65 feet (17 to 20 meters).

Wheelchair divers who paddle dive-kayaks will find easy access at Okeover Ramp.

To get to Malaspina Road and Okeover Inlet
From Powell River head north on Sunshine Coast Highway 101. Past Sliammon, watch for signs to Okeover Arm Provincial Park at Malaspina Road. Turn right and

drive 2⅓ miles (3¾ kilometers) to the park signs. Do not continue straight into the campground but turn right to the government dock and launching ramp.

Comments: Superb winter dive. The inlet is usually protected. When winter winds are blowing up in the strait, it can be calm here.

Diver at entry of shallower cave

NOT TO BE USED FOR NAVIGATION: For information
on obtaining navigational charts see page 318.
This is a portion of 3559.

500 Yards

Coming from underwater wrecks at Seabeck Bay

From Z's Reef to East Wall, Mount Rainier behind

Off *Vertigo* to Possession Point Wreck

Pink and white anemones on wreck at Edmonds

Columns of plumose anemones at Edmonds Underwater Park

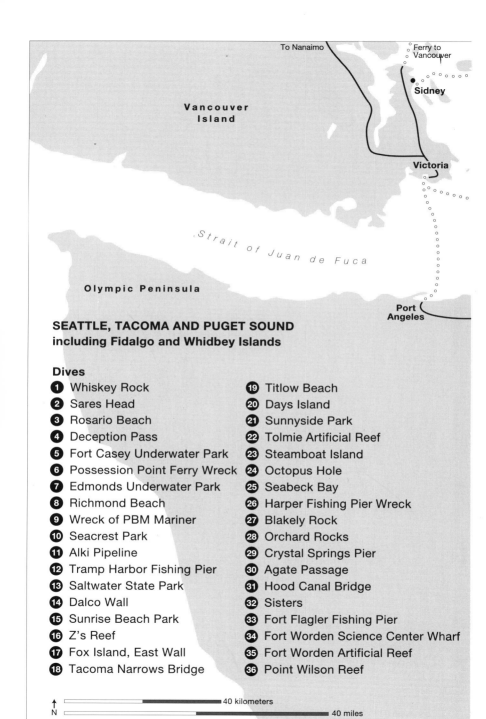

SEATTLE, TACOMA AND PUGET SOUND
including Fidalgo and Whidbey Islands

Dives

1. Whiskey Rock
2. Sares Head
3. Rosario Beach
4. Deception Pass
5. Fort Casey Underwater Park
6. Possession Point Ferry Wreck
7. Edmonds Underwater Park
8. Richmond Beach
9. Wreck of PBM Mariner
10. Seacrest Park
11. Alki Pipeline
12. Tramp Harbor Fishing Pier
13. Saltwater State Park
14. Dalco Wall
15. Sunrise Beach Park
16. Z's Reef
17. Fox Island, East Wall
18. Tacoma Narrows Bridge
19. Titlow Beach
20. Days Island
21. Sunnyside Park
22. Tolmie Artificial Reef
23. Steamboat Island
24. Octopus Hole
25. Seabeck Bay
26. Harper Fishing Pier Wreck
27. Blakely Rock
28. Orchard Rocks
29. Crystal Springs Pier
30. Agate Passage
31. Hood Canal Bridge
32. Sisters
33. Fort Flagler Fishing Pier
34. Fort Worden Science Center Wharf
35. Fort Worden Artificial Reef
36. Point Wilson Reef

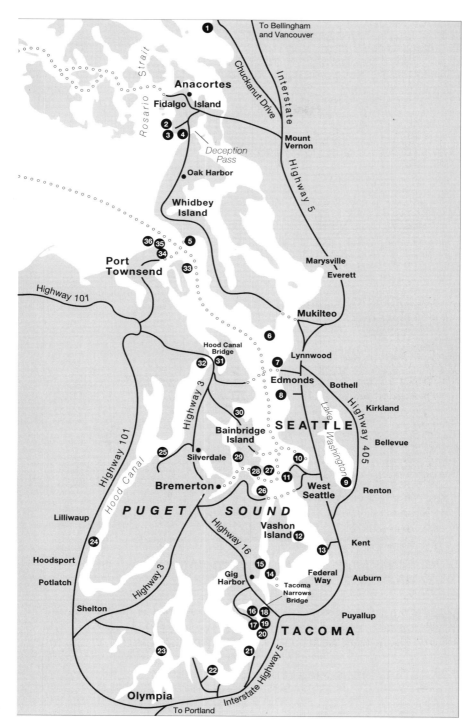

SERVICE INFORMATION *
Seattle, Tacoma and Puget Sound
including Fidalgo and Whidbey Islands

Charts: United States of America NOAA National Ocean Service
- 18421 Strait of Juan de Fuca to Strait of Georgia
- 18423 Bellingham to Everett including San Juan Islands (small-craft folio)
- 18427 Anacortes to Skagit Bay
- 18440 Puget Sound
- 18441 Puget Sound–Northern Part
- 18445 Possession Sound to Olympia Including Hood Canal (small-craft folio)
- 18446 Puget Sound–Apple Cove Point to Keyport
- 18447 Lake Washington Ship Canal and Lake Washington (small-craft folio)
- 18448 Puget Sound–Southern Part
- 18449 Puget Sound–Seattle to Bremerton
- 18450 Seattle Harbor, Elliott Bay and Duwamish Waterway
- 18457 Puget Sound–Hammersley Inlet to Shelton
- 18458 Hood Canal–South Point to Quatsap Point Including Dabob Bay
- 18464 Port Townsend
- 18471 Approaches to Admiralty Inlet–Dungeness to Oak Bay
- 18473 Puget Sound–Oak Bay to Shilsole Bay
- 18474 Puget Sound–Shilsole Bay to Commencement Bay
- 18476 Puget Sound–Hood Canal to Dabob Bay
- 18477 Puget Sound–Entrance to Hood Canal

Tide and Current Tables
United States of America NOAA National Ocean Service
Tide Tables – West Coast of North and South America and *Tidal Current Tables – Pacific Coast of North America and Asia North*

Tidal Current Charts, Puget Sound, Northern Part, and *Tidal Current Charts, Puget Sound, Southern Part*
or
Canadian Hydrographic Service
Tide and Current Table, Volume 5

Diving Emergency Telephone Numbers
Dial 911: Say "I have a scuba diving emergency".
Virginia Mason Hospital: To reach the hyperbaric unit, dial (206) 624-1144, ask for Emergency Room, then say "I have a scuba diving emergency".

If medical personnel are unfamiliar with diving emergencies, ask them to telephone DAN (Divers Alert Network): (919) 684-8111, then say "I have a scuba diving emergency".

Other Useful Numbers
Weather Service Forecast: (206) 526-6087
Red Tide Hotline (shellfish infoline): 1-800-562-5632
Sportfishing Hotline (nominal charge to use the number): In Washington, 1-976-3200

• Dive Shops and Air Stations
Seattle

Seattle Skindiving Supply
1661 Harbor Avenue SW
Seattle WA 98126
(206) 937-2550; fax (206) 935-1661

Adventure Diving Technical Dive
  Center
Pier 70
2815 Alaskan Way, Suite 5
Seattle WA 98121
(206) 441-8223

Lighthouse Diving Center
8215 Lake City Way NE
Seattle WA 98115
(206) 524-1633

Underwater Sports
10545 Aurora Avenue N
Seattle WA 98133-8811
(206) 362-3310

Greater Seattle – North
Underwater Sports
264 Railroad Avenue
Edmonds WA 98020-4133
(206) 771-6322

Lighthouse Diving Center
5421-196th Street SW, Suite 6
Lynnwood WA 98036
(206) 771-2679; fax (206) 771-5959
Toll-free throughout North America:
1-800-777-3483.

Underwater Sports
205 East Casino Road, #4
Everett WA 98203-2830
(206) 355-3338

Blue Dolphin Diving Center
1375 State Avenue
Marysville WA 98270
(206) 653-2834

Greater Seattle – South
Lighthouse Diving Center
24860 Pacific Highway S
Kent WA 98032
(206) 839-6881

Underwater Sports
34428 Pacific Highway S
Federal Way WA 98003-7325
(206) 874-9387

Another World Diving
620 Auburn Way South, Suite L
Auburn WA 98002
(206) 939-7787

Northwest Divers
7824-E River Road E
Puyallup WA 98371
(206) 845-5350

Greater Seattle – East
Underwater Sports
12003 NE 12th Street
Bellevue WA 98005-2455
(206) 454-5168

Silent World Diving
13600 NE 20th Street
Bellevue WA 98005
(206) 747-8842; fax (206) 747-5905

West of Seattle – Bainbridge Island to Bremerton
Exotic Aquatics Scuba & Water Sports
154 Winslow Way E
Bainbridge Island WA 98110
(206) 842-1980; fax (206) 842-1761
(Also dive guiding, dive-kayak rentals.

Silverdale Scuba
2839-A Kitsap Place
PO Box 644
Silverdale WA 98383
(206) 692-1086

Sound Dive Center
(Old Town Watersports)
3423 Byron Street
Silverdale WA 98383
(206) 692-0737
(Also dive guiding, dive-kayak rentals.)

• Dive Shops and Air Stations (continued)

Sound Dive Center
990 Sylvan Way
Bremerton WA 98310
(206) 373-6141
Toll-free in USA: 1-800-392-3483
(Also dive guiding.)

Puget Sound Dive Enterprises
1921 Wheaton Way
Bremerton WA 98310
(206) 377-0554
(Also dive guiding.)

Tacoma

Miller's Dive & Marine
3005 Harborview Drive
Gig Harbor WA 98335
(206) 858-7989
(Waterfront air fills.)

Northwest Divers
4815 North Pearl Street
Tacoma WA 98407
(206) 752-3973

Pacific Reef
7516 Twenty Seventh Street W
Tacoma WA 98466
(206) 564-0356

Lighthouse Diving Center
3630 South Cedar Street
Tacoma WA 98409
(206) 475-1316

Underwater Sports
9608 Fortieth Street SW
Tacoma WA 98499-4302
(206) 588-6634

Lakewood Scuba
9109 Veterans Drive SW
Tacoma WA 98498
(206) 588-8368

Fort Lewis Sport Diving Program
Building 3236
Fort Lewis WA 98433-5000
(206) 967-4298; fax (206) 967-7222
(Air fills only, and only for NATO military personnel and family members. Telephone to arrange for fills.)

Olympia

Underwater Sports
9020 Martin Way E
Olympia WA 98516-5997
(206) 493-0322

Hood Canal – West Side

Mike's Diving Center
North 22270 Highway 101
Shelton WA 98584
(206) 877-9568
(Dive shop. Located north of Potlatch State Park, 1 mile [1½ kilometers] in Potlatch WA.)

Sunrise Motel & Dive Resort
North 24520 Highway 101
PO Box 554
Hoodsport WA 98548
(206) 877-5301
(Resort air station; also dive packages including accommodation.)

Mike's Beach Resort
North 38470 Highway 101
Lilliwaup WA 98555
(206) 877-5324
(Telephone to arrange for air fills. Also motel accommodation and camping; restrooms and telephone outside office. Concrete launching ramp, good at all times except extreme low tides.)

Quimper Peninsula, near Port Townsend

Orca Divers
1761 Irondale Road
PO Box 193
Port Hadlock WA 98339
(206) 385-5688
(Best to telephone to arrange for air fills. Open Saturdays and most evenings, Sundays and holidays.)

• Dive Shops (continued)
Olympic Peninsula
Angeles Dive & Sports Center
134 East Lauridsen Boulevard
Port Angeles WA 98362
(206) 452-3483

Olympic Divers
509 South Lincoln Street
Port Angeles WA 98362
(206) 452-5264
(Telephone to arrange for air fills.)

Whidbey Island to Bellingham
Whidbey Island Dive Center
9050-D 900th Avenue W
Oak Harbor WA 98277
(206) 675-1112
(Also dive-kayak rental.)

Anacortes Diving & Supply
2502 Commercial Avenue
Anacortes WA 98221
(206) 293-2070

Adventures Down Under
701 East Holly Street
Bellingham WA 98225
(206) 676-4177
(Also dive-kayak rentals.)

Washington Divers
903 North State Street
Bellingham WA 98225
(206) 676-8029; fax (206) 647-5028
(Also dive guiding, dive-kayak rentals and charters.)

Bellingham Dive-N-Travel
2720 West Maplewood Avenue
Bellingham WA 98225
(206) 734-1770

• Boat Charters to Puget Sound
Out of Greater Seattle and Tacoma
Caldo
Caldo Charters
Contact Underwater Sports
34428 Pacific Highway S
Federal Way WA 98003-7325
(206) 874-9387
(Day, night, overnight and short live-aboard charters out of Tacoma in summer, fall and winter to Puget Sound. Out of Anacortes, in spring and summer, to the San Juans.)

Genie Aye
Down Time Ltd.
14404 SE 128th Street
Renton WA 98059
(206) 277-9069
(Day charters throughout Puget Sound; also day and occasional dive-package charters in the San Juan Islands.)

Kingfisher
Kingfisher Scuba Adventures
PO Box 779
Kingston WA 98346
(206) 598-3569
(Custom day charters throughout Puget Sound and the San Juan Islands. Pick up at your location.)

Subsea Explorer
Adventure Diving Technical Dive Center
Pier 70
2815 Alaskan Way, Suite 5
Seattle WA 98121
(206) 441-8223
(Day charters throughout Puget Sound. The boat is trailerable and will go anywhere in the Sound.)

Vertigo
Pacific Rim Diving, Inc.
13217 SE 54th Place
Bellevue WA 98006
(206) 643-6584; fax (206) 643-9730
(Custom day charters year-round to Lake Washington, Puget Sound and the San Juan Islands. Trailerable boat – will go anywhere, meet you anywhere. Accommodate wheelchair divers with prior notice.)

• Boat Charters to San Juan Islands
Out of Anacortes

Caldo
Caldo Charters
Contact Underwater Sports
34428 Pacific Highway S
Federal Way WA 98003-7325
(206) 874-9387
(Day, night, overnight and short live-aboard charters in spring and summer to the San Juans; out of Tacoma in summer; fall and winter to Puget Sound.)

Genie Aye
Down Time Ltd.
14404 SE 128th Street
Renton WA 98059
(206) 277-9069
(Day and occasional hotel-dive-package charters in the San Juans; also day charters throughout Puget Sound.)

Kingfisher
Kingfisher Scuba Adventures
PO Box 779
Kingston WA 98346
(206) 598-3569
(Custom day charters to the San Juans and throughout Puget Sound. Pick up at your location.)

Narcosis
Newport Aero Marine
12510 SE 63rd Street
Bellevue WA 98006
(206) 747-7931
(Day charters year-round to San Juans.)

Out of Bellingham

Washington Diver I
Washington Divers
903 North State Street
Bellingham WA 98225
(206) 676-8029; fax (206) 647-5028
(Day charters year-round to San Juans; also dive-kayak rentals and guiding.)

Sea Wolf
Discovery Charters
PO Box 636
Anacortes WA 98221-0636
(206) 293-4248
(Weekend liveaboard trips to the San Juans. Also 5-day and 7-day liveaboard charters to the San Juans and the Gulf islands.)

Starfire
Starfire Charters
849 NE 130th Street
Seattle WA 98125
(206) 364-9858
(Day trips and occasional liveaboard charters to the San Juans.)

Vertigo
Pacific Rim Diving, Inc.
13217 SE 54th Place
Bellevue WA 98006
(206) 643-6584; fax (206) 643-9730.
(Custom day charters year-round to the San Juans and Puget Sound. Trailerable boat – go anywhere, meet you anywhere. Accommodate wheelchair divers with prior notice.)

• Boat Rentals
Bainbridge Island to Bremerton
Exotic Aquatics Scuba & Water Sports
154 Winslow Way E
Bainbridge Island WA 98110
(206) 842-1980; fax (206) 842-1761
(Dive-kayak rentals; also dive guiding.)

Sound Dive Center
(Old Town Watersports)
3423 Byron Street
Silverdale WA 98383
(206) 692-0737
(Dive-kayak rentals; also dive guiding.)

Tacoma
Point Defiance Boathouse Marina
Point Defiance Park
5912 North Waterfront Drive
Foot of Pearl Street
Tacoma WA 98407
(206) 591-5325
(Boat rentals. No reservations, easier to obtain on weekdays or in winter out of fishing season. Mostly for fishing, but the boats work for diving. Wheel your gear by handcart from curb to boat and they lower you to the water. Also launching nearby south of ferry landing; café and restrooms. Telephone outside next to restroom and marina store, another in parking lot north of marina, and one at ferry landing ticket office.)

Olympia
Zittel's Marina Inc.
9144 Gallea Street NE
Olympia WA 98506
(206) 459-1950
(Boat rentals. Also a launching ramp plus a sling-launch. It is located 1 mile [1½ kilometers] south of Johnson Point. Restrooms; telephone at the northeast corner of store building.)

Whidbey Island and Bellingham
Whidbey Island Dive Center
9050-D 900th Avenue W
Oak Harbor WA 98277
(206) 675-1112
(Dive-kayak rentals; also air fills.)

Adventures Down Under
701 East Holly Street
Bellingham WA 98225
(206) 676-4177
(Dive-kayak rentals; also air fills.)

The Great Adventure
201 East Chestnut Street
Bellingham WA 98225
(206) 671-4615
(Dive-kayak rentals.)

Washington Divers
903 North State Street
Bellingham WA 98225
(206) 676-8029; fax (206) 647-5028
(Dive-kayak rentals; also charters, dive guiding and air fills.)

BOAT RAMPS AND SLINGS

• Launching for Lake Washington

Coulon Beach Park
1201 Lake Washington Boulevard NE
Renton WA
(Concrete ramps, good at all times – no tides in Lake Washington. A great deal of parking space for a fee; restrooms with hot showers; and telephones, one beside the restrooms, one at the top of Ramp 8.)

Off Highway 405: take Exit 5 following signs to Issaquah and Sunset Boulevard NE. Turn toward the lake onto NE Park Drive and follow signs to Coulon Beach Park – only ⅓ mile (½ kilometer) off the highway.

Bellevue Public Ramp
Foot of SE 40th Street
Factoria
Bellevue WA
(Concrete ramps, good at all times – no tides in the lake. Roadside parking on 40th Street, toilets, and telephone north side of road near ramp.)

Off Highway 405: take Exit 10. Go for ½ mile (1 kilometer) toward the water on Coal Creek Parkway which becomes Lake Washington Boulevard SE. The 40th Street turnoff is marked with signs saying Public Boat Launch, Mercer Marine, Newport Yacht Basin. Turn left and go ⅓ mile (½ kilometer) to the foot of 40th Street. Past 40th, the boulevard changes names to 118th Avenue SE; if you find yourself on 118th, you have gone too far.

• Launching for Puget Sound
At Seattle

Don Armeni Public Ramp
1600 Block Harbor Avenue SW
West Seattle WA
(Concrete ramps, good at all except minus tides. Plenty of room to park; restrooms. Telephone across road.)

From I-5 (Interstate Highway 5), it is 5 minutes to the ramp: take Exit 163A onto West Seattle Freeway, and Harbor Avenue Exit off West Seattle Freeway. Turn right and go around the waterfront to Seacrest and Don Armeni parks.

At Bainbridge Island

Fort Ward State Park Ramp
Bainbridge Island, south end
(Concrete ramp, good at all tides. Parking space; wheelchair accessible toilets. Telephone at Lynwood center in front of theater; this is 1½ miles [2½ kilometers] from ramp.)

From Highway 305 heading south or immediately off the ferry from Seattle, follow signs to Winslow city center. From here, 5 miles (8 kilometers) – 15 minutes to Fort Ward Park. Go west on Winslow Way to the stop sign at Madison Avenue. Turn right. At Wyatt Street, turn left. Then go straight and follow signs up Bucklin Hill Road toward Fort Ward State Park boat ramp. Past Lynwood, continue straight on Pleasant Beach Drive. When you reach a "Dead End" sign, keep going. From here only ½ mile (¾ kilometer) to the ramp.

Eagle Harbor Waterfront Park Ramp
Foot of Shannon Drive SE, Winslow
Bainbridge Island WA
(Concrete ramp, that is good except with extreme low tides. Limited in-town parking; restrooms and picnic tables in the park; telephone at roadside, foot of Madison Avenue.)

From Highway 305 heading south or immediately off ferry from Seattle, follow signs to Winslow city center. Go west on Winslow Way to the stop sign at Madison Avenue and turn left. Take first left at Bjune Drive, then right on Shannon Drive and go to the water.

• Launching for Puget Sound (continued)
At Bremerton
Evergreen Park Public Ramp
Foot of 14th Street, Bremerton WA
(Concrete ramp, good at 2-foot [⅔-meter] tides and greater. Restrooms; telephone.)

Off Highway 303 (Warren Avenue): located in city of Bremerton *south* of Port Washington Narrows – from Warren Avenue Bridge, 1 minute to the ramp. At the traffic light at Warren Avenue and 11th Street, head east on 11th: go to Park Drive. Turn left to 14th Street; then right to the ramp.

Lions Field Public Ramp
Lebo Boulevard, Bremerton WA
(Concrete ramp, good at 5-foot [1½-meter] tides and greater; restrooms and telephone back beside Lions Field parking space.)

Off Highway 303 (Warren Avenue): located in city of East Bremerton *north* of Port Washington Narrows. From the bridge, 5 minutes to the ramp. At north end of Warren Street Bridge, curve eastward downhill on Wheaton Way to Lebo Boulevard. At bottom of the hill, turn right onto Lebo and go under the bridge. Pass Lions Field parking on your left; shortly beyond it, you will see a second sign for Lions Park. Boat trailer parking on your left beside the ramp.

Illahee State Park Ramp
Sylvan Way, Bremerton WA
(Concrete ramp, good at medium to high tides. Lots of parking, toilets and picnic tables beside ramp. Hot showers in campground. Telephones at entry to the park.)

Off Highway 303 (Wheaton Way): when *north* of Warren Avenue Bridge in East Bremerton, continue straight along Wheaton to Sylvan Way. Turn east following signs to Illahee State Park. Go on Sylvan Way for 1½ miles (2½ kilometers); turn left into Illahee Park. In the park, stay right and follow the launching ramp signs. The curving road winds through the park between tall trees, goes down a steep hill to the water.

South of Bremerton
Port of Manchester Public Ramp
Foot of Main Street, Manchester WA
(Concrete ramp, good at all tides for small boats. For boats 14 feet [4 meters] and greater, good at medium and high tides. Parking north of Main Street, west of grocery store. Picnic tables beside ramp at Pomeroy Park. Toilet on dock. Telephones by grocery store.)

Off Highway 160 between Port Orchard and Southworth; from the highway, 5 minutes to the ramp. When 2 miles (3 kilometers) north of Harper, turn right off Highway 160 and follow signs to Manchester. Go 1½ miles (2½ kilometers), turn right onto Main Street and go to the water.

• Launching for Southern Puget Sound – At Tacoma
Narrows Marine Center
9007 South 19th Street
Tacoma WA 98466
(206) 564-4222
(Concrete ramp, good at all except extreme low tides. Located immediately south of Titlow Beach. A great deal of parking space. Restrooms and telephone outside bait shop at marina.)

Point Defiance Park Public Ramps
Foot of Pearl Street, Tacoma WA
(Concrete ramps, good at all tides. A great deal of parking space. Restrooms and telephone at ferry landing.)

Wollochet County Ramp
Foot of 10th Street, Wollochet Bay
(Concrete ramp, good at all tides. It is located near Point Fosdick. You will find parking space for four or five cars at the roadside. No toilet, no telephone.)

Off Highway 16: immediately north of the Tacoma Narrows Bridge take the Wollochet-Point Fosdick Exit. From the bridge, 2½ miles (4 kilometers) to the ramp: follow the road under bridge and turn left heading west on Stone Drive NW past the Tacoma Narrows Airport to Point Fosdick Drive. Then go south: from Stone Drive, go ⅔ mile (1 kilometer) to 10th Street NW. Turn right. Go on 10th to the water.

If you approach from the Olympic Drive exit off Highway 16, go south on Point Fosdick Drive for 7 miles (11 kilometers) to 10th Street NW, turn right and go on 10th to the water.

At Olympia
Luhr Beach Public Ramp
Foot of Meridian Road, Olympia WA
(Launching at head of Nisqually Reach: concrete ramp, good at all except extreme low tides. Located east of Olympia. Picnic tables, a great deal of parking space; restrooms, telephone.)

From I-5 (Interstate Highway 5) take Yelm-Marvin Road Exit 111: cross I-5 heading south and go to the traffic light at Martin Way SE. Turn left and proceed to the top of Nisqually Hill to Meridian Road. Turn left and go 2½ miles (4 kilometers) on Meridian. Turn right following "Public Fishing" signs to Nisqually Head. Ten minutes from I-5.

Zittel's Marina Inc.
9144 Gallea Street NE
Olympia WA 98506
(206) 459-1950
(Launching at Nisqually Reach: concrete ramp, good at all except extreme low tides of minus 3 feet [minus 1 meter]; plus a sling-launch. Also boat rentals. Restrooms; telephone at northeast corner of store building.)

Located 1 mile (1½ kilometers) south of Johnson Point.

Boston Harbor Public Ramp
Located near top of Budd Inlet.
Olympia WA
(Launching for southwestern Puget Sound: steep concrete ramp. Launching at 2-foot [⅔-meter] tides and greater. Toilets and telephone across road from ramp and marina.)

From I-5 (Interstate Highway 5) take Exit 105 and follow signs to City Center and Port of Olympia: stay right and take "B" Exit. You will be on Plum Street. When you cross State Avenue, do not turn left to East Bay Marina. Continue straight. From here, head north along east shore of Budd Inlet for 7 miles (11 kilometers). Plum Street becomes East Bay Drive, then Boston Harbor Road. Go to Main Street. Turn left onto Main at the sign to Boston Harbor Marina and go ⅓ mile (½ kilometer). The launching ramp is immediately past the marina. From I-5, it takes 15 or 20 minutes.

East Bay Marina Ramps
Port of Olympia
1022 Marine Drive NE
Olympia WA 98501
(206) 786-1400
(In-the-city launching for southwestern Puget Sound: concrete ramps, good at all tides; at the head of Budd Inlet. Restrooms with wheelchair access, hot showers; telephones.)

Arcadia Point Public Ramp
Off Highway 3
Shelton WA
(Launching near Shelton for southwestern Puget Sound: concrete ramp, good at all except minus tides. A great deal of parking space a fair walk from the water. No toilets; no telephone.)

Off Highway 3: from the top of the hill in Shelton, head east on Arcadia Point Road. Drive for 15 minutes to the end of the road.

• Launching for Agate Passage
Charles Lawrence Memorial Ramp
Foot of Suquamish Way, Suquamish
(Steep concrete ramp; good at midtides to high tides. Suquamish Dock where people fish, lots of parking space and a tiny beach for picnics. Toilets are ⅔ mile [1 kilometer] away at Old Man House; go back up Suquamish Way to Division Avenue, turn left and follow signs to Old Man House at foot of McKinistry Street. Telephone is outside grocery store in shopping center at southeast corner of Division Avenue and Suquamish Way.)

Located 5 minutes off Highway 305: immediately west of Agate Pass Bridge at traffic light, go north 1½ miles (2½ kilometers) to end of Suquamish Way. Ramp is below Chief Sealth's grave.

• Launching for Hood Canal

Salsbury Point County Park Ramp
Foot of Whitford Road NE
North of Hood Canal Bridge (east end)
(Concrete ramp, good at all except extreme low tides. Huge parking area, toilets and telephone.)

Off Highway 104: located north of the east end of Hood Canal Bridge. From junction of Highways 3 and 104, head north toward Port Gamble. Go ½ mile (¾ kilometer) to Wheeler Street with signs to Salsbury Point County Park. Turn left down Wheeler which curves back toward the bridge. Go to Whitford Road NE. Turn right.

Hood Canal Bridge Ramp
Off Paradise Bay Road
North of Hood Canal Bridge (west end)
(Concrete ramp, good at all tides. Limited parking. Pit toilets and primitive camping at adjacent Shine Tidelands State Park. No telephone – telephone across bridge at Salsbury Point Park.)

Off Highway 104: located north of the west end of the Hood Canal Bridge. To reach it, turn north into Paradise Bay Road, which is the first road at the west end of the bridge; immediately turn right again and head downhill. At the "Y", bear left to Shine Tidelands State Park or go straight to the ramp.

William Hicks County Park Ramp
Hicks Road
South of Hood Canal Bridge (west end)
(Concrete ramp, good at medium and high tides. Limited parking, pit toilets and a picnic table. No telephone – telephone across the bridge at Salsbury County Park.)

Off Highway 104: located south of the west end of the Hood Canal Bridge. To reach it, turn south into Hicks Road, which is the first road at the west end of the bridge. Go 1¼ miles (2 kilometers) and turn left into the park.

• Launching for Admiralty Inlet

Fort Worden State Park Ramp
200 Battery Way
Port Townsend WA 98368
(206) 385-4730; fax (206) 385-7248
(Launching for a fee: concrete ramp, good at all tides. Lots of parking space. Fast food. Camping with hot showers year-round – reserve for camping. Restrooms with wheelchair-accessible flush toilets. Telephone across road, outside the refreshment stand.)

Off Highway 20: in Port Townsend, go along the waterfront on Sims Way to Kearney Street and follow signs to Fort Worden State Park. At Fort Worden, turn left through the main gate of the park, which is opposite Cherry Street, onto Fort Worden Way. Turn right at Eisenhower Avenue; and continue straight to a large anchor, then turn left and head down the hill to the ramp.

• Launching for Northern Puget Sound

Port of Edmonds
336 Admiral Way
Edmonds WA 98020
(206) 774-0549; fax (206) 774-7837
(Sling launches. Plenty of room to park; restrooms, coin-operated hot showers; telephone outside marina office. Next to Anthony's Home Port.)

Edmonds Marina Beach
Admiral Way, south end
Edmonds WA
(Car-top boat launching across beach. Limited parking space; toilets but no telephone. Nearest telephone at Port of Edmonds.)

Off I-5 (Interstate Highway 5): take Exit 177 and follow signs to Edmonds-Kingston ferry. When almost at the ferry lineup, continue straight toward the water on Dayton Street. Cross the railway tracks, turn left onto Admiral Way and follow signs to the beach. It is 15 minutes off I-5.

Possession Beach Waterfront Park
    Public Ramp
Foot of Possession Road
Whidbey Island, south end
(Concrete ramp, good except with very

• Launching for Northern Puget Sound (continued)

low tides. Parking, picnic tables, wheel-chair-accessible restrooms with flush toilets and telephone next to it.)

Reach from Highway 525: you turn off the highway at Cultus Bay Road. It is 2½ miles (4 kilometers) northwest of Clinton at Columbia Beach, south tip of Whidbey Island; and 22 miles (35 kilometers) southeast of the Port Townsend Ferry-Keystone junction. From Highway 525, go 6 miles (10 kilometers) to the park. It takes 20 minutes.

Turn south onto Cultus Bay Road following the signs to Possession Beach: Cultus Bay Road becomes Possession Road. When you reach a sign saying Possession Beach Waterfront Park, do not go straight. Turn right and head downhill to the water.

Mukilteo State Park Ramp
Foot of Front Street, Mukilteo WA
(Concrete ramp, good at all tides. Great deal of parking; picnic tables; restrooms with flush toilets. Telephones one-half block away at Front Street and Mukilteo Speedway beside ferry landing.)

From I-5 (Interstate Highway 5), takes 15 or 20 minutes to Mukilteo.
• Heading south on I-5, take Exit 189 onto Highway 526 and go to Mukilteo Speedway. Turn right.
• Heading north, take Exit 182 onto Highway 525.

Follow signs to Mukilteo Ferry. Just before the ferry landing you will see a sign to Mukilteo State Park: turn left and go one-half block south of the ferry landing to the ramp.

• Launching for Rosario Strait and Deception Pass at Fidalgo and Whidbey Islands

Cornet Bay Public Ramp
Deception Pass State Park
Whidbey Island, north end
(Concrete ramp: good at all except extreme low tides. Restrooms and hot showers. Telephone at top of privately owned dock at Cornet Bay. It is opposite Canyon Road and ⅓ mile [½ kilometer] west of the public ramp.)

From Highway 20, when 1½ miles (2½ kilometers) *south* of Deception Pass Bridge, go east on Cornet Bay Road for 1¼ miles (2 kilometers) to ramp.

Bowman Bay Public Ramp
Deception Pass State Park
Fidalgo Island, south end
(Concrete ramp for a fee: good only at high tides. Lots of parking space; picnic tables. Telephone and restrooms at the CCC Interpretive Center.)

Off Highway 20: immediately *north* of Deception Pass Bridge and south of Pass Lake, turn west. Then follow signs to Bowman [Reservation] Bay.

Washington Park Ramp
Fidalgo Island, north end
Anacortes WA
(Launching at Fidalgo Head, near Anacortes ferry terminal: steep concrete ramp, good at all tides for small boats but can be difficult for larger boats; coin-operated gate to it. Restrooms and hot showers. Telephone in front of the park superintendent's home beside curve of drive out.)

Washington Park is 4 miles (7 kilometers) west of Anacortes off Highway 20. Follow signs through Anacortes toward the San Juan ferry. From Commercial Avenue and 12th, go for 3 miles (5 kilometers) toward the ferry. You will see a marina sign: just past it, bear left – do not go straight to the ferry which is ⅔ mile (1 kilometer). Bear left through the stop sign onto Sunset Avenue. It is the same distance again to Washington Park Ramp at the end of the road.

Cap Sante Marine
Cap Sante Boat Haven
Next to Harbor Office
PO Box 607
Anacortes WA 98221
(206) 293-3145; 1-800-422-5794
(Sling launch at Fidalgo Bay in city of Anacortes. Restrooms and hot showers; telephones beside marina office.)

• Launching for Rosario Strait and Bellingham Bay (continued)

Skyline Marina
2011 Skyline Way
Anacortes WA 98221
(206) 293-5134; fax (206) 293-9458
(Sling launch at Flounder Bay, south of Fidalgo Head near Anacortes ferry terminal. Restrooms and hot showers; telephones beside marina office.)

Wildcat Cove Public Ramp
Larrabee State Park
Foot of Cove Road, off Chuckanut Drive
(Concrete ramp; good at medium and high tides. Pit toilets, picnic table and lots of parking space. Telephone at the campground, south on Chuckanut.)

Located 15 to 25 minutes off I-5 (Interstate Highway 5) between Bellingham and Mount Vernon at Wildcat Cove, south of Bellingham Bay.
• Heading south from Bellingham, take Exit 250 and follow signs to Chuckanut Drive (Highway 11) and Larrabee State Park. The road becomes narrow and curves alongside the water to the park. You will see signs to the launching ramp at Cove Road. From Bellingham, 15 minutes to Wildcat Cove.
• Heading north, past Mount Vernon and Burlington take Exit 231 to Chuckanut Drive (Highway 11) and head north – takes 25 minutes to the launch point. When 10 minutes past Bow-Edison Road and shortly past the two Larrabee campground entrances, you will reach Cove Road. Turn left to Wildcat Cove.

Fairhaven Public Ramp
Harris Avenue, immediately east of 355 Harris (across from 6th Street)
Bellingham Bay, south end
Bellingham WA
(Concrete ramp, good at all except extreme low tides. Limited parking. Restrooms; telephone outside restrooms.)

In Bellingham, just east of the Alaska ferry dock. From I-5 (Interstate Highway 5), take Exit 250 and follow signs to the Alaska ferry. The ramp is 2 miles (3 kilometers) off the highway. Go on Old Fairhaven Parkway to 12th Street. Turn right, then left onto Harris Avenue. The ramp is at the south end of the harbor.

Squalicum Harbor Ramp
Foot of Thomas J. Glenn Drive
Bellingham Bay, north end
Bellingham WA
(Launching for a fee at Bellingham Bay, north end: concrete ramps, good at all tides. Large parking space; freshwater taps in parking area to wash gear. Restrooms and telephones at the north end of Harbor Center. At the top of the ramp, turn left and walk 80 yards [75 meters] through Harbor Center to the facilities.)

In Bellingham, 5 to 10 minutes off I-5 (Interstate Highway 5): the ramps are at the north end of Bellingham Bay. Turn off Roeder Avenue at Thomas J. Glenn Drive and then turn right at Boat Launch Parking sign and go to the ramps.
• Heading south on I-5, take Exit 256. Turn right at Meridian Street and go to traffic light at Squalicum Way. Turn right and follow the Squalicum Harbor signs toward the water; the road curves left into Roeder Avenue. Go on Roeder for just over ⅔ mile (1 kilometer) passing various harbor facilities. Go to the south end of Squalicum Harbor and turn right into Thomas J. Glenn Drive.
• Heading north on I-5, take Exit 253 to Lakeway Drive and go back under I-5. Go along Lakeway following Squalicum Harbor signs: follow Holly Street and go through the city center to F Street, turn right on Roeder Avenue, then left at Thomas J. Glenn Drive.

• More Information for Boat Divers and Kayak-Divers

Explore for new sites on your own; additional launching ramps, public beaches where you can land and facilities are listed in the following publications:

Henning's Guide to Boat Ramps, Elevators, Slings edited by Henning Helstrom. No date. Helstrom Publications, 3121 SE 167th Avenue, Portland OR 97236, (503) 761-

3139. (Scope: Access directions and descriptions, with photographs, to launching facilities in Washington and Oregon.)

Morgan's Guide: Boat Launches & Ramps on Puget Sound edited by Bill Hanson, 1991. Sound Publishing, PO Box 7192, Tacoma WA 98407, (206) 565-6568. (Scope: Well-organized user-friendly information, useful for boaters with large craft and with dive-kayaks; well indexed. Covers Puget Sound and the San Juan Islands.)

Puget Sound Public Shellfish Sites booklet compiled by Washington Department of Fisheries, 1989. Obtain free copy from some dive stores, the Department of Fisheries or the Department of Natural Resources, DNR Photo and Map Sales, 1111 Washington Street SE, PO Box 47031, Olympia WA 98504-7031, (206) 902-1234. (Scope: Maps showing launching ramps, access to public beaches by road and water, and artificial fishing reefs from southern Puget Sound through San Juans.)

Washington Atlas & Gazetteer, 1988. DeLorme Mapping, PO Box 298, Freeport, ME 04032. Toll-free in USA: 1-800-227-1656 or (207) 865-4171. (Scope: Parks, beaches, boat launch sites, moorage, campgrounds throughout Washington State.)

Washington Public Shore Guide: Marine Waters by James W. Scott and Melly A. Reuling, 1986. University of Washington Press, PO Box 50096, Seattle WA 98145-5096, (206) 543-8870. (Scope: launching and beaches throughout Washington.)

• More Dive Facilities
Discover Scuba
PO Box 33512
Seattle WA 98133
(206) 362-3863
(Guiding services throughout Puget Sound and the San Juan Islands; specialize in Whidbey Island dive packages including accommodation.)

• Ferry Information
Washington State Ferries
Colman Dock/Pier 52, 801 Alaskan Way
Seattle WA 98104-1487
(206) 464-6400: recorded schedules with touch-tone menu choices.
Toll-free in Washington State: 1-800-843-3779
(Ferries between Seattle and Bremerton on Kitsap Peninsula; Seattle-Bainbridge Island [Winslow]; Edmonds and Kingston on Kitsap Peninsula; Mukilteo and Clinton [Columbia Beach] on Whidbey Island; Port Townsend on Olympic Peninsula and Keystone, Whidbey Island; Fauntleroy in West Seattle and Vashon Island; Fauntleroy in West Seattle and Southworth on Kitsap Peninsula; Point Defiance in Tacoma and Tahlequah, Vashon Island; Anacortes and San Juan Islands and Sidney, British Columbia.)

Victoria Line Ltd.
185 Dallas Road
Victoria BC V8V 1A1
(604) 480-5555; fax (604) 480-5222
Toll-free in western USA and western Canada, for information only: 1-800-668-1167.
(Summer sailings between downtown Seattle and downtown Victoria from mid-May through mid-September.)

Black Ball Transport, Inc.
10777 Main Street, Suite 106
Bellevue WA 98004
(206) 622-2222
Port Angeles: (206) 457-4491
Victoria: (604) 386-2202
(Ferries between Port Angeles, Washington, and Victoria, British Columbia.)

• Tourist Information

Washington State Tourism
101 General Administration Building, PO Box 42500
Olympia WA 98504-2500
1-800-544-1800: Toll-free throughout Canada and the USA, including Hawaii and Alaska, for *Travel Kit (Lodging/Travel Guide* and seasonal *Field Guide)* only.
(206) 586-2088 or 586-2102 for travel counselling.
Parking is very difficult – it is easier to telephone or write.

Washington State Parks
Public Information
7150 Cleanwater Lane
PO Box 42650
Olympia WA 98504-2650
(206) 753-2027, message-taking mach-ine and respond by mail. To reach a per-son on the telephone, contact each park.

Seattle-King County Convention
and Visitor Bureau
Level 1, Galleria
Located at 800 Convention Place
8th and Pike Streets
520 Pike Street, Suite 1300
Seattle WA 98101
(206) 461-5840

How to go – Seattle, Tacoma, Olympia, Bremerton, Port Townsend, the Olympic Peninsula, Fidalgo Island, Whidbey Island and Bellingham comprise an enormous area. But because these locales are so interrelated they are all included in one chapter. Time to travel from place to place is included in access directions for divers unfamiliar with Washington State; these times are approximate. If my truck will take the curves, I usually travel at posted speed limits. But times vary depending on traffic and ferry line-ups – travel at uncongested times to meet the times given.

Washington State is surrounded by water – one reason it is such a rich region for diving. And today, as well as in historic Puget Sound days, boats are an important part of the transportation system. Car ferries connect many communities within Puget Sound in addition to connecting Washington State with Vancouver Island. Landmarks used for directions are bridges, ferry landings and the large cities where the greatest number of people live: Seattle, Tacoma, Olympia, Bremerton and Bellingham.

• Seattle is one hub: distances measured from here are from I-5 (Interstate Highway 5) at Denny near the city center.

• Tacoma and Olympia are at the southern end of I-5 and many dives can be reached from these centers. Distances from these cities are usually from Exit 132 in Tacoma and Exit 104 in Olympia.

• Bremerton is the hub of Kitsap Peninsula: car ferries and roads approach Bremer-ton from all directions. Road distances given are from Highway 3 or 303.

• Hood Canal Bridge and Agate Pass Bridge are important locator points.

• Port Townsend seems at the center of this guidebook. Car ferries and roads converge on it: you can drive north from Tacoma and Bremerton via the Hood Canal on Highways 3, 104 and 20 to Port Townsend. Drive from Olympia and Shelton on Highways 101 and 20. Go by way of the car ferry from Keystone, Whidbey Island-Port Townsend; from Victoria, British Columbia-Port Angeles, Olympic Peninsula; or from Edmonds-Kingston or Seattle-Bainbridge Island by car ferry and then follow signs via Hood Canal to Highway 20 and Port Townsend.

• Bellingham is the northernmost location in Washington State from which directions are given for this chapter.

But don't stop at the border. Lots more diving is north in Canada. It is described in the foregoing chapters. When you have dived Puget Sound, explore – head north!

* All of this service information is subject to change.

WHISKEY ROCK
Kayak Dive or Boat Dive

Skill: All divers

Why go: Whiskey Rock is great for a first-kayak-dive because you can anchor your dive-kayak next to the rocky shore, climb onto rocks that are convenient at the tide height you find, gear up, and dive. It is a 15-minute paddle and current free.

A bonanza of red sunflower stars – many like huge platters. Also purple stars and yellow stars around this giant jumble of rocks riddled with nooks and crannies. Going down, we saw perch. Heading up, lots of empty clam shells – possibly an octopus's lair. Or the clam shells could be leavings of voracious sea stars. They were feeding.

The occasional isolated plumose anemone is on the rocks, pink anemones on the sand. We saw a few giant barnacles under rocky overhangs. Dungeness crabs all over the sand and red rock crabs around and over and beneath the rocks. Inviting dark holes to look into, overhangs to look under at Whiskey Rock – take a light.

An even easier kayak-dive is at Seagull Rock, the first rock around the corner to the right of Wildcat Cove. It is similar to Whiskey Rock but closer, shallower and easier to gear up. At low tides, you can anchor in 1 foot (⅓ meter) of water in a sandy cove, step in the water, gear up, and dive – a gentle entry. But shallow diving requires careful buoyancy control, and visibility can be very poor. Yet, it *is* easier to gear up at Seagull Rock, good for divers who like to progress in tiny increments . . .

Before or after diving, interesting to paddle to Clarks Point. Go into the small bay at the end of the point and see petrified trunks of palm trees in the rock wall on the eastern shore. Two of these palmettos have large trunks, about 9 inches (23 centimeters) in diameter. Another clump of smaller palms is between the two larger ones. A wonder to see evidence of semi-tropical life in this region. Diving here when palms flourished, you might have met turtles and crocodiles.

These palms grew in the Paleocene or Eocene time – they are about 55 to 60 million years old. You can easily view them from your boat.

Bottom and Depths: At Whiskey Rock, you will find a jumble of rocks, undercut and slit with hiding places. A wall at the north end. Depth of 30 to 40 feet (9 to 12 meters) at the base of the rocks, with silty sand between the rocks and at their base.

At Seagull Rock, depth of 20 to 30 feet (6 to 9 meters), depending on tide height.

Hazards: Silt. Weight yourself adequately so you can stay down without effort, yet hover over the bottom and not stir up silt.

Telephone: At Larrabee Park campground. From Wildcat Cove, return to Cove Road and go south just over ⅓ mile (½ kilometer).

Facilities: None at Whiskey Rock. Launching, pit toilets, picnic table and lots of parking space at Wildcat Cove. Camping with hot showers at Larrabee State Park ⅓ mile (½ kilometer) south of Wildcat Cove. Launching at south end of Bellingham Bay.

Access: Whiskey Rock is south of Chuckanut Bay at the north end of Samish Bay. It is ½ nautical mile (1 kilometer) northwest of the launching ramp at Wildcat Cove in Larrabee Park. Launch a dive-kayak, or boat, at Wildcat Cove. Paddle 5 minutes to Seagull Rock – 15 minutes to Whiskey Rock. Climb onto the rock, gear up and dive around the outside. Wheelchair divers who paddle dive-kayaks could dive Seagull.

Clarks Point, for sightseeing, is at the north end of Chuckanut Bay. On a calm day, you could reach it by dive-kayak from Wildcat Cove. Go 3 nautical miles (6 kilometers) from Wildcat Cove across open water at the entrance to Chuckanut Bay. On the way, pass Seagull and Whiskey rocks, and you could check out more potential dive sites at Governors Point, Chuckanut Island, where you can land, and Chuckanut Rock. At high tides of 6 to 9 feet (2 to 3 meters), you could paddle a dive-kayak from Chuckanut Park at the north end of Chuckanut Bay to the petrified palms – 20 to 25 minutes. It is only 1 nautical mile (2 kilometers) but you go when the tide is flooding. Paddle beneath the railway bridge and close along the shoreline to Clarks Point. At lower tides, this paddle is not possible as the head of the bay is a mud flat.

To reach Chuckanut Park: in Bellingham, turn off Old Fairhaven Parkway, following signs to Highway 11 or Chuckanut Drive. Go 1¼ miles (2 kilometers) south on Chuckanut Drive to 21st Street. Turn right and go a short way to the road end of Fairhaven Avenue. Here there is parking space for four or five cars at the edge of the mud flat.

Comments: Governors Point is a progression: it is for advanced kayak-divers who can anchor, gear up in the water and dive. It would be easy for divers with boats.

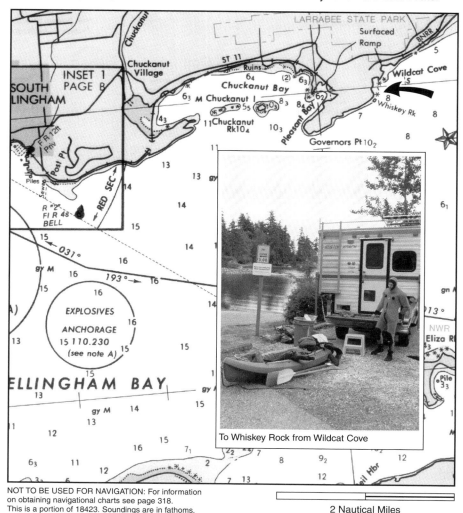

To Whiskey Rock from Wildcat Cove

NOT TO BE USED FOR NAVIGATION: For information on obtaining navigational charts see page 318.
This is a portion of 18423. Soundings are in fathoms.

2 Nautical Miles

SARES HEAD
Kayak Dive or Boat Dive

Skill: Intermediate and expert divers. All divers with guide. Advanced kayak-divers.

Why go: A cascade of white plumose anemones spills over Sares Head like a gigantic waterfall. A dark cavern is beneath it. Basket stars are scattered like giant snowflakes at its entrance. Swimming scallops, too – some clap up around us. Inside the cave, basket stars in shadowy corners.

We look up beneath another overhang, a small one. In the darkest corner, see slipper cucumbers like red lace. Swim away from the wall, lie back and look up: white froth of plumose anemones burgeons from the black bulge of rock. Sares Head appears like the prow of a ship breaking waves. A black rockfish swims past. Yellowtail rockfish. A lingcod. You might see tiger rockfish. On the way up we see lined chitons dotting the rocks. Giant purple urchins between boulders. A rock scallop. We see broken shells on the bottom – must be an octopus. We look for it in the crevice above the shells. We are rewarded by finding a decorated warbonnet, nearby a painted anemone on a rock, and a 1½-foot (½-meter) lingcod cruises past in the thicket of kelp.

So much! But basket stars, shallow and deep, are the best things to me about Sares Head. They're extravagant.

Bottom and Depths: The rock wall at Sares Head bulges like a gigantic monolith and drops to sand at 90 to 100 feet (27 to 30 meters). A cavern at its base. Rocky ledges stairstep up from the cave to the narrow ledge south of Sares Head that is at a depth of 30 to 40 feet (9 to 12 meters). Boulders scattered from deep to shallow. Basket stars start at 30 to 40 feet (9 to 12 meters). In summer, thick curtains of kelp.

Hazards: Current; bull kelp and boats, especially in summer. Dive on the slack. Carry a knife. Listen for boats. Ascend close to the wall all the way to the surface.

Telephones: • Bowman Bay, beside road. • Cornet Bay Marina, top of the dock.

Facilities: None at Sares Head. Air fills and dive-kayak rental in Oak Harbor; air fills in Anacortes. While in Deception Pass State Park you will find launching at Bowman [Reservation] Bay; launching, restrooms and hot showers at Cornet Bay; in summer, restrooms and hot showers at Rosario Beach. Camping year-round – hot showers, too, in the Cranberry Lake area of the park. To reach it, turn west off Highway 20 between Cornet Bay Road and the south end of Deception Pass Bridge.

Access: Sares Head is on Rosario Strait at Fidalgo Island. It is 1½ nautical miles (3 kilometers) north of Deception Pass. At the time of writing, you know you are there by the dead tree snag on the point at Sares Head.

Charter out of Oak Harbor or Anacortes; or launch at Bowman [Reservation] Bay, Cornet Bay or Anacortes. Kayak-divers can hand-launch at Rosario Beach (see road directions to it on page 230): walk 22 yards (20 meters) down a trail to the water and paddle to Sares Head in 15 minutes. Easier to paddle with the flooding current and dive on high slack; then coast back with the ebb. At Sares Head: divers with inflatables and kayak-divers can anchor in a cove immediately south of Sares Head where there is a narrow ledge at 30 to 40 feet (9 to 12 meters). In summer, a forest of bull kelp marks it. In winter, thin wisps of kelp. Larger boats cannot anchor at Sares Head because of depth, and must leave a boat tender on board.

Cornet Bay, Bowman [Reservation] Bay and Rosario Beach are all in Deception Pass State Park which is open year-round. But access to Rosario is limited: in winter, the gate to it is open only on holidays and weekends.

Comments: Explore on land, too: hiking trails throughout Deception Pass Park.

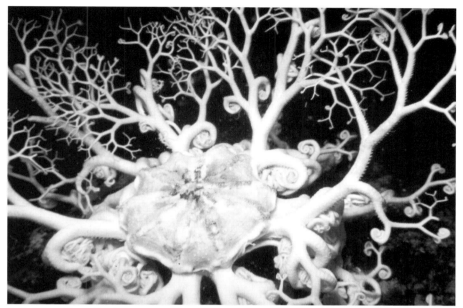

Basket star at Sares Head

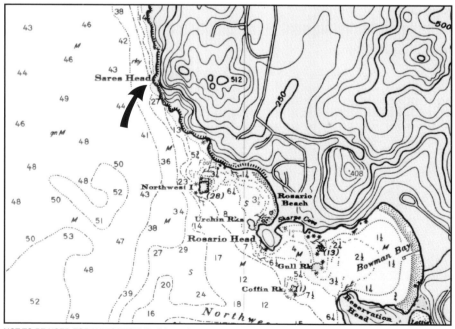

NOT TO BE USED FOR NAVIGATION: For information
on obtaining navigational charts see page 318.
This is a portion of 18427. Soundings are in fathoms.

½ Nautical Mile

ROSARIO BEACH
Shore Dive

Tide Table: Port Townsend

Skill: All divers

Why go: The underwater setting is wild, the surface civilized, the dive within the capability of all divers. This wilderness feeling is the unique offering of Rosario. Unlike many nearby sites, Rosario is a totally natural underwater scene. No man-made pilings to attract marine animals. No jetty. Just bottom kelp, bull kelp, red and green seaweed feathering up in the water. Many animals, too: big frothy white plumose anemones, kelp greenlings, grunt sculpins, octopuses, gum boot chitons, decorator crabs and thousands of spider crabs. Millions of transparent shrimp hop and skitter about – the bottom is like a field of grasshoppers in July. Look for juvenile wolf-eels and umbrella crabs.

If you've ever wanted to stroke a fish, Rosario Beach is the place you can probably do so. There are some red Irish lords here. And although I wouldn't say they *like* back scratching, they tolerate it. The waters at Rosario are within Deception Pass State Park, an underwater reserve. You must not take any marine life.

Rosario is good for underwater sightseeing with a civilized setting and amenities on the surface – both the good and bad. Huge evergreens are on shore. The sound of jets whistling and roaring overhead is ever-present – even under water. After diving, year-round camping and hot showers nearby in the park.

Bottom and Depths: Shallow and sandy in bay. Around Urchin Rocks, undulating rocky bottom covered with bull kelp to a depth of 40 to 50 feet (12 to 15 meters). Sand beyond.

Hazards: Current, bull kelp and poor visibility. Dive near slack; carry a knife. The water is usually silty with debris stirred up by currents through nearby Deception Pass. It is particularly turbid in spring because of Skagit River runoff. Visibility is best at high slack tide in very early spring or late fall.

Telephone: Bowman [Reservation] Bay picnic site, beside road. To reach it, go 1 mile (1½ kilometers) back almost to Highway 20; turn sharply right and follow signs to Bowman Bay.

Facilities: At Rosario, which is open on weekends only, parking and picnic tables. In summer, restrooms and coin-operated hot showers. In the park just *south* of Deception Pass – at the time of writing – camping with hot showers is available year-round.

Access: Rosario Beach is on Rosario Strait *north* of Deception Pass. It is at the south end of Fidalgo Island in Deception Pass State Park off Highway 20. You can go all the way to Rosario by road – no ferries. However, access to Rosario is limited. In winter, the gate to it is open only on holidays and weekends.

In Deception Pass State Park, just south of Pass Lake, turn toward the sea and follow signs to Rosario Beach and the marine center. Immediately past the marine center, you come to Rosario. Walk 240 yards (220 meters) down a groomed path past the pavilion to the beach where the entry is very easy over the sand. Walk up the beach to your left and snorkel out to Urchin Rocks.

To get to turnoff to Rosario Beach
• From Seattle, go north on I-5 (Interstate Highway 5) and take Exit 230. Go west on Highway 20 and follow signs to Whidbey Island and Deception Pass. Then turn left, still on Highway 20, and go 5 miles (8 kilometers) south to the Rosario turnoff. From Seattle, 2¼ hours to the dive.

• From Bellingham, go south on I-5 (Interstate Highway 5) and take Exit 230. Go west on Highway 20 and follow signs to Whidbey Island and Deception Pass. Turn left, still on Highway 20, and go 5 miles (8 kilometers) south to the Rosario turnoff. From Bellingham, 50 minutes to the dive.

• From Anacortes, go east on Highway 20 for 2½ miles (4 kilometers) to the turnoff to Oak Harbor and Port Townsend ferry. Turn right. Still on Highway 20, go for 5 miles (8 kilometers) south to the Rosario turnoff. From Anacortes, 15 minutes to the dive; from San Juan ferry, 25 minutes.

• From Oak Harbor, go north on Highway 20. Drive for 11 miles (18 kilometers) to the Rosario turnoff. It is just across the bridge at Deception Pass. Takes 20 minutes.

Comments: A luxurious place for camping and diving. With hot showers after!

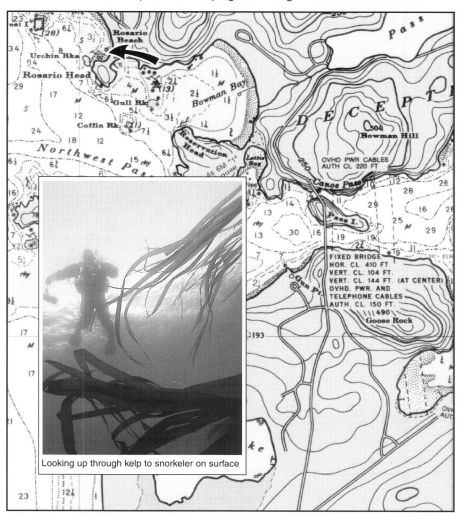

Looking up through kelp to snorkeler on surface

NOT TO BE USED FOR NAVIGATION: For information on obtaining navigational charts see page 318. This is a portion of 18427. Soundings are in fathoms.

½ Nautical Mile

231

Skill: Expert divers

Why go: An extravaganza of suspension feeders and fish looks like a surrealistic underwater painting down the steep rock walls of Pass Island.

Purple plume worms burst out along the entire wall in flamboyant bouquets, their purple tufts not even disturbed by divers. Masses of 2-inch (5-centimeter) red, pink and green dahlia anemones carpet the space between. Confetti-like bright red anemones and hot pink brooding anemones are scattered side-by-side in a splash of color. The brooding anemones spill over onto parchment-like plume worm tubes. Other feather duster tubes are completely encased in yellow sponges. Not enough room for all the life on the rocks!

Strange finger sponges poke out from the most current-washed parts of the wall like flabby pale yellow rubber gloves. We saw urchins, chitons, and white plumose anemones softening the deep crevices. Large lingcod, cabezons and huge kelp greenlings sweeping out of the dark and back again.

But the most striking feature is the splendrous wall of suspension feeders. A grand scenic tour.

Bottom and Depths: Steep rock wall drops from the island to a depth of 100 to 110 feet (30 to 34 meters) in the pass, depending on tide height. Deep crevices and overhangs. Some bull kelp by Pass Island.

Hazards: Current, downcurrents, whirlpools, boats and poor visibility. Very swift currents. Dive on a day with a small tidal exchange – best at the turn before ebb and precisely on slack. Arrive at the site 45 minutes before the predicted turn at the end of the flood. As with all current predictions, slack may not happen as scheduled. Watch the water and when it slows down, go in. Have a "live" boat ready to pick you up if you are swept away. Listen for boats and ascend close to the steep sides of the island well out of the way of those boats.

Visibility can be poor, particularly when the Skagit River is in flood in springtime or after heavy rain. Also, Deception Pass is different from most places. The ebbing tide carries flotsam and jetsam out of the bay into the pass. For best visibility, dive on the tail end of a flooding current.

Telephones: • Cornet Bay Marina, top of dock. • Bowman [Reservation] Bay, beside road.

Facilities: Launching in the park at Cornet Bay where there are flush toilets and coin-operated hot showers, and launching at Bowman [Reservation] Bay.

Access: Deception Pass is between Fidalgo and Whidbey islands in Deception Pass State Park. Charter out of Oak Harbor or Anacortes; or launch at Cornet Bay south of Deception Pass or Bowman [Reservation] Bay north of it. Then go by boat to Pass Island under the bridge. Leave someone in your boat as a pickup while you dive.

Before diving, try to see Deception Pass in action. Go when the 5- to 8-knot (9- to 15-kilometer/hour) current is running: See the impressive whirlpools, the wild current whipping through. Park at a scenic overlook at the north end of the northernmost bridge over the pass. Pass Island is below. To reach Deception Pass by road: from I-5 (Interstate Highway 5), take Exit 230. Go west on Highway 20 to signs pointing south to Deception Pass State Park. From Anacortes, go east on Highway 20 to signs pointing to it; turn right. Drive south for 10 minutes to the park.

Comments: In 1792 Captain Vancouver named this waterway Port Gardner. When he discovered it was not an inlet but a pass between two islands – he renamed it Deception Pass.

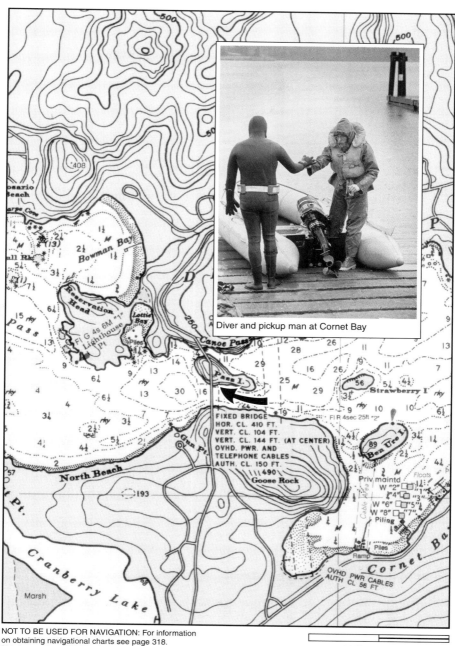

Diver and pickup man at Cornet Bay

FIXED BRIDGE
HOR. CL. 410 FT.
VERT. CL. 104 FT.
VERT. CL. 144 FT. (AT CENTER)
OVHD. PWR. AND
TELEPHONE CABLES
AUTH. CL. 150 FT.

NOT TO BE USED FOR NAVIGATION: For information
on obtaining navigational charts see page 318.
This is a portion of 18427. Soundings are in fathoms.

½ Nautical Mile

233

FORT CASEY UNDERWATER PARK
Shore Dive

Tide Table: Port Townsend

Skill: All divers and snorkelers first half of jetty. All divers with guide to end of jetty and to wharf.

Why go: Fort Casey Underwater Park, better known as Keystone, is a "must" for anyone who wants to dive all the best sites in the northwest. Especially popular with photographers.

Keystone jetty concentrates life. The fish are fat in this current-washed area. And very tame, too. The fish seem to know that Keystone has been a wildlife reserve for years. Many divers actually hand-feed kelp greenlings that live beside the jetty. One photographer says the painted greenlings are tame to the point of being a nuisance. "They get in the way when you're taking pictures!"

Gorgeous white plumose anemones are heaped on the riprap at the base of the jetty like dollops of whipped cream. Other colorful invertebrates, too. Countless rockfish in crevices. An octopus in a dark hole. Wolf-eels. Life stacked on life. Even divers are accepted as part of this underwater scene. On weekends, expect to meet lots of divers.

The abandoned wharf at the left of the jetty provides more shelter for marine life, but watch the current. Dive here on slack. I love drifting with schools of seaperch between these pilings covered with purple plume worms.

Bottom and Depths: The jetty made of heaps of rock or riprap is 75 yards (70 meters) long. It is a solid breakwater structure and you could not slip beneath it into the path of the ferry. Maximum depth at the tip of the jetty, 50 to 60 feet (15 to 18 meters). The abandoned wharf (east of the jetty) harbors much life on its 30- to 40-foot (9- to 12-meter) deep pilings. Smooth sand and pebble bottom between the wharf and jetty.

Hazards: Current, southeast wind, ferry, broken fishing line and bull kelp. Look for people fishing before you go in. Dive on slack, especially at the wharf and when current is ebbing. Be careful not to be swept around the end of the jetty into the path of the ferry. Stay down, hold onto rocks and pull yourself along the jetty back towards shore. Do not dive when southeast wind blows surf onto the exposed beach. Carry a knife; if caught in kelp or fishing line you can cut your way free.

Telephone: On ferry building.

Facilities: Picnic tables, a great deal of parking, cold-water showers for rinsing gear, restrooms with wheelchair-accessible flush toilets and coin-operated hot showers, and launching ramp – all right at Keystone. Camping close-by at Fort Casey Historical Park, also with coin-operated hot showers. Dive guiding at Whidbey. Dive-kayak rental and air fills in Oak Harbor; air fills in Anacortes.

Access: Fort Casey Underwater Park is at Keystone Harbor on Admiralty Bay, Whidbey Island. It is 20 minutes south of Oak Harbor at the end of Highway 20; follow signs to Port Townsend Ferry and Fort Casey State Park.

Take Keystone turnoff from Highway 20 and Highway 25 junction, and go 3 miles (5 kilometers) along Keystone Spit. Turn left into the parking area for the underwater park. The Port Townsend ferry landing is just past the parking area. If you reach it, you have gone too far. Enter the water at the left of the jetty.

Wheelchair access is possible for divers with able-bodied help to cross a short stretch of gravel sloped like a driveway. It is excellent for divers with wheelchairs who also paddle dive-kayaks. From the launching ramp in the parking area: paddle around the jetty and back to the beach on the other side. Total distance is 220 yards (200 meters). Not far to paddle, but do not try to swim it. Too much current and you are exposed to ferry traffic. Leave your dive-kayak on the beach and enter the water on the left of the jetty.

To get to turnoff for Keystone
• From Seattle to Keystone turnoff: a choice of two routes. *Drive all the way:* go north on I-5 (Interstate Highway 5) and take Exit 230. Go west on Highway 20. When signs point to Deception Pass and Whidbey Island, turn left. Head south through Oak Harbor; follow the signs to Port Townsend ferry. *Driving and ferry:* go north on I-5. Take Exit 182. Go to Mukilteo-Clinton ferry on Highway 525; sail to Columbia Beach at Whidbey Island in 20 minutes; then drive north on Highway 525. From Clinton, it is 22 miles (35 kilometers) to the Keystone turnoff: then follow signs to Port Townsend ferry. Both routes take 2 hours or more, depending on traffic and ferry lineups.
• From Bellingham, drive south on I-5 (Interstate Highway 5) and take Exit 230. Go west on Highway 20 to signs pointing to Deception Pass and Oak Harbor. Turn left. Still on Highway 20, follow signs through Oak Harbor to Port Townsend ferry: from Oak Harbor, 15 miles (24 kilometers) to Keystone turnoff. From Bellingham, 1½ hours.
• From San Juan ferry at Anacortes, go east on Highway 20. When 2½ miles (4 kilometers) past Anacortes, turn right. Still on Highway 20, follow signs to Whidbey Island, Port Townsend ferry and Keystone turnoff. Takes 1 hour.
• From Oak Harbor, go south on Highway 20: follow signs to Port Townsend ferry; go 15 miles (24 kilometers) to Keystone turnoff. Takes 20 minutes.

Comments: After diving, walk uphill to Fort Casey; see the fortifications that guarded the entry to Puget Sound in the 1890s.

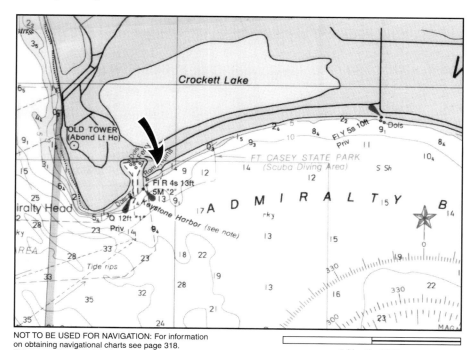

NOT TO BE USED FOR NAVIGATION: For information on obtaining navigational charts see page 318.
This is a portion of 18471. Soundings are in fathoms.

1 Nautical Mile

POSSESSION POINT FERRY WRECK
Boat Dive

Skill: Intermediate and expert divers

Why go: To be surrounded by fish. To cruise over a bower of tiny white anemones, over a lacy looking wreck. To explore this former Washington State ferry.

The *Kehloken* – ex-*Golden State,* was built in 1926. The wreck is impressive because of its sheer size. Its wooden hull is 240 feet (73 meters) long by 50 feet (15 meters) wide. It stands upright on its keel. You swim over it, look down onto a big coil: that is one of the diesel-electric motors. Those who know about engines and wrecks can poke around and see things like the sacrificial zinc or the electric motors that are still there and tucked away, hidden but findable. Still one rudder at the northeast end when we dived this double-ender ferry. The superstructure on top where passengers used to eat doughnuts and drink coffee in the café burned before sinking. Much of what you relate to as a ferry is no longer there, but part of the deck where the cars used to drive on remains. This wreck is big, it's fun to prowl around. And even if there were no wreck, it's worth going to see the marine life.

The ferry was sunk on February 15, 1983, to create a fishing reef for hook-and-line fishermen. The ferry was chosen for the reef because it is a large, high structure particularly suitable for black rockfish. It has been down long enough for lots of life to collect. Seaperch – schools of them – hang around you above the wreck. We saw black rockfish, a humongous cabezon dart into the depths of the hull, two lingcod by the rudder. A couple of swimming scallops. Tube worms all over the wreck. A few orange plumose anemones. And thousands of tiny white ones on the deck. At the time of writing this artificial reef is one of ten such reefs created by Washington State Fisheries to enhance fishing potential. Some are made from scrap concrete blocks, some from quarry rock – this is the most dramatic one for divers.

Bottom and Depths: You reach the top deck at 55 to 65 feet (17 to 20 meters), depending on tide height. The hull rests on silty sand at 75 to 85 feet (23 to 26 meters). Concrete blocks and sand bags used in sinking the ship are around it.

Hazards: Current; fishing boats, especially in summer; the wreck itself and transparent fishing line. Dive on slack, but even then the current is unpredictable and there is almost always current on the surface. Throughout the dive, be aware of where you are on the wreck. When time to ascend: find your anchor line, be sure it is free of the wreck and go up it – a protected place to ascend out of the way of boats. The anchor line is also useful during a safety stop and could save you from being washed away.

The wooden ferry is splintered and crumbling. Unsafe to enter. Advisable, also, not to swim beneath the overhangs of the bulging outer sides. Pieces of it are falling off. Carry a knife; if caught in fishing line you can cut your way free.

Telephones: • Possession Point Ramp, up hill beside restroom. • Mulkilteo ferry landing. • Port of Edmonds.

Facilities: None. Air fills in Edmonds and Oak Harbor.

Access: Possession Point Ferry Wreck is in northern Puget Sound off the southern tip of Whidbey Island. It is 200 to 300 yards (185 to 275 meters) directly west of the green navigational buoy at Possession Point and south of three homes on the bluff on Whidbey.

Charter out of Seattle or launch at Edmonds north of Seattle, at Possession Point Ramp on Whidbey Island, or Mukilteo State Park south of Everett. Pick a calm day.

The site is exposed to west and southeast wind. Possession Point Ramp, the closest launching point, is 2½ nautical miles (5 kilometers) northeast of the site. Edmonds and Mukilteo State Park are both 4½ nautical miles (8 kilometers) away. Marker buoys might be in place at the wreck but do not count on it.

The wreck is shown as a Fish Haven on the chart. To find the ferry, line up on a right-angle with you in the corner of it, the green navigational buoy at one end, the houses on the bluff at the other end. Or, if you have a depth sounder and Loran-C equipment, the following Loran-C coordinates will help you find it: Lat 47 53.87 N, Long 122 23.52 W. The wreck lies at a slightly skewed angle: one end to the southwest, the other to the northeast. Weave back and forth at right-angles to find it; look for a very visible lump on the screen at a depth of 75 to 85 feet (23 to 26 meters).

Anchor and throw something over to check the current. When we rolled off the boat to enter, we held onto a line attached to the bow, pulled ourselves to the bow, then down the anchor line.

Comments: Anchoring tips from the Department of Fisheries: to avoid snagged anchors, pass a biodegradable, hemp line through a concrete building block, keeping *both* ends in the boat. Slide the block down the looped line until it snags the reef. Attach the line to the boat. If the block cannot be retrieved, simply release one end of the line and pull it through the block.

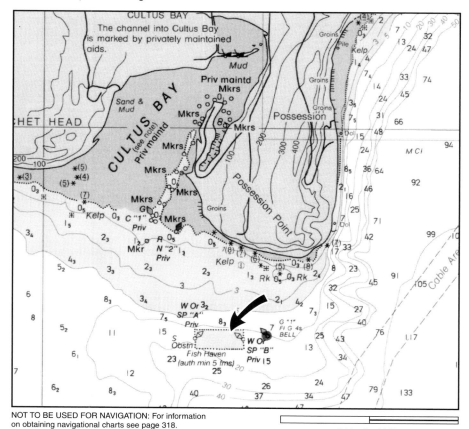

NOT TO BE USED FOR NAVIGATION: For information
on obtaining navigational charts see page 318.
This is a portion of 18473. Soundings are in fathoms.

1 Nautical Mile

EDMONDS UNDERWATER PARK
Shore Dive

Skill: Intermediate and expert divers. All divers with guide.

Why go: An underwater Disneyland-type park with heaps of marine life, wrecks and more easy-to-find attractions. To see them, follow underwater paths, trails of rope held in place with pipes, rocks, and yellow road cones. Probably the most-dived site in the Pacific Northwest, Edmonds is a mecca for photographers, a great place to meet new divers.

The park began in 1935 – before modern scuba gear was invented – with the sinking of the 300-foot (90-meter) DeLion Dry Dock. It was the first dry dock on the west coast with a concrete keelson and you can still see the keelson today. In 1970 Edmonds was officially designated an underwater park, the first marine sanctuary on the West Coast. In 1972 the 94-foot (29-meter) tug *Alitak* was scuttled. For years, the two wrecks have sheltered so much life – and still do.

On my first visit I saw rockfish, red Irish lords, painted greenlings and decorated warbonnets ranging the wrecks. A wolf-eel, in the open. An octopus, too. Archways of fluff rose around us as we swam through plumose-covered ribs of the *Alitak,* past the sunken dry dock. In 1982 the 76-foot (23-meter) *Fossil* was added to the park; in 1992, the 28-foot (9-meter) *Sky Hi.* Wrecks and marine life abound. During a recent dive my buddy and I met a huge lingcod guarding eggs. We saw at least 20 giant cabezons cruising the wrecks. Copper rockfish. Pipefish. Clown nudibranchs. Purple tube worms. Hermit, kelp and Dungeness crabs – too much to name!

A gigantic concrete-block-and-steel dinosaur – perhaps the ultimate Disneylandish underwater creation that could be conceived of – is due to be completed in 1994.

Bottom and Depths: The dry dock rests on silty sand at 25 to 35 feet (8 to 11 meters), depending on tide height. It is northwest of the ferry pier between the ferry (when it is in) and the rest-float. Some bull kelp, in summer, attached to the dry dock showing where it is. Boundary buoys mark the 32 acres (13 hectares) of park where boats are prohibited. Between the underwater enhancements and shore you will find eelgrass, moon snails, flounders and all the other life associated with a sandy bottom.

Hazards: Long swim (long walk, if tide is out), some crosscurrent and close proximity to the ferry dock, the underwater trail itself. Poor visibility in early summer and in fall. Some bull kelp, some red jellyfish. Current is created by wind, tides and the ferry propeller-wash. Watch current direction and notice whether you are being swept sideways. Unless you are very familiar with the dive, stay on the underwater trail. Do not go near the ferry slip; the underwater park boundary is marked by a row of tires. Use your compass. The trail lured me far out to sea; remember to turn around and come back. Watch your air, avoid a long surface swim and save some sights for a second dive. On the surface, look for buoys with tails that show current direction. Carry a knife. If you have seen jellyfish, check for tentacles before removing mask and gloves.

Telephones: Main Street, across railway tracks from anchor and beside restaurant. Also, in emergencies, at ferry dock ticket booth.

Facilities: Restrooms and changerooms; cold-water showers for gear. Limited parking space, including handicapped parking, and a drop-off zone. Air fills just down the street in a dive shop in Edmonds.

Access: Edmonds Underwater Park is in Puget Sound at Edmonds. The dive is 15 minutes west of I-5 (Interstate Highway 5). From Seattle, go north 15 minutes; from Bellingham, drive south 2 hours to the I-5 turnoff to Edmonds-Kingston ferry.

From I-5, take Exit 177 onto Highway 104 and follow signs to Edmonds city center. When nearing the water, turn right at Sunset Avenue. Go to Main Street. Turn left and move to the right-hand side. Cross the railway tracks, you will see a big anchor; turn right into Brackett's Landing Park. For easier entry across the beach, and for the most silt-free water, dive at high slack. In the water, follow the submerged system of ropes. It starts at the base of the piling closest to the ferry pier. You will swim past the *Alitak* on your way to the dry dock and the many attractions.

To learn where highlights of the park are, and for information about new additions, see the map near the changerooms. Or obtain a brochure: Edmonds Parks & Recreation, 700 Main Street, Edmonds, WA 98020, telephone (206) 775-2525.

Comments: Photographers will find best visibility on weekdays in early- to mid-August, then again in winter when plankton levels are low and fewer divers stir the silt. Remember, it's a marine preserve and sanctuary.

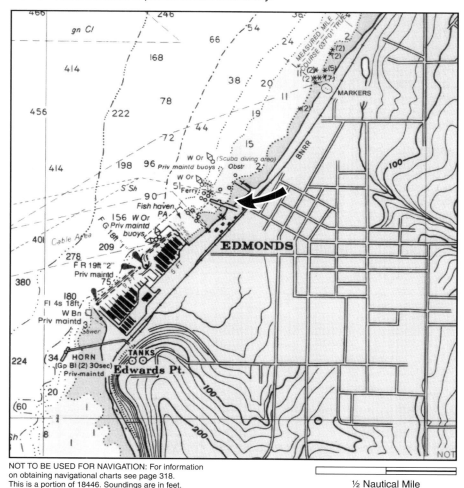

NOT TO BE USED FOR NAVIGATION: For information on obtaining navigational charts see page 318. This is a portion of 18446. Soundings are in feet.

½ Nautical Mile

RICHMOND BEACH
Shore Dive

Skill: All divers and snorkelers

Why go: Old bottles and scraps of the steamer *Utopia* are underwater treasures you might find at Richmond Beach – if you are very lucky. All in a lovely natural setting.

The *Utopia* was built in 1893 for Tacoma-Seattle freight service, rebuilt as a passenger vessel in 1898, then made several voyages during the Gold Rush to Alaska. In 1906 or 1907, this sturdy 124-foot (38-meter) ship bumped a dock at Anacortes and knocked it into the bay. The ship was not damaged. In 1929 it was finally burned for scrap metal at Richmond Beach. You can see photographs of the *Utopia,* and many Mosquito Fleet vessels, in *Pacific Steamboats* and *The H.W. McCurdy Marine History.* Both books are chock-a-block with tales of early days on Puget Sound.

On a summer dive at Richmond Beach, we saw hermit crabs and moon snails in the eelgrass. Schools of small black rockfish, striped seaperch and pile perch between the bull kelp. Decorator crabs, sea stars and sea cucumbers. Some large shrimp. Gobies. Plumose anemones. Painted greenlings. Dungeness crabs. Millions of miniature sea pens. And lots of flounders. The dive is a shallow, relaxed one. And Richmond Beach is an attractive place to spend the day. After diving, you could walk along the rolling sand dunes.

Long walk to the water – but once at the water, it's an excellent beginner's dive.

Bottom and Depths: In summer, bull kelp attached to crumbling metal wreckage and small rocks scattered over the bottom. Most of the life is in the kelp, 10 to 20 feet (3 to 6 meters) deep, sloping to a depth of 30 to 40 feet (9 to 12 meters), depending on tide height. Beyond the kelp, look for bottles where the steeply sloping, smooth sand bottoms out at 55 to 65 feet (17 to 20 meters).

Hazards: Some current. Boats. Red jellyfish, in the fall. Long walk to the water. You could carry gear to the beach in stages. Dive near slack. Listen for boats and ascend close to the bottom all the way to shore. If you have seen any red jellyfish, check one another for stinging tentacles before removing your masks and gloves.

Telephone: At 20th Avenue NW and NW 195th Street, southeast corner. From Richmond Beach, go back toward NW Richmond Beach Road to it.

Facilities: Richmond Beach County Park offers parking space, picnic tables, restrooms and a beach to walk on. Changerooms and food concessions, in summer only.

Access: Richmond Beach is on Puget Sound. It is 10 minutes off I-5 (Interstate Highway 5) between Everett and Seattle. From Seattle, drive north 15 minutes to Exit 176. From Bellingham, drive south 2 hours to it.

From I-5, take Exit 176 and go west on 175th Street to the first light. Turn right and go north to 185th Street. Turn left and continue west on 185th Street which changes its name to NW Richmond Beach Road. At 20th Avenue NW turn left and continue to the lower parking lot at Richmond Beach. From here walk 330 yards (300 meters) over a footbridge to the water. Easy entry over sand directly in front of the bridge. Follow the broken off pilings straight out into the water and head down. Look for bottles at the base of the ledge. On your way up, look for pieces of the wreck of the *Utopia* which, as noted, was burned on the beach in 1929. The wreckage is in the shallows north of your entry point.

Comments: Park hours are from 8:00 a.m. until 5:30 p.m., so no night diving.

Sand at Richmond Beach

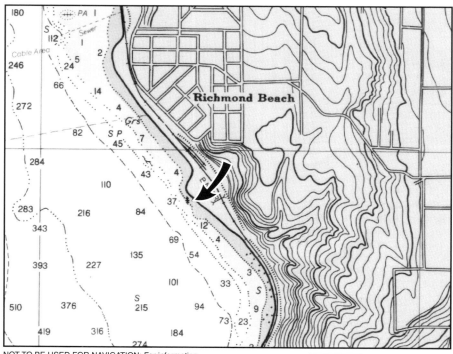

NOT TO BE USED FOR NAVIGATION: For information
on obtaining navigational charts see page 318.
This is a portion of 18446. Soundings are in feet.

½ Nautical Mile

WRECK OF PBM MARINER
Boat Dive

Tide Table: None, non-tidal freshwater lake

Skill: Intermediate and expert divers

Why go: Unique aircraft, unique dive. The only other PBM-3 Mariner flying boat known to survive is owned by the Smithsonian Institution. And this one, deep in Lake Washington, is rumored to have been an admiral's.

The Martin PBM-3 is a World War II twin-engine patrol bomber. Machine guns were on this model when it was first built in 1942. Accommodation for a crew of seven to nine was provided. Later in 1942, PBM-3s were adopted as naval transport and all military equipment and turrets were removed. The Mariner could carry forty passengers. Its wingspan is 118 feet (36 meters); length 77 feet (23 meters); height 17½ feet (5 meters). It is about the size of a Boeing 737 but is a seaplane. It is large. The hatch covers are off this one and expert wreck divers could penetrate and explore; however, no salvage is permitted.

On its last flight, the Mariner had returned from Sand Point Naval Air Station on May 6, 1949. It landed safely but was blown by strong winds into a piling and sank. Damage is minimal: One pontoon lies on the lake floor about 100 feet (30 meters) out from the wreck. A challenge to find it on the dark silty bottom.

Freshwater diving is different in two unexpected ways, another reason to dive here. Often you can see layers in the water as you go down – cloud levels because of changing temperature. The lake can be very warm. Or very cold. Also you experience the expected; less weight is needed in the lake.

Bottom and Depths: Flat mud bottom: 65 to 70 feet (20 to 21 meters). The lake height rises in spring with river runoff.

Hazards: Dark and silty: visibility of 15 to 20 feet (5 to 6 meters) is a good day. The best visibility is in early fall. Avoid diving December through March when the Cedar River silts up the south end of Lake Washington.

Telephones: • Coulon Beach Park, top of launching ramp #8. • Coulon Beach Park, beside restrooms.

Facilities: None at the wreck. Launching ramp, picnic tables and restrooms with hot showers at Coulon Beach Park.

Access: The PBM Mariner is in the south end of Lake Washington in Renton southeast of Seattle. It is close to Highway 405.

Custom charter out of Seattle or launch at one of the boat ramps on Lake Washington – the closest is Coulon Public Ramp next to the Boeing hangars at the south end of the lake. The flying boat is 300 feet (90 meters) offshore from the Boeing center hangar. To find the Mariner from there, sight west to a telephone pole lined up with a tall tree on a hillside at Mercer Island. Go on a clear day as fog could make it impossible to locate. A depth finder is essential: the Mariner lies north to south in 65 to 70 feet (20 to 21 meters). Loran readings are no help as the wreck is very silted over and the exposed part is not large enough to spot. Best to go the first time with someone who knows it.

As you descend, stop to let your eyes adjust to the darkness. Look for the Mariner lying upside down on its back like a big gray whale. Its wings are buried in silt, but you can see the tips of the propellers.

Comments: Quickie different dive right in the city.

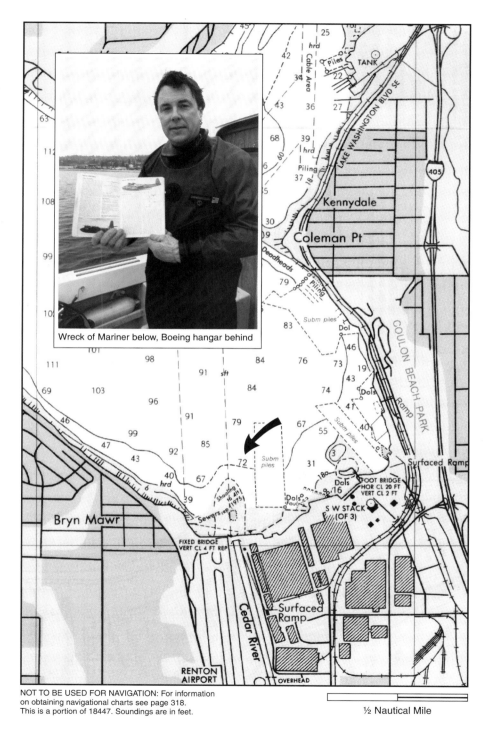

Wreck of Mariner below, Boeing hangar behind

NOT TO BE USED FOR NAVIGATION: For information
on obtaining navigational charts see page 318.
This is a portion of 18447. Soundings are in feet.

½ Nautical Mile

243

SEACREST PARK
Shore Dive

Skill: All divers

Why go: The wreck of the *Honey Bear,* treasure hunting, and a bottom that drops off quickly are three good reasons to dive along this north-facing shore which is usually protected from stormy winds.

Seattle's first settlement was here in 1851. Shortly after, many settlers moved into the area of Seattle now called Pioneer Square. They named Seattle after Chief Sealth of the Duwamish tribe. Later a ferry service connected Seattle and Duwamish Head in West Seattle. For years it was the only way between these two points.

Today two new parks, Seacrest and Don Armeni, occupy this historic strip of land offering excellent access to divers searching for bottles and other valuable old junk from early Seattle days. Even old Indian artifacts. The steep underwater cliff is unstable and periodically whole chunks fall away to reveal new bottom. It is a constantly renewing treasure-hunting ground. And the wreck of the small cabin cruiser *Honey Bear* in 25 to 35 feet (8 to 11 meters), depending on tide height, is a new addition.

A night dive at the old sawmill at the west end of Don Armeni Park turns up an amazing variety of fish. On one night dive I saw a dozen sailfin sculpins, several painted greenlings, flounders and sturgeon poachers. Look for marine life around the decaying wood of the old sawmill.

It's a perfect place for new divers. Many open-water certification dives are done here. Interesting diving – night or day.

Bottom and Depths: Muddy bottom drops off steeply at Seacrest. Some bull kelp attached to pilings.

Hazards: Boats and broken fishing lines are potential hazards. Listen for boats and ascend up pilings or else close to the bottom all the way to shore. Carry a knife.

Telephone: Harbor Avenue SW, south side; opposite the east exit of Don Armeni parking lot.

Facilities: Parking, picnic tables, restrooms and launching ramp at these grassy parks. Cafés and a pub across the road.

Access: Seacrest Park is on Elliott Bay in West Seattle off I-5 (Interstate Highway 5). From Seattle, go south 5 minutes to the West Seattle Freeway turnoff. From Tacoma, go north 30 minutes to it.

From I-5, take Exit 163A and go west. Move to the right-hand lane of West Seattle Freeway and take Harbor Avenue Exit. Turn right; continue around the waterfront to the 1600 block Harbor Avenue and Seacrest Park. Public access all along Seacrest and Don Armeni parks to Duwamish Head.

• To dive the *Honey Bear,* enter at the east end of the cove. Go in southeast of Seacrest Boathouse and find the wreck between the pilings.

• To look for relics, dive from Seacrest Boathouse west toward Duwamish Head but avoid ramps at the boat launch. The old ferry landing was halfway between. You will probably find the best junk farther out along the ledge where fewer divers have been.

Wheelchair access possible at Don Armeni Ramp for night diving year-round, perhaps during the day in winter when fewer boats. Use a compass to return along the contours of the bottom to shore and ascend up the riprap, then snorkel to the ramp.

• To dive at the old sawmill, go west of Don Armeni Park near the seawall at the northwest end of the park, and climb a few steps down slippery riprap rocks by the seawall. Once in the water – it's easy! Swim a short way west to the pilings, which project from the water at low tides, and go down.

Comments: When wind blows at Alki Beach, Seacrest is often sheltered.

Diving class at Seacrest Park, *Honey Bear* past dive flag and down

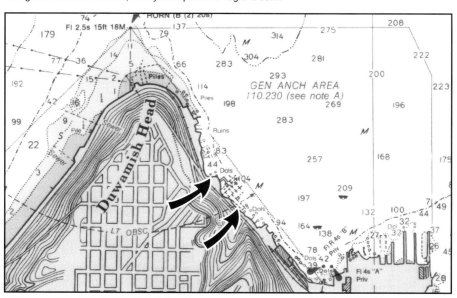

NOT TO BE USED FOR NAVIGATION: For information on obtaining navigational charts see page 318. This is a portion of 18449. Soundings are in feet.

½ Nautical Mile

ALKI PIPELINE
Shore Dive

Skill: All divers

Why go: Popular for good reasons – Alki Beach is a pretty place, easily accessible and easy to dive. A good night dive.

The main attraction is the "tubular reef", or Alki Pipeline, at the south end of 63rd Avenue and Beach Drive around on the south side of Alki Point. Broken rocks are scattered over the pipeline that extends in a narrow 3- to 5-foot (1- to 1½-meter) wide pathway out over the clean white sand. We saw small pink swirls of tube worms, kelp crabs menacing us with their small pincers, sculpins, blood stars, sunflower stars, delicate nudibranchs on and under the long, low row of angular rocks. Orange and white plumose anemones tilt over the top of the "reef". A profusion of anemones is at the apparent end of the pipe about 200 yards (185 meters) offshore.

The pipeline reappears and actually ends about 50 yards (46 meters) beyond its apparent end. To look for it, follow your compass and continue in a straight line. This area used to have great holes and caves and hid a large octopus in its dark depths under the pipe, but the caves are filling with sand. The end of the pipeline is the most beautiful part of the reef and surely the least visited. It is difficult to find. I missed it altogether.

Finding myself in an orange jungle of sea pens I didn't even mind. And I enjoyed the moon snails, flounders and tube-dwelling anemones on the sand around. You might see harbor seals.

Bottom and Depths: A broken rock path, 3 to 5 feet (1 to 1½ meters) wide covers the pipeline extending out over clean white sand, gradually sloping to a depth of 25 to 35 feet (8 to 11 meters) at the end of the pipe. Some bull kelp.

Hazards: Surf. Shallow depth. Red jellyfish in the fall. Strong south wind sometimes blows up the surf, making entry difficult at Alki Beach. When windy, check nearby Seacrest Park which is sheltered from most winds. Dive on a high tide. If you have seen jellyfish, check for stinging tentacles before removing masks and gloves.

Telephone: At 63rd Avenue SW, north end.

Facilities: Pleasant beach for a picnic at the dive site beach, *south end* of 63rd Avenue SW. Restrooms at the beach, *north end* of 63rd Avenue SW and across the street from the telephone. Fast food, too.

Access: Alki Pipeline is in Puget Sound at Alki Beach Park in West Seattle. The site faces southwest. Reach it off I-5 (Interstate Highway 5). From Seattle, drive south to the West Seattle Freeway turnoff, takes 5 minutes. From Tacoma, 30 minutes north.

From I-5, take Exit 163A. Go onto West Seattle Freeway and move to the right. Take Harbor Avenue Exit. Turn right. Continue 4 miles (7 kilometers) around the waterfront to 63rd Avenue SW and Alki Beach. At 63rd Avenue SW, turn left and go to Beach Avenue. Turn right and park beside Charles Richey Sr. Viewpoint at Alki Beach Park. Walk down the gently sloping concrete ramp. Go a few steps to the left over cobbled beach and logs, but not onto the privately owned property, and enter the water in front of the concrete pump station. Snorkel out to the southwest, lining up with the wall at the pump station, for 150 yards (140 meters) or so until you see rocks. The rocks mark the beginning of the "tubular reef". Easier to dive at high tide.

Comments: I had heard so much about this one that I felt I didn't want to or need to do the dive. To my surprise, I loved it. Now I can't wait to see the sea pens at Alki Pipeline at night!

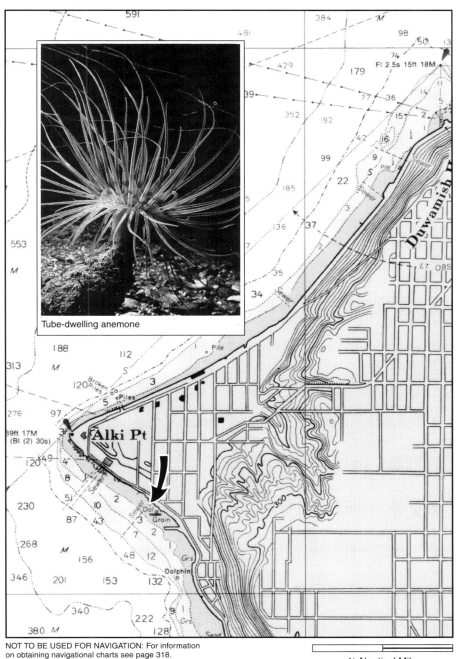

Tube-dwelling anemone

NOT TO BE USED FOR NAVIGATION: For information
on obtaining navigational charts see page 318.
This is a portion of 18449. Soundings are in feet.

½ Nautical Mile

TRAMP HARBOR FISHING PIER
Shore Dive

Skill: All divers

Why go: Bottle garden, easy entry, shallow diving safe from boats. Sheltered in all except north winds. Great for night dives.

Plumose anemones on the pilings are lovely, but we pushed off for the bottle garden. Then forgot it when we saw a small octopus in the open. With arms spread, it was the size of a golf ball. We spent half our dive observing it, and my dive partner photographed it. This small species of octopus, often seen at bottle sites, is the *Octopus rubescens*. Its scientific name refers to its red color. At the surface, I laughed when my dive partner referred to it as "ruby". I was rinsing a bottle I had picked up to show my partner when another octopus pushed its way out of the skinny neck of the bottle. Seeing these octopuses is one of the prime reasons I enjoy diving bottle sites.

Lots more marine life, too, at Tramp Harbor. Big day – a first sighting for me. I saw a skate. We also saw two ratfish in 13 feet (4 meters) of water. In summer, look for lion nudibranchs on the back of the kelp. In winter, Tramp Harbor is a stubby squid breeding ground.

Bottom and Depths: Flat sand bottom, with lettuce kelp, slopes gradually to a depth of 50 to 60 feet (15 to 18 meters), depending on tide height.

Hazards: Silt. Red jellyfish. Weight yourself for a shallow dive, and stay off the bottom. Best visibility is on outgoing tides. If you have seen jellyfish, check for stinging tentacles before removing masks and gloves.

Telephones: • Dockton Road, outside store at Portage, ½ mile (¾ kilometer) south of pier. • On Vashon Highway: return to the highway by Ellisport to 204th. At the highway, turn right and go one city block. Telephone is on left-hand side.

Facilities: Toilet and picnic table beside the pier. Parking space for four or five cars.

Access: Tramp Harbor Fishing Pier is in Tramp Harbor on the east side of Vashon Island. It is a 15-minute ferry ride from Seattle, Tacoma or Southworth, Kitsap Peninsula, south of Bremerton. Once on Vashon, the dive is 20 minutes away.

From Vashon Highway at the center of Vashon Island, head east on 204th Street for 1 mile (1¾ kilometers) to the dive. Follow 204th Street, which becomes SW Ellisport Road, to the water. Turn right at Dockton Road SW to Tramp Harbor Fishing Pier. At higher tide, six or eight stairsteps to the water – wheelchair divers could "bum it". At low tide, 16 stairsteps to the beach and a few paces across it. Swim out on the right-hand side of the pier to the ladder. Take a sighting on Robinson Point on the right, set your compass and head down:10 to 30 kicks and you're in the bottle garden.

To get to Vashon Highway at the center of Vashon Island
• From Tacoma, take the ferry to Tahlequah at the south end of Vashon, go 7 miles (11 kilometers) to 204th Street. Turn right.
• From Seattle, go to West Seattle, take the Fauntleroy ferry to the north end of Vashon, go 7 miles (11 kilometers) to 204th Street, then turn left.
• From Bremerton, drive to Southworth, take the ferry to the north end of Vashon, go 7 miles (11 kilometers) to 204th Street and turn left.

Comments: Rich, varied diving at Vashon. North of Tramp Harbor off Point Heyer, giant octopuses – but treacherous current. Go when a long slack. Off the south end of Vashon, go by boat to Dalco Wall – a drop-off.

Bottles, logs and frilly plumose anemones

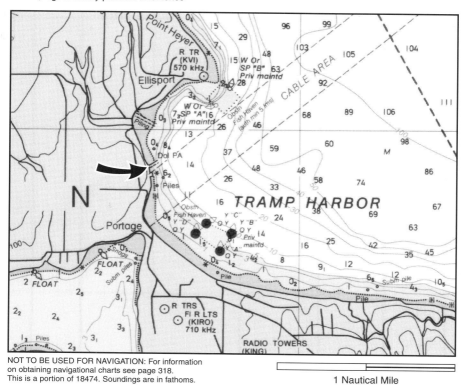

NOT TO BE USED FOR NAVIGATION: For information
on obtaining navigational charts see page 318.
This is a portion of 18474. Soundings are in fathoms.

1 Nautical Mile

SALTWATER STATE PARK
Shore Dive

Skill: All divers

Why go: The sunken barge at Saltwater Park is shallow, with minimal currents and marked with a buoy. Fish seem to know they're protected at this underwater reserve, and the barge is easy for all divers to find. Despite the fact that there is very little left of the barge – it's being eaten away by shipworms – the site still attracts fish and divers.

Striped seaperch, shiners, copper rockfish, painted greenlings or convict fish, sculpins, dusky rockfish and cabezons are some of the fish to look for. Some nudibranchs, too. Sailfin sculpins and an octopus hide under the dark edge of the hull. Flounders, stars and sea pens flourish on the silty sand around. Clusters of plumose anemones cling to tires in the area.

As the old wooden gravel barge is gradually eaten away by shipworms, its shape becomes more interesting. The interior of the barge originally measured 110-by-40-feet (34-by-12-meters) but has now nearly disintegrated. Nevertheless it still attracts life. Placed here in 1971, this is one of the first intentional artificial reef habitats in Puget Sound.

Bottom and Depths: The barge rests on silty sand at a depth of 45 to 55 feet (14 to 17 meters).

Hazards: Heavily used recreational area. Before ascending, listen for jet skis and boats. Fairly long swim to the barge. Only dive on the barge if you are fit or if you have a dive-kayak or a boat. Park is open from dawn till dusk, so no night diving.

Telephones: • Saltwater Park picnic site, by park concession stand. • Saltwater Park campground, beside restrooms.

Facilities: Picnic tables and shelters, restrooms with wheelchair-accessible toilets, food concession, and plenty of parking space beside the beach. Campground in the woods behind the beach with coin-operated hot showers. At the time of writing open all summer but weekends only in winter.

Access: Saltwater State Park is on East Passage near the southern end of Puget Sound. It is south of Des Moines – only 10 minutes off I-5 (Interstate Highway 5). From Tacoma, go north 20 minutes to Exit 149. From Seattle, head south 20 minutes to it.

From I-5, take Exit 149 and go west 1¾ miles (3 kilometers) on Highway 516 to Marine View Drive in Des Moines. Turn left and go 1½ miles (2½ kilometers) more to the park. Straight out from the point with picnic tables on it, straight out from the cove and creek, you will see a red-and-white buoy marking the barge. It is 290 yards (265 meters) offshore. You might want a dive-kayak, an inflatable raft or other small boat to reach it. There is no ramp, but hand-launching is possible across the sandy log-strewn beach. The site is wheelchair accessible for divers able to get over a few feet (meters) of sand. Possibly logs too. A hard-packed earth ramp goes from the parking lot to the sand.

Comments: An underwater reserve. Don't take any marine animals, just take their pictures. And take a light to look for the big octopus under the south end of the hull.

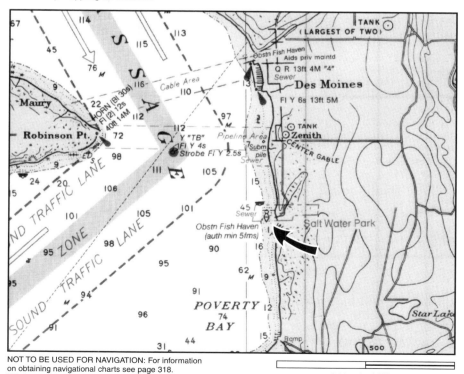

Sailfin sculpin rippling its dorsal fin

NOT TO BE USED FOR NAVIGATION: For information
on obtaining navigational charts see page 318.
This is a portion of 18448. Soundings are in fathoms.

2 Nautical Miles

DALCO WALL

Boat Dive

Current Table: The Narrows

Skill: Intermediate and expert divers on wall. All divers and snorkelers in shallows.

Why go: To plunge over a sheer wall – see undercut caves, columns sculpted by current, sandstone pitted like moonscape. Dalco is easy to get to. Good for deep divers making safety stops. Good for shallow divers, too, as well as snorkelers.

Wolf-eels abound. When heading down, we happened onto a mated pair in a shallow slot at 50 feet (15 meters). At least two more dens are along the wall. We dropped over the edge and hovered above darkness, enjoyed the vacantness, the space. It is stark. Then we started looking for things and saw a big lingcod, a tiny grunt sculpin, a ratfish. Swimming scallops at the base of the wall.

Gradually moving up, we passed columns of sandstone. Came to an old piddock clam area: the sandstone is pitted where piddocks have burrowed into it. In the kelp, we saw lots of piddock clams that were alive and well. Or we saw their paired siphons with dark hairs lining them – that's what you see of a piddock clam. In the shallows near the end of our dive, lots of big painted greenlings. Black-and-white pile perch. Striped seaperch. Schools of tube-snouts. Silver flashes of juvenile perch. A myriad tiny alabaster nudibranchs. A clown nudibranch. Tube worms. Shrimp all lined up beneath a ledge to defend themselves against us. Decorator, hermit and kelp crabs. A few white plumose anemones. And one water jellyfish. Later my buddy told me they glow in the dark when touched.

Bottom and Depths: Wall of glacial sandstone with till embedded in it sheers down to silty bottom at 120 to 130 feet (37 to 40 meters). Along the southeast end of the wall, depth at the top ranges from 30 to 50 feet (9 to 15 meters). There are plenty of big rocks and cubby holes for divers who just want to look over the edge. Heading northwest, we found undercuts and shallow caves at 110 to 120 feet (34 to 37 meters). At the center of the wall, the depth sounder shows 190 feet (58 meters).

Dramatic columns of sandstone are near the northwest end. Then shallow rocky crevices and ledges riddled with piddock holes at 20 to 30 feet (6 to 9 meters). Near shore, sand bottom with starry flounders, moon snails and all that goes with it. A good place to end a deep dive. Good snorkeling too. Bull kelp, in summer.

Hazards: Current, small boats and bull kelp in summer; water jellyfish, spring and summer. Dive on slack. The current in Dalco Passage sets west or northwest almost constantly. Easiest to start your dive at the southeast end of the wall and drift toward your anchored boat. Before ascending, listen for boats. Carry a knife for kelp. If you have seen any jellyfish, check for stinging tentacles before removing your masks and gloves.

Telephones: • Tahlequah at Vashon Island, near ferry landing. A short way up the road. • Point Defiance, beside ferry landing.

Facilities: None at Dalco Wall. Charters, boat rentals and launching in Tacoma.

Access: Dalco Wall is in Dalco Passage 100 yards (90 meters) offshore from Point Dalco on the southern tip of Vashon Island.

Charter, rent a boat or launch your own boat at Point Defiance Park and cross Dalco Passage. Go 1½ nautical miles (3 kilometers) to Vashon. Look along the shoreline: ½ nautical mile (1 kilometer) west of the Tahlequah ferry landing is a large home with a concrete retaining wall. Often a boat is moored in front of it. West of this home is an old shed, also with a concrete retaining wall. Anchor near the shed in 30 feet (9 meters). Swim southeast out past the mooring buoy. Head down. A short underwater swim and plummet over the wall. Or snorkel or dive shallow right around your boat.

Comments: At Tramp Harbor on the east side of Vashon Island, old bottles.

At Point Defiance Park: diver and gear lowered in rental boat for Dalco Wall

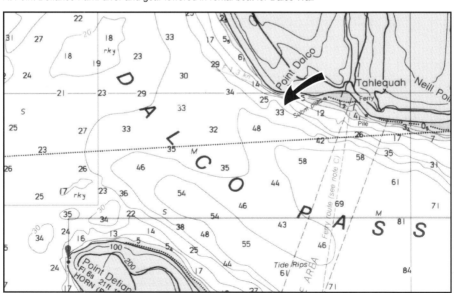

NOT TO BE USED FOR NAVIGATION: For information on obtaining navigational charts see page 318. This is a portion of 18474. Soundings are in fathoms.

1 Nautical Mile

SUNRISE BEACH PARK
Shore Dive

Skill: Intermediate and expert divers

Why go: Crevices in the wall hide wolf-eels, octopuses, mosshead warbonnets. The most vivid red-and-white warbonnet I have seen was at Sunrise. And the wolf-eels were exceptional. We saw one mated pair and a pale peach-colored one. A red Irish lord. Swimming scallops. Pink encrusting sponge on the rocks. Grunt, sailfin and buffalo sculpins and white cucumbers. Beneath the overhangs, barnacles thickly encrusted with yellow sponge, purple plume worms, red slipper cucumbers. Kelp crabs and decorator crabs. You will see painted greenlings, blue sea stars, blood stars, nudibranchs, chitons, green urchins. Look for gunnels, ratfish, dogfish. In the sandy shallows look for orange sea pens, hermit crabs, seaperch, and flounders. Mussels on the beach. So much in so little space at Sunrise.

Bottom and Depths: The top of the wall is at 30 to 40 feet (9 to 12 meters), depending on tide height. The wall is 20 feet (6 meters) high, riddled with undercut ledges and crevices. Boulders are below it from 50 to 60 feet (15 to 18 meters) down to 130 feet (40 meters) and beyond. In summer, the top of the wall is marked with bull kelp. Sandy bottom with no handholds slopes slowly from top of the wall to shore.

Hazards: Current, small boats, long walk, bull kelp and red jellyfish. Dive on a day with tidal exchange no greater than 8 feet (2½ meters). Dive at high water at the end of the flood. Start 1½ hours before *high slack* – do not dive at the end of ebb when it is almost impossible to predict slack and when there might be downcurrents. It is a circling current. The water almost constantly ebbs past Sunrise, flowing parallel to shore in a northerly direction through Colvos Passage.

Listen for boats; make your safety stop before leaving the kelp which is something to hold onto. Then stay close to the bottom almost to shore. Carry a knife. Past the kelp, you might need to "knife it" across the sand. If jellyfish, check before removing masks. If you have been swimming hard, take it easy walking uphill as the possibility of bends may be increased by overexertion after diving.

Divers who want a pickup boat can go by charter to Sunrise.

Telephone: Gig Harbor, west side of Harborview Drive by shops. It is 1 mile (1½ kilometers) past Crescent Valley Drive.

Facilities: Picnic tables, pit toilets and lots of parking space. The park closes at dusk: not only be out of the water at dusk, but also have your car out of the park.

Access: Sunrise Beach is on the west shore of Colvos Passage. It is just north of the town of Gig Harbor and 15 minutes off Highway 16 between Tacoma and Bremerton. From I-5 (Interstate Highway 5) and Highway 16 junction, 25 minutes to the dive. Plan to dive at the end of the flood – see current precautions in "Hazards" section.

From Highway 16, take Gig Harbor Exit to the city center. Go downhill on Pioneer Way to Gig Harbor. At the bottom of the hill, turn left onto Harborview Drive and you follow it around the water. When Harborview Drive heads uphill away from the water it becomes 96th Street. At the top of the hill, turn left onto Crescent Valley Drive and from there you can follow signs to Sunrise Beach Park.

Go to Drummond Drive and turn right. At the top of the hill turn right onto Moller Drive, then turn left down Sunrise Beach Drive and go down a long steep hill to the park. Lots of space but park where directed. Walk 225 paces on a well-graded path to a shed beside the cobbled beach. Swim south from the shed for 100 yards (90 meters). At the time of writing, you swim toward a tree that hangs out over the water. The north end of the wall is out from it. Past the tree, keep angling south as you start down. Swim across the sand and through the kelp.

To get to Highway 16 exit to Gig Harbor
• From I-5 (Seattle, Olympia or Tacoma) take Bremerton Exit 132. Follow the signs to Highway 16 West and Tacoma Narrows Bridge. From I-5, it takes 10 minutes to the Highway 16 turnoff. After crossing the bridge, do not take the first Gig Harbor-Olympic Drive Exit. Take the second exit to Gig Harbor City Center.
• From Bremerton, go south on Highway 16 East for 30 minutes; take Gig Harbor Exit to the city center.

Comments: Easier to follow road signs to Sunrise Beach than to go back again. My second trip, I felt I knew where I was going and got lost trying to return to Gig Harbor.

Early morning dive at Sunrise Beach

NOT TO BE USED FOR NAVIGATION: For information on obtaining navigational charts see page 318.
This is a portion of 18474. Soundings are in fathoms.

1 Nautical Mile

Skill: Intermediate and expert divers from boat. Advanced kayak-divers.

Why go: At the rocky reef, a great sculpin lazes on top of a ledge. During one dive, we see ten great sculpins, two pairs of mated wolf-eels, one lone wolf-eel, swimming scallops on the rocks and a red Irish lord. My buddy flashes his light. Between some boulders he's found an octopus with large suckers. On the same dive, we see four more octopuses as well as sunflower stars, blood stars and copper rockfish. Purple tube worms are beneath the undercut ledge. Crabs wave their claws at us. We see painted greenlings, a valley of rock heaped with leafy hornmouth whelks, a school of pile perch, and a dogfish shark at the edge of deeper water.

Water jellyfish pulse around us over reef and sand like puffy, white cumulus clouds.

Bottom and Depths: An undercut ledgy ribbon of rock parallels the shore of the cove for 200 yards (185 meters). It is 150 feet (46 meters) offshore and up to 20 feet (6 meters) high. Boulders are scattered along it. Depth at its base is consistently 50 to 60 feet (15 to 18 meters), depending on tide height. Gently sloping sand stretches into Hale Passage.

Hazards: Some small boats, current, and stinging jellyfish. Listen for boats and, if possible, ascend your anchor line. The reef is in the shadow of the island on the ebb. Dive any time from high slack through the ebb, but do not dive during the last half of the flooding current. If you have seen jellyfish, check for tentacles before removing your mask and gloves.

Telephones: By water: • Narrows Marina, beside bait shop. • Titlow Beach, across railway tracks outside pub.

By road: • Fox Island, at Fox Drive and 6th Avenue off Island Boulevard. From the East Wall beach, go nearly 4 miles (6½ kilometers) back toward the bridge onto Fox Island. Return as you came to 9th Avenue and then along the longer section of Island Boulevard. Around a corner past a church, you will see a sign to 6th Avenue. Go down 6th to Fox Drive. The telephone is in front of the shop.

Facilities: None at Z's Reef – not even a rock to stand on. Charters out of Tacoma and Gig Harbor. Dive-kayak rentals at Silverdale and Bainbridge Island.

Access: Z's Reef is in Hale Passage off the eastern shore of Fox Island near Tacoma. It is in the second cove 1 nautical mile (2 kilometers) northwest of Fox Point where there are a few homes and privately owned yachts at anchor, but no public access. Z's Reef is only accessible by boat or dive-kayak.

At Z's Reef, the southeast end closest to Fox Point is more or less marked by an orange float. It is not intended to show the reef and could be moved or removed, so do not count on it. Northwest of the orange float, when I dived, were two private swimming floats, and on the beach a small white building that marked the west end of the reef. Drop anchor 100 feet (30 meters) offshore and 100 feet (30 meters) east of the white building in 30 to 40 feet (9 to 12 meters), depending on tide height. Go down and swim straight out until you reach the reef. Do not descend any deeper than 60 feet (18 meters) or you will be too deep. Then head east.

To get to Z's Reef
• Charter out of Tacoma or Gig Harbor. Or launch at Wollochet Bay, at the ramp south of Tacoma Narrows or the ramp at Fox Island Bridge, and go 2 to 4 nautical miles (4 to 7 kilometers) to Z's Reef. The ramp closest to Z's is at Wollochet Bay.

• Kayak-divers can drive to the end of the road south of Fox Point (see Fox Island, East Wall on the next page) and launch at the cobbled beach. From the concrete dock, it is 1½ nautical miles (3 kilometers) to Z's Reef. Paddle around Fox Point and up Hale Passage past the first cove to the second, larger cove where a few private yachts are anchored. It took us 45 minutes each way.

Time your paddle as well as the dive. It is easier to kayak to Z's Reef with the ebb, dive on slack, then paddle back with the flood. The return may be difficult as far as Fox Point. After that you cruise. See the *Puget Sound Current Guide* (information about it on page 21) for the direction of the currents. An advanced kayak-dive, as there is no place to land. You must anchor and gear up on your boat or in the water.

Comments: Paddling back, we saw snowcapped Mount Rainier in the distance.

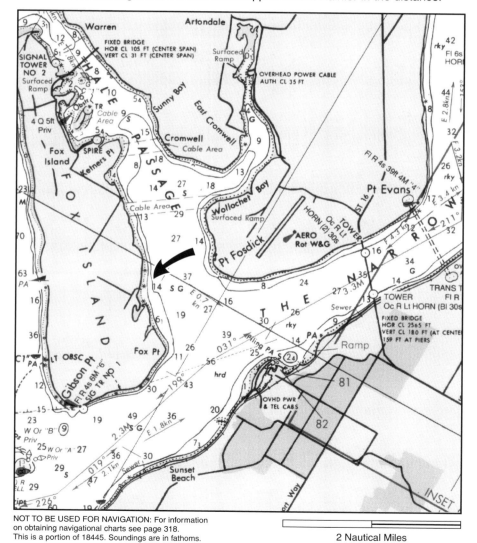

NOT TO BE USED FOR NAVIGATION: For information
on obtaining navigational charts see page 318.
This is a portion of 18445. Soundings are in fathoms.

2 Nautical Miles

FOX ISLAND, EAST WALL
Shore Dive

Tide Table: Seattle
Add 20 minutes

Skill: Expert divers

Why go: The east wall of Fox Island is the most beautiful wild seascape I've seen in Puget Sound. Canyons and crevices, overhangs and caves within a few feet of shore make marvelous homes for all kinds of life. Rockfish galore, red Irish lords, cabezons, perch, sunflower stars, painted greenlings, giant barnacles, decorator crabs, slime stars, hermit crabs, sea pens, rose stars and flounders. And the list could go on. We were chased by a huge octopus surely 10 feet (3 meters) across, the first time a shy octopus has become aggressive with me!

The east wall of Fox Island is one of those wild, wonderful places where you feel you might see anything – and do.

Bottom and Depths: Coarse gravel slopes rapidly to bull kelp in 20 to 30 feet (6 to 9 meters). Sandstone ledges intricately carved by the current form steps down to 50 to 60 feet (15 to 18 meters), then 100 feet (30 meters) and on. The east wall is not so much a bottom as a quick series of ledges cut by small canyons perpendicular to the shore, with current-carved crevices and deep overhangs.

Hazards: Current, current, current. Also a multitude of small boats and some bull kelp. Dive on slack on a small tidal exchange. Current is not as strong on outgoing tides. Always be ready to pull out if the current becomes too strong. Fishing boats come close to shore. Listen for boats, and hug the contours of the bottom all the way up to shore. Carry a knife. Best in the morning, when sun shines on the east wall, if you can coordinate sun and tides.

Telephone: Fox Island off Island Boulevard; it is in front of a shop at Fox Drive and 6th Avenue. Go nearly 4 miles (6½ kilometers) back toward the bridge. Return as you came via the twists and turns to 9th Avenue, then on Island Boulevard. Around a corner past a church, you will see a sign to 6th Avenue. Follow 6th to Fox Drive.

Facilities: None. Beautiful wild beach.

Access: The east wall of Fox Island, also known as the "concrete dock", is on the west side of Tacoma Narrows, east end of Fox Island. It is off Highway 16 between Tacoma and Bremerton. From Seattle, Olympia and Bremerton, 1 to 1¼ hours. From Tacoma at I-5 (Interstate Highway 5) and Highway 16, 30 minutes to the dive.

On Fox Island, follow the main road, which zigzags the length of the island and changes names several times. It takes 10 minutes to drive 5 miles (8 kilometers) to the East Wall. Follow Island Boulevard to 9th Avenue, and turn right. At Kamus Drive, turn left. When you see the water at Kamus and Island Boulevard, do not go straight. Bear right and go to the end of the arterial road. Island Boulevard becomes Mowitsh Drive. Follow Mowitsh to 14th Avenue; turn right. After ½ mile (¾ kilometer), 14th becomes Ozette. The road ends at a small turnaround and parking space for five or six cars. Walk 200 paces down a wooded trail, slippery when wet, to a coarse gravel beach. The concrete dock is on your left. Enter, swim a short way to the bull kelp, and go down; then work your way south.

To get to Fox Island
• From Olympia or Seattle, go on I-5 to Tacoma and take Exit 132. Follow signs to Highway 16 West and Tacoma Narrows Bridge. Just after crossing the Narrows, take Gig Harbor-Fox Island Exit. From I-5, 10 minutes to it. If you miss the first exit, take the second one. Both will work. Follow signs to Fox Island.

• From Bremerton, go south on Highway 16 East for 30 minutes, and take either of two exits to Gig Harbor-Fox Island. Follow signs to Fox Island.

Comments: After the dive, follow the signs back to Highway 16.

Into the kelp, then over the wall

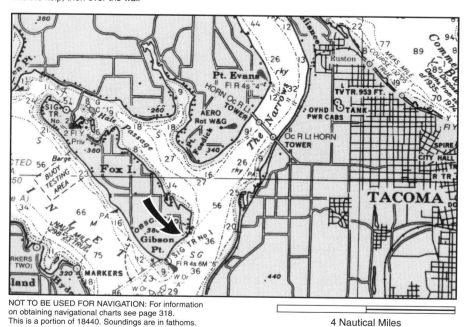

NOT TO BE USED FOR NAVIGATION: For information on obtaining navigational charts see page 318. This is a portion of 18440. Soundings are in fathoms.

4 Nautical Miles

TACOMA NARROWS BRIDGE
Shore Dive and Boat Dive

Current Table: The Narrows
Subtract 10 minutes

Skill: Intermediate and expert divers

Why go: Both beauty and fascination with disaster lure the diver to Tacoma Narrows Bridge. In November 1940 the first Tacoma Narrows Bridge, "Galloping Gertie", collapsed while cars were crossing. Twisted remains of the original bridge are still under water for divers to explore.

Marine wildlife is spectacular in The Narrows. Clay ledges carved and undercut by current offer hiding places for red Irish lords, hermit crabs, painted greenlings and buffalo sculpins. The Narrows is well-known for lingcod, octopuses and wolf-eels. We found one each living under the huge concrete anchor blocks of the bridge. Pale pink hydroids that look like powder puffs are scattered over clean-swept rock bottom under the bridge. Near shore, a thicket of bull kelp. South of the bridge, where the bottom is sandy, a forest of sea pens bends in the current.

When I dived The Narrows we did a short "drift" on the ebbing tide. Entering 45 minutes before predicted low slack, we were lucky, and our calculations worked well. Just as we reached the concrete anchor blocks of the bridge, the current slowed and was still, enabling us to stop and explore. A marvelous way to see The Narrows!

Bottom and Depths: Carved undercut clay ledges with glacial till line The Narrows down to a depth of 30 to 40 feet (9 to 12 meters), then smooth sand. Under the bridge, big boulders and concrete anchor blocks the size of a house. Bull kelp by the shore. Depths to 140 feet (43 meters).

Hazards: Big current, bull kelp, and tough walk. Dive on the slack. The current table correction is for "The Narrows, south end" on The Narrows. Dive on small tidal exchanges only. Carry a knife for kelp. After diving, if the gate is locked and you have to carry gear uphill, take it easy and avoid overexertion which might bring on bends.

Telephone: Titlow Beach, outside pub; go south on Jackson and turn right on 6th to Titlow.

Facilities: Parking above Treatment Plant, and possibly drive gear to the bottom of the hill. Charters and boat rentals in Tacoma and Gig Harbor, launching in Tacoma.

Access: The Tacoma Narrows Bridge dive is on the east side of Tacoma Narrows beneath the bridge. It is in Tacoma off Highway 16. From Seattle or Olympia, 45 minutes to it. From Bremerton, 40 minutes.

At War Memorial Park (south end of Tacoma Narrows Bridge), drive through the parking lot to the parking area outside Western Slopes Treatment Plant. The plant gate is locked on weekends, but is usually open on weekdays from 8 a.m. till 2 p.m. If the gate *is* open – no guarantee even on weekdays – drive ⅓ mile (½ kilometer) to the bottom of the hill, drop gear and return to the top to park. Then walk down the hill, and cross the railway tracks to The Narrows. If the tide is ebbing and you plan to drift to the bridge, enter here. Or walk down the beach and dive beneath the bridge.

When the gate is locked, some divers walk down the road – you could take a wheelbarrow for gear. Others cross the gravel space opposite the Treatment Plant parking lot and hike 300 yards (275 meters) down a steep trail to the water.

To get to War Memorial Park
• From Seattle or Olympia, go on I-5 (Interstate Highway 5) to Tacoma and take Exit 132. Go north on Highway 16 toward Tacoma Narrows. Just before the bridge, take Jackson Avenue Exit off Highway 16. Move to the right-hand lane; continue straight

across Jackson Avenue, head down 10th, and turn left into War Memorial Park.
• From Bremerton, go south on Highway 16 East. At Tacoma Narrows Bridge, move to the right. Take Jackson Avenue Exit at the far end of it. Then turn left and go back across Highway 16; turn left on 10th and left again into War Memorial Park.

Comments: Worth the trouble to dive it. Take a light!

Packing gear easier with wheels, Tacoma Narrows Bridge behind

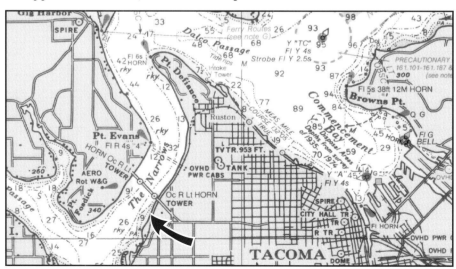

NOT TO BE USED FOR NAVIGATION: For information on obtaining navigational charts see page 318.
This is a portion of 18440. Soundings are in fathoms.

4 Nautical Miles

TITLOW BEACH
Shore Dive

Tide Table: Seattle
Add 20 minutes

Skill: All divers

Why go: Easy access to old pilings and natural ledges that provide attachment and hiding places for a great deal of life.

White plumose-covered piers of an abandoned ferry landing slip rise like columns of a Roman temple directly in front of the beach. They provide habitat for red Irish lords, cabezons, seaperch, giant sea stars. At the ledges, lots of little rockfish. Many giant octopuses used to hide here. Not so many now, but take a light for looking under ledges and into holes.

Always the chance for old bottles, too. And look for tiny octopuses in them, the *Octopus rubescens.* The total length of body and arms of a large one might measure up to 16 inches (40 centimeters). The scientific name refers to its color, which is red. These octopuses also have smooth skin. And they make bottles their homes. Before removing bottles from the water, check them out for any residents.

Bottom and Depths: Pilings of the ferry landing provide attachment, sandy bottom around them, 25 to 35 feet (8 to 11 meters) deep, depending on tide height. Ledges and caves are beyond buildings on pilings, 25 to 45 feet (8 to 14 meters) deep. A few rocks and bull kelp, flattening to shell and gravel at 45 to 55 feet (14 to 17 meters).

Hazards: Current; fairly strong back eddy from The Narrows. Red jellyfish, in the fall. Dive near the slack. If you see any jellyfish, you and your buddy should check one another for stinging tentacles before removing masks and gloves.

Telephone: Beside pub, across railway tracks from beach.

Facilities: Marine life information sign. Cold-water shower for washing gear, picnic tables, cooking shelters, playground and tennis courts. In summer, restrooms and swimming pool with hot showers in Titlow Park.

Access: Titlow Beach – its real name is Hidden Beach – is on the east side of The Narrows south of Tacoma Narrows Bridge in Tacoma. Approach from Highway 16. From Seattle or Olympia, 50 minutes to the dive; from Bremerton, 45 minutes.

At Titlow Park, cross the railway tracks to a drop-off stall near the beach. Parking space is provided along the approach to the beach. Walk 15 paces down a shallow path to the beach. On your right, pilings of an abandoned landing slip. On your left, a building on pilings over the water. There are a couple of pilings in front of it. Beyond this building and the pilings is a series of shallow rock ledges and small caves.

To get to Titlow Park
• From Seattle or Olympia, go on I-5 (Interstate Highway 5) to Tacoma and take Exit 132. Follow signs to Highway 16 West and Tacoma Narrows Bridge. Just before the Narrows Bridge, take the Jackson Avenue Exit. Turn left, crossing over the highway and go straight to 6th Avenue. Turn right and follow 6th down the hill to Titlow Park.
• From Bremerton, head south on Highway 16 East. When you reach the Tacoma Narrows Bridge, move to the right-hand lane; immediately across the bridge take the Jackson Avenue Exit. Turn right and go to 6th Avenue. Turn right again and follow 6th to Titlow Park and the water.

Comments: In summer, often two slacks close together during the day with low tidal exchange between. Then you can dive two times.

Tiny red octopus on sand, outside its bottle home

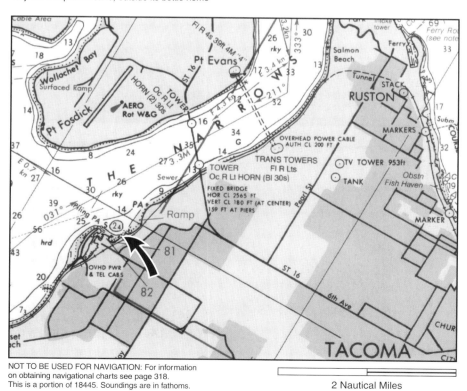

NOT TO BE USED FOR NAVIGATION: For information
on obtaining navigational charts see page 318.
This is a portion of 18445. Soundings are in fathoms.

2 Nautical Miles

DAYS ISLAND
Kayak Dive or Boat Dive

Current Table: The Narrows
Subtract 10 minutes

Skill: Intermediate and expert divers from boat. Advanced kayak-divers.

Why go: Rich marine life in a beautiful natural underwater setting and easy access are an unbeatable combination to me.

This area is especially noted for octopuses and wolf-eels and I was not disappointed when diving here. In less than an hour we saw two of each. We saw many other creatures, too. For example, beautiful pink tube worms under every rock in the shallows, moon snails, flounders, painted greenlings, plumose anemones. Rich in marine life in the shallows and dropping off dramatically into a bare rock canyon, Days Island invites all divers who love a wild underwater seascape.

On the surface it's a civilized scene with homes lining the clean, beautiful pebble beach.

Bottom and Depths: Small broken rock covered with bottom kelp and some sand between. From there, the bottom falls away fairly quickly. The wall roughly parallels the shore and goes farther from shore as you head south. Small slit ledges are all along where wolf-eels live. The top of the wall starts at 40 to 50 feet (12 to 15 meters) at its northern end, and at 60 to 70 feet (18 to 21 meters) as you work south. Cleanly scooped out sandstone ledges drop swiftly into a very deep canyon.

Hazards: Current, boats and unstable ledges. Very strong current in the canyon. Dive on the slack. Deeper than 60 feet (18 meters), be very careful of the current. When looking under ledges be careful not to disturb the bottom or rubble might fall on you. When ascending, hug the bottom all the way to the surface, then swim out to your boat or dive-kayak.

Telephones: • Narrows Marine Center, beside bait shop at marina. • Titlow Beach, across railway tracks beside pub.

Facilities: None at Days Island. Charters out of Tacoma and Gig Harbor. Launching nearby at foot of 19th Street. Kayak-launching at Titlow Beach and dive-kayak rentals at Bainbridge Island and Silverdale. In summer, restrooms and hot showers at Titlow Beach.

Access: Days Island is on the east side of The Narrows in Tacoma. It is just over ½ nautical mile (1 kilometer) south of Titlow Beach where kayak-divers could launch. From Seattle or Olympia, takes 50 minutes. From Bremerton, 45 minutes to Titlow Beach to launch (see directions to Titlow Beach on page 262). The island is separated from the mainland by a very narrow stream of water – Days Island looks like a peninsula.

Boat divers could launch at the marina at the foot of 19th Street and go less than ½ nautical mile (1 kilometer) to Days Island. Kayak-divers could launch at Titlow Beach Park and paddle just over ½ nautical mile (1 kilometer) to the dive. Allow 15 minutes to paddle. Probably easier if you go at the end of a flood, but the water is usually ebbing at Titlow and you might have to break out of that eddy. An advanced kayak-dive, only for divers who can anchor, gear up and dive from their kayaks.

Comments: Take a light for looking under ledges.

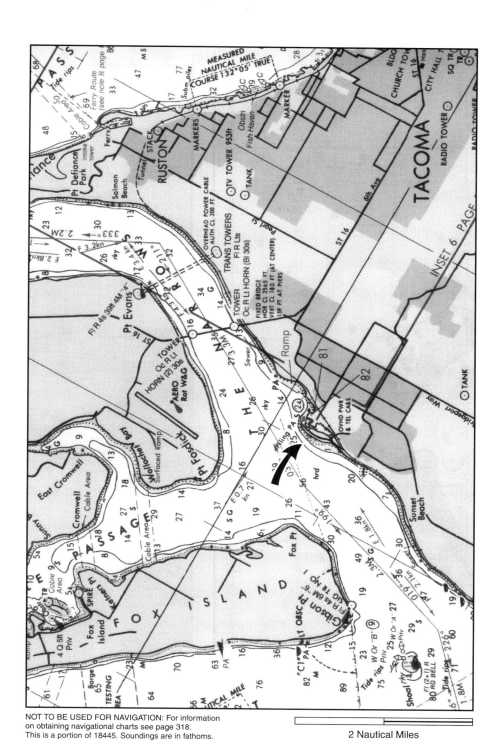

NOT TO BE USED FOR NAVIGATION: For information
on obtaining navigational charts see page 318.
This is a portion of 18445. Soundings are in fathoms.

2 Nautical Miles

SUNNYSIDE PARK
Shore Dive

Skill: All divers

Why go: A resident octopus hides under the pipeline. Orange and white plumose anemones, red rock crabs and encrusting sponge are at the pipeline – guaranteed. Beside the pipeline, tube-snouts slide in smooth jerks through the open water. Flounders swoop over the sand. Hermit crabs scuttle across the bottom. We saw a moon snail. Black-and-white striped pile perch and other perch. Geoduck clams – pronounced "gooey duck" – sucked into the sand as we swam over them. I saw two lingcod, a white-spotted greenling.

A totally hassle-free dive. Easy, sloping, short walk to the beach at low and high tides, the shortest of snorkels, a submerged line to follow to the pipeline. Current free. Good place for all divers to drop into anytime for a quickie dive on your way to anywhere. Or try it at night – you might find the octopus in the open.

Also, since I dived this site, a 32-foot (10-meter) trawler has sunk here.

Bottom and Depths: Sandy bottom slopes very gently to one quick smooth slope close to shore, then almost flattens again at a depth of 25 to 35 feet (8 to 11 meters). An abandoned pipeline that is 2 feet (⅔ meter) in diameter provides attachment and hiding places for marine life. The metal pipeline appears offshore at a depth of 20 to 30 feet (6 to 9 meters) and gradually deepens to a maximum depth of 90 to 100 feet (27 to 30 meters). It goes far out; you could not swim to the end of it.

Hazards: Small boats might be in the area in summer. Listen for them. Return to shore close to the bottom along the pipeline.

Telephone: Steilacoom, outside post office on south side of Lafayette Street. Go ½ mile (¾ kilometer) from the park toward the city center to it.

Facilities: Parking – take dollars for the parking machine. Picnic tables, flush toilets in spring, summer and fall.

Access: Sunnyside Park is in the southeast corner of Puget Sound. It is 10 minutes off I-5 (Interstate Highway 5) in Steilacoom, which is pronounced Stil´a·cŏom. The turnoff is midway between Tacoma and Olympia: from either, 25 minutes to the dive. From Seattle and Bremerton, 65 minutes.

From I-5, take Steilacoom-Dupont Exit 119 and follow signs to Steilacoom. When you see the "U.S. Army, North Fort Lewis" sign, keep going. Head down the hill. You will see a ferry dock. Turn right at the last street before the ferry landing, Lafayette Street. Drive on Lafayette through historic Steilacoom to Sunnyside Park. At the parking lot, you will find a smooth, gently sloping, tarmac path across the railway tracks to the grassy park. Immediately across the tracks, pass a picnic table and a broadleafed maple. Then walk three or four paces down a gentle gravel slope to the sandy beach.

Swim straight out and down. If you have a compass, follow a 270-degree bearing. You will come to a submerged line. Follow it to the right to a concrete block at the head of the pipeline. If the line is not there, swim straight out. Near shore, the bottom swishes down in a short quick slope. Past that, at a depth of 25 to 35 feet (8 to 11 meters), turn right and go to the pipeline.

Wheelchair access to the water is anticipated in the near future. For more information contact the Town of Steilacoom, 1715 Lafayette Street, Steilacoom, WA 98388, telephone (206) 581-1900 or fax (206) 582-3463.

Comments: Today Steilacoom is a neat looking Victorian town. And it's "for real". Incorporated in 1854, it is the oldest municipality in Washington State. In the 1850s and 60s it was the busiest port in Puget Sound. Probably bottle and artifact collectors could find rich hunting grounds nearby.

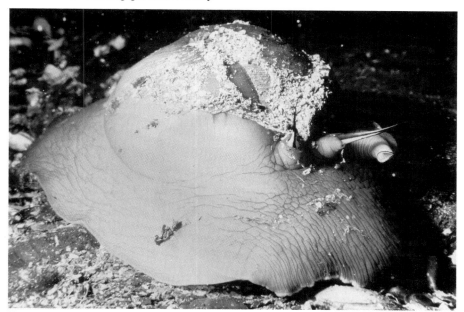

Moon snail creeping across sand

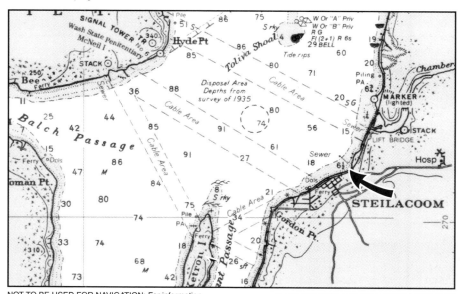

NOT TO BE USED FOR NAVIGATION: For information on obtaining navigational charts see page 318. This is a portion of 18448. Soundings are in fathoms.

2 Nautical Miles

TOLMIE ARTIFICIAL REEF
Kayak Dive, Boat Dive or Shore Dive

Skill: All divers with dive-kayak or boat. Generally called a shore dive, but this is a shore dive for very strong swimmers only.

Why go: Two intact barges – two dives at this uncomplicated current-free site.

A great place for new divers who are fit. The barges are loaded with rockfish – some large ones. We stumbled over young cabezons. And it's fun to explore these old wooden gravel barges with metal bins. The largest is 110 feet (34 meters) long, is in 40 to 50 feet (12 to 15 meters) of water, and has a high picturesque wooden railing. The other one is 90 feet (27 meters) long and rests farther out, at 50 to 60 feet (15 to 18 meters) deep. There used to be a third barge but it is now buried in silt. There is, however, a tire reef. Masses of geoduck clams are in the sand all around.

Dive on weekdays in summer due to heavy use of this marine state park. Dive anytime in winter, except Monday and Tuesday when the park is closed.

Bottom and Depths: Smooth sand slopes gently to the barges which are marked with red-and-white buoys. The closest barge is in 40 to 50 feet (12 to 15 meters). The other one is 50 to 60 feet (15 to 18 meters) deep, depending on tide height.

Hazards: Long swim, long walk, small boats and jellyfish. If you have seen jellyfish, check for stinging tentacles before removing masks and gloves. Shore dive for very strong swimmers only. All divers with a dive-kayak or boat; easier at high tides in winter which are usually mid-day. Listen for boats and ascend up the chain to the buoy. Take care not to exhaust yourself. Rest during the swim and take it easy walking back to the parking lot because overexertion after diving may increase the risk of bends.

Telephone: Gas station at I 5-Marvin Road interchange.

Facilities: Parking, restrooms, changerooms, cold-water shower for divers to wash gear, picnic tables, kitchen shelters, hiking trails. Launching ramps at Johnson Point and Luhr Beach. Dive-kayak rentals in Silverdale and Bainbridge Island.

Access: Tolmie Artificial Reef is in Nisqually Reach northeast of Olympia in Tolmie State Park. You reach it off I-5 (Interstate Highway 5). From Seattle, 1 hour. From Tacoma, 25 minutes. From Bremerton, 1¼ hours. From Olympia, 10 minutes to the Yelm-Marvin Road turnoff. At the time of writing, the park is closed during winter on Mondays and Tuesdays. To check on access, telephone (206) 456-6464.

From I-5, take Exit 111 at Yelm-Marvin Road and follow the well-signposted route to Tolmie State Park. Go 5 miles (8 kilometers) to the park – from the highway, 10 minutes. When you reach the park, continue past the top parking lot. Head down the hill to where you can see the water. Go to the lower parking lot. Walk 100 paces across a footbridge to the sandy beach. As you look out from the beach you will see mooring buoys on the left-hand side and red-and-white buoys marking the barges on the right-hand side. Paddle or swim out to one of the buoys marking a barge.

In summer, when the tide is out, you can walk two-thirds of the way. Still a long swim, but possible. In winter when the tide is in, the swim is more than 550 yards (500 meters). A dive-kayak, boat, small raft or air mattress would be a help to stop and rest on; however, the craft must be hand-launchable as there is no ramp at the park. Or else launch at Luhr Beach at Nisqually Head or north at Johnson Point. Once in the water, no current to fight, but the artificial reef is a shore dive for very strong swimmers only. Kayak-divers could launch over the sand and quickly paddle out to the reef.

Comments: Camping nearby at an RV park on Nisqually Flats.

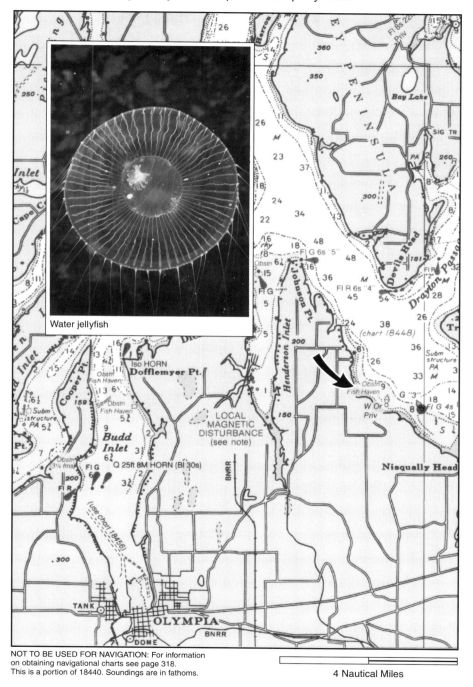

Water jellyfish

NOT TO BE USED FOR NAVIGATION: For information
on obtaining navigational charts see page 318.
This is a portion of 18440. Soundings are in fathoms.

4 Nautical Miles

STEAMBOAT ISLAND
Kayak Dive or Boat Dive

Current Table: The Narrows
Subtract 20 minutes

Skill: Intermediate and expert divers from boat. Advanced kayak-divers.

Why go: Dropping quickly in steep giant steps, the sheer clay corrugated cliffs with narrow ledges carved by the current at Steamboat Island make a most unusual dive for this area where gently sloping sand is the norm.

The beautiful nooks and crannies carved in the clay offer hiding places for all types of marine animals. We found whole pockets of life stashed here and there. In one, half a dozen red Irish lords. In another, a handful of painted greenlings, or convict fish. But my biggest thrill was seeing a 6-foot (2-meter) wolf-eel lying right in the open. Usually you see dogfish at Steamboat Island and always a mass of peculiar invertebrates.

A different and interesting site. Well worth the bother of taking a boat or dive-kayak.

Bottom and Depths: Clay cliffs drop in steep steps to a depth of 100 to 110 feet (30 to 34 meters). Some big boulders at 30 to 40 feet (9 to 12 meters). Narrow, scooped-out undercut ledges all the way down. Visibility often limited because of silt. A dark dive. Take a light.

Hazards: Current and whirlpools. The current is weird at Steamboat Island, probably because of the labyrinth of waterways. Dive on the slack. The current table correction is "Totten Inlet entrance" on The Narrows. Kayak-divers who dive deep should rest before paddling back as overexertion after diving may increase the risk of bends.

Telephone: The closest public telephones I could find are at the launching ramps at Boston Harbor or Port of Olympia. In an emergency you might try one of the many privately owned homes on Steamboat Island.

Facilities: None at Steamboat Island. No place to land at the site; it is all privately owned property. Wild undeveloped beaches to land on at Hope Island State Park which is ½ nautical mile (1 kilometer) away. Charters out of Olympia. Launching and air fills at Shelton and Olympia. Dive-kayak rentals and air fills at Silverdale and Bainbridge Island.

Access: Steamboat Island is located near Olympia and Shelton at the northern entry to Squaxin Passage. It is 6 nautical miles (11 kilometers) northwest of Olympia. A maze of inlets is in the region and there are many launch points. Access is easy for both power boaters and kayakers. Anchor near the north end of Steamboat and go down.
• Charter out of Olympia and go to Steamboat Island.
• Rent a boat or launch your own boat at Olympia: from the Port of Olympia, 6 nautical miles (11 kilometers) to Steamboat Island; from Boston Harbor, 4 nautical miles (7 kilometers); from Johnson Point, 9 nautical miles (17 kilometers).
• Kayak-divers and boats can launch at Arcadia Point outside Shelton: from Highway 3 at Shelton, drive 15 minutes to the ramp at the end of Arcadia Point Road. Launch and paddle 1 nautical mile (2 kilometers) south to Steamboat. Anchor and go down. This is an advanced kayak-dive because you have to gear up on your kayak, dive, then climb back on.

Wheelchair divers who paddle dive-kayaks will find it easy to launch at Arcadia Point Ramp. But parking is two city blocks from the ramp.

Comments: For me, a real "turn-on" dive.

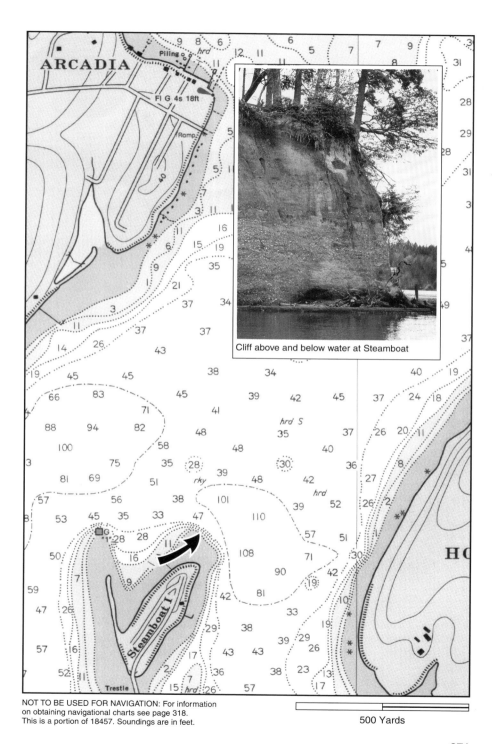

ARCADIA

Piling

Fl G 4s 18ft

Ramp

hrd

Steamboat I

Trestle

Cliff above and below water at Steamboat

hrd S

rky

hrd

G
"1" 28

HO

NOT TO BE USED FOR NAVIGATION: For information
on obtaining navigational charts see page 318.
This is a portion of 18457. Soundings are in feet.

500 Yards

271

OCTOPUS HOLE
Shore Dive

Tide Table: Seattle

Skill: All divers

Why go: Easy access, minimal currents, and an attractive rock wall dropping from 30 to 60 feet (9 to 18 meters) make this a popular open-water certification site.

Octopus Hole is excellent for new divers. We saw rockfish in crevices, lots of bright orange encrusting sponges splashed over the wall, rocks capped with picturesque white plumose anemones, an octopus and sunflower stars. One weird invertebrate that was a "first" for me that day – a galatheid crab sometimes called "tuna crab" or "squat lobster". Also look for another slightly unusual marine animal sometimes seen in Hood Canal that looks more like a giant tarantula than anything else, the hairy lithode crab.

Octopuses are gone at the time of writing except for some young ones but they are coming back. And you always have to look hard to find one of these shy creatures because so many divers scatter along this shore. To find an octopus, look in holes and under ledges. And look for small piles of bits and pieces of crabs, telltale signs of the entrance to an octopus's lair. You might find two or three wolf-eels, too.

Bottom and Depths: Rocky beach gives way to silty sand bottom which slopes rapidly to a ledge at 20 to 30 feet (6 to 9 meters) that is marked by a buoy. From the ledge, the rock wall drops to 50 to 60 feet (15 to 18 meters), depending on tide height. The wall parallels the shore. Slightly farther offshore the bottom drops off quickly again. Very deep water in Hood Canal.

Hazards: Red jellyfish, in the fall. If you see any, you and your buddy should check one another for stinging tentacles before removing your masks and gloves.

Telephone: South of Octopus Hole; go ¾ mile (1⅓ kilometers) south and look on east side (water side) of highway.

Facilities: None. Air fills in Potlatch, Hoodsport and north of Lilliwaup. Camping, cold-water showers for divers to rinse gear, and coin-operated hot showers to warm up in at Potlatch State Park, 7 miles (11 kilometers) south of Octopus Hole. You will find a variety of motels and cafés close-by.

Access: Octopus Hole is on the west side of the Hood Canal next to Highway 101 between Olympia and Port Townsend. It is 35 miles (60 kilometers) north of Olympia; 60 miles (100 kilometers) south of Port Townsend.

You will know you are there when the road comes down close to the water and you see a sign on the tree: "Private Property, No Shellfish Harvesting". Roadside parking for two cars at a lay-by. Park, climb over the guard rail at the north end of the lay-by, and walk down a few stairsteps to an easy path to the water. The rock wall starts south of this point. To find the wall, walk down the beach or snorkel south 75 yards (70 meters) before going down. At the time of writing, this access to Octopus Hole is owned by the dive shop owners in Potlatch and they make it available to all divers. They have placed an orange buoy to mark the wall and ledge. No fee for use of the access, but the dive shop requests no removal of marine life by divers.

To get to Octopus Hole next to Highway 101
• From Hoodsport, heading north on Highway 101: from the bridge in Hoodsport, measure the distance. Go 3⅔ miles (5¾ kilometers) to Octopus Hole.
• From Lilliwaup, heading south on Highway 101: from the bridge in Lilliwaup, measure the distance and go 1 mile (1½ kilometers) to Octopus Hole.

Comments: Great place for new divers. But just look, don't touch. Treat Octopus Hole like an underwater reserve as the locals do. "No Shellfish Harvesting" – and remember, octopuses are shellfish.

Galatheid crab, or squat lobster

NOT TO BE USED FOR NAVIGATION: For information
on obtaining navigational charts see page 318.
This is a portion of 18448. Soundings are in fathoms.

2 Nautical Miles

SEABECK BAY
Shore Dive

Tide Table: Seattle

Skill: All divers and snorkelers

Why go: Balls and chains clank and rattle at Seabeck Bay. "It's like music, under-water wind chimes," says one diver who showed me the multitude of wrecks at Seabeck. "Rugged water makes wonderful music – it's best in a storm!"

"Underwater playground" to another diver who loves to swoop up and over the giant balls in an underwater ballet.

Wrecks of pleasure boats and fishing boats that sank in the marina at Seabeck in a windstorm on December 18, 1990, are still scattered beneath the balls and chains which form a breakwater for the marina. Gusts up to 80 knots (150 kilometers/hour) were reported that evening. Eighty of the 88 vessels at the marina were either sunk or tossed on shore – many were recovered, but there are still remains to explore. The intact wrecks range in length from 25 to 40 feet (8 to 12 meters): a fiberglass sailboat with keel, a wooden cabin cruiser, a purse seiner of wood, a 25-foot (8-meter) cruiser that sank in 1993 with lots of gear and another boat with some gear still on it. Many giant balls have gone down, too. They are orange with a diameter of 4½ feet (1⅔ meters). The floating balls and the chains that hold them are richly coated with mussels, orange sponges and yellow ones, purple tube worms and minute shrimp. The hulls of the wrecks provide homes for pile perch, painted greenlings, striped perch, blackeye gobies, decorator crabs. We saw lingcod, copper rockfish – big ones. White sea cu-cumbers, sunflower stars, fat brown cucumbers. Moon snails and opalescent nudi-branchs in the eelgrass. Oysters in the shallows. Hermit crabs rolling around in no-man's-land out on the sand.

Seabeck Bay is interesting for marine biologists: it is a breeding ground for stubby squid.

Bottom and Depths: The bottom slopes gently from shore to the breakwater of balls. Beneath the balls, the depth is 30 to 40 feet (9 to 12 meters), depending on tide height. North of the balls, the silty sand and eelgrass slopes gradually to a depth of 40 to 50 feet (12 to 15 meters).

Hazards: Small boats and visibility. Check in at the marina office and fly your diver's flag – you should do so at all sites, but at this one it is a must. Stay between the breakwater of balls while snorkeling out, descending and ascending. Do not surface beyond the balls in marina traffic lanes. To stir up less silt, weight yourself carefully to stay down at shallow depths.

Telephone: Seabeck, beside post office, highway and store.

Facilities: Fast food snacks; toilets at end of dock. Hot showers nearby at Scenic Beach State Park picnic site and at the campground with camping year-round.

Access: Seabeck Bay is on the east side of Hood Canal in the village of Seabeck. It is next to Seabeck Highway off Highway 3. The Highway 3 turnoff to Seabeck High-way is midway between Bremerton and Hood Canal Bridge. From either point, it is 30 minutes to the dive.

From Highway 3, take Newberry Hill Exit and follow signs toward Scenic Beach State Park. From this Highway 3 junction, 12 minutes to reach the dive: go nearly 3 miles (5 kilometers) and turn right; continue 4 miles (7 kilometers) more to Seabeck. Park by the roadside and check in at the marina office. Enter the water down the bank at the sign that says "The Marina at Seabeck". Snorkel out to the giant balls that

274

form a breakwater for the marina: 100 yards (90 meters) to the first ones. Then snorkel between them for protection from small boat traffic.

To find the sunken sailboat, go down at the ball in the southwest corner of the breakwater near the buoy light with the sign that says "Come Back". A cluster of wrecks is nearby. Look 30 feet (9 meters) southeast of the sailboat for a sunken cruiser. Another wrecked cabin cruiser is 75 feet (23 meters) south of it. The purse seiner is directly north of it. Follow a compass bearing to them. The last wreck we found was straight out from shore and north of the ball closest to shore. I call this part no-man's-land because it is so flat, sandy and featureless. But divers often see skates here as well as the wreck – and dogfish sharks.

The marina and breakwater are privately owned property. Diving is not permitted within 300 yards (275 meters) of the marina but is allowed at the breakwater. At the time of writing the owner of this marina is happy to welcome divers who dive with a flag and who do not harvest or salvage. Again, check in at the marina, so the dive remains available. And do not dive during shrimping season – late May or early June.

Comments: From Scenic Beach, a view of the Olympic Mountains across Hood Canal. A fishing reef is nearby at Misery Point; strong swimmers and kayak-divers could go to it from the public launching ramp at Scenic Beach Park.

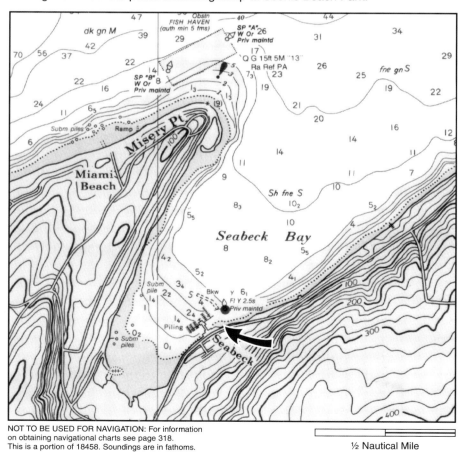

NOT TO BE USED FOR NAVIGATION: For information on obtaining navigational charts see page 318.
This is a portion of 18458. Soundings are in fathoms.

½ Nautical Mile

HARPER FISHING PIER WRECK
Shore Dive

Tide Table: Seattle

Skill: All divers and snorkelers

Why go: A lot to see at Harper, including a shallow, penetrable easy-to-find wreck. At very low tides, the mast projects from the water. It's a quick and easy dive in a quiet place. Uncomplicated. Good for new divers or anyone who wants to unwind.

The fishing boat has sunk north of the pier. Its oak and cedar hull is 50 feet (15 meters) long and 16 feet (5 meters) high, and there is lots to explore. The head is intact and recognizable. The motors have been pulled but the shaft is there. Divers experienced in penetrating wrecks can enter the captain's cabin, the storage and berthing areas and the engine room. Marine life is excellent. Within six months, white plumose anemones and purple tube worms were on the wreck, an octopus had moved on board, and poachers and shrimp were all over it. Schools of slim silvery juvenile tubesnouts spurt forward in unison and seaperch swim through the wreck. Flounders are all around on the sand. Inside and outside, lots to look for and explore.

If the wreck should be towed away or if you still want more after the wreck, go sightseeing along the plumose-covered pilings of the pier. We saw pink anemones, lots of horse crabs, moon snails, horse clams and sea stars. This site is where I first saw an octopus shoot its ink. Popularity has not spoiled this spot, but for best visibility go on a weekday when fewer divers are stirring up the silt.

Bottom and Depths: The wreck rest on silty sand in 20 to 30 feet (6 to 9 meters), depending on tide height. The top of the wreck is so shallow it projects from the water at extreme minus tides. Silty sand slopes gently from beach to wreck and end of pier.

Hazards: Small boats and transparent fishing line. Before diving, look for people fishing from the pier. When diving, listen for boats. Ascend up the mast of the wreck, up a pier piling, or use a compass and swim close along the bottom all the way back to shore. Carry a knife and be careful of fishing tackle, but do not disturb the crab traps.

Telephones: • Harper, across road from sea wall. • Southworth ferry landing.

Facilities: Toilets on Harper Pier. Camping nearby at Manchester State Park off Highway 160, between Harper and Port Orchard. In winter, open only on weekends.

Access: Harper Fishing Pier Wreck is in Puget Sound near the east end of Yukon Harbor. It is on Highway 160, Kitsap Peninsula, north of Southworth and south of Bremerton. From Seattle by car ferry and road, 45 minutes to the pier. From Tacoma, 55 minutes. From Bremerton, 20 minutes.

Just north of Harper Fishing Pier, space for one or two cars to park beside the seawall. Climb three or four steps down the rocks piled beside the seawall to the cobble beach and snorkel 300 yards (275 meters) to the wreck. At the time of writing, you can find the wreck by the mast. If the mast is destroyed, follow a 40-degree compass bearing from seawall to wreck. The wreck is 50 yards (46 meters) directly north of the end of the pier.

To get to Southworth
• From Seattle, Olympia and Tacoma by road: go on I-5 (Interstate Highway 5) to Highway 16. Head north on Highway 16 to Sedgewick Road (Highway 160) and go east on Sedgewick to Southworth and Harper.
• From Seattle by ferry and road: head south on I-5 (Interstate Highway 5) and take Exit 163A onto West Seattle Freeway. Move left. At the end of the freeway continue on Fauntleroy Way, following signs to the Vashon ferry and go from Fauntleroy to

Southworth. Off the ferry, bear right on Highway 160 and go nearly 2 miles (3 kilometers) to Harper.
• From Bremerton, head south on Highway 3/16 through Gorst to Port Orchard, then southeast on Highway 160. From the Highway 3/16 junction, go nearly 5½ miles (9 kilometers) through Colby to Harper Fishing Pier.

Comments: Great for a night dive.

Shallow, easy-to-find wreck at Harper Fishing Pier

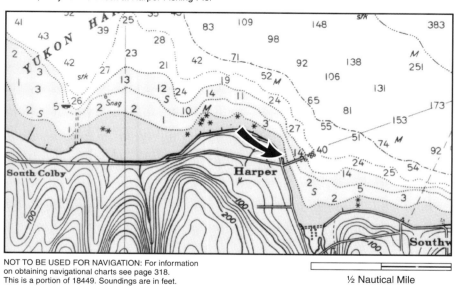

NOT TO BE USED FOR NAVIGATION: For information
on obtaining navigational charts see page 318.
This is a portion of 18449. Soundings are in feet.

½ Nautical Mile

BLAKELY ROCK
Boat Dive

Current Table: Admiralty Inlet (Bush Point)
Subtract 20 minutes

Skill: Intermediate and expert divers and snorkelers. All divers with guide.

Why go: Blakely Rock is the closest place with rocks, and Blakely must be the most beautiful natural dive site – unassisted by people – in the immediate Seattle area. It is particularly worthwhile for available light photography. You'll find grottoes thick with white plumose anemones in only 10 feet (3 meters) of water. Lots and lots of fish. It's like an aquarium.

Dusky perch, big black rockfish, silver shiners, striped seaperch, red Irish lords, giant painted greenlings, often called convict fish, and small blennies swim about in the sunny shallows. We saw gorgeous nudibranchs of many varieties: white ones with white tips, orange ones with white tips and white ones with orange tips, the clown nudibranchs. Also interesting shells. Leafy hornmouths and Oregon tritons. The area is supposedly good for octopuses, wolf-eels, and the occasional lingcod and cabezon which has escaped the hunter up until now, but I saw none of these.

The unique beauty of Blakely Rock to me is in the shallow grottoes and caves. Yet you will find diving shallow and deep. Blakely Rock sits on the east-west trending Seattle fault located between Restoration Point and Winslow on Bainbridge Island. Millions of years of geologic activity have lifted these layers and tilted the bedrock almost vertically, so the jumble of ancient and new rocks at Blakely is next to a steep wall. Diving near the surface you might find ancient fossil clams or petrified wood in the rocks – you might see rock that is 25 to 37 million years old.

Bottom and Depths: Silt-covered sandstone and shale. At the southeast corner of Blakely Rock, ledges drop in steps to a depth of 60 to 70 feet (18 to 21 meters), bottoming out deeper than you want to go off – it quickly plunges to 120 feet (37 meters), then to 360 feet (110 meters) on the chart. Caves and grottoes from 10 to 20 feet (3 to 6 meters) right up to the surface on the eastern and northern sides. There is a very shallow forest of bull kelp on the northwest side of Blakely Rock.

Hazards: Current, boats and bull kelp. Fishing line and gill nets. Red jellyfish, in the fall. Dive on slack. Listen for boats. Carry a knife. If caught in kelp, fishing line or gill nets you can cut your way free. If you have seen any red jellyfish, check for stinging tentacles before removing masks and gloves.

Telephones: • Eagle Harbor, Bainbridge Island ferry landing. • Don Armeni Boat Ramp in Seattle, across street.

Facilities: None at the site. Charters out of Bainbridge Island, Seattle, Bremerton and Kingston. Launching at Don Armeni Park in Seattle with air fills across the road. Launching at Fort Ward State Park, camping and hot showers year-round at Faye Bainbridge State Park, air fills and guiding in Winslow – all on Bainbridge Island.

Access: Blakely Rock is in Puget Sound 1 nautical mile (2 kilometers) off the east side of Bainbridge Island and 6 nautical miles (11 kilometers) west of Don Armeni Ramp at Duwamish Head in West Seattle. Bainbridge Island is a 35-minute ferry ride from downtown Seattle.

Charter out of Bainbridge Island, Seattle, Bremerton or Kingston. Launch from Don Armeni Boat Ramp at Duwamish Head in Seattle or take the Seattle-Bainbridge Island Ferry to Winslow and launch at Eagle Harbor or at Fort Ward State Park on the southeast corner of Bainbridge. From Fort Ward, go around Restoration Point to Blakely Rock which has a marker on it – about the same distance as from Duwamish

Head. Anchor south of the rock and dive from the deeper southeast corner around the east side to the shallows on the northern side.

Comments: Blakely Rock is well worth the effort of taking a boat!

Looking east from Blakely Rock to Seattle

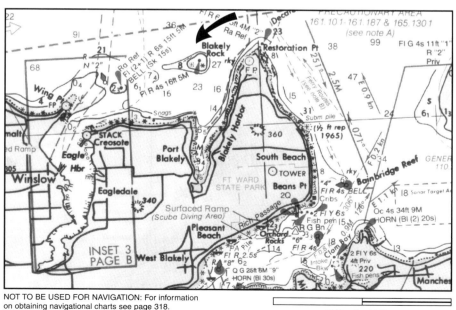

NOT TO BE USED FOR NAVIGATION: For information on obtaining navigational charts see page 318. This is a portion of 18445. Soundings are in fathoms.

2 Nautical Miles

ORCHARD ROCKS
Kayak Dive or Boat Dive

Current Table: Admiralty Inlet (Bush Point)
Subtract 15 minutes, turn to flood
Add 35 minutes, turn to ebb

Skill: Intermediate and expert divers. All divers and snorkelers with guide.

Why go: Vast territory to explore at Orchard Rocks. You have to see it at low tide to know how much.

Great kelp forest in the shallows from spring to late fall with red rock crabs, kelp crabs, green urchins, orange sea cucumbers hiding in it. From there, go to whatever depth you want to. Ledges stairstep down from Orchard Rocks. A jumble of rock, sand and surf creatures live here.

We saw green anemones, giant barnacles, pillow stars the color of half-baked cookies. Also feather stars, sunflower stars, leather stars. Maroon-and-gray striped painted greenlings. Snakelock anemones. Moon jellyfish. China rockfish. Metallic blue kelp. Moon snails, sea pens, big brown sea cucumbers. Shrimp. A mosshead warbonnet. Lingcod, cabezon, kelp greenlings. Water jellyfish. Also a large octopus, probably 75 pounds (34 kilograms). And we only got to the second ledge.

Bottom and Depths: Orchard Rocks are covered at high tides; a great deal of rock is exposed at low tides. The bull kelp forest is thick, in summer, and shallow. In 20 to 30 feet (6 to 9 meters). Ledges stairstep down into Rich Passage. One ledge at 45 feet (14 meters), one at 50 feet (15 meters), and at 70 feet (21 meters). You can go deeper to 110 feet (34 meters). Pools of sand between ledges.

Hazards: Very swift current, boats, bull kelp, especially in summer and fall; stinging jellyfish in spring and summer; and fishing line – we also found a rope, tangled gill net, a large chain. Dive on slack. However, it is largely unpredictable. Boat divers should dive with a "live" boat. Kayak-divers – be aware of what the water is doing to you while you are down. The Washington State Ferry passes during almost every dive – do not become alarmed by the roar. But *do* listen for small boats. At low tides, ascend up the rocks. At high tides, if you hear a boat, stay down until it passes. Carry a knife for kelp and fishing line. If you have seen jellyfish, check for stinging tentacles before removing masks and gloves.

Telephones: • Manchester, 1½ nautical miles (3 kilometers) south of Orchard Rocks. • Lynwood Center, Bainbridge Island, in front of theater. From Fort Ward Park ramp, go by road 1½ miles (2½ kilometers) to it.

Facilities: None. Launching and wheelchair-accessible toilets nearby at Fort Ward State Park; camping and hot showers at Faye Bainbridge State Park – both on Bainbridge Island. On the Kitsap Peninsula, launching at the town of Manchester; camping at Manchester State Park, but in winter on weekends only. Camping with hot showers year-round at Illahee State Park, Bremerton. Also launching. Dive-kayak rentals at Silverdale and Bainbridge Island. Dive guide at Bainbridge Island.

Access: The Orchard Rocks site is near the east end of Rich Passage between Bainbridge Island and Kitsap Peninsula. Easy to find at all tides because of the red navigational marker. At low tides, Orchard Rocks are exposed. Pick a spot in the kelp or on the inside of the rocks – and try it. Expert divers with a pickup boat could dive on the outside of the rocks in Rich Passage.
• Charter at Bainbridge Island, Bremerton, Kingston or Seattle to Orchard Rocks.
• Launch your boat or dive-kayak at Fort Ward State Park on Bainbridge Island and go to Orchard Rocks. From Fort Ward, just over ½ nautical mile (1 kilometer) to the

dive. Launch at Manchester and go 1½ nautical miles (3 kilometers); or launch at one of many ramps in Bremerton and go to Orchard Rocks.

• Kayak-divers can paddle from Fort Ward to the dive in 15 minutes. Easier at low tides when you can land on the rocks to gear up. We dived at high tide, anchored in kelp, geared up and rolled off our dive-kayaks. Gently sloping ramp for wheelchair divers.

Comments: A "repeater" dive: so much I did not explore yet. And want to.

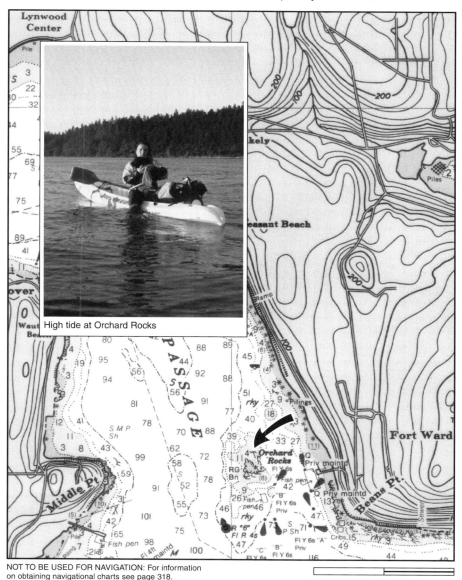

High tide at Orchard Rocks

NOT TO BE USED FOR NAVIGATION: For information
on obtaining navigational charts see page 318.
This is a portion of 18449. Soundings are in feet.

½ Nautical Mile

CRYSTAL SPRINGS PIER
Shore Dive

Current Table: Admiralty Inlet (Bush Point)
Subtract 45 minutes, turn to flood
Add 45 minutes, turn to ebb

Skill: All divers and snorkelers

Why go: Sand dollars – only the second dive where I've seen live ones. Crystal Springs Pier has the advantage of current. That's what makes it different from most sandy-beach-type places. And access is extremely easy, climb across two or three logs to the sand.

The collection of creatures I saw on one dive at Point White was varied, including two "firsts" for me – always special, plus lots of old friends. Orange and white plumose anemones decorate an old cartwheel at the end of the pier. You will see blue striped seaperch, tube-snouts, gunnels, flounders. Dungeness crabs, hermit crabs and lots of red rock crabs. More everyday stuff, too: giant barnacles, tiny purple and pink tube worms. Mussels. Lots of razor clams. Big smooth moon snails, lumpy sea cucumbers, wispy tube-dwelling anemones. Sea lettuce. Coon-striped shrimp. Metallic ribbon kelp, shimmering blue. Moon jellyfish. Geoducks. Leafy hornmouth whelks. Sunflower stars, leather stars, mottled stars, purple stars heaped on the pier pilings. We saw lots of juvenile sea pens that looked like frayed rubber. And many brown-striped nudibranchs – they go with sea pens like bacon and eggs as they feed on them. Look for skates, sometimes here. When I dived here I had still not seen one in the wild.

The "firsts" for me this dive: a pink scoop-shovel nudibranch on the sand. It was the size of my hand, but frilly and delicate. The other was a sturgeon poacher lying with its whiskers on the sand. A sharp angular little character with a small, pointed nose.

Bottom and Depths: Sandy bottom slopes gently from the beach to a depth of 10 to 20 feet (3 to 6 meters) at the end of the pier, depending on tide height. Pier pilings provide attachment for barnacles, shelter for fish. Most life is around the pier and down to 30 feet (9 meters). We reached 50 feet (15 meters) maximum. You could go deeper.

Hazards: Current and shallow depth. Dive on slack. But be aware that predictions are unreliable at Crystal Springs Pier. The current table correction is "Rich Passage, west end" on Admiralty Inlet (Bush Point). Pick your time, go to the site and look at the water. You might have to wait or even give up on the dive. If diving with slight-current, start your dive west of the pier pilings. Weight yourself well so you can stay down at shallow depths. That is where the life is.

Telephone: Lynwood Center, in front of theater. Go 2 miles (3 kilometers) back to junction and turn right.

Facilities: Parking for eight or ten cars at Crystal Springs Park, Point White; camping at Faye Bainbridge State Park, north end of island. Air fills and dive guide in Winslow.

Access: Crystal Springs Pier juts into Port Orchard Narrows just north of Point White. It is on Bainbridge Island, 15 minutes from Winslow. From Bremerton via Highways 3 and 305 to Winslow on Bainbridge takes 50 minutes; from Hood Canal Bridge (also via Highways 3 and 305) to Winslow takes 50 minutes; by ferry from downtown Seattle to Bainbridge Island takes 35 minutes.

At Winslow, off the ferry from Seattle (or heading south into town on Highway 305), follow signs to the city center. From Winslow Way and Highway 305 it is 5½ miles (9 kilometers) to the dive. Go west on Winslow Way to the stop sign at Madison Avenue. Turn right. At Wyatt Street, turn left. Go straight to the end of Wyatt and the road curves left. At the "Y" turn right and follow signs up Bucklin Hill Road toward Fort Ward State Park. At Lynwood Center turn right into Point White Drive which becomes Crystal Springs Drive. Wind your way past waterfront homes – from Lynwood Center, 5 minutes to Crystal Springs Pier north of Point White.

Enter at the left-hand side of the pier – if current is ebbing, enter at the right. Access is especially easy at high tide because the walk is so short. And there is *no* swim. When you've got your boots wet, you're there. If entering at low tide be careful not to walk on live sand dollars. The gray ones are dead, the dark purple ones alive.

Comments: The Mosquito Fleet used to call here; might be old bottles.

Plumose anemones on cartwheel and pilings

NOT TO BE USED FOR NAVIGATION: For information
on obtaining navigational charts see page 318.
This is a portion of 18474. Soundings are in fathoms.

1 Nautical Mile

AGATE PASSAGE
Shore Dive or Boat Dive

Current Table: Admiralty Inlet (Bush Point)
Subtract 50 minutes

Skill: Expert divers. Intermediate divers with pickup boat.

Why go: Tumbling and flying through a fantasy-land of fish and rocks, travel ⅔ mile (1 kilometer) through current-swept Agate Passage without kicking a fin. This is the best site for a "drift" dive that I've ever seen.

Access to the water at both ends of the passage makes three dive plans possible. Dive on slack at either end. Take two cars, leaving one at each end, spend the whole day and drift both ways. Or take a boat and dive from either access without having to plan the timing. A heady trip however you do it.

Starting the rollercoaster ride you fly through giant pile perch schooling around the piers of the bridge. Sweeping on, you hurtle towards a bright white hedge of horse clams. A gentle push of your hand and you're over it, slowing down, picking up a red Irish lord in your palm. Then off again. Past large rocks encrusted with bright yellow sponges and millions of miniature white anemones. A big rock. You're going to hit it! The current carries you up and over. Looking behind boulders in the lee of the current you see large lingcod staring back at you. A cabezon on eggs. There's no way to stop. You somersault for the sheer joy of it, floating upside down to see where you've been. The motion's enough to make the dive.

Bottom and Depths: The bottom is 25 to 35 feet (8 to 11 meters) through Agate Passage. Mostly sand and gravel. Rocks and boulders north of the bridge. Bull kelp around the bridge piers.

Hazards: Currents and boats. Currents run up to 7½ knots (14 kilometers/hour). The current table correction is "Agate Passage, south end" on Admiralty Inlet (Bush Point). Current is greater at the southern end of the passage and on flooding tides. Dive on slack around the piers of the bridge but safest with a pickup boat.

Plan a "drift" dive carefully according to current and available pickup boats. Listen for boats and ascend with a reserve of air. If you hear a boat you can stay down until it passes. When drifting do not take a camera, spear gun or goodie bag; extra gear will be in the way. Hold hands with your buddy, and tow a dive flag to show the pickup boat where you are.

Telephone: Suquamish, in shopping center at southeast corner of Division Avenue and Suquamish Way.

Facilities: At north end of Agate Passage: Launching ramp at end of Suquamish Way at the water's edge below Chief Sealth's grave. Picnic tables, fire ring, drinking water, a pit toilet and interpretive display at the historic site at Old Man House where Chief Sealth lived for years. Some house posts remain from about 1800. No facilities at access on the Bainbridge Island side of the bridge. Just a nice wild beach.

Access: Agate Passage is between Bainbridge Island and the Kitsap Peninsula. The dive is reached off Highway 305. From Seattle by ferry and car, 50 minutes. By road from Bremerton, 35 minutes. From Hood Canal Bridge, 25 minutes.

Go on Highway 305 to the *south end* (Bainbridge Island side) of Agate Pass Bridge. Immediately east of the bridge, turn north down Reitan Road, then bear left to park under the large power pole – space for one or two cars at the most. Gravel steps go 100 feet (30 meters) down to the shore just north of the bridge. We launched our inflatable beneath the bridge where you must start if drifting with an ebbing tide.

Drive to the northern end of the passage by going west across Agate Pass Bridge to the Kitsap Peninsula. Just across the bridge, turn right onto Suquamish Way and go 1 mile (1½ kilometers) following signs to Old Man House and Chief Sealth's grave. At a sign pointing to Old Man House Park, turn right into Division Avenue. When you reach McKinistry Street, turn left to a parking space for two cars at the road end at Old Man House. Walk a few steps to the water. A red buoy marks the northern end of Agate Passage.

To get to Agate Pass Bridge
• From downtown Seattle, take Seattle-Bainbridge Island ferry to Winslow and drive north on Highway 305 to Agate Pass Bridge.
• From Bremerton, drive north on Highway 3 to Highway 305. Turn right and go to Agate Pass Bridge.
• From Hood Canal Bridge, drive south on Highway 3 to Highway 305; turn left and go to Agate Pass Bridge.

Comments: A thrilling flight!

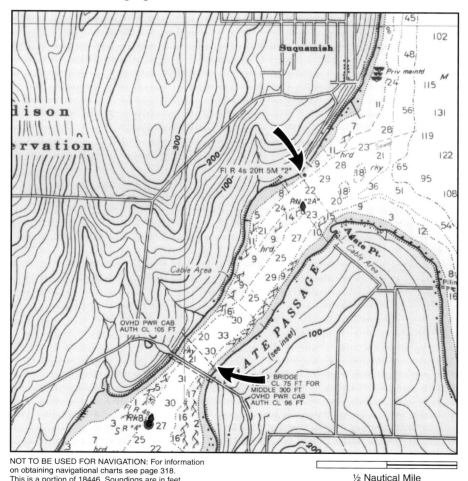

NOT TO BE USED FOR NAVIGATION: For information on obtaining navigational charts see page 318. This is a portion of 18446. Soundings are in feet.

½ Nautical Mile

HOOD CANAL BRIDGE
Shore Dive

Current Table: Admiralty Inlet (Bush Point)
Subtract 30 minutes, turn to ebb

Skill: Intermediate and expert divers

Why go: Where else can you dive from shore and see such magnificent feather duster worms? Fast currents feed these giant purple bouquets. Elegant plumose anemones, countless enormous sea stars and other invertebrates are heaped around the bridge piers. Not an inch of concrete to be seen.

Swimming out to the piers and back, we were fascinated with ranks of sand dollars studding the clean white sand. They feed on fuzzy amber-colored diatoms hanging quietly in grooves of sand while current rushes over the top of them.

Bottom and Depths: Perfectly smooth, silty sand slopes gradually to the bridge piers. At the first submerged pier (which is the second pier), 10 to 20 feet (3 to 6 meters) deep. At the next pier, 30 to 40 feet (9 to 12 meters) deep.

Hazards: Current. Dive on high slack. The current correction is "South Point" on Admiralty Inlet (Bush Point). Sandy, smooth bottom offers no handholds to grasp to pull yourself along against the current. You cannot, therefore, go far during the very limited slack tide under the bridge. Beyond the second submerged pier, a pickup boat is advisable. Carry a knife so you can "knife it" back to shore if all else fails. But take care not to damage the dark-colored sand dollars – they are alive.

Telephones: • Salsbury Point County Park. • Port Gamble Country Store: go to Highway 3 and north from Salsbury Park turnoff for 1 mile (1½ kilometers) to Port Gamble; turn left to the Country Store.

Facilities: Launching ramp, toilets and telephone at Salsbury Point County Park. Camping with hot showers year-round at Kitsap State Park which is 3 miles (5 kilometers) back along Highway 3 toward the Highway 305 junction and Bremerton. Camping year-round with pit toilets across bridge at Shine Tidelands State Park.

Access: The dive is beneath Hood Canal Bridge (east end) near the entrance to Hood Canal. It is off Highway 104. By ferry and car from downtown Seattle, takes 1¼ hours. From Bremerton, 35 minutes. By ferry and car from Edmonds, 50 minutes. From Port Townsend, 30 minutes.

At Hood Canal Bridge (east end): go north ½ mile (¾ kilometer) on Highway 104 and follow signs to Salsbury County Park. Go down Wheeler Street which curves back toward the bridge. Two roads go from Wheeler Street to the beach. The first one is Whitford Road to Salsbury Point Park where you will find a huge parking area, boat launching and toilets. However, if you go to the second road end which is ⅕ mile (⅓ kilometer) farther, the swim is shorter. Snorkel south to the bridge, and swim to the first submerged pier. Descend and continue under water to the next pier.

To get to Hood Canal Bridge
• From downtown Seattle: take Seattle-Bainbridge Island ferry; 35 minutes to cross. Then drive north 21 miles (34 kilometers) from Winslow to the Hood Canal Bridge: go on Highway 305 and cross Agate Pass Bridge; continue on Highways 305 and 3 following signs to Hood Canal Bridge.
• From Bremerton: go on Highway 3 to Hood Canal Bridge.
• From Edmonds, north of Seattle: take Edmonds-Kingston ferry for 30 minutes; then drive 10 miles (16 kilometers) to the dive. From the ferry, follow signs on Highway 104 to Port Gamble. From there, go 1 mile (1½ kilometers) to the turnoff to Salsbury County Park. This is the turnoff to the dive and is before Hood Canal Bridge.

• From Port Townsend, 25 miles (40 kilometers) to the dive: go on Highway 20 to Highway 104. Then east on Highway 104 to Hood Canal Bridge.

Comments: A wealth of invertebrate life, but frustrating for the photographer because the current stirs the silt and creates poor visibility.

Purple sand dollar

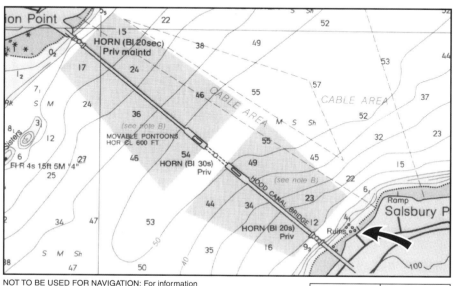

NOT TO BE USED FOR NAVIGATION: For information
on obtaining navigational charts see page 318.
This is a portion of 18477. Soundings are in fathoms.

½ Nautical Mile

SISTERS
Kayak Dive or Boat Dive

Current Table: Admiralty Inlet (Bush Point)
Subtract 45 minutes, turn to flood
Subtract 30 minutes, turn to ebb

Skill: Intermediate and expert divers from boat. Advanced kayak-divers.

Why go: Underwater seamounts are incredibly rich in marine life. The Sisters pair is no exception. The color is intense.

Pink soft coral and transparent glassy tunicates are around the rocks. We saw a clown nudibranch, red Irish lords, a bright green gunnel, a grunt sculpin. A sailfin sculpin was lying sideways in a slit in the rocks. We saw gray colored sponges, keyhole limpets, large white plumose anemones and octopus dens, but nobody home. Rock scallops. And fields of juvenile white sea whips on the flat sand stretching out to forever between the Sisters and shore.

Bottom and Depths: Two seamounts at the Sisters. One is marked with a light; the second is north of it with a flat sandy stretch between that is 20 to 30 feet (6 to 9 meters) deep, depending on tide height. At the big Sister on the shore side, rocky ledges with crevices and some boulders pyramid down to 70 to 80 feet (21 to 24 meters). On the channel side, the bottom drops to 110 feet (34 meters) and deeper. A great deal of marine life from the surface down to a depth of 30 to 40 feet (9 to 12 meters).

Hazards: Current, boats and transparent fishing line – we also saw a net. Dive on slack. The current table correction is "South Point" on Admiralty Inlet (Bush Point). Listen for boats. Carry a knife. If caught in fishing line you can cut your way free. Kayak-divers who dive deep should take it easy paddling back. Bends might be brought on by energetic exercise after diving.

Telephones: • Salsbury Point County Park: go to east side of bridge by water, then north to the launching ramp. • Port Gamble Country Store: go by road to east side of bridge, then north 1¼ miles (2 kilometers) and turn left to the Country Store.

Facilities: Dive-kayak rentals in Silverdale, Bainbridge Island and Oak Harbor on Whidbey Island. Launching immediately north of Hood Canal Bridge (west end). Launching and pit toilets south of Hood Canal Bridge (west end) at Hicks County Park. Camping year-round with picnic tables and pit toilets at Shine Tidelands State Park just north of Hood Canal Bridge (west end). Camping year-round nearby at Kitsap State Park with flush toilets and hot showers. It is 10 minutes away.

Access: Sisters is near the entry to Hood Canal. It is ½ nautical mile (1 kilometer) south of Hood Canal Bridge (west end). A marker is on the Sister that breaks water.

Take a custom charter boat or launch at the ramp immediately north of Hood Canal Bridge (west end) and go south beneath the bridge to the Sisters. Kayak-divers can anchor close to the big Sister and, at the end of the dive, ascend up the rock. Larger boats anchor north of the marker between the Sisters. Plan to be at the site ready to dive 30 or 45 minutes before slack. Currents whirl around the Sisters even on slack, but you can usually find a place to hide from it. Also hold onto the rocks. First trip, dive the big Sister. Second time, look for the little Sister.

Kayak-divers can launch at the ramp beside the bridge or at Shine Tidelands State Park – that's what we did. When diving at high slack, you get help from the flooding current. It took us 15 minutes to paddle ½ nautical mile (1 kilometer) to the Sisters. If diving at low slack, you might paddle 1 nautical mile (2 kilometers) from Hicks County Park. I have not done that but it's worth a try. Allow time. With ebbing tides a counter-clockwise eddy forms in Squamish Harbor – you might have to break out of it.

Comments: One diver finds the little Sister by watching diving birds. If you know your birds, you can go where the shallow-diving birds are and land right on the underwater seamount.

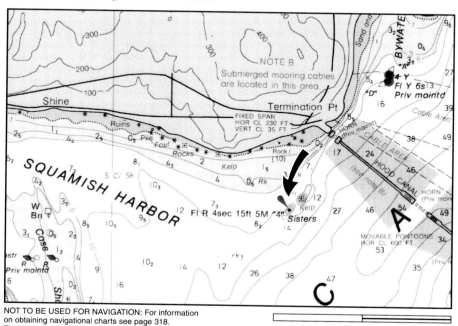

Upping anchor after diving, Sisters Marker behind

NOT TO BE USED FOR NAVIGATION: For information on obtaining navigational charts see page 318. This is a portion of 18476. Soundings are in fathoms.

1 Nautical Mile

FORT FLAGLER FISHING PIER
Shore Dive

Skill: Intermediate divers. All divers with guide.

Why go: Fort Flagler is off the beaten path – few divers visit this park. Wild roses crowd the roadside. Under water it feels like wilderness, too, unspoilt and remote. As you swim along the line to the artificial reef, gunnels dart from the kelp, flounders ripple away, iridescent blue kelp shimmers.

At the reef, it's rich, rich – so rich you cannot see the concrete cylinders that offer attachment and shelter for the life. On one dive we saw six red Irish lords, one big lingcod and four more smaller ones. We saw hermit, spider and Dungeness crabs. Moon jellyfish. Hard yellow sponges, flabby finger sponges, leafy hornmouth whelks, gum boot chitons, a clinging jellyfish, kelp greenlings and lots of silvery fish. Quillback rockfish, painted greenlings, giant barnacles, swimming scallops, rock scallops, plumose anemones, Christmas anemones, plume worms, cemented tube worms, orange cucumbers and white ones, at the reef. Sea pens at its base. Egg cases of moon snails and pink anemones on the mucky bottom.

The current can be strong, yet the line to the reef, as well as the concrete cylinders themselves, give handholds to divers caught by surprise.

Bottom and Depths: The sandy bottom gradually deepens to a depth of 40 to 50 feet (12 to 15 meters) at the reef.

Hazards: Current, fishing line and silty bottom. Dive on slack. Visibility is better on an ebbing tide. Carry a knife for fishing line.

Telephone: On the Interpretive Display Building near Marrowstone Point. Return to junction near park entry, and go north ⅔ mile (1 kilometer) toward the lighthouse.

Facilities: Picnic table on pier; space for 12 cars to park and a picnic table at top of trail; flush toilets and more picnic tables across from the gun emplacement. Camping in the park, and a long stretch of beach to hike, from the pier to Marrowstone Point.

Access: Fort Flagler Fishing Pier is on Admiralty Inlet, southern end, at the entry to Puget Sound. It is at Marrowstone Island but connected by two bridges to the Quimper Peninsula at the town of Port Hadlock. One bridge goes from the Quimper Peninsula to Indian Island, the second to Marrowstone. From Port Townsend ferry terminal to the dive takes 30 minutes. From Hood Canal Bridge, 60 minutes.

At Flagler Road, head north. Go 8 miles (13 kilometers) – the length of Marrowstone Island – to a junction in Fort Flagler Park. Three roads: one goes to the campground, one to Marrowstone Point, and one to the fishing pier. From this junction, ½ mile (¾ kilometer) to the pier. Walk down 25 stairsteps and 30 paces on the trail to the beach. Swim between the pilings. Find a submerged line at the eighth piling, 60 yards (55 meters) as you swim out under the pier. Look sharply, the line is covered with kelp. Follow the line to the reef, which is off the left-hand end of the pier and beyond it.

To get to Flagler Road
• Arriving in Port Townsend from Whidbey Island, turn left onto Water Street which becomes Sims Way then Highway 20. From the ferry, go just over 4 miles (7 kilometers) to the Airport Cutoff Road. Turn left. Follow signs to Fort Flagler and go 3½ miles ((6 kilometers) to Ness Corner. Turn on Highway 116 East (Ness Corner Road) following signs to Mystery Bay and Fort Flagler. When you reach the town of Port Hadlock, go nearly 1 mile (1½ kilometers) on Highway 116 East and turn left into Flagler Road.

• From Olympia or Port Angeles, go to junction of Highway 101 and 20. Head north for 7 miles (11 kilometers) to the Airport Cutoff Road and turn right. Then follow directions from Port Townsend to the dive as given on the previous page.

• From Hood Canal Bridge, head east on Highway 104 for 4 miles (7 kilometers) and turn right onto Beaver Valley Road (Highway 19). Go on it 8 miles (13 kilometers) to Chimacum Road. Turn right and go 1½ miles (2½ kilometers) to the town of Port Hadlock. Turn right onto Highway 116 East (Ness Corner Road) following signs to Fort Flagler State Park. Go nearly 1 mile (1½ kilometers) and turn left into Flagler Road.

Comments: Usually you will have this dive all to yourself.

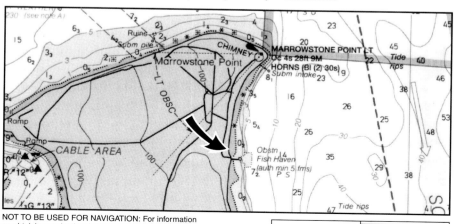

Fort Flagler Pier, Marrowstone Light and ship entering Admiralty Inlet in distance

NOT TO BE USED FOR NAVIGATION: For information on obtaining navigational charts see page 318.
This is a portion of 18471. Soundings are in fathoms.

1 Nautical Mile

FORT WORDEN SCIENCE CENTER WHARF

Shore Dive

Skill: All divers and snorkelers

Why go: Elegant grandiose hallways – bright white plumose-covered columns rise from the dark world beneath the wharf, broken shells like sawdust on the floor of a market place. Wolf-eels, octopuses and dogfish sharks at the edge of it.
  The shell-littered bottom is rich with life. We see lots of sculpins. A sea lemon. A gang of hermit crabs tumbling onto and over a tire. An octopus hiding in it. We see two decorated warbonnets. Decorator crabs covered with stuff – "party" crabs my buddy says when we ascend. We see orange cucumbers, a dahlia anemone, giant barnacles, yellow sponges. A white-spotted greenling, painted greenlings, a school of shiner perch flashing past. Sunflower stars. Lots of shrimp. A rust-colored juvenile wolf-eel stops in the open. Another juvenile wolf-eel follows. A pale gray dogfish shark lies on the bottom in sunshine at the edge of the wharf. Eyes me. Looks into cool darkness beneath the wharf. Another smaller dogfish shark swims slowly toward us, then away. A third, even smaller dogfish, hurries past.
  Snorkeling in, after ascending at a piling, we look down and see a sailfin sculpin.

Bottom and Depths: Bright white sand slopes gently from cobbled beach strewn with silvery logs to silty bottom littered with broken shells and bottom kelp beneath the wharf. Depth at end of wharf is 20 to 30 feet (6 to 9 meters), depending on tide height. Gradually deepens beyond the geometric hallways beneath the wharf.

Hazards: Shallow depth, small boats, current and fishing line. Weight yourself so you can stay down. Listen for boats. If you hear one, stay down until it passes. Throughout your dive, keep the pilings in view because of boats and because of current – that is where the life is anyway, and ascend up a piling. Or stay close to the bottom and navigate by compass to shore. Dive near slack, especially with large exchanges. Carry a knife for fishing line.

Telephone: Refreshment stand, outside; across road from wharf.

Facilities: Camping by reservation and coin-operated hot showers in the park year-round. Dive-kayak rentals at Bainbridge Island, Silverdale and Whidbey Island.

Access: Fort Worden Science Center Wharf is on Admiralty Inlet in the outskirts of Port Townsend. From Port Townsend ferry terminal to the wharf takes 10 minutes.
  At Fort Worden State Park, turn left through the main gate opposite Cherry Street into Fort Worden Way and turn right on Eisenhower Avenue. Continue on Eisenhower to a large anchor; then turn left. Go downhill to the Marine Science Center. Parking is across the road. Walk 60 yards (55 meters) across cobbled beach *south* of the wharf, swim out and follow a piling down.
  Wheelchair access at the launching ramp immediately *north* of the wharf. Strong swimmers could snorkel 75 yards (70 meters) from the launching ramp to the end of the wharf and go down. This swim is cut in half in summer when very low tide, but safer in winter when fewer boats. Wheelchair divers with dive-kayaks could paddle from the launching ramp around the wharf to the beach on the south side of it – the distance is 220 yards (200 meters) in all. Land your kayak on the beach at the south side of the wharf and go down.

To get to Fort Worden State Park
• Arriving in Port Townsend from Whidbey Island, turn left onto Water Street and go ½ mile (¾ kilometer). Turn right up Kearney Street and follow signs to Fort Worden.

• Arriving in Port Townsend on Highway 20 (from the Olympic Peninsula), head down the hill into town; Highway 20 becomes Sims Way. Go along the waterfront on Sims. Past the Chamber of Commerce you come to Kearney Street with a sign to Fort Worden – if you reach the ferry turnoff you have gone too far. Turn left up Kearney and follow the signs to Fort Worden Park.

Comments: I found colorful marine life postcards in Fort Worden Science Center.

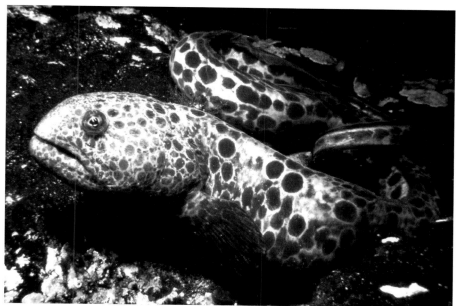

Juvenile wolf-eel

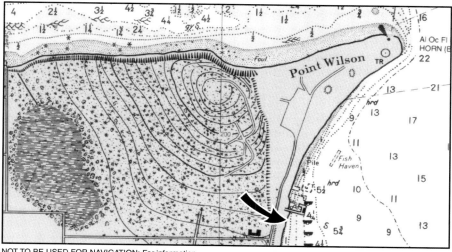

NOT TO BE USED FOR NAVIGATION: For information on obtaining navigational charts see page 318.
This is a portion of 18464. Soundings are in fathoms.

½ Nautical Mile

FORT WORDEN ARTIFICIAL REEF
Shore Dive

Skill: All divers in winter. Intermediate and expert divers in summer.

Why go: Easy in, easy out, easy to find the artificial reef. But no spearfishing – this marine state park is a fish haven.
We saw the always-beautiful white plumose anemones, hermit crabs in their adopted shell homes, decorator crabs festooned to hide themselves in the kelp. Giant barnacles, a gum boot chiton, shrimp, a rose star, sea cucumbers – even a couple of swimming scallops. Yellow encrusting sponge brightens the reef. Quillback rockfish, kelp greenlings, and painted greenlings are around it. We also saw clam shells and sand dollar shells but no live ones.
And the most incredible views on a calm sunny day ranging from Mount Baker through the Skagit Valley to Mount Rainier.

Bottom and Depths: Gently sloping eelgrass and silty sand from beach to artificial reef made of tires at 20 to 30 feet (6 to 9 meters), depending on tide height. A 10-foot (3-meter) long concrete pipe is at south end of the reef. Some bull kelp in summer.

Hazards: Shallow depth, silt, small boats in summer, current, fishing line and some bull kelp. Easier to dive this site at higher tides in winter when no boats. Weight yourself carefully so you can stay down in the shallows yet stay off the bottom and not stir up silt. Do not ascend unexpectedly, as the reef is near boat moorage. Listen for boats. Ascend up the reef marker-buoy or dive with a compass and swim along the bottom to shore. Dive near slack, especially with large exchanges. Carry a knife for fishing line.

Telephone: Refreshment stand, outside; across road from wharf.

Facilities: Air fills on the way to the dive at Port Angeles, Bainbridge Island, Bremerton or across the ferry route at Oak Harbor on Whidbey Island. Sometimes air fills at nearby Port Hadlock but best to telephone and check it out.

Access: Fort Worden Artificial Reef is at the edge of Admiralty Inlet in the outskirts of Port Townsend and is shown on the charts as a Fish Haven. From Port Townsend ferry terminal to the park takes 10 minutes.
At Fort Worden State Park, turn left through the main gate opposite Cherry Street into Fort Worden Way and turn right on Eisenhower Avenue. Pass the park office and continue on Eisenhower to a large anchor, then turn left. Go down the hill and past the Marine Science Center. The artificial reef is 190 yards (175 meters) north of the launching ramp. An Underwater Park sign points toward the reef. It is a short walk across sand to the water, the distance depending on tide height. The artificial reef is 100 feet (30 meters) offshore. A white cylindrical marker with an orange stripe marks it. Other buoys are around for boats to tie up to – you can arrive by boat, too. But stay away from those mooring-buoys when diving. Enter over the sand, swim out over eelgrass to the artificial reef marker-buoy and go down. Wheelchair divers with dive-kayaks could enter at the launching ramp and paddle 190 yards (175 meters) north along the beach, land and swim to the reef.

To get to Fort Worden State Park
• Arriving in Port Townsend from Whidbey Island, turn left onto Water Street and go ½ mile (¾ kilometer). Turn right up Kearney Street and follow signs to Fort Worden.
• Arriving in Port Townsend on Highway 20 (from the Olympic Peninsula), head down the hill into town; Highway 20 becomes Sims Way. Go along the waterfront on Sims.

Past the Chamber of Commerce you come to Kearney Street with a sign to Fort Worden – if you reach the ferry turnoff you have gone too far. Turn left up Kearney and follow the signs to Fort Worden Park.

Comments: Discovered in 1792, the first fort was built here in 1855 and named Fort Wilson; renamed Fort Worden in 1900.

Victorian home, Port Townsend

NOT TO BE USED FOR NAVIGATION: For information
on obtaining navigational charts see page 318.
This is a portion of 18441. Soundings are in fathoms.

2 Nautical Miles

POINT WILSON REEF
Boat Dive

Current Table: Admiralty Inlet (Bush Point)
Subtract 68 minutes, turn to flood
Subtract 47 minutes, turn to ebb

Skill: Expert divers

Why go: A rich dive on the few days of the year you can visit this current-swept, kelp-covered reef at Point Wilson. White rocks make a bright background for pale lavender anemones, dark red sculpins, hot pink and yellow-and-white-striped dahlia anemones. Boulders crusted over with chitons and giant barnacles and capped with small white plumose anemones make good hiding places for wolf-eels. Mauve coralline algae and large yellow bath-like sponges fill any space that's left. Big ling-cod are all over the place. Some divers say they have seen 60- to 70-pound (27- to 32-kilogram) lingcod at Point Wilson, particularly in the fall when the salmon are around. We saw schools of big black rockfish, copper rockfish and kelp greenlings on the reef. Loads of flounders between the reef and shore.

After the dive walk around historic Port Townsend, one of the oldest settlements in Washington State. Each Victorian home is as well painted as the day it was built. Signs on more than 200 homes indicate the date of building and original owner.

Bottom and Depths: The bright white rock reef is clean-swept with no silt, 25 to 35 feet (8 to 11 meters) deep. Some big boulders, scattered white sand, and thick bull kelp.

Hazards: Extremely dangerous current as well as bull kelp, in summer. Dive on the slack. The current correction is "Pt. Wilson, 0.5 mile northeast of" on Admiralty Inlet (Bush Point). All the water going into Puget Sound pours past Point Wilson. The reef can only be dived on small tidal exchanges and exactly on slack. Rip tides are vicious and could sweep you out into the big shipping lanes in Admiralty Inlet. Dive from a "live" boat at Point Wilson Reef. Carry a knife for kelp.

Telephone: Fort Worden Park, across road from ramp, outside refreshment stand.

Facilities: None at the reef. Launching ramp, fast food, restrooms with wheelchair-accessible toilets and coin-operated hot showers at the beautiful natural beach at Fort Worden. Plus historic remains of Fort Worden, housing in old Victorian homes that were once officer's quarters, as well as camping year-round. Many vacation homes are furnished with fireplaces and reproductions of Victorian furnishings. Inquire about campsite reservations, and vacation housing. Contact Fort Worden State Park Conference Center, 200 Battery Way, Port Townsend, WA 98368. Telephone (206) 385-4730; toll-free from Seattle, (206) 464-7542; and fax (206) 385-7248.

Wonderful wild beach walk from Point Wilson all the way to North Beach.

Access: Point Wilson Reef is close offshore from Point Wilson at the entry to Admiralty Inlet. You can reach it from Fort Worden State Park in the outskirts of Port Townsend. It takes 10 minutes to drive from the ferry terminal in Port Townsend to Fort Worden where you can launch (see directions on page 294).

Charter with a custom operation or launch your own boat. Go to the north shore of Point Wilson where bull kelp marks two reefs. The kelp is most easily seen at low tide. The best reef is 300 yards (275 meters) offshore under the kelp bed closest to the red buoy. Do not anchor. Dive from your "live" boat, leaving a pickup person to follow if you are swept away by the current.

Comments: Approach Point Wilson Reef with respect and have a good dive.

At Fort Worden Park, preparing to dive Point Wilson Reef

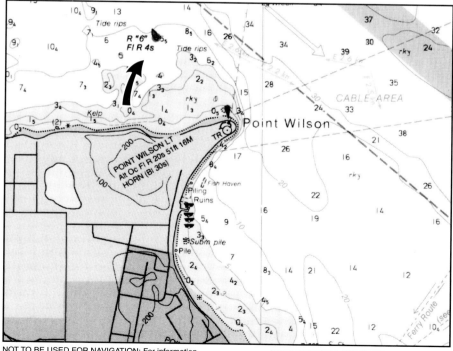

R "6"
Fl R 4s

Tide rips

Tide rips

Kelp

POINT WILSON LT
Alt Oc Fl R 20s 51ft 16M
HORN (Bl 30s)

Point Wilson

TR

CABLE AREA

rky

Fish Haven

Piling
Ruins

Subm pile

Pile

Ferry Route

NOT TO BE USED FOR NAVIGATION: For information
on obtaining navigational charts see page 318.
This is a portion of 18471. Soundings are in fathoms.

1 Nautical Mile

INDEX TO PLACES, MARINE LIFE AND DIVES, DIVING ACTIVITIES, CONDITIONS AND FACILITIES

including bottle dives, night dives, snorkeling sites, drop-offs, reefs, underwater parks and wreck dives

DIVE NOTES

T-shirt with map: use fabric paint to mark where you dive – let it dry before touching the shirt. Puget Sound is on the front; the San Juan and Gulf islands on the back.

DIVE NOTES

MORE DIVE NOTES

MORE DIVE NOTES

ACKNOWLEDGMENTS

Today I think of Christmas as I wear a sweatshirt given to me then by my son Doug and family – it is a bright, happy red color and a Christmas-tree-pattern of many colorfully wrapped gifts is on the front. This book is like that tree.

Gathering information for – which translates into diving – and writing this guidebook has turned every day into Christmas for me for the past seven years. Gifts of shared diving experiences, useful information to pass on to divers, and ideas on how to best present the information have come my way from so many different people. The fun of putting together this guidebook, and its companion volume, and the information that is in them, are gifts to you and me from the following people:

Thanks to Mike Clement and Gerry Millar for sharing their love of bottle, china and junk diving when we went to the Old Customs House, the first dive described in this book. Before diving, I visited the library to find historical photographs – a treasure hunt of one sort. Under water, another treasure hunt as we fanned the muck and found interesting artifacts. Before and after diving, we talked with local residents at Britannia Beach and the dive became a "people" thing. Since diving this site, I have enjoyed returning again and again to the library to read the most fabulous books about the marine history of the region. The interest in history stirred in me by this total experience is a great gift that will enrich the rest of my life.

Ken Roberts persisted and dived with me several times at Porteau Cove Marine Park, the second dive described in this book. He wanted to share one of his favorite places with me. I will remember our first attempt at this dive as the only dive I have completely pulled out of. Bad luck? Yes. Waste of time? No way, a good time was had by all – even on a "washed out" dive. After an energetic snorkel to the float, descending the buoy line of the *Nakaya* to a depth of 75 feet (23 meters) to find only faceplate visibility, and then snorkeling back, we felt good from the exercise. We had an appetite and went to a waterfront café to eat oysters. Our second attempt at this dive, we arrived too late to enjoy the best visibility, because many divers had already entered. Be warned! The marine park can be very crowded on weekends, so that day we dived another part of Porteau. Our third dive at Porteau we visited all of the wrecks, saw a variety of marine life and the dive was a singular success – each dive was. That is part of the point. Diving often is not so much the arriving as the getting there. Thanks, Ken.

My thanks go to many others who have shared the dives in this guidebook with me. Katrina Ringrose and Jeff Cuneo were excellent buddies for a number of dives in Washington. Many thanks, too, to Pam Auxier, Robin Battley, Bill Brooks, Dan Eason, Judy Freesom, Cheryl Gittens, Laura James, Chuck Lewis, Ovid Mac, Gary Mallender, Lenny Marriott, Nancy Mills, Jim Oakley, my husband John and our son Brian, Tom Sheldon, Ron Stead, Monika Schittek, Rene and Tim Street, Kailyn Swanson, Gwyneth Taphouse, Don Tietz, Fred West, Chris Woodcock, and Kim and Frank Zarick for good times diving.

I am grateful to those who have given me feedback about dives they have gone on which I wrote about in *141 Dives*. What a treat, when diving for this update, to meet Albertans Tish Soley, Phil Fraser and Al Williams at Texada Island. Their enthusiasm gave me impetus to keep going on driving around and checking distances from ferries to dives and other of the less-inspiring parts of the update. They reminded me that, yes, of course I am filling in important facts about how to get there, but most of all I am relating to fun and the joys of diving. I appreciated that timely refocusing on what it's all about.

Advice from local divers and experts has been forthcoming from many directions. I am most grateful, once again, to Neil McDaniel who read the entire manuscript and who helped me with many questions regarding marine life; to Mike Woodward at the